The Northern Connection

Ontario Northland Since 1902

The Northern Connection

Ontario Northland Since 1902

Best wishes to Nora Elliott.

*Robert J. Surtees
20 June 1992*

Robert J. Surtees

Captus Press

THE NORTHERN CONNECTION:
ONTARIO NORTHLAND SINCE 1902

ISBN 0–921801–83–1

Canadian Cataloguing in Publication Data

Surtees, Robert J., 1941–
    Northern connection : Ontario Northland since 1902

Includes bibliographical references and index.
ISBN 0–921801–83–1 (bound)   ISBN 0–921801–85–8 (pbk.)

1. Ontario Northland Railway – History.
2. Railroads – Ontario – History.   I. Title.

HE2810.05S8 1992   385'.0971314   C92–093570–2

0 9 8 7 6 5 4 3 2 1
Printed and bound in Canada

to

My Parents,
Robert Manion Surtees and
Annie Ellen Luella (McCarthy) Surtees,
who brought me into the North

and

Helen H. Tanner, James A. Clifton
and S.R. Mealing
who trained me to write about it.

Table of Contents

A List of Maps

Foreword

NTARIO NORTHLAND, originally known as the Temiskaming and Northern Ontario Railway Commission (T&NO), is described today as an agency of the Ontario government. It is a term that is difficult to define, because the organization's relationship to government does not fit the norm. It is not a crown corporation, because it lacks both the full benefits and the full set of restrictions associated with such a body. It is certainly not a department or ministry of the provincial government, because it has no cabinet minister at its head. While it currently resides within the portfolio of the Minister of Northern Affairs and reports through that office, it tends to operate through its own government-appointed commission, quite separately from the ministry's channels. It is an organization of some commercial and economic consequence, for it has recently been selected for membership in *Fortune* magazine's prestigious "500" list. Yet it cannot be viewed as an independent enterprise, for it is clearly owned by the province.

It is unique in other ways as well. Through its various and wide-ranging operations, it can claim to be a service-oriented body with many of the characteristics of a public utility. This can be most easily identified in its efforts to provide a variety of services to such isolated places as Attawapiskat and Moosonee and other not so isolated locations such as Marten River and Bear Island. The public-service feature can also be observed in the efforts and the mind-set of its employees who, while performing their particular jobs, often reveal a desire to ensure that particular services be maintained in the North. Yet Ontario Northland also accepts and often seeks the restrictions, challenges, and motivations of a commercially oriented enterprise. Its tariffs, its transportation routes, and its general range of services all conform in most instances to the operations of a free market economy.

In these two concepts—sometimes conflicting, sometimes complementary—Ontario Northland occupies a unique and special role with respect to its principal geographic area in the North. For the most part its various operations—rail, highway, marine, air, telecommunications—have a commonality in that they all concern transportation and communication. As the title of this book indicates, Ontario Northland is a connector within the North and between the North and the rest of the world. Here too, however, there are irregularities. Ontario Northland at times has gone beyond its obvious mandate and engaged in or undertaken activities that require attention in the North, but which do not by definition fall easily into any of the organization's normal activities. One little-known example would be the special metal-testing laboratory which T&NO mining engineer Cole maintained at Haileybury in the 1930s. Temiskaming Laboratories, while largely independent, had a close connection to the railway. Likewise, the T&NO for several years assisted the town of Cochrane with an annual grant and for a time accepted responsibility for maintaining the public water pump at Englehart. Its special role with respect to mining and land management for the provincial government, also largely unknown, receives treatment in chapter 2.

These several aspects of Ontario Northland have inspired a considerable range of responses and opinions regarding the organization. It has been both praised and condemned for its adherence to the profit motive. It has also been praised, and condemned, as an instrument which advances socialism. It has been praised for directing special attention and concern towards the interests of the North; yet it has been condemned for that same sentiment, because, in doing so, it has used a government agency to promote a particular region at the expense of the province as a whole.

The explanation for this multifaceted corporate personality, and the resulting diversity of opinion regarding its activities, can be found in the company's 90-year history. It began with a simple purpose: to construct a railway into the North from near North Bay on Lake Nipissing to New Liskeard at the north end of Lake Timiskaming. It did that in less than three years. The first train made its initial run on 16 January 1905, but it was soon called upon to do much more. The railway's presence became a catalyst for a burgeoning new mining frontier. This frontier began with the Cobalt bonanza of 1903 and extended to include Lorrain, Gowganda, and the Porcupine and grew further into Kirkland Lake, Larder Lake, and Rouyn.

Nothing had prepared the Ontario government, or anyone else, for this. Since no infrastructure existed to control the boom, the mantle of responsibility fell to what little there was: the T&NO. From that point on there developed an intimacy between the T&NO and the North. Matters that were normally well beyond the ken of a railway—mining policy, land management, fire ranging—fell into the lap of the T&NO Commission. Because the commissioners accepted the tasks and because of the personal relationships between those commissioners and the government of the day, the T&NO became and continues to be a truly special agency for the provincial government. Sometimes by default, sometimes by design, sometimes by accident, the T&NO became much more than a railway. It became an integral factor in the development, promotion, growth and moulding of the North and of northern society.

Yet it began as a railway, it grew as a railway, and it continues to include a railway. For most of its 90-year history, furthermore, its public image continued as a railway, and in portions of the North—notably Englehart or Moosonee—it continues to be seen as such. Certainly its greatest notoriety on the provincial and even the national stage came during the era of the T&NO expansion. The most notable accomplishments, notwithstanding the significance of the branch lines to Charlton, Elk Lake, Iroquois Falls, Lorrain, and the Porcupine, came with the controversy regarding its move into Quebec in 1925–27 and the romantic images that surrounded the achievement of a salt water railhead at Moosonee on James Bay in 1932.

In those years and beyond—perhaps as late as 1960, but certainly until 1950—the T&NO and the ONR enjoyed a stature that accrued to the railway industry during its golden age. As such, it deserves the attention of the historian in terms of its role in northern expansion and growth. Two other features warrant comment. The first concerns the railway's subliminal influence. Stations became vital centres of communication. They were also social centres. Train schedules dictated business, private affairs, social and cultural events, and athletic contests. A derailment or collision could disrupt any of them, and because of the isolation that might result from either, such mishaps were commonly the cause of inconvenience and often were matters, literally, of life and death. It is hardly surprising, therefore, that news of train movement, accidents, and excessively late arrivals often figured prominently in northern newspapers. Nor is it surprising that "railway talk" figured extensively in general conversation.

Our language continues to possess idioms and expressions in common usage by a generation that knows little of their origins. Students, for example, are told to get "on track" (or that they are "off track") or not to get "side tracked" if they hope to "make the grade." A football running back is most feared if he "gets up a full head of steam"; a driver might "highball it" on a long trip; passengers on a bus trip seek to avoid "milk runs"; a dedicated person has "a one-track mind"; new employees are urged to "come on board"; and no one wants to lose "Brownie points." Terms like "pulling the pin" (to retire), or "deadheading it" (travelling with no cargo or at one's own expense and time) are less common but still used. An expression, still in vogue is the sardonic remark used most often by managers, that when working with a railway, "if you haven't heard a rumour by 10 a.m., start one!" One suspects that this could work its way into the jargon of many organizations.

The second feature that warrants mention concerns the nature of the railway itself. Its main task and the multiple operations required to carry it out required that the railway procure equipment and establish procedures unique to its operations. Some of these remain, but many of them, especially those that pertain to the age of steam, have faded into the past. Those operations caused the emergence of attitudes and a manner of behaviour among the men and women who performed the many jobs designed to keep the trains rolling. Many of these have also faded into the past.

The railway certainly had heroic aspects to its grand design. The idea of linking small communities, of maintaining a lifeline for them, and of playing a major developmental role in the North carried with it a certain nobility of purpose, like that of a liberating army which marches into a region to restore freedom and strike down the oppressor. But like the soldiers in such an army, railroaders had to attend to the countless mundane features of the general goal: loading freight, checking train orders, switching track, spotting cars, repairing track, enduring the cold or heat, ordering food, etc. While never doubting the importance of their grand corporate role, they also had their own work and private responsibilities. The railway might indeed be a vital northern institution, but it was also a means of making a living. Within this framework, the T&NO employees—as many as 2000—devised methods of playing the rules, while performing their jobs and interacting with their workmates within the railway's structure.

The following pages seek to record these several facets of Ontario Northland's past. For the most part it is a proud record, as pioneering organizations often are, and it is an interesting one. To include it all within the covers of a single volume lies beyond the talents of this writer. The matter of labour relations, for example, has

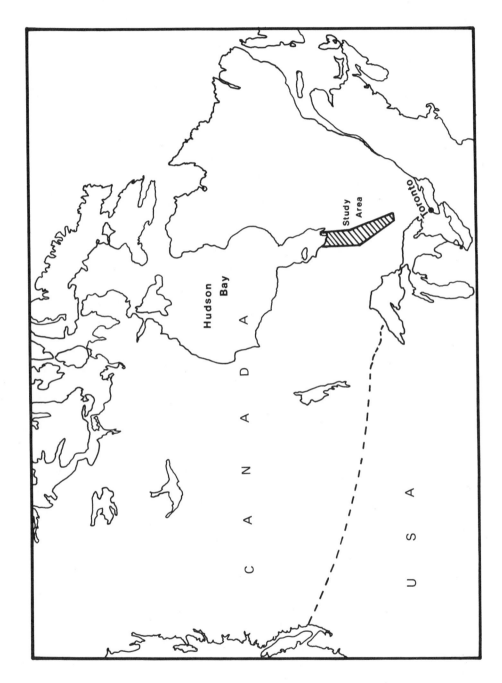

Map 1. *Outline map of Canada showing the study area*

been largely neglected, and some significant decisions, such as that in 1938 of awarding the T&NO the right to operate trucks, buses, and airplanes, are inadequately explained because the records are incomplete. What has been included has been arranged chronologically. Part One seeks to explain its genesis and its early growth during the initial stages of the northern mining frontier; Part Two follows the more notorious story of its extensions into Quebec and towards the salt water of James Bay; and Part Three attempts to narrate the Commission's response to the changing circumstances of the mid-20th century and the transformation of the T&NO into a complete communications system. Part Four constitutes this writer's effort to present at least a partial record of the tasks, the goals, the methods, and the attitudes of the men and women who worked the line, largely through their own words, during the age of steam and beyond. Here too the record may be considered incomplete, for the multiple tasks and experiences of certain sections, such as the repair shops or food services, have not received the attention accorded to the running trades. Yet it is hoped that the reader will lay down this book with a better understanding of the way in which Ontario Northland has evolved to its present form and of its special relationship with the North.

It has often been observed that the task of the historian is a lonely one, for he or she must rummage alone in the vestiges of the past, make constant choices regarding what to include or omit, and then present the story, also alone. Ultimately this is true, and I accept full responsibility for the choices, the arguments and the conclusions found in this study. Yet I did not work without assistance from institutions and from individuals.

Although naively confident that my task could be accomplished in two years, three at most, I soon realized that Ontario Northland's past and that of northeastern Ontario has been far more dynamic and considerably more dramatic than first estimated. So the project dragged on, much to the chagrin, I expect, of the two men who suggested that it be done, to the point that by the time you read this, six years will have passed. One of those men, Don MacDougal, at that time the Assistant General Manager, has since retired. Peter Dyment, the General Manager, remains, though his title has changed to the more modern one of President and CEO. In extending my gratitude to Peter for his patience, I wish also to observe that throughout the extent of this project I have received two things that are precious to the scholar: the complete co-operation of all persons from whom I requested assistance within the organization, and a similarly complete absence of any effort to direct my searchings. Commissioned studies are sometimes awkward to prepare because of preferences held by those who commission them. This was not one of those. I was told at the beginning to tell the full story, "warts and all." At no point was that attitude altered.

Three general areas of resource materials provided the data. Although the historiography of northern Ontario remains in a formative state, the curious student can find a considerable range of local studies or specialized accounts which collectively provide a reasonably sound backdrop for the North's past. It is not my intention to provide a bibliography of northeastern Ontario's history, but certain studies warrant attention. Among them is *Arrow North* (New Liskeard: Highway Book Shop, 1976), George Cassidy's too little-known study of the Temiskaming district. Other local histories provide a rich source of details about the North's past: Alice Marwick, *Northland Post* (Cochrane, 1950); Leslie Roberts, *Noranda* (Toronto; Clarke, Irwin,

1956); Andre Witjen and L.H.T. Irvine, *The Kirkland Lake Story* (Cobalt: Highway Book Shop, 1988); *The Book of Timmins and the Porcupine* (Timmins: Lions Club, 1937).

The mining industry has received somewhat more attention. Early accounts by Anson Garde (*The Real Cobalt, Silverland and Its Stories*, and *The Story of the Temiskaming and Hudson Bay Mining Co.*, all by Toronto's Emerson Press in 1908 and 1909) and later ones by S.A. Pain (*The Way North: Men, Mines and Minerals* and *Three Miles of Gold: The Story of Kirkland Lake*, published by the Ryerson Press in 1964 and 1960), provide a good amalgam of the major events and places and of the peoples who were involved. D.M. LeBourdais' *Metals and Men* (Toronto: McClelland and Stewart, 1957) provides a sound record of Canadian mining and *Harvest from the Rock* (Toronto: Macmillan, 1986) by Philip Smith is a more recent and more comprehensive study of mining in Ontario. Resource development in the North in general and the government's approach to it is dealt with in H.V. Nelles' *The Politics of Development* (Toronto: Macmillan, 1974). The labour relations feature of mining has received some attention, notably by Laurel S. MacDowell, '*Remember Kirkland Lake': The Gold Miners' Strike of 1941–42* (Toronto: U of T Press, 1985) and by B. Hogan, *Cobalt: Year of the Strike, 1919* (Cobalt: Highway Book Shop, n.d.)

Ontario Northland itself has received attention, and the present study has benefited from the trail blazed by others. The railway aficionado will find pleasure in Frank N. Vollhardt's *The Locomotives of the Ontario Northland Railway* (Calgary: The Calgary Group of British Railway Modellers, 1985) and in Patrick C. Dorin's pictorial study *The Ontario Northland Railway* (Burbank, CA: Superior Publishing, 1987). Two studies by Michael Barnes, *Link with a Lonely Land* and *Polar Bear Express Country* (Toronto: Boston Mills, 1985 and 1988), provide illustrated survey accounts, while R.D. Tennant's *Ontario's Government Railway: Genesis and Development* (Halifax: Tennant Publishing, 1973) gives a clear and complete survey of the Commission's past and evolution. The widest trail has been cut by a previous commissioned study: Albert Tucker, *Steam Into Wilderness* (Toronto: Fitzhenry and Whiteside, 1978). Dr. Tucker integrated the stories of the emerging North and the emerging railway system and analysed these largely through the medium of provincial politics and political changes. *The Northern Connection* makes no claim to supplant these earlier works. Rather, the hope is that it supplements them and broadens the trail through the sources in preparation for the next scholar who chooses to travel along this path.

The second major source of data has been the recollections of longstanding and former Ontario Northland employees and other northeners, including those which were collected by Tucker and deposited in the Archives of Ontario. In addition, I am grateful to the following who granted me interviews and shared their experiences with me: E.A. Audet, C.L. Bailey, Joseph Belanger, A. Bentley, Basil Boisvert, Ralph Brill, Jack Campbell, Albert Cant, Evelyn Chivers, Lorne Daigle, Peter Dyment, Lorne Fleece, Art and Kathleen Houghton, Jack Huntington, Britt Jessup, Buck Kyle, Bill Landsdell, John Kennedy, Isabelle Labreche, Bob Lee, John and Margaret Lloyd, Jack McCarthy, Don McDougal, Bob Moore, Ken Moorehead, Fred Nabb, Orville Nichols, Eric Nicholson, Les Nicholson, George Payne, George Pullen, Clem Ruttan, Dan Ruttan, Clara Seguin, A.E. Simms, Charlie Spence, W.L. Spooner, Arnold Sullivan, Robert and Luella Surtees, and Charlie Warner. Copies of these interviews have been deposited in the Ontario

Northland Archives. While these have been used largely to create Part Four of this book, the stories, information, opinions, and insights provided by the men and women interviewed are reflected throughout.

For the first three parts, the bulk of the data has been obtained through archival research, especially at two locations. One was the Archives of Ontario. I wish to use this venue to extend gratitude to the Provincial Archivist, Dr. Ian Wilson, who showed particular sensitivity towards the trials of a scholar conducting research from Toronto and who was ingenious in finding ways to overcome them. His entire staff of archivists and assistants deserve praise. This project, however, owes special debts to three of them: Bennett McCardle, Paul McIlroy, and Leon Warmski. The reports of various government departments—Mines, Highways, Natural Resources, Northern Affairs—have invariably found their way to the provincial archives and naturally provide a sound basis of data for the researcher. For more intimate social, personal, and political details, the collected papers of the premiers and other individuals, such as J.L. Englehart, are invaluable. This was especially so for the T&NO, because so many of the corporate records have not survived as a result of unfortunate fires, insufficient care, and a tendency to destroy out-of-date documents.

But by no means were all of them destroyed. The Commission's legal department and some others have been meticulous in maintaining a corporate record. In addition, concurrent with the start of this project, Ontario Northland undertook to establish a formal department of archives. Lorne Fleece, a longstanding member of the Communications branch, for the two years before he retired, turned his avocation into his livelihood by starting to set up this new department. To him, I extend my appreciation for the assistance and co-operation he extended in that time. Similar gratitude must go towards his successor, Janet Calcaterra, who has taken a personal and even proprietary interest in this project. Located in the former T&NO head office building in North Bay, the Ontario Northland Archives has, in just six years, emerged as a significant repository. It houses documents, photographs, artifacts, reports, books, and newspaper collections concerning both Ontario Northland and Ontario's northland. Other northern repositories have also managed to emerge and grow despite chronic shortages of money and personnel. Regrettably, I did not get to them all, but I wish to applaud those I have used: the Timmins Museum in South Porcupine, the Teck Public Library in Kirkland Lake, the Cobalt Miners' Museum, and the North Bay and Area Museum. These demonstrate how hard work and interest can overcome the incessant shortage of resources.

Others warrant acknowledgment of their contribution to this project. Professor S.R. Mealing of Carleton University guided me through two theses only to find himself saddled with me once again when the final editing and organization of this book loomed. The Nipissing University Board of Governors granted me a sabbatical leave for the 1988–89 academic year to work on this project. Research assistants included Martha Hancock for two summers, Kathleen Hynes for one summer, and Joe Goski on an occasional basis. Bob Moore not only conducted four interviews but also spent three days on the line to instruct me on the nuances and produced the story of the Moosonee run. Ken Moorehead, the Director of Rail Services, and Chief Engineer George Payne offered assistance whenever asked regarding terminology and railway organization. Peter Dyment, already overwhelmed with the task of managing the entire Ontario Northland organization, made time to read and comment on most of the manuscript. Fred Nabb, a retired mining engineer, extended his assistance by explaining mining terms which seemed alien. A former student, Malcolm Clark, designed and prepared the maps, and my colleagues Ken Stange and Bob Bergquist introduced me to the world of word processing. Professor Bergquist also assisted by reading and commenting on substantial portions of the text. My good friends John Follis, Stan Lawlor, and Phil Taylor all assisted in ways which they know and need not be detailed here.

It has been stated often, but should be again, that a writer's family pays a significant price for any project. Four of my daughters—Jennifer, Rebecca, Allison, and Victoria—assisted in a variety of tasks—typing, collating, proofing, and researching—and they did so in spite of their father's changing moods. My pleasure in obtaining their help and in observing the quality of their work has been considerable. Their younger sisters—Sarah, Laura, and Deborah—have rewarded their father with their enthusiasm, if not direct help, for the enterprise. My debt to Margaret, my wife, runs deeper than can be declared by a few words of acknowledgement.

Preface

Professor S.R. Mealing, Carleton University

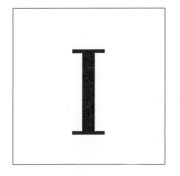

N THE HISTORY of transcontinental countries like Canada, the railway has a special place. The combination of steam power and steel rails, while it may seem in retrospect to have been a rather simple technological advance, had national consequences as yet unmatched by more recent and sophisticated inventions. It was the means by which Australia, Canada, India, Mexico, Tsarist and Soviet Russia, and the United States were able to exert effective control over the wide lands which they claimed, to move people and goods throughout them, and to extend government authority from sea to sea. It was also the means by which the narrower countries of Europe and South America were first linked in transportation and communications networks which have transcended and in time may possibly obscure national boundaries. Wherever it has appeared, the railway has been at once the instrument and the symbol of the two forces that, more than any others, have transformed the world of the 19th century into that of the 20th century: national growth and material progress.

The global role of the steam railway had probably reached its peak during the 1930s. It has been calculated that in 1932 there were 790,552 miles of track in operation throughout the world. The Canadian share, only 42,409 miles, would seem to suggest that in this country the railway game was played for small stakes. The Canadian total was almost twice as much as that found in the limited confines of Great Britain and Ireland (24,360 miles), but less than one seventh of the mileage in the United States (251,210) or in western continental Europe (249,663). Comparing mileage figures to population, however, gives a different impression. In that same year there were only 248 Canadians for every mile of track, just a little more than half as many people per mile as in the United States (497), about one eighth as many as in Great Britain and Ireland (1,991) or in western Europe (2,026), and about one tenth of the world average (2,414). The Canadian national commitment to railways and our dependence on them has in fact been unique.

It is therefore not surprising that Canadian writing about railways has very often emphasized the great transcontinental lines or the transcontinental ambitions of earlier lines, with their national consequences and the politics of their construction. From the time that steam power was first used in Canada to haul loads over rails, in the construction of the Quebec citadel in 1830 and in the opening six years later of the first little portage line, the Champlain and St. Lawrence Railroad, the most usual perspective on the history of Canadian railways has been a nationalist one. It must be admitted that the nationalist perspective is entirely reasonable. In the history of Canada railways have, after all, shown themselves to be the most tangible expression of a national will.

This book offers a very different perspective, not entirely novel but nonetheless both topical and refreshing. It emphasizes that the Temiskaming and Northern Ontario Railway, while it periodically attached importance to transcontinental connections, was always directed towards local development. Its most effective leaders in the past, whether ebullient like Jake Englehart or quietly persistent like George Lee, saw it primarily as a means of exploiting the resources and promoting the growth of the region identified in this book as Ontario's northeastern corridor. Its expectations of profit and of social utility, like its claims to government support, were based on a vision of its role in regional development. The changes in name, organization, and technology that have turned the steam railway into the Ontario Northland Transportation Commission have maintained the same vision. It has not been abandoned by the shift from steam to diesel power, nor by the greater shift from reliance on the railway itself to a more flexible use of technological advances in the means of transportation and communication. The purposes of regional development, once served almost exclusively by the railway and its attendant telegraph, now rely increasingly on newer developments in road and air transport and in telecommunications.

Yet it is clear that it was the steam railway that first organized both the economic and the social life of Ontario's northeastern corridor. Originally intended to promote rather speculative hopes of agricultural settlement, the railway responded very quickly to a remarkable bonanza of mineral discoveries. It supplied and organized the exploitation of those discoveries and in doing so became the dominant institution in the region. Not only did many people work for the railway; almost everyone depended on its services and led lives regulated by its timetable. The imperatives of the railway—the awareness of schedules, the necessity of shift work and of dealing with emergencies, the calculation of transportation costs, even the acceptance of bureaucracy in the use of printed forms— were a fundamental part of everyday life in the northeastern corridor. The railway was, often in fact and always in symbol, the centre of the region's hopes for material progress and of its sense of a distinctive identity.

There is as yet no entirely clear method by which to assess the full social impact of an institution like the Ontario Northland Transportation Commission on its region. That is a problem over which academics will continue to agonize. This book provides effective answers to three parts of that problem: it describes in perceptive detail the process of building the line; it describes the experience of those who operated the railway; and it is careful to offer, very sympathetically, a series of local points of view. The author has the twin advantages of a formal training in social history and an upbringing in South End. He is therefore able to explain not only how the railway served the northeastern corridor, but also how it came to be for many people an object of pride and even affection. Perhaps a personal commitment to a regional ethos is necessary to appreciate the role of such an agency as the Ontario Northland Transportation Commission and its predecessors. However that may be, readers interested in the history of railways will find this book as informative and interesting as those whose interest, nostalgic or analytical, is in the history of Ontario's northeastern corridor.

The Northeastern Corridor

T O THOSE WHO merely travel through or look at a map of Ontario between the Great Lakes and Hudson Bay, northeastern Ontario usually seems a single northern region, rich in natural resources but forbidding in its landscape and climate, neither populous nor variegated enough for local differences to command an outsider's attention. The people who live there, and who are apt to regard this southern viewpoint with varying shades of amusement and resentment, know better. Marked differences in topography and resources divide the land north of the Great Lakes into a number of regions, the differences being reinforced for each by a distinctive historical experience and resulting in a sense of local pride and local uniqueness. Of particular importance in the last hundred years of Ontario's economic expansion northwards has been the area, nowhere more than eighty miles wide, that stretches from North Bay on Lake Nipissing to Moosonee and Moose Factory on James Bay. The region could be called "Northeastern Ontario," except that it includes a slice of western Quebec. Its residents today refer to themselves as "Northerners" and to their region as "Northern On-

tario." Around the turn of the century it was both officially and commonly called "New Ontario."

Those terms are imprecise: they have been applied also to the Sudbury Basin, the Sault Ste. Marie hinterland, the Thunder Bay district, the borderlands of Ft. Francis, the northwestern region of Lake of the Woods and Kenora, and the western coasts of Hudson Bay and James Bay. The North Bay–Moosonee area is a natural passageway through the Canadian Shield and the northern forests. North-south and east-west routes, used both by Europeans for over three hundred years and by Indians for generations before that, cross just east of Lake Nipissing. The region is the obvious means of access to the lands north of the Great Lakes; the name that best indicates its place in geography and its role in history is the "northeastern corridor" of Ontario. When such terms as "Northern Ontario," "New Ontario," or "the North" are used in the following pages, often in quotations from people who have lived there, they should be understood in that limited sense.

The corridor's eastern edge is formed by the Laurentians, which continue northward beyond the Mattawa River and Lake Nipissing, mostly covered by heavy forests or muskeg for about 90 miles. They then slope into a gentler and flatter terrain. This reasonably arable land, called the Little Clay Belt, stretches westward from Lake Timiskaming until the terrain becomes rocky again near Gowganda. Its northern limit lies 40

1

miles beyond the Wabi River. The Canadian Shield, though not the Laurentians, surrounds this enclave; but after extending some 80 miles further north across the Arctic watershed, it opens up once more into a larger agricultural belt some 100 miles wide. Discovered later than the first, this is generally called the Greater Clay Belt. North of it for about 70 miles lie the forests, mostly pine, of the Lake Abitibi region. About 100 miles from salt water, the terrain remains flat but begins to slope gradually down through the marshy lowlands that border James Bay.

The corridor's first importance as a transportation route stemmed from the fact that rivers drain into it from three directions. On the western fringe the Sturgeon flows from the Gowganda highlands into Lake Nipissing, which in turn drains into Georgian Bay via the French River. Lake Nipissing is also connected via the LaVase and a short portage over a low height of land to the Mattawa, a tributary of the Ottawa. The headwaters of that great river rise in the Des Quinze sector of Quebec, swing in a northwesterly arc, and then run south into the elongated widening known as Lake Timiskaming. From the west its greatest tributary is the Montreal River, but other significant streams like the Blanche, the Wabi, and the Amable also serve to fill the Ottawa system. The Montreal, in turn, receives the waters from the extensive Temagami Lake system through Lady Evelyn Lake. Beyond the Arctic watershed, the Abitibi, the Frederick House, the Mattagami, and the Moose rivers drain sluggishly into James Bay.

The first European commercial activity in Canada was the fur trade. Competitors of its two principal centres, Hudson Bay and the St. Lawrence River, met first in the northeastern corridor. The meetings sometimes were hostile. In 1686, for example, Chevalier de Troyes led a French expedition up the rivers of the corridor to temporarily capture the Hudson Bay Company's bayside posts on the Moose, Rupert, and Albany rivers. But the corridor remained a side show in the fur trade. The Hudson Bay Company (HBC) and its Montreal-based rivals—first the licensed traders of New France, then the independent traders called "pedlars," then the Northwest Company—put their main efforts into westward expansion. In the corridor some independent traders survived the union in 1821 of the HBC and the Northwest Company; the Revillion brothers endured to transfer their capital from furs to cosmetics, as the Revlon Corporation. In general, though, the local fur trade after 1821 was dominated by the HBC posts at Moose Factory and Fort Timiskaming.

Older than the European fur trade and vital to it were the trade routes established by the Indians. The corridor lay on the northwestern edge of the Huron's great trading circle, along which agricultural bands exchanged their products with hunters. After the dispersal of the Hurons and the decline of Iroquois power in the 17th century, the Arctic watershed of the corridor remained the territory of the Cree. To the east were the Algonkian groups, stretching from the upper Saguenay and Lac St. Jean to Lake Timiskaming. In the 18th century, the Ojibwa people, as they expanded eastwards along the north shores of the Great Lakes, took over the Lake Temagami region. All three groups remained the primary middle-men and producers of the fur trade.

By the 1830s, the HBC began to encounter what proved to be the harbinger of its demise—lumbering. The two activities were incompatible: lumbering brought with it larger numbers of people, and its principal purpose was to cut down trees. Naturally it drove off the fur bearing game. It was the vanguard of a new economy that would shoulder aside the trade in furs and the centuries-old lifestyle of the native people whose commerce had come to depend on fur. The first lumber firm to arrive was that of the McConnell family from Hull. Other prominent lumbering names followed, pushing west from the lower Ottawa valley in search of pine: Booth, Gillies, McLaren, Bronson, and Eddy. Inevitably, "civilization" was reaching the northeastern corridor.

One of its standard features was the establishment of permanent missions among the Indians. The earliest missionaries were the Sulpician priests who started a mission at Des Joachim on

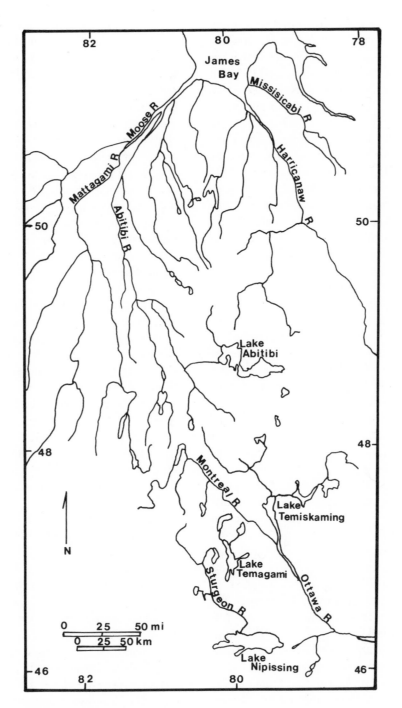

Map 2. *The northeastern corridor*

the Ottawa River and who in 1836 proposed another at Fort Timiskaming, with others as far north as Moose Fort and Fort Albany. The Oblates of Mary Immaculata (OMI) maintained the travelling missions throughout the corridor when they replaced the Sulpicians in this field in 1844. In 1864 they established what came to be called "the old mission" on the right bank of the Ottawa River directly across from the HBC post at Fort Timiskaming. Two years later, the first Grey Nuns joined them there. Reconciled to the inevitability of missions and to a government policy whose ultimate aim was to assimilate Indians into white society, the HBC gave its support to missions that were English and protestant. In 1850 the Church of England created a diocese for Rupert's Land and sent its first missionary, James Horden, to the Moose River post.

In 1886 the Oblates moved their headquarters to a new settlement at the Baies des Pères, in effect ceding a foothold among the Cree on the Arctic watershed of the northeastern corridor to the Anglican missions. While they continued to evangelize Indians from their "old Mission," their main concern shifted to the influx of agricultural settlers from the long-established centres of the province of Quebec. The CPR main line westward had reached Mattawa in 1880, opening up the comparatively arable land on the left bank of the Ottawa River. Through the energetic efforts of Father Paradis and Father Gendreau's Colonization Society of Timiskaming, two new communities emerged 25 miles apart: Ville Marie, around the OMI mission at Baies des Pères, and Notre Dame du Nord. The two were joined by a wagon road and, in 1894, the Timiskaming Colonization Railway (part of the CPR system) reached Lake Timiskaming from the main line at Mattawa. The TCR was to be extended to Ville Marie in 1925 and to Angliers in 1927. In the agricultural settlement of the northeastern corridor, the early initiative lay with the province of Quebec.

Until 1884 the Ontario government's main northern concern was jurisdiction. Specifically, the province claimed for itself the right to administer the lands and resources of all the territory that lay north of Lakes Huron and Superior,

northward to the Albany River, and westward as far as Lake of the Woods. The federal government wished to confine Ontario to the region south of the height of land between the Great Lakes and Hudson Bay. The disputed territory was very large and believed to be very rich in resources. Known as the Ontario Boundary Dispute, this classic dominion-provincial struggle lasted a decade. In 1884 Ontario obtained all that she had demanded. (See Map 2 on p. 3.) Her present western boundary, beginning at a point on Lake of the Woods, was confirmed. Her eastern boundary was defined as running from a point in James Bay "where a line drawn due north from the head of Lake Temiscamingue would strike it..."[1] The line then ran south through the middle of the lake and then along the middle of the Ottawa River. This definition of the Quebec-Ontario border had the effect of splitting jurisdiction over the northeastern corridor.

One jurisdictional matter remained: that of Indian land entitlement. In 1850 the Robinson-Huron Treaty had secured to the government the lands of the corridor as far north as the height of land (i.e. the Arctic watershed) at Sesekinika. North of that point, however, the Cree bands still held aboriginal entitlement. Their claims were purchased as far north as the Albany River in 1905 when the federal government concluded the James Bay Treaty (Treaty No. 9). Since then a dispute has arisen and is still unresolved. In 1973 the Bear Island Indian band challenged the 1850 agreement. Arguing that it had not been involved in that treaty, the band claimed to retain aboriginal title to a substantial area, including the Temagami lake district. That claim has since been denied by the Supreme Court of Canada, but as of this writing a judicial caution has been removed from only a small portion of the land in question, and the band continues to negotiate with the province.

During the drawn-out Ontario boundary dispute, while lawyers and politicians wrangled, provincial survey parties trekked over the disputed territory. From their reports, a Crown Lands Department pamphlet in 1883 described the arable land at the northern end of Lake

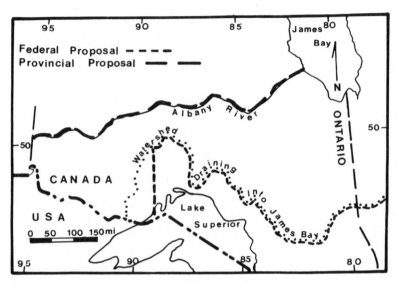

Map 3. *The Ontario boundary dispute*

1890 with a survey party, returned to stay there two years later. With him came a man named Paget, who, when registering his lots, gave the location as "Liskeard," in honour of his home town in Cornwall County in England. In 1897, when the post office there required a name, the local people chose Liskeard. Post office officials objected since it could be confused with the eastern Ontario town of Lisgar. When no other name could gain local approval, the federal officials arbitrarily selected the name "New Liskeard."

Both communities grew slowly, rather too slowly to suit Farr, who journeyed out of the north to urge the government of A.D. Hardy to assist the region, wrote two promotional pamphlets, and made a trip to England to attract immigrants. The region's population, however, was only 910 in 1891.[3] In fact, long as the history of European enterprise in the northeastern corridor had been, by the end of the 19th century, its visible results were not especially impressive. There were only about 2000 white residents north of North Bay, almost all of them in the four settlements on Lake Timiskaming: Haileybury and New Liskeard on its northwestern shore, and Ville Marie and Notre Dame du Nord on the east.[4] The southern end of the corridor had been crossed by the transcontinental Canadian Pacific Railway, which reached North Bay in 1881; and a link to southern Ontario was provided when the Northern and Pacific Junction Railway (part of the Grand Trunk Railway system) reached a point near Nipissing Junction from Gravenhurst in 1886. The route northward into the corridor itself, despite the best efforts of the colonization societies, remained inadequate for any large-scale movement of people or commodities.

Yet things were about to speed up. The Ontario government had been awakened to the

Timiskaming, which later came to be called the Little Clay Belt. The province responded to this news by ordering the area to be surveyed into townships and land there were offered for sale.

Among the first purchasers was Charles C. Farr, a graduate of Haileybury College, London, England, currently serving with the HBC. In obtaining some 1200 acres, Farr acquired a personal stake in the agricultural development of the Clay Belt, an interest directly injurious to that of the company's fur trade. In 1884 he left the company to devote his considerable energy to promoting the area, especially that sector which contained his land and which came to be known as Haileybury. On the shores of Lake Timiskaming he built his own home which "held the first religious services, the first baptism and the first marriage in the district."[2] That same home also witnessed the trial of the first criminal case in the new country. In 1889 he arranged for a grist mill and a sawmill, and the next year Haileybury obtained the first post office on its side of the lake. Another early arrival was John Armstrong, the Crown Lands agent, who moved his office from Novar to Haileybury in 1894 and then moved again to another small settlement that had been started a little to the north at the mouth of the Wabi River. William Murray, who had arrived in

5

possibilities of the northeastern corridor. New Liskeard and Haileybury, represented in the Ontario legislature as part of the new constituency of Nipissing since 1889, were vocal enough to draw attention. The industrial development of the province, to which its government was committed, would soon require improved access to northern resources. It counted for something, too, that Premier Ross in Toronto understood the advantage of taking some reasonably dramatic action in an election year. And in an era when the imperative of material progress was accepted as both beneficial and exciting, what could be more dramatic than to build a railway to Ontario's last frontier?

Nothing in the history of the northeastern corridor was more important than the decision in 1902 to construct the Temiskaming and Northern Ontario Railway (T&NO). Indeed, it has often been said that the history of this part of northern Ontario *is* the story of the railway. That is of course an over-simplification: it neglects the significance of such other vital factors as mining, lumbering, and trapping, and it ignores the longest period in the corridor's recorded history. The railway, after all, followed the path of traders, warriors, and migrants who had discovered its advantages long before railways or even wheels had come to North America. The engineers of the T&NO were more scientific than their predecessors, with more sophisticated technology at their disposal, but they were hardly more effective in their selection of the route. Their starting point was chosen for human—some would say political—reasons rather than from natural or geographic considerations. Railway technology broadened the corridor, both at its southern end and at Elk Lake, Timmins, and Rouyn by the addition of branch, spur, and connecting lines. Being an Ontario enterprise, the T&NO also kept its main line west of the Ottawa River and Lake Timiskaming.

Once the line pushed north of Lake Temagami, however, it followed very closely the route which was already centuries old.

It was not merely the application of new technology to an old route that made the railway so vital to the northeastern corridor. Originally conceived as a simple colonization road, a somewhat belated response to initiatives on the Quebec side of the border, the T&NO was transformed by the spectacular discovery of silver at Cobalt into the first public utility of the province. It has been the instrument by which the economic development of much of Ontario's North has been organized and fostered. The range of the services it provides has expanded quite as rapidly as technological change itself. To begin with, the T&NO simply ran the railway, with incidental attention to such ancillary services as the telegraph, telephone, and express. Other matters—land management, mining, and road services—accrued to its original relatively simple responsibilities. Known since 1946 as the Ontario Northland Transportation Commission, this provincial corporation now includes rail, bus, truck, air, marine, and telecommunications divisions. It influences the economy and social fabric of communities throughout the northeastern corridor from North Bay to Cochrane and Moosonee, from Swastika to Rouyn-Noranda, from Porquis Junction to Timmins. Its commitment to the region, symbolically declared by the location of its headquarters at North Bay in 1921, remains undiminished. Its own success in promoting economic growth has left it a less dominant factor than it was when its line began operation, but that success made it the central institution in the critical period of the development of Ontario's northeastern corridor. Moreover, in the strategy of Ontario's economic development, it had a unique and sometimes even dramatic place.

Notes
1. H. Nicolson, *The Boundaries of Canada, Its Provinces and Territories*, Ottawa: Queen's Printer, 1964, p. 64.
2. G. Cassidy, *Arrow North*, Cobalt: Highway Bookshop, 1976, p. 106.
3. Canadian census for 1891.
4. Cassidy, *Arrow North*, pp. 97–107.

Part One

Establishing the System

T&NO skeleton track, c. 1905 (ONA 19882215)

Chapter 1

The First Commission

O N 15 JANUARY 1902, Frank Latchford announced an new era in the history of the north-eastern corridor. Neither he nor his audience could anticipate the enormous changes that would result. To Premier George Ross and the rest of the Ontario legislature, the Commissioner of Public Works was simply declaring the government's intention to provide for the construction of a government-owned railway to run from a point near North Bay on Lake Nipissing to a point near New Liskeard on Lake Timiskaming and to be known as the Temiskaming and Northern Ontario Railway.[1] It would be managed by a commission of between three and five persons appointed by the province.

His announcement was not surprising, for the project had been broached almost a year earlier during the budget presentation of 28 February 1901. Moreover, the government had already through the Department of Public Works provided for a series of explorations and surveys in the lands north of North Bay in the District of Nipissing. These reports had described the presence of lands rich in timber resources and, more significantly, a rich farming area known as the Clay Belt. They simply confirmed, in other words, what the people of the two small agricultural communities of Haileybury and New Liskeard had been saying for more than one and a half decades. These factors, combined with the extension of the province's boundary north of the height of land and Ontario's fairly recent concern to assert its authority in New Ontario,[2] had made the construction of such a railway at some point almost a certainty. Latchford's statement, therefore, did not surprise anyone.

The project was not very large. The thought of a track running some 110 miles from one small town in the wilderness to a much smaller town even further into the wilderness did not strike forcibly on anyone's imagination. Most no doubt viewed the announcement as either a symbolic gesture or an obvious political ploy, or perhaps as both. Even the one unique feature of the announcement, the decision to build the railway as a publicly owned government venture did not arouse much interest or discussion. It was certainly a departure from the norm since other Ontario lines were privately owned, albeit usually assisted in part by public support through subsidies or land grants. It would certainly give the government in office an additional source of patronage, a factor that could usually arouse passion among the opposition benches. Private capital had not shown sufficient interest to date, however, and the scale of patronage to be gained from the project appeared rather small. Opposition, therefore, was minimal. Even the leader of the opposition Conservatives, James P. Whitney, confined his comments to suggesting that a commission of three could do that job as well as five and to expressing surprise that the government did not provide precise cost estimates. Another member of the opposition declared that the proper way to build the line would be to provide subsidies or other encouragements to the private sector. Such entrepreneurs as Mackenzie and Mann of the Canadian Northern Railway had the expertise and the experience to do the job properly, while the government did not.[3] It was at most a token opposition.

One suspects that Whitney played it deliberately in a low key in order to limit the political mileage that the Ross Liberals might obtain from the enterprise. And in a symbolic sense, there was considerable political hay to be made. The Liberals had grown old in office, having been there through the tenures of Oliver Mowat (1872–96), Arthur Hardy (1896–99), and the incumbent George Ross, who had not yet won a general election. The major issues of separate schools, prohibition, and hydro were old, and the Liberal majorities had dwindled. In the 1898 election, the Conservatives had actually won a larger percentage of the popular vote than had the Liberals (48.1% vs 47.3%; 4.6% voted for independent candidates).[4] The Liberal hold on office was tenuous. Ross needed a new issue, a new project, something that would be completely his, something that could catch the imagination of the voters. While the northern railway was neither startling nor grand, it did have some potential, especially if it were used properly. For one thing, Ross could present it as a beginning of the government's redemption of the fairly longstanding Liberal promise to develop the North. Ross could also claim that the railway would promote the interests of the agricultural community. That sector had for some time viewed with alarm the growing urbanization of Ontario at the expense of the farmers. The new railway, it was argued, was designed to promote a new agricultural region in the

province, a step that would strengthen and expand the industry. Finally, the railway had some political potential in the constituencies that would be affected directly. This potential was increased by *An Act Respecting the Representation of the People in the Legislative Assembly*. This statute, which coincidentally received royal assent on the same day as the railway act, divided the electoral district of Nipissing into Nipissing East and Nipissing West.[5] Two seats, not one, were therefore directly at stake. Whitney knew this. To object too strongly to the northern railway might raise the project's stature and leave the impression that the Conservatives were opposed to progress. Thus, having registered his token opposition, Whitney concentrated his campaign on other issues. The Liberals, for their part, used the issue as best they could, especially in the North.

The *Act to Authorize the Construction of the Temiskaming and Northern Ontario Railway* received royal assent on 17 March 1902.[6] The first sod of the new lines was formally turned at a ceremony on Trout Lake, just outside North Bay, on 10 May 1902.[7] As it turned out, an election had also been called, which explains the presence at the sod-turning ceremony of the Commissioner of Public Works, Frank J. Latchford. It probably also explains the absence of J.W. Richardson, the mayor of North Bay, who might otherwise have been expected to be there. Richardson was a Conservative who wished not to be seen as supporting the Liberal candidacy of either Michael James (Nipissing East) or Joseph Michaud (Nipissing West), both of whom were certainly present. Ten days later, through the Department of Public Works, tenders were called for the task of clearing the first 20 miles of the railway's right-of-way. And on 24 May 1902, the day before the provincial election, a local contractor, Patrick Furlong, received the clearing contract, the first to be issued in connection with the construction of the new railway.[8] In the election, Ross managed to secure a majority government, but it had been a close race. The effect of the promise to build the northern railway on this outcome is difficult to assess; it certainly did not hurt. The return of both Liberal candidates in Nipissing and of Liberals in Algoma and Sudbury assured the Liberals of their five-seat majority. There was bound to be a close connection between the railway and the machinations of partisan politics. This surprised no one, either then or since. The expenditure of public money has always been, and continues to be, a matter highly charged with the potential of patronage and accusations of favouritism and abuse. At the turn of the 20th century, some of the major recipients of such patronage were the railways; and a government-owned railway could be expected to offer special advantages to the political group that could secure the reins of power.

If the railway fitted easily into old political practices, it also raised new questions of public policy. The mission or purpose of the railway became a matter for open and public debate. Should the operations of the railway be expected to turn a profit? And if that happened, should those profits be spent for the benefit of the province as a whole? Or should they be used in the area that created them? Over the years these questions would receive various answers.

First the railway had to be built, along with the telegraph and the telephone lines called for by the enabling legislation of 17 March. In the creation of something as heavy or permanent as a railway, the first decisions made can become largely unalterable. The story of the first decade, therefore, is a vital one.

Three stages can be identified in the first decade.

1. The first Commission: 1902–05.
2. Unexpected prosperity: 1905–09.
3. The second northern boom: 1909–12.

The stages overlap. The Liberal commissioners appointed in 1902 guided the T&NO into the first phase of its prosperity. The personality of J.L. Englehart, which came to dominate the Commission by 1906 soon after his appointment in 1905, continued to do so until 1920. Yet each of these three time segments was characterized by its own prevailing mood and tempo. When the decade opened, the focus for the project was a small set of offices that the Commission rented in Toronto. Few people in Toronto were interested in or affected by the decisions made in those offices. Two hundred miles north, however, it was a far different story. The Commission had the power to influence the future of an entire district for at least 100 miles. From the beginning, there were two centres of activity, with the one acting and the other reacting to Commission decisions. As the events unfolded, the roles began to reverse: the commissioners more and more found themselves reacting to conditions in the North. In particular, when the mineral wealth of the region became known by 1906, it excited the entire province and actually caused the Ontario government to restructure its entire mining policy.[9] No longer was this new enterprise with the small offices largely ignored. It had become important and newsworthy. The focus, in other words, gradually shifted north. Southern control of the T&NO did not disappear, but a trend had begun. "Go North, young man," became a common expression, inferring that opportunity and prosperity lay on the northern frontier. The federal government may have concentrated its efforts in the Canadian West, but for Ontarians, the great prospects lay to the north. And those who followed the pull to the north discovered that the single-most significant institution there was the Temiskaming and Northern Ontario Railway.

In the summer of 1902, however, none of this was apparent. The Ross government, having narrowly survived at the polls, carried on. Its promise to build a northern railway had to be honoured. Accordingly, Ross appointed five men to the Commission and assigned them that task. The group comprised the following: A.E. Ames of Toronto, who had been personally selected by the Premier to act as chairman; E. Gurney, also of Toronto; F.E. Leonard of London; B.O. Folger of Kingston; and M.J. O'Brien of Renfrew. P.E. Ryan of Toronto was chosen to serve as Secretary-Treasurer. Both Ames and Ryan resigned in 1904 and were replaced respectively by Robert Jaffray and H.W. Pearson, both of Toronto.[10]

The original government promise had simply called for a colonization line into the northeast in order to assist anyone who wished to go up there to live. The province of Quebec had been promoting its northern frontier for several years, and now Ontario was doing the same. Little else was expected. It is true that the rhetoric of the day, both political and otherwise, had spoken of exploiting the mineral wealth in the northeast and perhaps even of extending the line all the way to the salt water of James Bay. In most minds, however, that was simply rhetoric. For the moment, the goal was to build a rail transportation system to link the two tiny agricultural communities of New Liskeard and Haileybury with the southern reaches of the province by rendering them less dependent upon the water route via Lake Timiskaming and the Ottawa River. This might indeed lead to further agricultural settlement in the much touted Clay Belt; it was also expected that the line would assist the lumber industry. The railway would serve notice that Ontario, like Quebec, was ready to claim control of its own hinterland.

It was intended that this control should be exerted from Toronto. A brief flurry of lobbying by eastern Ontario and Ottawa Valley interests tried to promote the idea that the line should connect with the CPR at Mattawa, thereby pulling the northeast into the metropolitan influence of Ottawa. This, it was argued, had been the historical and traditional route, and it was logical to continue to use it. It would also have involved a pull towards Montreal, however, and the Ontario Government was determined to avoid that. It is true that the line into the northeast was secondary in importance to the grand issues of hydro-electric power at Niagara Falls, the extension of Yonge Street, the University of Toronto, the prohibition movement, or even the burgeoning commercial interests of the Clergue empire in Sault Ste. Marie. Yet, while there may not have been much in the northeast, whatever might be there was going to be controlled by Toronto, not by Montreal.[11]

It was with this limited frame of reference that the five recently appointed members of the T&NO Commission gathered for their first meeting on Tuesday, 29 July 1902, in the office of the Assistant Commissioner of Public Works. None of them had much knowledge about New Ontario; nor were the commissioners especially inspired by railways. Apart from O'Brien, who had done some rail contracting, none had any real experience with railways other than that of riding on them. Moreover, they all had other interests and their own careers. The annual honorarium of one thousand dollars was not, in the commercial circumstances of the day, a paltry sum, but neither was it a consideration that would inspire these men to devote an inordinate amount of time to the enterprise. They were certainly prepared to do the job properly and with energy, for they were all energetic men, but it was a peripheral interest for them. Yet, from all appearances, they performed their jobs in a competent, formal, and businesslike fashion.

It was clear, even before the Commission was struck, that the major decisions would be made on the advice of trained professionals in the field of railroading and railroad engineering. Through the Department of Public Works, under the direction of Latchford, who retained both his seat and his portfolio after the 1902 election, surveys had been run north of North Bay, and a right-of-way had been located. A contract had even been let for clearing the right-of-way from Trout Lake northward. The survey and location work had already been undertaken by an engineer, W.B. Russell, engaged in 1901 for that purpose.[12]

The inexperience of the commissioners in the actual construction, supplying, stocking, and operation of a railway was not, therefore, a severe handicap. There was apparently a plentiful supply of trained professionals like Russell (who was, from the evidence, a good one). There were, moreover, scattered within Ontario and without, a variety of suppliers, either manufacturers or their representatives, who were eager to secure any new business that might come open. Even the hint of new construction in a newspaper article would bring inquiries concerning the job along with requests that the inquiring firm be considered. The commissioners did not have to expend much effort seeking out suppliers, but they did have to make choices among the various competitors, and they had to make decisions regarding the systems to be adopted. In these they depended heavily upon the expertise and advice of the professionals. The only restriction placed on them in this regard was one written into the enabling legislation, viz. that the railway "as far as practicable, be constructed, equipped and operated with railway supplies and rolling stock made, purchased or procurable in Canada..."

Their collective inexperience made it logical to choose the contract system for actual construction. None of them had either the time or the imagination to supervise all facets of such a project. That, it was felt, should be assigned to a single contractor who would be responsible for the "proper and satisfactory execution" of the job. As they stated in the annual report for 1902:

> This method, it was felt, would relieve the Commission of a great deal of the detail work necessarily attached to organization, which would involve the necessity of having a large clerical staff to look after the purchase, receipt and distribution of supplies for the men, etc., and it was thought that the contract system would, in the end, prove more economical, as were the Commission to undertake directly the construction of the road it would be necessary to purchase a complete construction plant, which might have to be disposed of at a loss after the work of construction should have been completed.[13]

In the meantime W.B. Russell, now the Chief Engineer, had prepared two significant reports. One recommended that the line be run in an arc, northeasterly from Trout Lake; the second outlined in precise detail the building specifications of the railbed along the right-of-way. There was an alternative route westward in a similar arc to take advantage of the railbed that had been prepared a few years earlier but abandoned when the Nipissing and James Bay Railway failed. An arc in one direction or the other was necessary because of the sharp rise of some 550 feet in the escarpment that lies directly north of North Bay. The Commission hired George A. Mountain, Chief Engineer of the Canadian Atlantic Railway, to comment on Russell's report. Mountain concurred that the western approach to the north followed a much rougher terrain and involved several water crossings, a matter of some consequence, for bridges were very expensive. The eastern route, in contrast, would require fewer water crossings, contained plentiful timber and agricultural resources, and would permit a better and more gradual grade from north to south. These advantages, said both men, would more than compensate for the extra length of six miles.[14] The Commission accepted this judgement. Mountain's considerable applause for Russell's report seems also to have reinforced the Commission's confidence in their own Chief Engineer. They accepted his elaborate set of specifications and directed him to "enlarge his staff as he considered necessary for properly staking the line and supervising future construction work."[15]

Thirteen major firms responded to the Commission's call for tenders for the construction contract. The lowest bid of $1,464,600 came from the Montreal firm of A.R. Macdonell. Because it was the lowest bid, and possibly also because the firm was known to Commissioner O'Brien as a competent one, this company and the Commission concluded a construction agreement on 3 October 1902. The Macdonell company agreed to build a complete road bed for a single track railway according to T&NO specifications from a point near North Bay to a point on Lake Timiskaming, a distance of approximately 110 miles. The first 60 miles were to be delivered to the Commission on or before 31 December 1903 and the remainder by 31 December 1904.[16]

With that settled, the commissioners turned their attention to other matters, the most important of which were questions of locomotive power, grades and curvature, and the quality of the steel. At the turn of the century, the relative merits of steam and electric locomotion were being argued. Steam had been the preferred method throughout the 19th century, but with the evolution of electric power, its adoption by the lighter radial railways,[17] and the emerging developments in hydro power such as the plant at Niagara Falls, the question was not simply academic. It was argued that the supply of potential hydro-electric power was great in the North and, in view of the dangers of forest fires in the wilderness, it would be sensible to harness that renewable energy rather than burn coal and risk fires. The Chief Engineer, however, declared that there was not a suitable or convenient source of hydro-electric power along the proposed route of the new railway. Moreover, he reported that if proper care were taken in screening emissions from engines, if the right-of-way were cleared properly, and, if, during the dry season, good fire ranging were implemented, the fire hazard was indeed small. During the operation of the railway, he said, "the greatest and perhaps the only danger, lies in carelessness or negligence on the part of the trackmen, engineers, tramps, or the travelling public, and this danger will not be reduced any by an electrically operated road."[18] Once again the Commission consulted outside experts. Mr. T. Hay, Claims Agent for the CPR, and George Mountain agreed with Russell. Consequently, the Commission declared in favour of steam locomotion, but the issue continued to be debated for half a century. As a further precaution, in conjunction with the Department of Lands, Forests and Mines, the Commission made an arrangement for fire rangers to be stationed along the T&NO right-of-way. It marked the beginning of the provincial government's venture into this forest preservation activity.

For a brief time the Commission considered the possibility of using 72-pound relaying steel rails for its sidings. Since this was a government line and therefore should be something of a show piece, and since the extra cost for new 80-pound steel was said to be "infinitesimal,"[19] it chose the higher quality rails for use on sidings as well as on the main line. In the bidding for the steel rail contract, the Algoma Steel Company in Sault Ste. Marie quoted the highest price: $34 per gross ton, f.o.b. cars, North Bay. There were lower quotations of $27.67, $28.85, and $28.95 from other com-

panies, all foreign (from England and Germany). When given a chance to reduce its price, the Sault firm could only go as low as $32. Despite this, the commissioners were inclined to accept that offer, but asked the Premier if his government would approve the action. In a carefully worded response to Secretary-Treasurer Ryan on 11 December 1902, Premier Ross agreed that the Commission would, in the opinion of his government, be justified in awarding the contract to the Algoma Steel Company. He went on:

> The Algoma Steel company has invested a large amount of capital in a steel plant, which I believe is capable of producing rails of an approved pattern and design, and in the manufacture of these rails Canadian ore is largely required. The Company, therefore, serves a double purpose, (1) of utilizing our own ores and (2) of furnishing employment to a large number of people. Both of these objects the Government has endeavoured to advance by legislation, as well as by substantial aid in the form of subsidies, etc. You may, therefore, assure the Commissioners that in the action they propose taking they will have the most cordial approval of the Government.[20]

In this, both the Premier and the Commission were acting in accordance with Article 9 of the T&NO Act, which called for preference to be given to goods manufactured in Canada. It is also likely that Ross wished to see the order go to a riding and to a business that had consistently supported the Liberal party.

Even with this advantage, Algoma Steel could not fulfill its contract. Its best steel, at that point, could not meet the T&NO's chemical specifications, even when these were relaxed somewhat. The problem actually lay with the supplier, the Consolidated Lake Superior Company, which could not be certain that its mines could supply enough pig iron. Also it was uncertain that the Algoma blast furnaces would be operating in time to complete the order. The company's Vice-President, Theodore Search, made a special trip to Toronto for a T&NO Commission meeting in order to explain why the offer had to be declined and to apologize to the commission for the six-week delay in the proceedings.[21] Everyone, it seems, was disappointed with the outcome, but the steel had to be laid. After a second round of bidding, arrangements were then made with the J.W. Cooper Company of Montreal, representing the English firm of Charles Cammell and Sons.[22] In subsequent bidding, the Algoma Steel Company fared much better.

The contract called for a single-track railway. North American railways were seldom double tracked: the distances were simply too great and the costs too high. This meant that railway companies were at all times running trains towards one another. Therefore the operation of a single-track railway required that strategically placed sidings be installed and that provisions be made for a proper signalling system to prevent collisions. More detail regarding signals and rules will follow in chapters 16 and 17; here it is noted merely that such a system was vital and required a good telegraph system. This too was tendered by the Commission, as were other significant but not so dramatic requirements: ties, spikes, tie plates, angle bars, coal, track bolts, nut locks, switches, frogs, fencing, and ballast. All of these, as well as such matters as rolling stock, steam locomotives, and the inspection of ties and other equipment were also handled through tender. In all instances the commissioners sought professional advice either from their own chief engineer or from experts in other companies, notably the CPR, the Grand Trunk Railway (GTR), and the Canadian Atlantic Railway. Such direction was given willingly and quickly. In short, the pre-operational activities of the T&NO proceeded through 1902 and 1903 in a very organized and logical fashion.

While they were making arrangements for equipment, locomotion, and rolling stock, the commissioners were heartened by the news coming from the North, where progress seemed to be as consistent and rapid as one could expect. The Commission's solicitor in North Bay, E.S. Senkler, reported no delays in acquiring land for the right-of-way, except for terminal arrangements at the southern end. Likewise, Russell, working closely with the contractor, reported generally happy progress. In other ways as well, the new line was beginning to have a definite impact on the town of North Bay and on the lands in the area along the line's right-of-way.

The significance of the railway was quite obvious to the people of North Bay, especially to the business community and the town council. It was also patently clear that the greatest advantages would accrue if the new government line were to locate its southern terminal, with its yard, shops, roundhouse, and principal station, in the town of North Bay. In terms of payroll income, town development and property, the effect on a small town of only 2500 persons would be tremendous. It was, however, equally clear that the location was by no means a certainty. Indeed, the nearby village of Nipissing, while much smaller, was a definite possibility for these facilities, since it was already the junction point of the Grand Trunk Railway and the Canadian Pacific Railway. The former ran south to Toronto from that point; the latter ran eastward to Montreal and westward through North Bay to Sudbury and beyond. Connections with those lines at Nipissing Junction would give the T&NO access to both major Canadian centres. It was also clear that the Ontario government meant to have a connection between New Ontario and Toronto. The new road would definitely run through the junction. The question was whether or not it would run into the town of North Bay or merely skirt it at a distance of perhaps three miles.

In the early instructions given to Chief Engineer Russell, the Commission directed him to locate a line from Trout Lake northward, but also one to the town limits of North Bay as well as one directly to Nipissing Junction; and the company's solicitor was also directed to secure options on rights of way for the same purposes. The North Bay town council was certainly anxious to secure these new services for the town. And it is likely that they also remembered that J.W. Richardson, the mayor, had snubbed the Liberal Minister of

Public Works, Frank Latchford, by neglecting to attend the sod-turning ceremonies during the recent provincial election. It was probably with some political fence-mending in mind, therefore, that the town council wrote in time for the Commission's meeting on 11 August 1902 to request a meeting with the Commission, either in North Bay or Toronto, to express the town's views regarding the railway's southern terminus. Three months later, on 7 November, the commissioners did indeed travel to North Bay. In the morning they inspected the CPR yards there, travelled the line between North Bay and Nipissing Junction, and then hired carriages to examine the first five miles of the new railway route. That afternoon they met a deputation representing the town council and the local Board of Trade, who were anxious that their town be made the southern terminus of the railway.

The council declared its hope that the proposed line would run from the Trout Lake starting point and through the town to connect with the CPR which ran along the Lake Nipissing shoreline. By doing so, the new railway could use the CPR tracks to reach Nipissing Junction, which would give the T&NO its desired connection to Toronto via the GTR. The plan would also require less construction since the route through the town would be half the distance as one running six or seven miles to the junction. The Commission could use the facilities of the CPR station in the centre of the town or establish its own on the property it had purchased—known as the Metcalfe property—at the town's east end. It could also construct its repair shops on that same property. The council undoubtedly felt that these suggestions made good sense, and they did. The commissioners, however, were inclined to make the town's leaders squirm somewhat. They responded with the suggestion that "it might be useful...if the Town would make an offer...of $5000 in cash..." to encourage the choice of a route into the town and "an additional amount contingent upon the railway putting their repair shops in the same locality."[23] It was clear that the Toronto-based Commission had the upper hand.

In subsequent meetings, the town offered some very generous concessions in terms of tax exemptions. Ultimately, it was rewarded with a major commitment to the community. This included a terminal, yard, repair depot, and roundhouse. These arrangements, however, took three years to complete; they were complicated by the building of the Nipissing spur and were probably delayed less by concessions negotiation than by the change in government in the 1905 provincial election.[24]

The early impact of the line was considerable. The original contractor, Furlong, worked through the summer of 1902. In the end he could not fulfill his contract, largely, it seems, because he had bid too low. This matter was settled in October when the new building contract was awarded to Macdonell. Both arrangements, nonetheless, had the effect of increasing employment opportunity in the area. Macdonell's forces first broke ground on 14 October; by 1 December, the work force numbered 780 men, and, by 1 January, it had grown further to total 1200.[25] Concurrently, the chief engineer's staff increased both at North Bay and on the line, and, as the work on the line increased, the Commission had to add to its northern staff. Payrolls increased accordingly. Also, it was at this point that local suppliers began to benefit from the newest railway in town. Because some of the major tasks of railway building were within the competence of local contractors, this too assisted the local economy. One example was the contract for 175,000 railway ties which was won by the local firm of Thomas Wallace.[26] Indeed, it would seem that very early on the Commission had made every effort to award contracts locally. By 1907 it had become a declared policy. Such awards once again increased the employment opportunities and the general prosperity of the region.

All of this was very exciting. For 18 months or so, all ran rather smoothly. In that period, the commissioners, acting very much like absentee proprietors, depended very heavily on their men on the spot, the chief engineer and the contractor. This, it no doubt seemed to all concerned, was sensible and logical. The appointment of Chief Engineer Russell seemed to have been a good one, for he had been applauded by his colleague from the Atlantic and Dominion Railway, and his reports were clear, thorough, and competent. The contractor also appeared to have been a good choice, for the progress on the road, according to the chief engineer, was rapid and sound. Some minor difficulties appeared from time to time, but these were settled easily, usually through direct contact between the chief engineer and the contractor's men on the spot. Indeed, events were so obviously proceeding evenly and were so clearly under control that the Commission debated the advisability of holding their meetings every three weeks instead of every two weeks.

Several unexpected events broke that calm. As first envisaged, the T&NO was expected to link the two small communities of Haileybury and New Liskeard with the central part of the province. It might also promote further use of Lake Temagami which had even then become known for its beauty and for its camping opportunities, and there was also a hope that it might encourage further settlement in the Clay Belt. When Col. Matheson, a Conservative member in the legislature, declared that "the first 80 or 90 miles of the route the road would not pay," no one challenged him.[27] The expectations were not great. Yet, as it turned out, the line inspired entrepreneurs to exploit the new opportunities which the steel tracks were offering in the new wilderness. The first to appear were those seeking to pursue fortunes in all phases of lumbering. Thus, the Commission, from very early on, received requests for sidings and short spurs to service this industry. Among the first was William Milne Lumber Company, which wanted a special siding to service the mill it planned to build on Trout Lake. Another request came from the Empire Lumber Company of J.R. Booth for siding facilities at the Montreal River.

The Commission responded quickly and rather well to this unexpected demand. In particular, it established a policy regarding sidings, notably a formal agreement whereby the applicant would agree to pay the costs of constructing the siding but allow the Commission's forces do the actual work. With respect to spurs, the Commission also set down certain conditions: the spurs would have to be profitable. Profit was not, however, the railway's prime consideration. The goal was to promote colonization of the provincial hinterland; and railways were therefore seen as a form of provincial subsidy for that promotion. Because the T&NO was actually owned by the province, it was not long before such terms as "the people's railway" were applied to it. This seemed to make even more legitimate the opinions, demands, and suggestions of the people who came to live and work along the line and who saw it mainly as a means of serving their needs and their interests. Yet, in an age when it was considered that government involvement in the economy of the state should be at best limited, it was also logical that the men who were responsible for the operations of the line would have a mind-set which would limit the extent of the province's subsidization. Demands for services beyond the original and rather restricted goals of the enterprise were entertained with hesitation and even with suspicion. The provincial tax payer could be expected to provide only up to a point. Establishing that point was difficult. To assist them in finding it, the commissioners brought into play a principle which they all understood very clearly: that of commercial viability.

Forces from without had concurrently greatly altered the ambitions of the original T&NO legislation. These emerged from the growing belief that the CPR should not be left alone in its monopoly of the east-west continental link. There were two leading contenders for the completion of a second transcontinental connection: the Canadian Northern Railway (CNOR)[28] and the Grand Trunk Railway (GTR). Through judicious purchase and a careful construction programme, the Canadian Northern Railway, controlled by Donald Mann and William Mackenzie, had a continuous rail connection from Alberta eastward to Port Arthur. This ambitious firm then began seeking out smaller lines in the east with the ultimate goal of stretching its enterprise from coast to coast. In the

Turning the first sod, 10 May 1902   Hon. Frank Latchford, with shovel. (ONA-19923278)

Rock Cut, 1903 (ONA-199113)

Temagami Station, 1905   This Station burned in 1909. Its replacement (see photo on p. 239) vied with that at Englehart as the most picturesque on the line. (ONA-1991119)

East, the Grand Trunk Railway had developed a series of lines that stretched across southern Ontario and extended as far west as Nipissing Junction. Here too, the principal partners, Charles Rivers Wilson and Charles M. Hays, declared their intentions in 1902 of building across the Canadian West through a newly created subsidiary called the Grand Trunk Pacific Railway (GTPR).[29]

In the meantime, the Laurier government in Ottawa was very anxious to see some competition for the CPR and its strong connection with the Conservative party. Some effort was made in 1902–03 to bring the Canadian Northern Railway and the Grand Trunk Pacific Railway into an agreement and thus avoid a duplication of construction. With a federal election on the horizon in 1904, Laurier's government was anxious to announce a clear railway policy. The two groups were rather more recalcitrant than expected, however, and Laurier also had to contend with pressures from Quebec city, where the commercial class was hostile to any support that the federal government might give

to the GTPR to run westward from Nipissing Junction. The lower St. Lawrence, it was pointed out, would be unlikely to benefit from this line. Goods moving from the West, it was felt, would be directed southward from North Bay to Toronto and Buffalo rather than trans-shipped via the CPR to Montreal.

In the end, Laurier came up with a compromise, as he so often did. It was sound politically, but financially disastrous. The federal government would undertake to build a new railway to be known as the National Transcontinental Railway (NTR) from Moncton, N.B., to Quebec city, and thence via northern Quebec and Northern Ontario to Winnipeg, a distance of 1800 miles through a region that was largely uninhabited and underdeveloped. From Winnipeg, the GTPR would build west to the Pacific. Once the NTR was finished, it would be leased to the GTPR for 50 years at an annual rate of 3 per cent of the cost of construction.[30] The first seven years, however, were to be rent free. The plan was a financial disaster, as many predicted at the time, but the full meaning of this would not be clear for almost 15 years. For the moment, another great railway project had begun.

For the T&NO, the plan was both a danger and an opportunity. On the one hand, a federal railway was to run across the northern fringe of New Ontario. If uncontested, the NTR could be the catalyst that developed Ontario's new frontier and drained its resources into Quebec. On the other hand, the new line provided a new northern destination for the government line. If the T&NO could make a junction with the new line, it would have far-reaching connections. It could hope to draw western traffic south to Toronto from wherever the junction was made. It could, furthermore, should the T&NO be extended northward to a seaport on James Bay, draw ocean-going traffic from and to that direction as well.

On 30 July 1903, Charles Hays announced formally the unique arrangements that his company had made with the federal government. Clearly, some announcement of this kind had been anticipated, for a mere nine days later the Commission's secretary reported that he had (as instructed at the 11 July Commission meeting) met the Premier, from whom he had requested, on behalf of the Commission, an appropriation of $10,000 to conduct surveys northward from New Liskeard towards the newly proposed National Transcontinental Railway. The Premier had assured him that the money would be forthcoming.[31] From this opening gambit, a series of events culminated in the first extension of the young T&NO to points beyond the northern height of land at Sesekinika.

It was clear that Premier Ross favoured the plan to build northward in order to cut into the proposed transcontinental railway. To the west, the Algoma Central Railway, designed to run from Sault Ste. Marie towards the James Bay lowlands, was also expected to link up with the new line. These two railways would mark the first concrete efforts by Ontarians to claim, through effective control, the lands that lay beyond the height of land and which had been awarded to the province of Ontario in the boundary settlement of 1884.

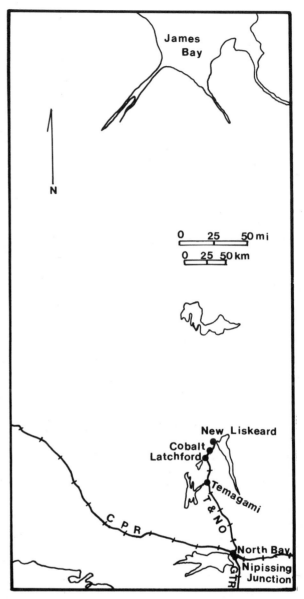

Map 4. *T&NO Evolution, 1905*

After securing, through the Premier's promise and a subsequent order-in-council, the authority and the money to conduct the northern surveys, the Commission then instructed Russell to undertake the task.[32] Concurrently, a deputation of the T&NO met National Transcontinental officials in Montreal to discuss the principle of establishing a junction. The NTR people did not, apparently, perceive any real threat to their traffic from this small provincial line. Rather, it would appear that they viewed the T&NO as being of potential assistance: supplies for the construction of the NTR could be transported into the wilderness by way of the T&NO. Furthermore, the T&NO would link the NTR with its sister company, the Grand Trunk Railway near North Bay, thereby providing the new transcontinental railway with links to both Toronto and Quebec. The two companies, therefore, saw mutual advantage to a junction, an advantage that would be reinforced if a similar connection could be made at the southern terminus of the T&NO by having the provincial line join the Grand Trunk Railway at Nipissing Junction.[33] Indeed, these opening talks regarding the northern terminus fed on the good relations between the two groups that had begun when the first agreements regarding the links at Nipissing Junction had been arranged in 1902–03. The CPR, however, frowned on the NTR/Grand Trunk ambitions. As hostility between the GTR and the CPR became more intense in the next few years, the T&NO and the GTR drew closer.[34]

At the Montreal meetings, the two groups had confirmed their common agreement that the northern junction was a good idea and that it should take place about 80–100 miles north of New Liskeard, somewhat to the west of Lake Abitibi. Further details would have to wait until more complete knowledge of the northern terrain had become known. There was nothing, however, to prevent the Commission from beginning to build towards that as yet unknown destination, and they decided to do just that.

Here the Commission faced a minor dilemma. The contractor who was already in place on the southern division of the line would have a definite advantage in bidding on the contract for the extension. In an effort to be fair, the Commission declared that it would absorb the cost of transporting, from North Bay to New Liskeard, the goods and supplies that would be needed to build the new section from New Liskeard.[35] This, it was felt, would obviate the apparent advantage of the Macdonell firm. Macdonell's bid was nonetheless lower by $157,675 than that of the next lowest bidder, the firm of Larkin & Sangster of St. Catherines. Thus, the Macdonell company (which had, perhaps shrewdly, listed its address at North Bay) officially signed the new contract on 7 June 1904.[36] The Commission's efforts to place all bidders on an equal footing was, incidentally, a wise move, for the unsuccessful firm of Battle, Conlon & Armstrong from Thorold and St. Catherines would subsequently protest the awarding of the contract to Macdonell. This protest, lodged with the Commissioner of Public Works, was not successful; but the Commission's efforts regarding the bidders was obviously a good precaution. In any event, a mere two years after assuming the task of pushing a line into the wilderness for some 100 miles, the Commission had contracted to double its commitment in the northeastern corridor; and it had done so before even a single train had travelled over the first section. The times did indeed seem propitious for the young enterprise.

Three unexpected developments jolted this complacency: increased difficulties with the contractor, the election of 1905, and the surprising bonanza at mileage 103. The first was, in the long run, the least crucial. It created some delays and some serious headaches and finally resulted in litigation, but these were all settled in time. The second resulted in a new provincial government and a new commission. The third exploded all previous plans, all previous expectations, and all sense of complacency. The silver finds at Cobalt began a process that would force a re-thinking of the entire enterprise, for they created a new frontier, a mining frontier, in the northeastern corridor. On that frontier the T&NO would both serve and shape the society that was created there. The North had begun to assert itself in earnest.

The contractor experienced serious difficulties as he moved his work crews far enough into the northern terrain to encounter sink holes. The term refers to the soft muskeg that would rise and fall and perhaps shift under heavy weight.[37] For the tracks to be secure, the

21

Widdifield Station, 1905 (ONA-1991118)

Sawmill at Mileage 14, 1903 (ONA-199118)

A track laying gang between Hailebury and New Liskeard in 1904 (ONA-19923280)

holes had to be filled extensively with ballast; but the sink holes were often so large and the muskeg so volatile that more than one filling was required. Worse, the filling could be done effectively only during periods of prolonged dry weather, which limited such work to the months of May through September. The first indication that something might be amiss came at the Commission's meeting of 24 September 1904. The chairman, Robert Jaffray, stated that in a recent conversation with Macdonell he had inquired about the non-completion of some sections of the road within the specified time, and, although Macdonell had promised to write to him on this matter, no correspondence had yet come. When the letter did arrive, it contained a request for an extension of the contract's time limit, specifically for "three months of seasonable weather."[38] Macdonell was in effect asking for an extension of almost a year. This was not a trivial request, for the original contract contained a performance clause calling for a penalty of one hundred dollars for each day that the builder ran behind deadline. The amount would have therefore been considerable, especially if one remembers that at that time a family could live on $500 a year. A special committee was struck: Jaffray, O'Brien, and the Commission's lawyer. In discussing the matter with Macdonell, this committee was inclined to

be lenient. Emphasizing that it was not required to do so, the Commission granted the extension. It would take over the line on schedule, but there was to be no inference that the Commission was accepting it as a completed project. The affair was settled, for the moment, by means of a new contract dated 19 November 1904. It called for the completion of the line to the satisfaction of the Commission by 15 August 1905.[39]

Although this action would later haunt the Commission, it is easy to understand why the new deal was struck. For one thing, in suggesting the new terms, Jaffray and O'Brien were likely confident that Macdonell would be able to deliver on his promise and finish the ballasting by 15 August 1905. He had, after all, completed 57 miles of track and 76 miles of graded road bed by 31 December 1903, when his contract had called for only 60 miles of each. He was on schedule with his second contract for 100 miles beyond New Liskeard, where his crews were actually laying the track. Indeed, at the 3 December meeting of the Commission, the chief engineer reported that the rails had reached six miles north of New Liskeard and that they would reach the 25th mile by mid-December. The feeling seems to have been that the contractor had simply encountered difficulties which could not have been anticipated. There was

Unloading ballast, 1903 (ONA-199116)

Sink hole (ONA-198825122)

ice to that point had not been by any means regular, but Macdonell's work crews had accepted some freight and some passengers on a sporadic basis. Even that had been a great boon to the area, and it was hoped that it could continue over the winter. The request, however, had been denied with regret and for very good business reasons; but it had been denied by five men sitting comfortably in Toronto. The image was not a good one.

Northerners had seen and to some extent had used the trains travelling north and south on the track during the summer and fall of 1904. These were the work trains, of course, operated by the contractor for construction purposes, but their presence and their occasional service to others had whetted northern appetites for this transportation service. To deny the use of the line for a second winter would be cruel and perhaps also risky. The Commission acknowledged these thoughts in their annual report for 1904.

"Barney" Morgan   Among the first to operate T&NO engines was Thomas "Barney" Morgan. When he transferred to the T&NO from the CPR, he began a family tradition. His son Frank, grandson Gerry, and great grandson Tim have all served as enginemen on the T&NO-ONR. (Kelly Morgan, North Bay)

every indication that Macdonell, with this little bit of help, could fulfill the committee's expectations.

Pressures from a variety of sources also called for the Commission to grant the extension and to assume the operation of the railway. Anticipation of regular train service was very high in the North, especially in Haileybury and New Liskeard, but also in Temagami and Cobalt. As early as 1903, the Lake Timiskaming communities had asked that the partially completed line of approximately 60 miles be kept open to serve them during the winter of 1903–04.[40] The serv-

> There was an urgent demand by the public including not only settlers to the north but numerous parties interested in lumbering, or desirous of establishing businesses of different kinds on the line of railway for an efficient service. The contractor was without the equipment, organization or staff essential to give a satisfactory service, nor was it possible then to establish a tariff of rates or to make traffic arrangements with other roads on the permanence of which those desiring to establish industries on the line of railway could depend. Under these circumstances the Commission considered the interests of the public would be best served by granting the Contractor the extension of time asked, subject to the right of the Commission to operate the road meantime without thereby relieving the Contractor from the obligations of his contract.[41]

Also, by the fall of 1904, other features of this very exciting project had begun to mature. The track was down; the telegraph line had been strung; stations were nearing completion at Widdifield, Temagami, Montreal River, Cobalt, Haileybury, and New Liskeard; some

An early train crew   This was not the original crew that ran out of North Bay in 1905, but it could be.
In addition to the 5-man crew, a yardman and one of the yard office staff posed for this shot.
Note that the three men who will meet passengers are in uniform. On freights, the conductor and
trainmen (brakemen) were not required to wear uniforms. (Kelly Morgan, North Bay)

townsites had been planned and surveyed; the locomotives had arrived and more had been ordered; rolling stock—coaches, flat cars, box cars—was in place and more had been ordered; and the road's principal officers had been engaged and had begun enlisting their staff. The Premier had shown interest, members of the legislature had toured the line, agreements had been negotiated with the CPR and the GTR, tariffs (i.e., a list of prices for travel or transport) had been established, and inquiries for

mill sites and living lots had begun to come in. Furthermore, the chief engineer and the recently appointed superintendent had both predicted that the line would be able to cover operating expenses immediately and in three months would be turning a profit. Everything was set to go. A few sink holes should not be permitted to stop it. The Commission assumed control of the line at 12:01 a.m. on 16 January 1905.[42] The first train ran later that day, at noon.

Notes

1. Newspaper Hansard for Ontario, 15 January 1902. Archives of Ontario (AO).
2. See p. 4 of this text.
3. Newspaper Hansard for Ontario, 27 February 1902. AO, p. 25.
4. *Electoral History of Ontario: Candidates and Results 1867–1982*. Compiled and Published by the Office of the Chief Elections Officer. Toronto. 1982, p. J3.
5. *Electoral History of Ontario: Redistribution 1867–1896*. Compiled and Published by the Office of the

Chief Elections Officer, Toronto. n.d., pp. 45–48. The constituency was joined again in 1908 and selected only one representative. In that year, a new riding, Temiskaming, was created from the Nipissing district which had, until then, included the whole northeastern sector of the province. The official spelling for the new district, until 1954, was Temiskaming. After that both the district and the lake were called Timiskaming. In 1914, the Temiskaming district was reduced to create the new electoral district of Cochrane. In 1926, Cochrane, in turn, was divided into two ridings known as Cochrane South and Cochrane North. See *ibid*, pp. 8, 12, 14.

6. Chapter 9 of the *Statutes of Ontario*, 1902.

7. Latchford to Lee, 16 April 1927. Ontario Northland Archives (ONA), B-8203. "25th Anniversary—Turning of the First Sod."

8. The contract to Patrick Furlong was actually issued through the Department of Public Works because the T&NO Commission had not yet been appointed.

9. See pp. 36–39 of this text.

10. See Albert Tucker, *Steam into Wilderness: Ontario Northland Railway 1902–1962*. Toronto: Fitzhenry & Whiteside, 1978, pp. 9–10.

11. *Ibid*.

12. Various correspondence between W.B. Russell, Engineer, and A.V. Campbell, Assistant Commissioner Public Works, for the period June–December 1902 was retained with the opening volume of the T&NO minute books. Entitled "Temiskaming and Northern Ontario Railway Commission, Minutes," the first 19 volumes covering the years 1902–1934 have been deposited in the Archives of Ontario, Record Group 14, Acc. 11444. The Ontario Northland Archives (ONA), North Bay, has obtained microfilm copies. The minutes since 1934, vols. 20ss, are located at head office for Ontario Northland in North Bay. ONA has copies of these. In this study this source will be noted simply as *Minutes*.

13. *First Annual Report of the Temiskaming and Northern Ontario Railway Commission to December 31, 1902*. Toronto: King's Printer, 1903, p. 9. The Commission's annual reports, especially those for the first 20 years, which are splendidly detailed and comprehensive, constitute a highly valuable source for the student of the Commission's past and indeed for the student of Northern Ontario history. A complete set resides at the ONA. References to them henceforth will be referred to as *AR*.

14. *AR*, 1902, pp. 5–8.

15. *Minutes*, 2 September 1902.

16. *AR*, 1902, pp. 12–38.

17. See pp. 154–57, 186–87 of this text.

18. *AR*, pp. 7–10.

19. *Minutes*, 27 October 1902. The two terms may require explanation. The term 80-lb. steel meant 80 lbs per yard. The rail has been upgraded consistently and most of the railway's tracks are now made

of 120-lb. steel. Relaying rail refers to track which has been moved from one place where it was no longer needed and then used (i.e., re-laid) again in another location. In its simplest meaning it refers to used track. Most sidings would be constructed with relaying rails taken from a portion of the main line that was being upgraded.

20. *AR*, 1902, p. 43.

21. *Minutes*, 7 February 1903.

22. *Minutes*, 7 March 1903.

23. *Minutes*, 7 November 1902.

24. See pp. 29, 64–66 of this text.

25. *AR*, 1902, p. 46.

26. *AR*, 1902, p. 38.

27. Newspaper Hansard for Ontario, 25 February 1902. AO.

28. Both the Grand Trunk Railway and the Canadian Northern Railway were systems which included several separate units, some of which the parent company had built and some which it had purchased. The section of the Canadian Northern's line that ran from Toronto to North Bay and was to continue through the Shield to the west was known as the Canadian Northern (Ontario) line. (CNOR).

29. A.W. Currie, *The Grand Trunk Railway of Canada*. Toronto: U of T Press, 1957, p. 395.

30. *Ibid*., pp. 396–404.

31. *Minutes*, 8 August 1903.

32. *AR*, 1903, p. 39.

33. See pp. 66–67 of this text.

34. In 1904 the GTR loaned its Chief Engineer, Joseph Hobson, to the T&NO to inspect the surveys of the line proposed north of New Liskeard. Hobson declared it to be "a very good one" (*AR*, 1904, p. 60). Earlier in the year the T&NO had agreed to lease two, and later all four, of its locomotives, as yet unused and being stored at the locomotive company in Kingston, to the GTR until they were needed (*Minutes*, 9 February 1904 and *AR*, 1904, p. 73).

35. *Minutes*, 7 May 1904; 21 May 1904.

36. *AR*, 1904, pp. 27–29.

37. See p. 24 of this text.

38. *Minutes*, 15 October 1904.

39. *AR*, 1904, pp. 7–9.

40. *Minutes*, 26 September 1903.

41. *AR*, 1904, p. 7.

42. *AR*, 1905, p. 12.

Chapter 2

The Cobalt Bonanza and Beyond

B Y THIS TIME Ontario was reaching the end of an election campaign. Concurrent with these northern developments, province-wide issues were changing the political mood of Ontario. The Liberal party had governed since 1872, but the most recent election had reduced its majority status to five. Subsequent scandals such as the *Minnie M.* affair in Sault Ste. Marie and an apparent inability by the government to handle such thorny issues as prohibition or the university question threatened this slim majority to the point that Premier Ross felt compelled to call an election in January 1905. The result of this election was significant for the T&NO.

First, James Pliny Whitney became the Premier of Ontario. His Conservative party won 69 seats in the legislature, compared to the 29 seats retained by the Liberals of George Ross.[1] Whitney would retain power in Ontario until his death in September 1914. The mantle then passed to William Howard Hearst from Sault Ste. Marie, the first person from Northern Ontario to occupy that post. Hearst held power until 1919, when the Farmer–Labour coalition of

Ernest Charles Drury ended the 14-year Conservative reign. Drury's victory, however, had little effect on the T&NO, because the commissioners were not replaced. And when in 1923 Drury gave way to Howard Ferguson, who had been Hearst's Minister of Lands and Forests, the Conservative tenure was re-established. It remained in place through the terms of Ferguson (1923–30) and George Stewart Henry (1930–34) until the Liberals ended their long drought with the victory of Mitchell F. Hepburn in 1934.[2] This almost continuous 30-year reign had the effect of entrenching Conservative personalities in the senior T&NO posts.

More immediately, as a result of the 1905 election, the original Commission, all Liberal appointees, resigned. This did not happen immediately. Rather, having assumed control of the line on 15 January, the five commissioners continued for three months to complete the task of preparing the road for regular traffic. They depended heavily, as before, on Chief Engineer Russell and on the recently appointed Superintendent and Traffic Manager, J.H. Black, who had come to the T&NO from the Kingston and Pembroke Railway.[3] Indeed, these two men had, in effect, the practical and day-to-day responsibility for the railroad. This situation had actually been set in place earlier.

At the meeting of 3 December 1904, it had been determined that the management of the road should be divided under two heads,

Operating and Engineering (i.e., construction). The latter had been the charge of the chief engineer from the beginning, and Russell retained that responsibility. His principal task was to see through the completion of the line as far as the junction with the National Transcontinental Railway. As events turned out, construction projects would continue unabated for almost a decade until the exigencies of the First World War halted all expansion. The Operating branch would take effect upon the assumption of control of the line from the contractor. This was a new area, and the responsibility for it fell to Black, who would be assisted by John Judge as Trainmaster. Both men had already been employed for several months and had begun the task of recruiting staff and trying to prepare for the first trains. This required some time: when the trains of the T&NO began operating in January 1905, the service could best be described as *ad hoc* or sporadic. The line was not yet in full order, stations were still under construction, and the trains were run largely by men who had been engaged by the contractor. Nonetheless, the railway had come to northeastern Ontario. Within a few weeks, the Commission issued its first official train schedule to take effect at 12:01 a.m. on 5 March 1905.[4] The five commissioners, therefore, could claim to have accomplished their original task: a rail service had been instituted between North Bay and Lake Temiskaming. On 11 March, they arranged for Robert Jaffray, the retiring Chairman, and Commissioner E. Gurney to hand over the business of the T&NO to the new Commission. Its members were Cecil B. Smith of Toronto selected as Chairman, Dennis Murphy of Ottawa, and J.L. Englehart of Petrolia. When Smith resigned 18 months later to become the line's consulting engineer, Englehart was chosen as Chairman. It was a fortuitous choice, for this elderly but energetic man would devote his remaining years to the government line. Why Whitney reduced the number of commissioners is not certain.

The succession was quite smooth, and, if not fully amiable, it was civil. It need not have

been. The original legislation had declared that the commissioners would hold their posts "at the pleasure of the government," and there was concern that this principle might also apply to the railway's personnel. To remove fears of a general blood-letting, the new Commission at its first formal meeting on 16 March 1905 announced that all employees would be retained in their current positions. There were a few casualties, for both Chief Engineer Russell and the company's lawyers would shortly be eased out, but the change of government caused minimal disruption.

Since the trains had actually begun to operate on a fixed schedule, the new Commission and its principal officers could devote full attention to two other areas of concern. The first was that of completing the apparatus of the railway, and the other was that of responding to whatever new services were demanded. Stations, for example, had begun to be erected: now these had to be completed and plans made for new ones as they were required. It was soon apparent that the schedule of two trains, each making three return trips weekly between New Liskeard and North Bay, would not be enough to satisfy the demand.[5] More equipment was needed immediately. The telegraph line needed improvement. Section houses were also needed, as were bunk houses, water towers, and additional sidings or small, private spurs. Requests for the latter had begun even before track had been laid, and, as the work on the line took place, more such requests had been received by the Commission. The new extension north, already contracted for, as well as other developments along the original right-of-way, would call for considerable and close attention. The new Commission, in other words, may have been presented with a line that was operable, but not with a line that was completed.

The original route had been set to include a connection with Lake Temagami, which was expected to draw tourists to the area and thus provide some passenger business for the railway. It was also expected that the railway would benefit as lumber operations extended northward. The

Lake Temagami, just south of the station, 1905 (ONA-1991124)

early requests for land at Temagami or for sidings or spurs to serve lumber interests were fully expected. Thus, through 1903 and 1904 and even the early part of 1905, the Commission was able to respond to the early demands without any real difficulty. Set-backs such as the sink-hole problem of the contractor were considered temporary. Once this was solved, the system could be expected to acquire the various trappings which were associated with a railway. This included an internal organization which would include the various trades, the managerial hierarchy, and the employee structure ranging from waterboys through the running trades, the dispatching system, and the maintenance department. It would also include stations, freight departments, water tanks, fuelling locations, sidings, perhaps some small spurs, and section houses. These were not simply pretty flourishes. They were all essential to the operation of the railway, to maintaining its right-of-way, to its commercial success. They were refinements on the basic line of steel, however, and could be added or developed as the railway conducted its tasks of freight and passenger service. They could be developed, in other words, in

an established pattern. It was also expected that small villages or hamlets would evolve, perhaps at a divisional point or at some of the stations or fuelling locations. This had been the case in dozens of instances along the colonization or development roads that had criss-crossed the province since the first small line, the Chippawa–Queenston road, had first opened in 1839.

But nothing could have prepared the commissioners, the government, or the general public for the explosion of activity that began in 1905. It centred around Cobalt or, as it was first known, mileage 103. The contractor had pushed north rather rapidly, and by the summer of 1903, the line had reached beyond Temagami and had work crews preparing to enter the long grade into the Clay Belt just to the south of Haileybury. There, three separate discoveries in 1903 began the process that would change the North.[6] On 7 August, James McKinley and Ernest Darragh, two lumbermen from Prescott County, walked along the T&NO right-of-way looking for timber they could use for railway ties. At a point on the southeast corner of Long Lake, they found a soft white metal that

Sawmill at Latchford, 1905 (ONA-1991127)

bent with a test bite. Although not certain what it was, the two men knew it was unusual and perhaps profitable, and they dispatched samples for testing. A few weeks later, a blacksmith working on the T&NO construction project also found a metal that was strange but intriguing. This was Fred LaRose,[7] who showed his find to his boss, Duncan McMartin. The two of them immediately staked claims even though neither was certain what the soft metal was. In October, a third find was made by Tom Hebert, who had crossed Long Lake to visit his cousin on the eastern shore. Hebert did not have to wonder for long about the metal: Dr. William Miller, the recently appointed Provincial Geologist, was in the area to investigate the LaRose discovery. He had already identified Fred's find as native silver, and upon seeing Tom's discovery, made the same identification. Needless to say, he encouraged Hebert to stake a claim. Also needless to say, Hebert did so. Subsequent assays confirmed that McKinley and Darragh had also found silver.

Convinced that a new mining bonanza was about to erupt, Miller advised the provincial government of his find. The government re-sponded by briefly suspending all claims in the region, by altering slightly the regulations regarding claim-staking, by declaring the Temiskaming region a "mining division," and then re-opening the right to stake claims there.[8] Ross's administration also appointed a mining recorder, George T. Smith,[9] who was given power to deal with claims and issue miner's licences. For his part, Miller tried to develop interest in the region by speaking publicly and by writing newspaper articles. Although he was probably somewhat disappointed, perhaps even frustrated, by the mining community's disinclination to share his excitement, Professor Miller remained certain that a rush was inevitable. In the spring of 1904 he returned to Long Lake with two assistants. He made straight for LaRose's camp, picking up two men who asked if they could share his cart from Haileybury. One was Alex Longwell, the other was William Tretheway. Both of these men very shortly afterwards made important silver finds which grew into the Tretheway Mine, the Coniagas Mine, and the Buffalo Mine. Miller assisted both of them, especially Tretheway, in their work. He actually provided the Coniagas name for Tretheway's mine, and, dissatisfied with the name of Long Lake, wrote the name Cobalt on a board and declared mileage 103 to be "Cobalt Station, T&NO Railway."[10] It was rather presumptuous, for no station existed and steel had not yet reached that point. When it did, however, the name, taken from the metal that was common in the surrounding rocks, was already in general use. Likewise, Cobalt Lake replaced the name Long Lake. While there is no remnant of Miller's name in the region, Queen's University, where he had taught before becoming the Provincial Geologist, named an important engineering building Miller Hall.

It took the whole summer of 1904 to awaken full interest in the Cobalt region, an interest that was delayed with the onset of the winter of 1904–05. It was clear, however, that things were going to start to happen there. Four mines had begun operating in 1904: the Tretheway, the LaRose, the Darragh–McKinley, and the Nipissing. This alone constituted a minor bonanza; it was expected, however, that this marked only the beginning, and may well have been another reason why the Commission had determined to start running

trains in January of 1905. There may also have been a sense of relief among the five commissioners when they were able to turn the T&NO operations over to Messrs. Smith, Murphy, and Englehart in March 1905. The Cobalt bonanza, which would continue for nearly a decade, was about to begin.

With silver so easily accessed, at least at first, and with the railway already available, hundreds of men made their way north. Most did not find silver, but enough of them did to keep the hopes of all alive and to keep the new hopefuls arriving. Prospectors spread out from mileage 103 in literally every direction. There was no way of knowing how far-ranging the rich deposits actually were. Did they run all along the T&NO line? Did they run east? Or west? By the summer of 1905, however, it was abundantly clear that the wealth was substantial and that men would be flooding into the region.

The new Conservative government of James P. Whitney clearly had acquired an unexpected bonanza. But it was equally clear that the administration, however delighted it may have been with the potential developments in

Prospectors ascending Montreal River, 1907 (ONA-1991161)

New Ontario, was uncertain about how it should manage the situation. While the potential benefits were indeed exciting, the attendant difficulties were equally frightening. First, there was the problem of land speculation. It had been latent all along, but the silver discoveries had brought the issue to the fore much sooner and with greater urgency than anyone had expected. A second problem was that of keeping order in the mining fields, particularly of preventing or regulating disputed claims. The appointment of Smith as a claims registrar in 1903 certainly had been a sensible step, but one man could not do it all. Third, some system had to be devised to distinguish between the bona fide settlers and the land speculator or the prospector. The basis of any settlement, it was generally felt, was the farmer who would work and develop his land or the freeholder who would improve his holdings and work to promote the region. Finally, it was felt that the riches of the province should in some measure accrue to the people of the province rather than to a few successful exploiters. Too much restriction would discourage the mining speculators; too little would prevent the public from securing any benefits. It was suggested at the time, and the Commission was to suggest again later, that

the government should simply undertake the management and control of the whole mining enterprise.

The Whitney government instead turned for assistance to the one presence which it already had in New Ontario: the T&NO. The young railway, barely able to run its own trains, became the principal government instrument for settling, developing, and promoting the new society that was taking shape in the northeastern corridor. To assist it, the Commission received some extraordinary authority for which it was responsible directly to the provincial cabinet. Through executive action—i.e., orders-in-council—and through some legislation, the Commission was vested with control over its right-of-way, over mining rights along the right-of-way, over several townsites along the line, and over mining rights within those townsites. These were extraordinary powers, but the circumstances were extraordinary.

Armed with this authority, the Commission took a series of steps in 1905 and 1906 designed to bring order and to maintain peace in the corridor. They first established the townsite locations at the spots that were most urgently in need of definition: Temagami, Latchford, and Cobalt. Following this, the townsites were surveyed into "railway lots" with areas in each designated as park land or recreation areas.[11] An upset price was placed on the lots after surveying, and lots were then offered for sale. This pattern was followed in subsequent townsites as they were designated, with occasional local differences. For example, at Englehart, the Commission assumed the responsibility of digging wells for the local water supply, and, at Latchford, Englehart, and Cochrane, the Commission took on the job of clearing the streets. In all cases, however, the mining rights were not included in the purchase price.

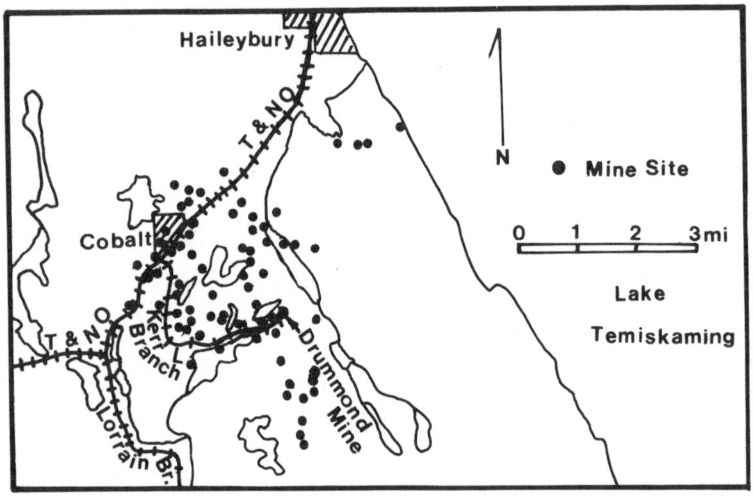

Map 5. *Mines in Cobalt area* Also showing is the Kerr Lake spur built in 1908 and the Lorrain branch, built in 1924.

T&NO Commission, 1906, in Toronto office   (Left to right) A.J. McGee, Sec. Treas.;
F. Dane; J.L. Englehart, Chairman; D. Murphy. (ONA-1988011)

The setting of upset prices required some thought. From the beginning some locations were more desirable than others. Lakefront property and lots close to the railway were considered most desirable. The prices reflected these considerations. In 1905 in Temagami, for example, the best lots lay on the west side of the railway—i.e., the lake side—and would sell for $150,[12] while those at a short distance from the lake were valued at $100. Those on the eastern and more barren side of the tracks were priced at $40.[13]

The prices set by the Commission and the regulations that accompanied them were designed to prevent, or at least to discourage, the perils of land speculation and to encourage the advent of true settlers. Prices varied from townsite to townsite, but in all cases the intent was to set a price high enough to prevent single investors from purchasing large blocks and then letting the land sit until the prices rose, but at the same time low enough for people other than the wealthy to afford. The matter of "sufficient price" was one that had long plagued settlement

agencies everywhere and was a current issue at the time in the Canadian West. The Commission was well-informed enough to include a requirement for improvement in its sale regulations. Any one person was permitted to purchase only three lots. This could be circumvented through the use of "dummy" buyers, so the terms also required the purchaser to erect a building valued at not less than $500 on at least one of the lots.[14] The rules, once again, varied somewhat from place to place and from time to time, but in all cases the intent was to discourage land speculation and to encourage the serious settler.

A certain amount of basic town planning can be seen in the early arrangement of the various townsites. Streets and road allowances were located in the original town plans, and park lands or recreation areas were usually set apart as well. Quite often, it seems, the park lands chosen were held in the highest regard by those planning to enter the community, and the commission received numerous requests for the purchase of lots in those designated areas. Such requests were consistently denied. Churches of all denominations, however, did receive a discount. This principle was first set in September of 1905, when the Methodist and Presbyterian congregations of Latchford were offered land at 60% of the upset price. (They had asked for it free of charge.) Later that same month the Commission decided that their cost should actually be 40% of the set value, and this became policy.[15] It was applied to other charitable, religious, and non-profit organizations such as the Salvation Army, the Camp Reading Associations, and the local schools. The Commission clearly intended to support any organization that would promote social order on the northern frontier, once again following the patterns set by older settlement agencies.

In setting prices and in establishing the conditions of sale, and even in determining the location of the several townsites, the Commission had virtually a free hand. The location of the townsites along the right-of-way were often rather arbitrary. Provincial proclamations vested the land in the Commission, and the commissioners could therefore put the townsites where they wished; and they did. Some, like Temagami, on the eastern arm of one of the most beautiful lakes in the province, or Latchford on the Montreal River, one of the region's most likely sources of hydro power, were obvious choices. Other selections like Tomiko, Uno Park, or Englehart were made on the basis of the railway's needs.[16] For the most part the selections preceded settlement, and thus objections or controversies with squatters were minimal and easily handled.

The big exception to this, and by far the biggest problem that was presented to the new Commission, was Cobalt. Here, hundreds of people had moved into the area before the T&NO took control of the line and before the commissioners could set down rules regarding land sales and townsites. Once the trains began running in January 1905, the number of newcomers increased dramatically. Few were settlers; fewer still were farmers. Most were young men, and almost all were fortune seekers. Exact numbers are difficult

to determine. The population grew from zero to an estimated 7000 in 1908. The 1911 census lists only 5638, but this must be considered low: the census takers were able to count only the people who were more or less settled. Many more, perhaps the majority, were transients or those who spent their time in the bush looking for silver. The Cobalt *Nugget* estimated the local population at 12,000 in 1909.[17]

At first glance, the task of organizing the Cobalt townsite must have appeared formidable to the de facto land branch of the T&NO. This body took official form when a minute of 12 April 1905 assigned the task of selling lots in the various townships to the Operating Department of the railway. Shortly afterwards, a Land Department became part of the T&NO fabric. It functioned until 1920. It would take some 18 months for the branch, assisted by some timely government action, to bring the situation under control.

It has already been noted that the Ross government had responded somewhat tentatively to the warnings of Professor Miller in the early months of 1904. After briefly closing the area to claims, the government had contented itself with simply declaring the Cobalt region to be a mining division and then re-opening it to staking. This declaration, made through an order-in-council on 6 April 1906, had the effect of reducing the size of a claim that a prospector could stake to an area of between 22.50 and 40 acres, down from a maximum of 320 acres.[18] This did not have the effect desired. The Cobalt region, because of unlimited staking by an aggressive few, became in effect a closed shop. Although the 6 April order-in-council had also restricted any individual to a total of four claims, it still meant that one person could tie up as much as 160 acres. When registering his claims, the prospector was required to certify that he had discovered "valuable mineral in place." Then, to obtain title to the staked area, he could choose from one of three options: purchase, lease, or exploration permit. All three, but especially the second, were easy conditions to satisfy. When the first considerable influx of hopefuls entered the region by way of the newly opened railway, they found that there was very little left to stake in the mining division.

To break the virtual monopoly of early speculative claims, the Conservative government of James P. Whitney took two decisive steps. First, it invoked the clause in the Mines Act which forbade a prospector from registering a claim "unless he had actually discovered a vein, a lode or other deposit of mineral."[19] Clearly designed to prevent idle speculation, this clause had been little imposed; a simple affidavit by the miner had been sufficient to satisfy that condition. This would no longer suffice. On 14 July 1905, a government order-in-council provided for the appointment of government inspectors to enforce the mineral-in-place condition.[20] Then a team of government mining engineers inspected the claims of the area. If a claimant could not satisfy the condition, the claim was thrown open. It was done very quickly, for the Mining Recorder, A.T. Smith (who probably had registered the original claims), was located on the spot in Haileybury. Charges of "government claim-jumping" were simply ignored as the process continued through the summer of 1905. It had the effect of re-opening the silver fields and rekindling the silver fever in the Cobalt camp. The new wave of prospectors, aware that they had to prove the value of their finds, were especially thorough in their searches. One observer commented: "It is doubtful whether any area of equal size anywhere on the continent has been prospected more thoroughly or intensely than the Cobalt Silver field."[21]

After taking these steps which created a virtual *tabula rasa* in Cobalt, Whitney turned the task of managing the land and the minerals there over to the Commission. The Cobalt townsite, including mining rights, having been deemed to belong to the Crown (i.e., the provincial government), was duly vested in the Commission.[22] This was done by orders in council issued in 1905 and 1906 and then reinforced by legislation.

Having received the task of sorting out the land question in the Cobalt region, the commissioners instructed the staff of the T&NO to survey the area, lay out the townsite, and examine the land there in order to report on its value. As this was being done, and as the licence commissioners proceeded to open up the Cobalt camp—Jake Englehart observed on 1 May that they were doing "great work"[23]—the Commission stayed in close contact with the government. On 26 June 1905, Chairman Smith and Commissioner Englehart discussed the status of the mining claims with members of the cabinet and with the Premier. Later that same day, the full commission struggled to no end with the problem of formulating a policy in the matter.[24] Two weeks later they came to the tentative conclusion that the land should be put up for sale in small holdings and that those persons interested should make offers on the lots they wished to obtain. Each offer was to contain the proposed purchase price as well as an indication of the percentage of gross receipts from the minerals that the buyer would be prepared to give to the Commission in exchange for the mining rights.[25] This solution, however, had the obvious fault that only the wealthy or those interested in mining, or both, would be in any position to submit bids. After yet another regular meeting, a trip into the region, and, one suspects, after more lengthy discussions, the Commission adopted a unique solution. They would split the problem. The lots in the townsite would be sold in much the same fashion as those in Latchford or Temagami, but the sales would involve only the surface rights.[26] In this fashion, the settler would have the opportunity to secure living space in Cobalt. The mining rights could be settled later, after the government had a chance to determine its policy.

The initial sale, it was decided, would take the form of an auction, to be held on 18 August 1905, at 1:00 p.m., in Cobalt. Advertisements of this event were placed in newspapers in Montreal (*Star*, *Gazette*, and *Herald*), Ottawa (*Citizen*, *Journal*, and *Free Press*), and Toronto (*Globe*, *Mail and Empire*, *News*, and *Star*), as well as the North Bay *Times*, the North Bay *Dispatch*, the Temiskaming *Herald* (of New

Liskeard), and the *Haileyburean*. Purchasers were expected to pay 25% of the purchase price at the auction and the balance within 30 days. After bidding successfully for one lot, the purchaser could purchase an adjacent lot for the same price, but a building clause also required that at least one building worth $500 should be built on every two lots.[27] This improvement condition was later removed.

Before any of this could take place, however, something had to be done about the buildings, both business and private dwellings, that had already been erected. Those structures were sitting on land vested in the Commission and which the Commission wished to sell. Yet, those same buildings had been put up in good faith during the hectic and unregulated days of the first strikes. Their owners had to be treated as fairly as possible. To accomplish this, the T&NO Superintendent was instructed to take the plan of the Cobalt townsite and endeavour to arrange with each building owner to locate upon the lot which he already occupied and to offer him the privilege of buying such a lot at the price which the adjacent one brought in the auction.

On the morning of the scheduled auction, the Commission held a meeting in the private car "Temagami" on the tracks at Cobalt, and set prices for the lots ranging from $350 for choice corner lots to $100 for the more distant locations.[28] These upset prices were to apply on all locations that did not sell that afternoon. Clearly, a purchaser, if he were already interested in obtaining Cobalt land, had little to lose by attending the auction.

As it turned out, some 75 lots were sold on 18 August 1905, and some of them were real bargains.[29] Someone named A. Rankin, for example, obtained three lots, valued at $675 (total) for $10 cash; the Bank of Commerce picked up five lots for a total cost of $473.50 against an upset value of $1300; and even Frank Latchford, the former Minister of Public Works and a prime mover behind the inauguration of the T&NO, obtained two lots in Cobalt. Latchford, however, paid the full price. He did not purchase land in Latchford! The total sales

General view of Cobalt, 1905 (ONA-1991125)

were not large and no doubt reflected the tran-
sient nature and temperament of the people
there. They were miners, not settlers. Although
the auction and subsequent sales of surface lots
through the T&NO offices in North Bay solved
only half the problem, they did establish a basis
upon which municipal institutions would be
built. It did not take long. Coleman Township
was organized in 1906 and the town of Cobalt
incorporated in 1907.

Over the winter of 1905–06, the Whitney
government scrambled to put together a sensible and fair mining policy. Cobalt was the first
apparently wealthy mining field in the province
since the Sudbury rush of 1882, where American entrepreneurs had gained control. There
was a strong wish that the new wealth be shared
more equitably and more within the province
than had been the case in Sudbury. From mining interests, both great and small, came other
pressures for a clear and streamlined policy.
The response was the Mines Act of 1906.

This statute extended the Mining Division
principle to include all of the province; it abandoned royalties and regulated working conditions. It strengthened the requirements of
discovery and inspection which Whitney had
used so effectively the previous year in the Cobalt camp, and it provided for a mining commissioner. In all of this, the miners generally
concurred. They did not, however, care for the
doubling of the licence fee to $10. The repudia-
tion of a royalty system payable to government
also pleased the miners, but there remained a
substantial body of opinion, both within government and without, that felt the public should obtain a portion of the wealth that was being
extracted from public lands.[30]

The Premier had, shortly after assuming
office and well before the introduction of the
Mines Act, indicated that the land and minerals
of the Cobalt townsite and the right-of-way
would be vested in the Commission, and the
Commission based its own activities regarding
land sales, etc. on the assumption that obtaining
the necessary authority was strictly a formality.
This lends significance to the Commission's ac-

tion in engaging an experienced prospector,
N.W. Parlee, to examine the right-of-way to determine the extent of the wealth that might lie
there. And as early as June 1905, the Commission discussed the possibility of actually engaging actively in mining. The same thought had
occurred to the government. It would certainly
have been one way in which the public could
secure its share of the wealth. The activities of
Parlee and independent prospectors reinforced
the belief that considerable wealth lay below the
ground at Cobalt.[31] Although his friend Commissioner Englehart supported the idea, Whitney hesitated to take such a bold and
unorthodox step.

Instead, in the fall of 1905 he withdrew
from prospecting all unclaimed portions of the
Cobalt region as well as the beds of Cobalt Lake
and Kerr Lake. He also forbade prospecting on
a tract of timber known as the Gillies Limit.
Then, after giving notice that a tax of some kind
would form part of a new mines management
programme, the government opened up the
area to prospecting again, excepting the beds of
Lake Cobalt and Kerr Lake, the Gillies Timber
Limit, and the T&NO right-of-way. Whitney announced his plans for these exempted areas in
April 1906. These had been developed and re-
fined by the Commission over the winter.

In January, with the reports of the chief engineer and the prospector Parlee before them
and with the general knowledge that they had
from their own northern investigations, the
T&NO Commission adopted two principles regarding the mineral rights on the unclaimed
portions of the townsite and right-of-way: the areas would be divided into substantial blocks,
and the blocks would then be offered for sale
by tender.[32] All information at the disposal of
the Commission—the assay reports on Parlee's
findings—would be furnished to the public,
presumably to give equal opportunity to all bidders. By March, the Commission had designated three parcels: the northwest 40 acres of
the townsite, the southwest 37 acres, and the
right-of-way between mileage 101 and 105.
The terms of any sale, furthermore, would have

to include an immediate payment for surface rights,[33] an immediate payment for mining rights, and subsequently a percentage of the gross receipts of the ore produced. All of these mining locations were taken up, though not without some difficult negotiations, in 1906, as were other locations along the right-of-way.[34] Subsequent agreements for the lake beds also served to exploit those locations as well as provide a share for the provincial treasury. These did not involve the T&NO, however, nor the arrangements regarding the Gillies Limit, which witnessed the provincial government's first foray into the realm of publicly owned mining ventures.

While the Commission struggled with the problem of finding the best way to settle the Cobalt lands in a fair, equitable, and orderly fashion, a natural process occurred in the camp. In brief, it gradually ceased to be a poor man's camp. The surface ore was sifted off. Much wealth remained, but it lay beneath the ground. No longer could a man work a claim with simple implements. It became necessary to dig for the ore, and, once found, the precious portions of it had to be separated from the waste. This task required either concentrators or smelters, or both. And this in turn meant the assertion of a whole new set of realities. The silver-bearing ore had to be dug from the ground, it had to be shovelled into the concentrators, then it had to be loaded onto ore cars for shipment to smelters which could extract the silver. These several steps required extensive labour and substantial capital investment. The day of the wild-catter was ending. The surrounding areas would continue to yield rewards for the persevering—or lucky—prospector, but in the Cobalt townsite, along the T&NO's right-of-way, the mining process became more orderly and much easier to control. This factor undoubtedly contributed to the success which the T&NO enjoyed in implementing its land and mining policies.

Much has been made of the relative absence of lawlessness in the Cobalt silver camp when compared to gold or silver rushes elsewhere. And if the Cobalt case is compared to that of Leadville, Colorado, or San Francisco of 1849, the claim would appear valid. The explanation for this circumstance usually rests on two considerations. The first is the argument that Canadians generally have been less violent than their American neighbours and generally have had greater respect for the upholders of the law. The second is that the police forces have been rather more competent and more sensible in their approach. In the case of Cobalt, considerable credit has been accorded the provincially appointed Inspector Caldbick and his assisting police officers.

Certainly Caldbick should receive kudos. His policy of collecting firearms from all incoming passengers of the T&NO was both sensible and effective.[35] His commanding presence and his effectiveness in dealing physically with troublemakers—potential or actual—also contributed towards teaching respect for law and order in a rough set of circumstances. So did other officers of the courts maintain law and order, such as Magistrate Atkinson, who was especially harsh in setting penalties for acts of excessive violence. The fate of the unfortunate Sam Spanelli no doubt also contributed towards a disinclination to commit violence. This young Italian immigrant died on the gallows in North Bay on 26 November 1909, after being convicted of killing a young Chinaman, Lung Chew, in a restaurant brawl in Haileybury the previous year on 13 July.[36]

The most irritating problem that prevailed in the Cobalt camp, and indeed throughout the length of the line, was that of liquor control. Prohibition had not yet come to Ontario—it would not until 1916—but the restrictions on the liquor trade in the mining camps were considerable. In response, the entrepreneurs stepped in. Bootlegging establishments, commonly known as blind pigs, came to be common in the north and especially in the mining camps where the sale of intoxicants was illegal. In some instances, a companion enterprise, the brothel, also operated concurrently. It was to be expected that these two related commercial activities would appear and flourish in a community which was dominated by young, single men. It is doubtful that anyone really felt that it would be possible to stop them. But because both were potential contributors to violence, it was necessary to try to control them, especially the blind pigs, which were much easier to establish and much more common.

Caldbick and his colleagues certainly attempted to provide such control, as did other persons in authority. Close restrictions were imposed, for example, on the shipping of liquor over the railway. In one instance, the recently appointed Travelling Agent for the line, George W. Lee, used the T&NO's influence to delay the granting of a liquor licence to an Englehart hotel until after the railway had completed building its station and yards there.[37] But the most publicized efforts against the liquor traffic of the region were the dozens of raids that the police authorities conducted against the blind pigs. These were dutifully reported in the area's principal newspaper, the Cobalt *Nugget*. From these reports and from other accounts in the *Nugget* regarding the liquor traffic, one gets the impression that the goal was control, not eradication. There was a rhythm to the raids, almost a schedule, as the inspector and his assistants moved about the area. The bootleggers themselves came to regard the raids and the resulting fines, which were also consistent, as business hazards and overhead expenses.[38] The incidents of violence remained remarkably low in a situation that was potentially explosive.

The Cobalt camp and those that followed it had two features which undoubtedly contributed to a reduction in violence and lawlessness. First, although to many it appeared that the provincial government moved forward in faltering steps towards a policy for the region, the indecision existed only on the question of dividing or distributing the wealth. In terms of civil control and the maintenance of order, there was really no hesitation. From the beginning, the area lay within the judicial jurisdiction of the District of Nipissing, centred in North Bay. The judicial system was already in place, complete with courts and even a gallows, as the fate of the unfortunate Spanelli clearly demonstrated. It was

simply a matter of appointing officers of the court such as Magistrate Atkinson, Inspector Caldbick, and Inspector Burke to exercise that authority in the new region. Local government, in the form of towns and organized townships, came very quickly also. In the interim, the important matters of land and mineral rights had been handed over to the T&NO Commission which dealt with them in 1905 and 1906. Other stabilizing institutions also entered the region with remarkable speed. Churches of several denominations, notably the Methodists, Baptists, and Roman Catholics, established themselves very quickly in 1905 and 1906 in Temagami, Latchford, and Cobalt. From North Bay, J.L. MacDougall, the school Inspector for the district, moved promptly to insure that lots be set apart for schools in all the townsites. The T&NO Commission, which had control of the townsites, fully concurred. The American Reading Association also began its activities along the line in 1905, as did the Salvation Army. Among the Army's early personnel in Cobalt was Leonard Miller, who enjoyed a curious notoriety from his previous career with the train-robbing gang of Jesse James.[39]

All of these stabilizers benefited in their efforts by the second feature: the presence of the T&NO. The same trains that carried the miners, prospectors the promoters, and entrepreneurs, also carried the ministers, preachers, teachers, policemen, and magistrates. Civilizing influences accompanied the boom in Cobalt; they did not lag behind. When a provincial proclamation decreed that the first municipal elections should take place in Cobalt on 7 January 1907, that same pronouncement declared that the polling station would be the Opera House! The railway, in other words, provided an easy access for all influences, and all of them came very quickly. Conversely, the railway also provided the only practicable exit from the region. A criminal could use this avenue to escape, of course, but he had better not hesitate, for once a crime had been discovered authorities could close the exit with great speed. Furthermore, since the T&NO had both its own policemen

Derailment of "Cobalt Special" at mileage 38, January 1909   Only minor injuries resulted. The railway, even today, boasts that it has "never lost a passenger." (ONA-1988084)

and its own telegraph system, a felon who sought to escape by train placed himself in considerable jeopardy. Order came quickly to the North, and it came on the railway.

The establishment of order in Cobalt was made easier as large and medium-sized mining corporations replaced the original surface operations. These companies naturally developed their own hierarchy for internal management which incidentally contributed to a more orderly society in general. Some of these firms designed and built their own somewhat rudimentary concentrators. These were intended to perform at least part of the task of separating the silver from the ore. Several such concentrators were operating by 1907.[40] The concentrates thus produced still required further refining, a process that involved either smelting or water flotation. A few years later the extraction process used either arsenic or cyanide. No plants capable of performing this function were established in Cobalt. The closest such refinery was that of the Montreal Smelting Company which began operating on Trout Lake near North Bay in 1907. Others were far more

distant, and in fact about 80% of the smelting was done at various points in the United States.[41] Regardless of the refinery locations, the concentrates had to be carried out of the Cobalt region over the T&NO. This type of freight had not been—could not have been—foreseen.

When the original Commission set about the task of ordering motive power and rolling stock, it had in mind the line's initial purpose of providing an avenue into the Clay Belt for agricultural purposes. Based on the assessments of its own engineer, the Commission expected that the principal products going north would be various types of supplies, machinery for farms or lumbering, household goods, and passengers. From the north it was expected that the trains would haul agricultural produce, lumber products, and passengers. That even this traffic was expected to be light can be seen in that the first purchases were limited to four engines, ten second-class passenger cars, 175 box cars, and 100 flat cars. No orders were placed for parlour cars or sleeping cars. And certainly no one even suggested ordering ore cars.

Here again the Cobalt strikes had changed everything. Hundreds, indeed thousands, of people made their way into the mining regions. The range of their motives was broad. Some continued to prospect, and some came for adventure, but many more came seeking work in the mines or on the railway, either in its operations or on construction. Others sought profit or other adventures through commerce or the service industries such as the power companies, timber operations, or education. There were even those who were involved in the entertainment business. Cobalt had an opera house by 1906, and there were other theatres in the region. Entertainment was live, of course. The *Nugget* of 4 June 1910, for example, reported on a three-day run of "The Irish Boarder," starring the well-known comedian, Tom Marks. The report also observed that "the vaudeville specialties introduced between acts are numerous and of the highest order."

Among the entertainers should be included professional hockey players. Cobalt very early on acquired a team, and as early as 1909, the Cobalt "Silver Seven" sought the right to challenge for the Stanley Cup, which Governor General Lord Stanley had recently donated as a symbol of Canadian hockey supremacy. It was a serious claim. Early that year, on 26 January, the Silver Seven (there was a seventh position then, known as the Rover) had defeated the Ottawa "Wanderers," the reigning cup champions, by a 4-2 score in a game played in Cobalt. Sceptics at the time may have downplayed the Cobalt victory by observing that the Wanderers may have been unnerved by having narrowly missed travelling on the T&NO's Cobalt Special which derailed at mile 38 out of North Bay (see photo on p. 42). It was the first mishap on a passenger train suffered by the young railway.[42] Other prominent, early tourists travelled to the Cobalt region by train. One was the poet Dr. Henry Drummond who was a shareholder in the Drummond mine. Once there, however, his medical background pulled him into ministering to the large number of typhoid sufferers in the town. His efforts to help stem this terrible epidemic cost Drummond his life, for he contracted the disease and died in the camp.[43]

Waiting Room, Cobalt Station, 1910 (ONA-19911128)

Banquet at the opera house, Cobalt, 1 January 1907   Social refinements came
quickly to the north. (ONA-19923282)

His death was noted, and regrets expressed, in the minutes of the Commission. Another famous visitor was the runner, Tom Longboat, recently returned from his Olympic triumphs, who came north in the summer of 1909.[44] He raced against a local lad named Harrison, who managed to stay with the Olympian for two miles of a five mile run. Lord Charles Beresford, the British Admiral, toured the Tri-town area in September of 1909 with a large party from the Ontario legislature.[45] A young Mary Pickford also came north in 1910. A group of six celebrated writers and editors from Chicago received special attention from the Mayor, J.H. Lang, and from Superintendent Black when they arrived in Cobalt in the morning of 9 September 1909. The combined press influence of these writers prompted special treatment: tours of the mines and a dinner at the Temiskaming Hotel. Like any local politician, Mayor Lang promoted his town whenever he could.

The list of famous visitors to Cobalt in the opening years of the camp is very long and can be obtained by reading the Cobalt *Nugget*. The arrivals of the famous, the influential, the unique, and the rich received special attention on the newspaper's pages. And it was likely this segment of the travelling public that caused the commissioners to add such railway amenities as parlour and Pull-man cars as well as additional sleeping cars and first-class coaches. The *Nugget* may have given disproportionate attention to the more notorious passengers; but the paper's highly chauvinistic editors were also careful to report the high rate of passenger patronage on the government line. Christmas of 1909, for example, saw 2369 passengers book out of Cobalt on 22–24 December. For those three days, reported the *Nugget*, "the platforms were crowded and the waiting rooms packed to the doors. Mr. Earle and his assistant worked morning, noon and night at the wicket."[46] In July 1909, passenger receipts on the line rose to $58,116, said the paper, as compared to $34,152 in July 1908. Freight revenues for the same months rose from $40,035 to $78,168, an increase of 95%. The paper observed that this rise in business was attributable to the T&NO's completion of its line to Cochrane in 1908, and once the NTR also completed its track, the Ontario line was able to increase its traffic. Reports such as these did not surprise T&NO officials. They received weekly and sometimes daily reports of traffic and were fully aware of the strain placed on the line's equipment and resources by the ever-increasing demands of the Cobalt camp and the surrounding area.

Notes

1. *Electoral History of Ontario: Candidates and Results...*, p. J4.
2. The results of these various elections can be found in *Ibid*, pp. J4–J7.
3. *Minutes, 25 May 1904, 24 September 1904, 3 December 1904.*
4. Train Schedules, A.E. Simms Collection, ONA.
5. See p. 47 of this text.
6. The most recent account, and a good one, of the early silver discoveries in the northeast is that of Philip Smith, *Harvest from the Rock*, Toronto: Macmillan, 1986. For Cobalt, see pp. 133–151. See also another recent account, Michael Barnes, *Fortunes in the Ground: Cobalt, Porcupine and Kirkland Lake*, Toronto: Boston Mills, 1986.
7. According to a story which was circulated widely in the north, Fred LaRose discovered silver by accident. While working at his blacksmith's forge near mileage 103 on the T&NO, he was harassed by a troublesome fox and threw his hammer to chase off the animal. He missed the fox but, as the story goes, hit a rock and revealed silver. Another version contends that LaRose spotted silver while answering a call of nature. The regular repetition of both stories irritated two northern ladies, Joan Nabb and Molly Lynch, who concluded wryly that clearly standard equipment for prospectors must include a supply of hammers and Exlax! It had been the intention of the writer to prepare perhaps the first account of the North which did not mention LaRose and the fox, but I felt that the wit of these two women should be credited.
8. Smith, *Harvest from the Rock*, p. 124.
9. *Ibid.*
10. *Ibid.*, p. 126.
11. The size of the lots was determined by the length of a surveyor's chain: 66'. A lot was one-half chain (33') by 2 chains (132'). Because railway surveyors and engineers performed the task of laying out the townsites in Northern Ontario and elsewhere in Canada, the term "railway lot" evolved.
12. *Minutes, 26 June 1905.*
13. *Minutes, 26 July 1905.*
14. *Minutes, 12–13 April 1905.*
15. *Minutes, 27 September 1905.*
16. *Minutes, 5 June 1905, 8 August 1905.*
17. Cobalt Nugget, 1 November 1909.
18. H.V. Nelles, *The Politics of Development: Forests, Mines and Hydro-Electric Power in Ontario 1849–1941.* Toronto Macmillan, 1974, p. 157.
19. *Ibid.*, p. 158.
20. *Ibid.*, Smith, *Harvest from the Rock*, p. 147.
21. Nelles, *Politics of Development*, p. 158.
22. Kerr to Hart, 14 November 1906. AO, RG8, J.L. Englehart, Box 10.
23. Englehart to Hanna, 1 May 1905, AO, RG8, J.L. Englehart, Box 10.
24. *Minutes, 26 June 1905.*
25. *Minutes, 11 July 1905.*
26. *Minutes, 8 August 1905.*
27. *Minutes, 15 August 1905.*
28. *Minutes, 18 August 1905.*
29. List of Cobalt Lots Sold. Whitney Papers, Box 5, RG3, AO.
30. Nelles, *Politics of Development*, pp. 159–66.
31. *Minutes, 10 November 1905, 24 November 1905, 13 December 1905.*
32. *Minutes, 26 January 1906.*
33. *Minutes, 27 March 1906.*
34. *AR*, 1906, p. 17.
35. Tucker, *Steam into Wilderness*, p. 16.
36. Cobalt *Nugget*, 18 September 1909.
37. Englehart to Hanna, 24 April 1907. AO, RG8, J.L. Englehart.
38. Cobalt *Nugget*, 26 November 1909.
39. *Ibid.*, 16 November 1909.
40. *AR*, 1907, pp. 90–104, contains a detailed report by Mining Engineer Cole regarding the systems established in Cobalt. Cole's reports for the next several years provide a running commentary on these developments.
41. *AR*, 1907, p. 97. Report of Mining Engineer Cole.
42. Cobalt *Nugget*, 25, 26, 27 January 1909.
43. D.M. LeBourdais, *Metals and Men*, Toronto: M&S, 1957, p. 144.
44. Cobalt *Nugget*, 1 September 1909.
45. Cobalt *Nugget*, 7, 9, September 1909.
46. Cobalt *Nugget*, 27 December 1909.

Chapter 3

Meeting Northern Demands

T WILL BE remembered that the Commission assumed control of the line on 16 January 1905. From there it required almost three months before an official schedule could be produced to take effect on Sunday, 5 March 1905. This called for the operation of two trains only. One was a first-class passenger train which would run north from North Bay to New Liskeard on Monday, Wednesday, and Friday and south from New Liskeard on Tuesday, Thursday, and Saturday. The second was a mixed train that ran north on Tuesday, Thursday, and Saturday and south on Monday, Wednesday, and Saturday.[1] No trains ran on Sunday. Since the railway in January 1905 possessed only four engines, seven coaches (3 first-class, 4 second-class), 3 baggage cars, 197 flat cars, 50 box cars, 10 stockcars, 2 flangers, 2 snow plows, 2 boarding cars, and 2 vans, the first timetable could hardly be much more ambitious, especially since the contractor was still using some of the rolling stock. Even so, that first year saw a second schedule providing daily passenger service in both directions. As equipment was withdrawn from the contractor, unscheduled freight trains—some of which from time to time could hook on a passenger car—

were run according to the demands of business and the availability of rolling stock. Even with these limited resources, the operating department managed to turn a profit from the very beginning. The profit for January 1905 was $526.49,[2] thereby meeting the predictions of Chief Engineer Russell and Superintendent Black.[3]

Five years later, in the Annual Report for 1910, Superintendent Black issued figures to summarize the line's traffic for the year.[4]

	Northbound	Southbound	
Passenger Trains	2,803	2,800	
Freight Trains	1,701	1,729	
Mixed Trains	314	314	
Non-revenue Trains	90	70	
Work Trains			969
Total	4,908	4,913	969
Total Trains		10,790	

	Northbound	Southbound
Loaded Cars	21,321	10,201
Empty Cars	3,611	14,765
Total	24,932	24,966
Total Cars		49,898

That same year the Commission reported total earnings of $436,130.31, of which $420,000 was paid to the Treasurer of Ontario. Ironically, this was $130,000 less than the amount paid in the 1909 fiscal year. In 1911, the net earnings rose to $593,152.69, of which the Commission sent $515,000 to the Treasurer.[5] These are amazing figures for a line still operating on half its total length. They reveal the incredibly heavy demands that had, in a very short space of time, been placed on the resources of the Commission.

The demands came from three sources: from the government of Ontario which came to lean more and more on the Commission for the solution of northern problems; from the fact that the Commission was in the railway business and that industry had its own distinctive challenges which might come from competition, technological change, or politics; and from the unique geographic characteristics of the North itself, which called for special accommodation from the corporation, from the people who ran it, and from the people who chose to live in the North. The Commission did not simply respond, however. In many instances, the Commission itself, or its employees, chose to initiate enterprises or to modify accepted practices in order to push forward on the new frontier.

Perhaps the greatest and most obvious challenge which faced the Commission was that of servicing and exploiting the new areas of growth to the northeastern corridor. The discoveries of 1903–04 at Cobalt were being repeated in other places. Some, like Kerr Lake, were close at hand; Charlton was somewhat more removed; Elk Lake lay further away; and Gowganda was further still. These locations had become well known by 1909, when news of the South Lorrain silver deposits began to command attention. Reports of promising mineral discoveries on the Quebec side of the border also started to filter into the public view, as did the first rumours regarding Larder Lake. And during the winter of 1909–10, exciting news of gold deposits in the Porcupine region kept the Cobalt camp in a state of constant excitement. Located as it was in the midst of proven riches and on the T&NO main line, Cobalt had become a centre for rumours and speculation as well as mining activity. One gets the impression of an entire camp during the months of February and March 1910 holding its breath waiting for the spring break-up to permit knowledge of the Porcupine to reach Cobalt, and then the world. Shortly after the Porcupine potential was confirmed, news of lignite coal finds north of Cochrane roused moderate new excitement.

The full potential of the new areas could only be surmised, for more than one promising gold or silver region had petered out after initial promise. Yet, the mood in the North was such that many felt that each new find could lead to another Cobalt. Moreover, each new area wanted what Cobalt had: a railway. The Commission found itself inundated with demands for new construction at a time when the link to Cochrane had only just been completed. Decisions had to be made regarding each new find, and, because railways were so expensive, the decisions had to be correct.

As a result of these fresh demands, the debate was renewed regarding the purpose and role of the T&NO. The T&NO, in one view, had been designed as a colonization road, and, as such, its purpose was to promote settlement and development. Profits were, at most, a secondary consideration. That being the case, the Commission should arrange to build whatever lines were warranted or demanded. The T&NO, in short, should operate as a service industry, not as a profit-oriented corporation. Among those who held this view early on was Robert T. Shillington, the MLA for Temiskaming. This new constituency had been created in 1908 and included the lands between Marten River and James Bay. Shillington held this seat from 1908 to 1914.[6] As a resident of Earlton, he had a special interest: he wished to see a branch of the T&NO built from his home town into the mining fields at Elk Lake. There is, however, no reason to doubt that Shillington, like many northern residents, sincerely held to the view that the line should operate as a major social force in linking and serving the North and that others should worry about its profitability.

In this he was fully supported by the Cobalt *Nugget*, whose editors viewed the railway not only as such a social force, but also as a means of redistributing wealth. The paper took considerable pleasure in observing that the North contributed mightily to the wealth and prosperity of Canada and Ontario. Sudbury, it noted proudly on 11 November 1909, had a virtual world monopoly on nickel, and Cobalt held the same status regarding silver. This wealth, however, found its way eagerly, said the editor, into general provincial coffers or into private hands in the south. By spending heavily on the T&NO and by reducing the tariffs on T&NO freight, passenger, telegraph and telephone services, the Ontario government could return some of that wealth to its source.

The opposite view, that the T&NO was simply a profit-seeking organization, found few, if any, supporters. Yet there was a strong body of opinion which felt that the railway should pay its way; it should not be a drain on the public purse. This was certainly the view of Jake Englehart, and he stated it publicly on several occasions. This view was probably not present in the first months of the Commission. Indeed, it probably did not appear important when the main task had been that of simply getting the line built. On one occasion, early on, the original group of five commissioners received a request from a small group that had settled north of Temagami at Milberta asking that the line be run near their location.[7] In response, the Commission instructed the chief engineer to investigate the request and if it were possible to do so, to run the line as requested. Obviously, there was no profit or commercial motive involved in that case. But the Commission changed, as did the conditions and the prospects in the North. What had been foreseen as a new farming region had become also a mining frontier. The former might not be flamboyant, but it was rather steady and more or less predictable. Mining was neither; more care, more planning, and more information were required. The Englehart formula, that the line should be expected to pay its own way, was therefore adopted. The adoption was never formal. Rather it probably came to be recognized as the chairman's choice and thus became the recognized principle for proceeding with any enterprise within the T&NO organization.

Such an attitude could be expected from a man who had been immensely successful in business, who could count the evolution of the Imperial Oil Company among his creations, and who

J.L. "Jake" Englehart, Chairman 1906–19 (ONA-1988095)

espoused the principles of hard work. Englehart, however, stopped short of complete rugged individualism. When Premier Whitney had seemingly suggested that his government would consider undertaking the mining task of exploiting the Gillies Limit, Englehart declared his approval.[8] Since this move was viewed by many as a step towards government commercial enterprise, Englehart obviously did not line up in the camp that opposed the tendency towards public ownership. Rather, he wished any enterprise, public or private, to follow sound business practices and accept business risks. No doubt, he also saw this approach as the best yardstick by which to measure the various demands for railway construction that became common as the north country increasingly revealed its wealth and charms. In any event, regardless of protest by the *Nugget*, Bob Shillington, or others, the T&NO became a publicly held company with a commercial motive.

49

An Apiary Demonstration, 1916   The original caption read, "Bees and clover actually go together. Temiskaming can produce more and better clover than any other part of the province." (ONA-19911413)

Healthy cattle owned by A.W. Skinner, Englehart, 1916 (ONA-19911399)

The two principal characteristics of the line —the commitment to serving the North and the commitment to follow sound business practices —would pervade its operations throughout its history. The two need not be incompatible, for the two goals often feed each other; at times, however, one dominates. In the years 1905– 14, the Commission was constantly receiving fresh requests for service; the traffic and profits grew annually, and throughout the railway's sphere of influence, economic conditions were generally good. At times they were better than good; they were booming. During this decade, therefore, when faced with the gargantuan task of managing the railway and simultaneously helping to supervise the inaugural years of an entirely new society, the Commission leaned towards following the principles of sound business. A basic policy or philosophy of some kind had to be in place to guide the Commission and its actions. It was this consideration, therefore, that guided them in first setting and then following four concurrent programmes defined in the yearly reports as "additions," "betterments," "beautification,"[9] and "expansion."

All four required the Commission to engage a very large force of personnel with far-ranging skills and talent. This force grew naturally, as the several requisite departments grew from the two basic units—engineering and operations—established in 1905. The precise organization varied somewhat at different stages in the railway's development—as it did with all railways—but it always provided for the integration and operation of such essential segments as yard services, shops, roundhouses, dispatching, car hire, demurrage, and train operations. The net result was the establishment—very quickly—of a powerful and prominent presence throughout the North.

The additions really constituted only the process of completing the railway's physical plant and its organizational infrastructure. They involved the construction of stations, passenger shelters, fuel depots, water stops, bunk houses, warehouses, and wyes, indeed the full range of buildings associated with the operation of a full-service railway. These tasks followed naturally

in response to the line's own needs and the needs of its clientele.

Officially the programme of betterments meant simply an upgrading of the T&NO's physical presence. It began with the decision to improve the track—in terms of its grade—by constructing the Widdifield division, a desirable project because of the heavier loads that resulted from the use of ore cars. Another early betterment was the stringing of a second telegraph line. This trend continued throughout the line's history. The most striking examples would include consideration of electrifying the line (1920), dieselization (1946), automatic block signal (ABS-1950), and, most recently, the use of continuous welded rail (CWR).

The programme of beautification seems to have been inspired by the active role that members of the second Commission took regarding the railway and the North in general. Before resigning as chairman, C.B. Smith had travelled the line many times, and, as a result of a tour of European railways he had undertaken in his first few months as chairman, he had obtained a solid basis of comparison between those lines and the T&NO. His successor as chairman, J.L. Englehart, was an almost constant presence in the North for the next 14 years. Frederick Dane, who took Smith's position on the Commission, involved himself heavily in the North from the very beginning. He made several exploratory trips along the line in late 1906 and in 1907—the minutes of the Commission record six such journeys, and there may have been more—and in 1908 he became even more active when he accepted the position of Land Agent for the Commission in addition to his other duties. In this post he travelled the line even more, usually in the company of the General Agent George W. Lee. Lee assumed Dane's place on the Commission when the latter resigned in 1914 to accept a position in Europe with the Canadian federal Department of Trade and Commerce.[10]

These men, through their northern travels and experience, came to realize the impact their railway was making and to understand the

Farm of William Schell—Dack Township, 1916 (ONA-19911390)

This portrait of a young girl appeared in the AR for 1911 This photograph and others like those on pp. 50, 52 and 53 which were also printed in the *AR* were designed to demonstrate the settlement opportunities in New Ontario. (ONA-19911174)

First public pump at Englehart, 1913 (ONA-19911308)

Women and children on the sections, 1905 (ONA-1991129)

importance of its image. They were very sensitive to negative press coverage, especially from the *Nugget*, which often complained that the "people's railway" was neglecting its full responsibilities to the North. The T&NO, in their view, must not only perform all the tasks that were set before it, but it must also be perceived to be doing them. The railway's buildings, property, and grounds should therefore not only function well, they should look good too. E.A. Audet remembered that, whenever the office staff at South Porcupine learned of an impending visit by Englehart, they would pay special attention to make certain the windows were all clean and that the station was clean and dust-free. He noted also that the chairman made a point of checking the glass on the framed pictures he had donated to the station.[11]

Paint and care can do much to promote beautification. So can flowers. Special attention, therefore, was given to the appearance of the railway's stations and other buildings. Because of the considerable tourist traffic to Lake Temagami, the station there received more attention

than most and became very quickly something of a showplace on the line. When it burned in January 1909, it was replaced with an even more attractive structure. Cobalt was another special case. Here the station facilities received a substantial upgrading and enlargement in 1909–10 to accommodate the heavy congestion that had developed there. That station was also among the first, along with Temagami, to have flower gardens attached to its grounds. The Cobalt *Nugget*, perhaps as penance for its highly critical stories over the previous few months regarding the railway, featured a picture of these grounds on its front page of 11 August 1910. This undoubtedly pleased both the station agent and the gardener. Their pleasure, one suspects, disappeared a month later when the *Nugget* ran another story telling how the entire flower bed had been eaten by a cow! Such set-backs did not stop the programme. Flowers became a prominent feature at all stations, and a mild competition developed among the station masters regarding their floral designs. While Temagami station may have remained the railway's

Diver Station, c. 1910   Station agent, Tom Baker, on platform.
Section gang on hand car. (ONA-1988231/Simms)

Englehart Station showing flower garden, green house, and water tower, 1911   The decision to establish a divisional point here meant that larger than normal facilities were required. (ONA-19911167)

Track at Lake Sesekinika, 1991   At this point, the T&NO track crossed the Arctic watershed. (ONA-19911163)

premier showplace, over the years a consistently strong rival was the station at Swastika. For years the leader in floral design was Englehart, where the line maintained experimental greenhouses. These were closed in 1934 following the Racine investigation.

The northern acclimatization of the second Commission also changed its attitude towards managing the line. Certainly the heads of the various departments, such as the Operations Branch of J.H. Black, the Bridges and Buildings Department of W.J. Oldham (which evolved from the Construction Department), and the Mining Department of A.A. Cole continued the tradition of making the day-to-day decisions. This had been set by the first Commission's heavy dependence on the expertise of Chief Engineer Russell and Superintendent Black. A very distinct change took place, however, in the years immediately following the selection of J.L. Englehart as Chairman. Jake adopted very much a "hands-on" approach. So did Dane. Later, George Lee followed this example. As time passed, therefore, the Commission came to be seen as part of the management team, rather than simply as an appointed group that would set policy but leave its application to others whom it hired. Englehart and then his successor came to be perceived as both Chairman and General Manager, although only Lee actually carried the two titles. It was an evolution made possible by the way these men involved themselves so closely with both operations and policy.

It was also made possible, in the beginning at least, by the close relationship—personal and political—among Premier Whitney, Englehart, Cochrane (Minister of Lands and Mines), and Hanna (Provincial Secretary). Whitney depended especially heavily upon Englehart and felt confident in doing so because of his friend's proven competence. What began as a personal modus operandi, however, became an established pattern that would persist until it was broken temporarily by Premier Mitchell Hepburn after 1934,[12] and then fully by Premier George Drew. The system had its detractors. It also had its faults. It is beyond dispute, for example, that it placed considerable—some said intolerable—power and authority in the hands of the chairman. It is also clear that there was a considerable supply of patronage available, and it was used. The Conservative party held office from 1905 to 1919 and again from 1923 to 1934. It held great advantages in the North, and T&NO appointments reflected that. Yet the system worked, and worked well, for almost 30 years.

Of the four new programmes adopted by the second Commission in its early years, the most dramatic was that of expansion and new construction. No one seemed to doubt that this would take place. Only questions of where and when had to be answered. Expansion had already begun, of course, for the first Commission had contracted for most of the line that was to be built north of New Liskeard to a northern junction with the National Transcontinental Railway. Once it was determined that this junction would take place at Cochrane, more definite plans could be made. The second agreement with Macdonell did not cover the full distance; a further section, which came to be known as the Northern Extension or the Forty Mile Extension, was needed. Accordingly, bids for that job were received in 1907, and the contract was awarded to the firm of McRae, Chandler & McNeil.[13] Macdonell did not bid. Had he done so and had his bid been the lowest, it is still unlikely that he would have won the job. He had been late in his first contract, he was late in the second, and was currently involved in litigation with the Commission on both of them![14]

McRae, Chandler & McNeil also experienced problems. It was probably not the firm's fault. Weather conditions for 1907 were extremely unco-operative. This point was made at length and with graphic detail by the chief engineer in his annual report for 1907.[15]

The McRae firm also suffered from a shortage of working capital and by January 1908 was in such straits that it had to renege on its contract. By special arrangements with the contractor, the T&NO, working through Chief Engineer McCarthy, appointed a new superintendent of construction, T.S. Scott. He would pursue the job with vigour with advice from a member of the

The weather conditions existing along line of railway since March 1907, have been, I believe, without parallel. The spring was the latest ever known. Snow-shoes were used to advantage by members of survey parties of National Transcontinental Railway near MacDougall's Chute as late as June 1st. Snow fell at Englehart to the depth of about nine inches on May 28th. Frost did not leave ground so that ordinary grading could be economically done until well on in June. By this time "rainy season" had set in and all operations of survey and construction were carried on under very adverse conditions.

At Englehart, it rained in July fourteen days, in August twenty days, in September twenty-two days, and in October seven out of first ten days of month. At Driftwood, rained in July sixteen days, in August twenty days, and in September twenty days. These records are from Engineer's diaries and can be relied upon.

Swamps were full of water all summer. Streams did not fall to ordinary summer level, and generally all conditions were abnormal.

When it is considered that on many other days of month after the heavy rains, clay cuttings and swamps were too wet to work, can be readily seen what a poor chance contractors had to get jobs done on time, or to carry on operations economically.

Until month of October laborers were exceedingly scarce at high prices. They kept moving continually from place to place and thus lowered their efficiency. For example, on Kerr Lake Branch in month of August there were employed 602 men. A force of 168 men, constantly employed, would have been sufficient to have performed same amount of work.

On Charlton Branch in month of July there were employed 760 men. 197 men, if employed constantly, would have been sufficient. In August there were on pay roll 595 men. The average number was 219.

The difficulties confronting contractors became greater as we got further north. Railway fares of greater proportion of men are advanced by contractor hiring them. It is very common for these men when they arrive at the different works to remain a very short time, often not working long enough to get out of the contractor's debt, and to seek work elsewhere. More men must then be brought in and this movement repeated. It can safely be stated that contractors in the North have lost thousands of dollars by their failure to hold men that were brought in...

Excerpt from Chief Engineer's Report, 1907 (AR, p. 29)

View of Cochrane, 1910 (ONA-19911156)

McRae firm acting in a consulting capacity and with McCarthy's men looking over his shoulder! The results were remarkable. Grading began in January 1908, tracklaying on 15 May, and ballasting shortly afterwards. By 26 November the wye at Cochrane was near enough to completion for trains to turn on it; and when the construction season ended on 30 November, the track was serviceable at moderate speeds.[16] The line was through to Cochrane, but it would require further improvements before it could handle extensive traffic. These were made in 1909.

Several other construction projects were affected by the inclement weather of 1907. These had been begun because optimism was high among northerners and the commissioners. When a mining area requested a branch line, the first assumption among most people was that it would probably be built. This attitude was one reason why the "pay as you go" principle came to be confirmed. Before any construction was authorized, the commissioners insisted upon three prerequisites: a survey to locate the route, a "trial run" to determine the grades and

curvature of the track, and a traffic estimate to determine the possible commercial return. It would seem that these requirements were more easily met in the first flush days of 1905 and 1906—the early days of the Cobalt boom—than would be the case a little later.

These prerequisites were nonetheless required even in those halcyon days before the Commission would endorse the need for rail access to Kerr Lake, Charlton, Elk Lake, and the waterfronts of New Liskeard and Haileybury. All of these had their special promoters in 1905 and 1906; all were approved; and all were ultimately built. But it took three years to complete the first and six years to finish them all. Each had its particular problems. The process followed by them all confirmed the sagacity of Englehart's "measure twice, cut once" mentality. At the same time, another northern reality was presented in concrete terms: the people of the North were indeed very grateful to have the railway, but they were not prepared to give the railway everything it wanted if that meant too much inconvenience. The clearest early case of this temperament would come from Hailey-bury,[17] one of the two significant communities that predated the railway, but the first example of it came when the T&NO decided to build the Kerr Lake branch.

The first requests for service into the mines to the south and east of the Cobalt townsite came in the summer of 1905. Traffic prospects appeared good, and in November the chief engineer reported on a trial run he had made from mileage 102 (between Short Lake and Cobalt Lake) in a southerly and then easterly direction through the Gillies Timber limit and thence along the shore of Giroux Lake to Kerr Lake.[18] There seemed to be little reason why the spur could not be built quickly. It was only about four miles. But all did not go smoothly. In particular, the owners of the McKinley-Darragh Mine made some substantial demands in return for the use of part of their sur-

face rights for a railway right-of-way. The Commission, disinclined to meet these demands, responded by testing alternative routes. One started at mileage 104, north of Cobalt Lake to the University Mine, the other ran from the main line directly eastward to the Drummond Mine near Kerr Lake.[19] When these did not prove suitable, the Commission finally agreed that the route from mileage 102 should be adopted.[20] To obtain the necessary surface rights, it had to provide, at its own expense, a 200-foot siding for the use of the McKinley-Darragh Mine.[21] There was some urgency, since the Commission had already advertised for tenders for the construction of the Kerr Lake branch, as well as for a spur into Haileybury and a branch into Charlton from Englehart.[22]

On the Kerr Lake line further delays resulted when the original contractor selected was

Temporary trestle, Kerr Lake branch, 1908   Trestle work served two functions. It provided a temporary means of spanning waterways or gulleys until a more permanent structure could be installed. This enabled crews to continue to lay track beyond the point where such a bridge was required. Also, trestle work could be used to keep a grade reasonably level. In this case, when the spanning structure was to be permanent, the trestle would be filled with earth and ballast, thus erecting an elevated roadbed. (ONA-199175)

Loading lumber, Charlton, 1914 (ONA-19911342)

unable to meet his obligations and when the new firm, McQuigge & Hunt of Arnprior, encountered some unforeseen problems. One was the need to re-route part of the line to avoid covering, by the railway's embankments, some of the silver veins on one of the mine properties! Two other problems, bad weather and a shortage of reliable labour, were enunciated by Chief Engineer McCarthy.

> The extremely wet season, and labor troubles among the miners of Cobalt Camp combined, caused contractors no end of trouble and delay. Men were openly hired off railway work to go to the mines. The management of all the mining properties paid more for ordinary labor than any railway contractor could afford. They thus got pick of all the men brought upon railway work.[23]

Blasting at the mines and along the railway also occasioned delay, as did the care that had to be taken by the construction crews when working in the same vicinity as the working mines. Here, as on other construction projects all along the T&NO right-of-way, even partially completed projects could be used to haul freight. On the Kerr Lake branch, however, this caused unacceptable delays. Because the grades were quite rough, the shunting of cars before the roadbed was fully ballasted often resulted in derailments, so service was discontinued.[24] By the end of 1907 the preparatory work—clearing, grading, etc.—had been more or less finished. The track laying was completed in 1908.

At about the same time, the spur into Charlton was also close to completion. This branch had first been requested by a petition presented to the Commission on 26 April 1906 from William Hugh and 83 other residents in the vicinity of the village of Charlton at the foot of Long Lake. Its main function was that of serving the Long Lake Lumber Company. After passing the requisite tests of cost, location, and commercial viability, this line also received the sanction of the Commission.[25] Although twice as long as the Kerr Lake branch, it was completed in about the same time. One reason was that the five recalcitrant property owners on parts of the desired right-of-way were treated much more abruptly than in the Kerr Lake case. After learning of the objections of these owners and of those of the lumber company, on

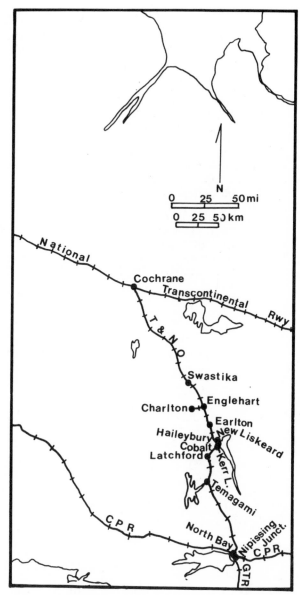

Map 6. *T&NO evolution, 1909*

Lumber Company at the Charlton end of the line.[26] This evidently overcame the local obstacles. It is also likely that workmen on the Charlton branch, situated westward from Englehart some 30 miles north of the Cobalt mines, were not as tempted to leave as were the men on the Kerr Lake branch. There was, however, as Chief Engineer McCarthy noted in his 1907 report, some labour trouble on that line during the summer months, and of course the wet weather affected work there as it did elsewhere.[27]

By the end of 1907, the eight miles of road bed had been completed; by the end of January, two miles of track was in place; and by the end of the year, the branch was fully operable. In fact, regular train service began on 24 October 1908.[28] The track on that branch, incidentally, had been upgraded from 60-lb. steel to 80 lb. on the advice of the chief engineer at the Commission meeting of 2 May 1907. It would seem that this change was made with a view to extending the Charlton branch in a southwesterly direction into James township towards Gowganda. Two months earlier McCarthy had been instructed to investigate such a plan because of the "recent developments" in that area.[29] These two moves—the upgrading of the track and the idea of an extension from Charlton—signalled the beginning of the debate regarding the route into the Elk Lake mining region in James township. This debate would heat up considerably after the Gowganda region also began to show promise of mineral wealth and to demand a rail link with the main line of the T&NO.

At this point four new construction projects demanded the Commission's attention: the Elk Lake–Gowganda branch, a branch into the Porcupine, spur lines into Haileybury and New Liskeard, and an extension or spur from North Bay to Nipissing Junction. Each was vitally important to the T&NO, each presented unexpected and awkward difficulties, and each was largely finished in 1911. The Nipissing Junction and Haileybury projects involved accommodating the presence and interest of other railways.

15 November 1906, the Commission declared that it wished to purchase the required right-of-way, that it was prepared to pay $5 per acre for it, and that it was inclined to instigate expropriation proceedings (which it had a right to do) in order to speed up the process. The Commission also stated, however, that it was prepared to negotiate, through its legal counsel, to provide the necessary accommodation for the Long Lake

Notes

1. Timetables, A.E. Simms Collection. ONA. A mixed train is one that carries both passengers and freight. Because freight had to be off-loaded along the way (i.e., way freight) the trip could get tedious for passengers. As the line became more active, therefore, most trains carried only one or the other.
2. *Minutes*, 9 February 1905.
3. See p. 26 of this text.
4. *AR*, 1910, p. 29.
5. *AR*, 1910, p. 7; AR, 1911, p. 7.
6. *Electoral History of Ontario: Candidates and Results...*, p. 459; *Electoral History of Ontario: Redistribution...*, p. 67.
7. *Minutes*, 20 February 1904.
8. Englehart to Hanna. Private. 3 April 1906. AO. RG8, J.L. Englehart.
9. *AR*, 1909, p. 11.
10. Maund to Lucas (Attorney General) 15 April 1918. ONA. B-2082. "Commissioner George Lee"; *AR*, 1914, pp. 6, 13.
11. Interview, E.A. Audet. 17 June 1991. North Bay.
12. See pp. 197–198, 202–204, 207 of this text.
13. *AR*, 1907, p. 5.
14. *AR*, 1908, pp. 10–11.
15. See p. 57 of this text.
16. *AR*, 1908, p. 19.
17. See pp. 69–74 of this text.
18. *Minutes*, 10 November 1905.
19. *Minutes*, 17 June 1906.
20. *Minutes*, 31 October 1906.
21. *Minutes*, 15 November 1906.
22. *Minutes*, 5 September 1906.
23. *AR*, 1907, p. 38.
24. *AR*, 1908, p. 20.
25. *Minutes*, 7 July 1906.
26. *Minutes*, 15 November 1906.
27. *AR*, 1907, p. 39.
28. *AR*, 1908, p. 20.
29. *Minutes*, 12 March 1907.

Chapter 4

Three Spurs and a Rival Railway

HE ONTARIO GOVERNMENT required the Temiskaming and Northern Ontario Railway to connect with Toronto. The obvious way of meeting that requirement was a link to the railhead of the Grand Trunk Railway (GTR), which in 1888 had taken over three similar lines whose tracks ran north from Toronto to the village of Nipissing, about six miles south of North Bay. There the GTR had arranged a junction with the Canadian Pacific Railway (CPR). The Commission had three options: it could build its own line from its point of origin on Trout Lake directly to the junction; it could run its line right through the town of North Bay to make a connection with the CPR there and then reach the junction by means of a running-rights agreement over the CPR tracks through it on the way to Ottawa and Montreal; or it could arrange to have the GTR extend its line from the junction to meet the T&NO. The apparently simple choice took almost a decade to make. It involved a decision on the location of the railway's southern terminus, a decision vital to the town of North Bay; and it drew the Commission into the nation-wide quarrel between the GTR and the CPR.

The CPR had been created specifically to build Canada's first transcontinental railway, a task which it had completed 16 years before the T&NO's foundation. It enjoyed and had no reason to surrender a monopoly of access to the Canadian West. The GTR was an older line, built by a different process and with a different traffic in mind. Its original line ran across the agricultural and population heartland of Ontario —then known officially as Canada West and popularly as Upper Canada—from Sarnia to Toronto and thence by way of Kingston, Brockville, Prescott, and Cornwall to Montreal. From Montreal it had sent a line eastward, one branch following southward through Sherbrooke to Portland, Maine. In the Ontario south-west it had other links with the United States at Port Huron and Buffalo. It had built most of the original main line itself, but much of its system, like the line north from Toronto, had been acquired by absorbing smaller railways. The whole collection, brought together over 30 years, was at the end of the 1880s still committed to the commerce of the St. Lawrence valley and the Great Lakes basin, with connections to transatlantic shipping and the United States. It had no access to the transcontinental traffic which offered the main prospect of future expansion, and it was therefore bound to attempt some sort of challenge to the CPR.

Lacking the capital to expand, the GTR management first sought a western link by an agreement with the CPR. Its northern terminus was already close to the CPR main line, and the two were connected at Nipissing village in 1889, and the connection point came to be called Nipissing Junction. At the same time, the GTR secured running rights for its traffic on its rival's transcontinental line.

The arrangement soon proved inadequate. The growing economy provided new sources of investment capital, which raised the Grand Trunk's ambition for westward expansion. With a change of parties in Ottawa, federal commitment to developing the prairies increased at the same time as the political influence of the CPR waned. In 1904, the Laurier government announced plans for a new railway, the National Transcontinental. It was to run from Quebec city across northern Quebec and Northern Ontario to the burgeoning West; and the management of the Grand Trunk was so heavily involved in the new company that it could expect to have effective control.

CPR officials, jealous of the GTR's new transcontinental monopoly, adopted a very hostile stance towards the GTR. It virtually declared war in the press, in politics and in business, and in the operation of the running-rights agreement from Nipissing Junction. They could not refuse to carry GTR rolling stock or traffic as long as the running-rights agreement existed, but they could refuse to renew it. And in the meantime, the CPR could, and did, make things awkward for its rival at the junction. As any railroader knows, it is possible for yardmen to misplace or forget about a boxcar, or several of them; it is also possible to do so deliberately! By this time, the T&NO depended on the failing co-operation of the CPR and the GTR for its links with Toronto. This circumstance resulted from the initial arrangements which the Commission had made with both lines with respect to securing a connection between its railway and the provincial capital and which had involved the town of North Bay.

Relations between the new Temiskaming Railway and the town of North Bay had had a rocky beginning. Years after the event, Frank Latchford, by then a federal judge, in response to

a question regarding the date of the sod-turning ceremony, recalled the early events.

> ...the date is beyond any question 10th, May 1902. As it was an important event in my life and in the history of this Province, the date is firmly fixed in my mind... May I refer to the ceremony which took place out at Trout Lake. At that time there was considerable hostility to the project, and it was necessary to turn the first sod at a point which would permit of the construction of the railway to Nipissing Junction, if certain necessary privileges as to crossing streets, etc. were not accorded by the Municipal Council of North Bay. Of course, when it became apparent that the road could have its terminus at Nipissing Junction, anything the Commission wanted was very promptly accorded by North Bay. The Mayor of the time, as I remember, was particularly hostile and refused to take any part in the ceremony.[1]

The hostility Latchford refers to was spawned by partisan politics and by the feeling that the long Liberal rule in Ontario was about to end. When the polls returned a Liberal majority, however, the predominantly Conservative town council moved quickly to try to mend its fences. On 3 July, before the Commission had even been appointed, A.G. Browning, the town's solicitor, wrote to Latchford, then the Minister of Public Works, "inquiring if it is the intention of the Government to place the terminus of the Temiskaming Railway at any point outside North Bay," and declaring that "the Town places itself at the disposal of the Company for the purpose of acquiring such lands as may be necessary for the Company's purposes, or negotiating with the CPR for the purpose of obtaining terminal facilities from that Company."[2]

It was probably galling to the council to do this, but it was felt to be necessary. A second railway would be a tremendous boom to the town which already owed most of its existence and growth to the presence of the CPR. To lose the new line would be a disastrous blow. The Commission played on that insecurity by instructing its solicitor on 8 August 1902 to obtain options for a right-of-way from Trout Lake to the town limits and for a second right-of-way from Trout Lake to Nipissing Junction.[3] The ploy was successful: the North Bay Council agreed, very quickly, that railway property in the town would be exempt from taxes. The Commission pushed a little harder by suggesting at a meeting held on 7 and 8 November 1902 in North Bay that the town offer an incentive of $5000 to the railway on condition that the T&NO run its line into the CPR station or put its station inside the town limits on the Metcalfe property contiguous to the town; and the chairman suggested further that the town "offer an additional amount contingent upon the railway putting their repair shops in the same locality." At that same meeting, the Commission continued to assert its right to place its southern terminus—with all that this involved—wherever it chose. It also suggested that this might be Nipissing Junction and sought options for land there as well as at North Bay. In turn, the town, at a special meeting, agreed to the $5000 bonus, but stopped short of promising more as the chairman had suggested.[4]

The commissioners, of course, had to consider factors other than the wishes and political affiliation of North Bay's officials. What was paramount was the absolute necessity to arrange for a rail connection to Toronto. There was little point in building a railway that could not provide such through service for both passengers and freight. This meant dealing with the people who could provide that connection: the officials of the Grand Trunk and the Canadian Pacific railways. After consulting with these two privately owned railways during the fall and winter, the T&NO Commission on 3 April 1903 reached an agreement with the CPR for the transhipment of freight and passengers between North Bay and Nipissing Junction.[5]

> 1 (a) The Pacific Company shall, during the continuance of this agreement, subject to the conditions hereinafter contained, allow the Commission to use the Pacific Company's track either way between Nipissing Junction and North Bay for trains, both passenger and freight.

> (b) And also to use the yard and facilities of the Pacific Company at the last name point.

> (c) The use of the said terminal facilities at North Bay shall include, amongst other things, the use of switching engines, the service of all the station and yard staff of the Pacific Company, the making up and setting away by the Pacific Company of the trains of the Commission, the conducting and handling by the Pacific Company of all the freight and passenger business of the Commission at North Bay, and the ordinary station accounting in connection therewith, the Commission providing its own blank forms.

The Commission had to pay for these services, but, under the circumstances, it was a realistic arrangement. For the CPR, it was not a matter of consequence, but this agreement did obtain a connection with a potential northern location, and it would receive payment for the use made of its facilities which had already been built and staffed. It was then, in a sense, "found money." For its part, the T&NO obtained its desired link with the south, and it did so without a capital expenditure which would have been heavy. According to the chief engineer, the capital cost would have been $35,400 and annual maintenance would have been $3000.[6] Since no one really expected the traffic to and from the North to be very heavy, it made good economic sense to lease the facilities, at least for the time being. The agreement was to run until 15 May 1904, and beyond that until terminated by either party after serving written notice at least 12 months in advance. The North Bay Town Council and the North Bay Board of Trade no doubt felt a sense of relief when this decision became known, for it meant that the first connection of the T&NO with a foreign railway would take place in North Bay,[7] and that would give the town something of an edge when the final decision regarding terminal facilities had to be made. The courtship of the T&NO continued, however, as did the T&NO's efforts to secure a full right-of-way between North Bay and Nipissing Junction.

The town had one final scare. At the Commission's meeting on 10 February 1905, a special committee reported having reached an agreement with the GTR to extend the T&NO line to Nipissing Junction, to make that point the line's southern terminus, and to construct a station and roundhouse there. But the Commission at this point was something of a lame duck, since the Conservative party of James Whitney had, just over two weeks earlier, won political control of the province. The move to make Nipissing Junction the southern terminus of the T&NO had been successfully resisted for over two and a half years; it could be resisted for another month or so until a new Commission was appointed.

The change in government and the subsequent change in the Commission coincided with the Cobalt bonanza. More and better services would be required from the T&NO, and its political importance rose accordingly. So did the political influence of the town of North Bay. Nipissing East and Nipissing West both returned Conservatives in 1905 and there was Conservative representation on the North Bay Council. The new Commission appointed by Whitney surprised no one when it declared North Bay as its southern terminus. The full extent of that decision became clear as, over the next few years, the town acquired the T&NO yards, repair depot, roundhouse and turntable, freight sheds, and blacksmith shop. A further, and pleasing, consequence came when the Commission moved its accounting department from Toronto to North Bay in 1906, and then in 1908 arranged to house that branch and other clerical services in a new General Office building at 195 Regina Street in the town's east end. A measure of the significance of this T&NO building boom was the growth of the town's population from 2530 in 1901 to 7737 in 1911.

The rivalry between the CPR and the GTR had meanwhile taken a new turn. In 1902 the General Manager of the GTR, Charles Hays, had agreed tentatively to build an extension of his line

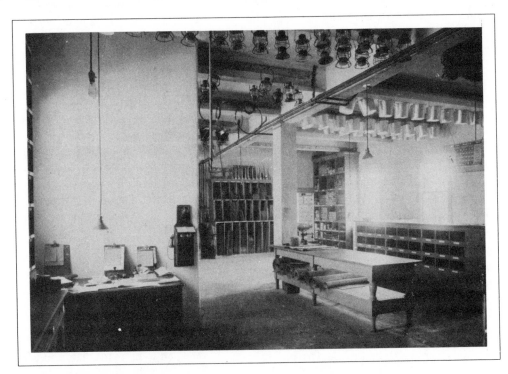

Inside the new stores building, North Bay, 1909 water buckets is clear. (ONA-1988077) The importance of signal lanterns and

from Nipissing Junction to meet the T&NO in North Bay; but he had insisted that the T&NO agree to a rental arrangement of at least five years if such a line were built.[8] By 1905, however, the Nipissing Junction link had assumed a far greater importance to the GTR. The reason actually lay 240 or so miles to the north where the T&NO would connect with the recently planned National Transcontinental, with which the GTR was intimately connected. With this new development, the GTR's dream of a transcontinental system could be realized by three simple arrangements: a junction with the T&NO and a union station at Cochrane; running rights over the T&NO railway; and a direct connection with the T&NO in North Bay. For the GTR, therefore, all that stood in the way of its transcontinental ambitions was a six-mile stretch of track! That same short track would also free the line from its dependence on the CPR.

The small, unfinished, and fledgling T&NO railway had suddenly secured some bargaining power. The Commission, and especially its chairman of November 1906, Jake Englehart, used it to considerable advantage. It helped, one suspects, that Englehart had already acquired national recognition as an entrepreneur through his assemblage of Imperial Oil, and also that relations between the two railways had thus far been good. The Commission, for example, had previously agreed, when the GTR experienced a shortage of motive power, to rent its engines temporarily to that line.[9] The modus operandi of the GTR—i.e., the practice of assembling a system of rail services through the purchase of other railways or by means of bilateral agreements with them—probably also made it easier for its officials to think in terms of such deals. And of course the animosity of CPR and the superior position which that line held in the existing agreement with the GTR regarding Nipissing Junction strengthened the position of the Commission.

The final deal varied somewhat from that arranged by the first Commission in 1905. The T&NO placed its terminus in North Bay; it used its own right-of-way on the north side of the CPR

track to construct the spur; and, upon completion, leased that spur to the GTR for a period of 20 years at an annual rate of 4.5% of the cost of construction. By this time the T&NO—once again, because of the Cobalt bonanza—had money available for capital expenditure. In the course of the agreement, the T&NO could recoup its capital costs and still own the spur and the right-of-way. Furthermore, as a provincially chartered railway, it did not have to seek the approval of the Canadian Board of Railway Commissioners. The GTR found the arrangements pleasing because it did not have to capitalize the construction or supervise it; it was released from its dependence on the CPR; and it acquired the running rights and the link it needed to North Bay and to its sister railway, the NTR, at the junction which by this time was named Cochrane. Indeed, although the two terminal agreements—at Cochrane and at Nipissing Junction—were quite separate and distinct, it is likely that the mutual dependence at each end of the T&NO line made the negotiations much easier. Even so, the full arrangements took several years and were finalized on 3 December 1911.[10]

In that time the commissioners had had considerable contact, for the most part agreeable, with GTR officials and especially with Charles Hays, the General Manager. When Hays died in the wreck of the *Titanic*, commissioners Englehart, Murphy, and Dane passed the following motion concerning Hays' funeral on 16 May 1912.

> Resolved—Chairman's actions in instructing that operations of T&NO should cease for period of five minutes, beginning at 11:30 a.m. Thursday April 25th, being the hour of memorial service at American Presbyterian Church, Montreal on that date. And further, that certain Officials of T&NO Railway should attend the service.

Through the T&NO–GTR agreements of 1911, the GTR became the third railway to enter North Bay. A fourth would follow two years later when the Canadian Northern (Ontario) Railway system would run its trains from Ottawa into its station at Second Avenue. The CNOR's route through town, now filled-in and ballasted, was originally supported by trestle work and formed a very impressive sight. This railway subsequently built westward through North Bay to Sturgeon Falls and then to Capreol. It formed part of the Canadian Northern Railway which, like the GTR, had dreams of a nationwide system and which, also like the GTR, tried to accomplish this partly through its own construction and partly by absorbing or making agreements with smaller local lines. The task proved too large for the company's resources, and this line, once again like its rival GTR, fell under the control of the federal government when the Canadian National Railway system took form in the years 1915–22. For a few years, however, with four rail lines operating through it, North Bay had become truly the railway hub of the north. As the T&NO's southern terminus, North Bay also claimed to be the Gateway to the North, a slogan which still persists. North Bayites had good cause to be pleased with the T&NO. One hundred miles to the north, however, Haileyburians had become split in their feelings for the railway they had lobbied to acquire.

It all started innocently enough. The people of Haileybury and New Liskeard, while delighted that the T&NO had begun running trains to their communities in the winter of 1905, nonetheless regretted that their respective railheads were actually located at a distance from their business and residential areas. It had always been assumed, once the enabling legislation had passed the provincial legislature in 1902, that the Temiskaming Railway (as it was often called) would run into those two small northern agricultural villages. The Commission had thought so as well. That changed when the Commission elected to run its main line 100 miles beyond New Liskeard to meet the proposed National Transcontinental. With that new objective the T&NO locating engineers chose a new path into the North. It ran several miles to the west of the original, passing very close to Haileybury and New Liskeard, but did not actually enter either town. It was possible to run the line through those communities by a route close to the shoreline of Lake Timiskaming and then

swing north after passing New Liskeard, but locating the track over the higher land slightly to the west and continuing north from there was considerably less expensive. By coming close to the two towns, furthermore, the Commission fulfilled its mandate to build a line into the Clay Belt near Lake Timiskaming; and by running northward from the New Liskeard it would be fulfilling its new mandate of connecting with the NTR.

The distance from New Liskeard and Haileybury to the steel was not great (approximately 1.5 miles in each case), but it did involve some inconvenience for both freight handlers and passengers, since roads from the town to the railheads were difficult to build, expensive to maintain, and awkward to travel. It was not surprising that individual and group petitions from both villages very early on made their way to the commissioners in Toronto. If it was not possible to serve these towns by the main line of the T&NO, was it not feasible to build short spur lines to do so? The first such request came from William Hartman of New Liskeard, who suggested constructing a spur from the station to the wharf on the lake. The Commission tabled this request at its 24 February 1905 meeting.

The commissioners were not unfriendly to the suggested spur lines; they simply lacked the resources to act. The Kerr Lake spur had already been proposed and the northern extension had been approved. These two projects fully occupied the manpower available at the time. When the petitions continued to arrive, however, the Commission responded by ordering trial runs,[11] and on 5 September 1906 resolved to advertise for tenders for the construction not only of the Kerr Lake and Charlton branches but also of the spur into Haileybury. While its engineering staff was engaged in a trial run for the Haileybury spur, the Commission also tried to assess the traffic that might result. It expected that freight for the railway could be obtained from the Quebec side of Lake Timiskaming and from other communities that had developed, or might develop, on the shores of the lake on the Ontario side.[12]

To capture this traffic, the Commission offered incentives to the town of Haileybury, in particular, to improve roads from the lake shore to the railhead. The townspeople were interested in the convenience of having a rail service; the railway was interested in freight. If the two coincided, a spur line made sense to Englehart and his fellow commissioners.

This appeared to be the case when the Imperial Lumber Company, with a huge supply of logs on Lake Timiskaming, required transportation to the sawmill of the Empire Lumber Company at Latchford. The obvious means to transport those logs was the Temiskaming and Northern Ontario Railway. When the two lumber companies indicated their willingness to guarantee freight of some $50,000 per year for seven years beginning in 1907,[13] the Commission agreed to construct a spur from its main line to a point in Haileybury where the logs could be loaded on to the railway. With this guarantee in hand, the Commission called for tenders and subsequently offered a contract to the Arnprior firm of McQuigge and Hunt. The spur was to be built by 1 July 1907.[14]

Because of the sharp incline from the station at Haileybury into the town, it was not possible to build from that point on the main line. After examining approaches from both the south and the north ends of Haileybury, the engineering department of the Commission determined that the better route would be an approach to the lake from a point on the main line north of Haileybury. The distance from the point chosen to the wharf at Haileybury was approximately 1.75 miles.

The spur into New Liskeard also received attention, and on 5 June 1905 the Commission agreed to its construction if the right-of-way into the town was provided free of cost.[15] As it turned out, it took several years for the town to comply with this condition. In the end, problems regarding the acquisition of the right-of-way, the matter of running the railway over the streets of the town, and the actual vesting of the right-of-way with the Commission were resolved, although the matter did require a hearing before the Ontario Railway and Municipal

Board on 9 September 1909.[16] Following that decision, the Commission awarded the construction contract to Canadian Contracts Limited.[17] This firm fulfilled its contract, one of the few construction contracts which passed without incident, and the 0.64-mile spur line was declared to be in operation in 1910.

Meanwhile, incidents were complicating the building of the Haileybury spur. Once the contracts had been signed with the lumber companies and an agreement had been reached with McQuigge, there seemed to be little to delay the spur line into Haileybury; but two developments appeared.

The first was the prosperity spillover from Cobalt. Haileybury prospered from the Cobalt bonanza partly because it was already an established centre of commerce. It was also an area where the mine workers, especially management, could obtain housing for themselves and their families and, while still close to the mines, could live away from the raucous Cobalt camp. Thus Haileybury expanded, particularly northward along the lakeside. It was along that same lakeside that the T&NO planned to build its spur line into the town. The north-end property owners attempted at first to convince the railway that the spur line should enter Haileybury from the south. When the T&NO remained adamant in its decision to build from the north, the people concerned about it organized opposition to the line in the town. To reach the Haileybury wharf, the line had to use part of the roadway through the town. When the work forces of McQuigge, after building easily for 1.64 miles from mileage 110 to Moore's Cove, reached the limits of the town of Haileybury in the summer of 1908, they were presented with a work stoppage injunction by a group of townspeople.[18]

A second development involved the appearance in the Cobalt and Lake Timiskaming region of rival railway corporations. Soon after it had been determined that the T&NO would construct north from North Bay, and once it became clear that mineral deposits were being found in the Cobalt region, a number of groups sought charters from the federal government to build railways in

Lake Temiskaming from Haileybury, 1906 (ONA-1991133)

the region of Lake Timiskaming. Several such charters were actually granted, but in the end only two of these groups actually began to put their plans into operation. One was the Nipissing Central Railway. This company, its principal owners based in Michigan, was chartered by the federal government in 1907. It had the right to construct a railway with lines running in several directions from Cobalt, including the right to move across the interprovincial border into the province of Quebec south of Lake Timiskaming.[19] By this time it was clear that the largest population base in the region would be located in the towns of Cobalt, Haileybury, and New Liskeard. The directors of the NCR conducted a series of surveys for an electric railway (also known as radial railways or light railways and best described as trolley or streetcar lines) among the three communities. Clearly, the directors were interested in passenger traffic. The company also negotiated with several of the municipal governments in the region in 1908. Although neither rights of way nor franchises were acquired immediately, the NCR could claim to be the first

to take a concrete and definite interest in the construction of a railway in that region.

It was a rival firm, however, which actually caused the pot to start boiling in the winter of 1909. This was the Cobalt Range Railway which had been created in 1903 but had allowed its charter to lapse. Several local shareholders sought to have the charter restored and build a trolley line to carry passenger traffic between Haileybury and the mining centre of Cobalt. Among them was Noah Timmins, formerly a storekeeper in Mattawa, who had won heavily in the Cobalt mining gamble and thus had a clear interest in providing good transport for the mine workers. Also involved were the Temiskaming Navigation Company which operated on that lake, and whose principal shareholder was C.C. Farr, the founder of Haileybury. The Cobalt Range Railway approached the town council of Haileybury on 23 February 1909 for permission to operate an electric railway over the streets of the town. The company promised to begin construction of the railway that year by September 1910. If it failed to meet these requirements, it would lose its franchise. On 2 March the council tentatively agreed.[20]

Three days later, however, a special meeting of the Haileybury town council, called for the express purpose of awarding the franchise to the Cobalt Range Railway, was interrupted just when the vote was about to be taken.[21] J.W. Fitzpatrick, one of the major shareholders of the Nipissing Central Railway, told the town that his company was prepared to build a railway from Haileybury to Cobalt, that it would begin construction by 15 May of that year (1909), and that it would have the line operating by November of that same year. The NCR, he said, was further willing to deposit a cheque of $2000 with the town council, to be forfeited to the town if the company failed to meet those requirements. The intervention of Fitzpatrick at that meeting caused the town council to give pause, and a two-week battle began between the two companies to secure the franchise from the town. Under the pressure of competition, both groups promised to perform the same tasks, offer the same guarantees, and meet the same deadlines. These included the depositing of a $2000 guarantee, the promise to begin work in May 1909 and complete the line to Haileybury by November, and the intent to operate trains between 7:00 a.m. and 11:00 p.m. daily with a fare of 10 cents for a return trip. In the process some harsh words were exchanged.

In all, it would seem that one particular factor and one particular individual provided the margin of victory for the Nipissing Central. The factor was the charter of the Cobalt Range Railway. When the Haileybury Town Council met on Tuesday 23 March 1909, the Cobalt Range Railway's representative, John McCracken of Ottawa, had to concede that his company's charter was currently under review by the Canadian Board of Railway Commissioners. He explained that the majority of such charters were granted, and he was fully sanguine that his company's charter would be renewed.[22] (In fact it was.) Alfred Jones, the lawyer for the Nipissing Central Railway, harped on this point. Indeed, he had been ad-

vised to do so by Robert McKay, the senior partner in the Toronto law firm which was promoting the interests of the Nipissing Central Railway. In a letter dated 13 March 1909, McKay advised Jones as follows:

> So far as opposition is concerned, it is a matter of tact of your promoters to meet them at every turn. You have to meet everything they say about you and say all the hard things you can about them, belittle their people financially, thoroughly discredit of their good faith and pursue methods which are quite unnecessary for me to outline to one who ever ran for municipal office in the city of Toronto...[23]

Jones took this advice to heart. He declared that the Cobalt Range Railway was a bogus company and had a bogus charter and a bogus board of directors.[24] To support this statement, he quoted telegrams which he had received recently from Ottawa declaring that the Cobalt Range Railway's charter had not yet been approved and would not be approved until at least the 25 March. He pointed out that it would not be advisable to franchise a company which might never have its charter renewed. It would be better, he said, to grant a franchise to a company that was already prepared to commence work. Another promoter of the Nipissing Central Railway, Fitzpatrick, also emphasized this point by declaring that the council should not deal with a dead company. These were harsh words, but they apparently had an effect on one particular ratepayer of the town. This was C.C. Farr, who declared:

> I am a share holder of the Temiskaming Navigation Company with whom the Cobalt Range Railway proposes to amalgamate, perhaps one of the heaviest, but I would sooner sacrifice that than see this town without an electric railway. The men are here who have the charter, and the other men only have hopes of getting a charter. Therefore, deal with the substance and not with the shadow.[25]

The effect of Farr's intervention can only be surmised, but it can be noted that the council that evening eliminated the Cobalt Range group and secured an agreement with its rival. The next day it prepared a by-law which gave the franchise for the town to the Nipissing Central. With this and other agreements with the townships between the two towns, the NCR had clearance to run from Haileybury southward to Cobalt. Here it ran into further obstacles.

The town of Cobalt was far less anxious than the other communities to grant a franchise to the electric railway. The town had been built very quickly, without any real regard for sanitary conditions or for careful planning. Mayor Lang's administration was doing what it could to correct that, and, under his leadership, the town council declared that before a railway could be constructed through the streets of Cobalt, it would be necessary to build proper sewers and drainage. This was a matter of some consequence; the typhoid epidemic that had claimed Dr. Drummond's life had not yet been fully brought under control, and the mayor's concerns were widespread.

The Nipissing Central Railway, through one of its spokesmen, J.W. Mahon, attempted to bully the town council by threatening to exercise its right of expropriation and build through the streets of Cobalt to the central square whether it had permission or not.[26] Aware that the decisions of the National Board of Railway Commissioners had consistently declared in favour of the towns in such disputes, the town council remained firm. The council was, in fact, quite prepared to have the railway come into Cobalt, provided that it would wait until proper sewage had been installed, and provided also that the line would extend as far as Kerr Lake.[27] The NCR wished only to enter the town as far as the town square. In any event, the railway placed its southern terminus on Argentite Street on the edge of town. This development really did not hurt the line because that location actually served to bring people sufficiently close to Cobalt's business centre and to the mines. Also, the company was spared the construction costs of building the line several blocks into the town's centre.

The company encountered more serious opposition in securing a right-of-way from Co-

balt to Haileybury, especially across privately owned lands in the townships of Coleman and Bucke. In four instances the railway had to invoke expropriation proceedings and go to arbitration: against John Darke, Argentite Townships Ltd., the Chambers-Ferland Company, and the Nipissing Mining Company. In all four cases the arbitrators declared in favour of the railway, but all involved expense and delay: the last award came on 30 September 1909. The Nipissing Mining Company insisted upon receiving $1000 over and above the amount awarded by the judge; the NCR paid to avoid the costs of further litigation.[28] There were other obstacles, such as the insistence by the Ulrica Mining Company that, in return for the right-of-way, the railway be required to build a station on the lands taken from the company, that this station be treated like others on the line, and that it be named "Ulrica."[29] The principal owners of the line, Fitzpatrick, Stack, and Utely, counting on local interest in getting their line built quickly, were undoubtedly surprised at the opposition they encountered from some of the mine owners.

A still more serious obstacle appeared on 19 July 1909 when the NCR sought permission from the T&NO to cross that company's tracks at mileage 105.25. The crossing was necessary because the NCR began its run at the Argentite Street terminus, a little west of the government railway's main line coming out of Cobalt. To approach Haileybury from the south and actually enter the town, the NCR had to swing eastward very close to Lake Timiskaming, and this meant crossing to the east side of the T&NO. The best spot to do so was at the Argentite Townships Company's site, and consequently it became known as the Argentite crossing. The T&NO was currently planning to double-track its run between Haileybury and Cobalt,[30] and an overhead crossing at that point would be very difficult to build safely. The NCR threatened an appeal to the federal Board of Railway Commissioners. The T&NO, as a provincially chartered railway, denied that it could be bound by the decisions of the national body. The Commission had made this claim very early on in its existence and was prepared to make it again.

The matter of the Argentite crossing was complicated by rivalry over the Haileybury spur. The T&NO, determined to secure the freight traffic from Lake Timiskaming, had committed itself to contracts with two lumber companies and the McQuigge construction company. It was prepared to use its rights of expropriation, if necessary, to extend the line as far as the government wharf, some distance inside the town. To overcome local opposition, the T&NO sought a hearing before the Ontario Railway and Municipal Board. Needless to say, Chairman Jake Englehart fully expected that the provincial board would rule in his favour.

Opinions regarding the desirability of the T&NO's Haileybury spur were still sharply divided. Generally speaking, those who had business interests in the northern part of Haileybury were in favour of the spur, while those who had homes in the region were opposed. One exception was C.C. Farr. He possessed extensive holdings in the region which would suffer as a result of the spur, but was prepared to see it go in because he felt it would benefit the community in general.

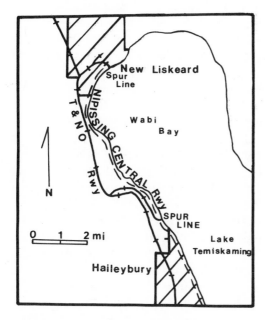

Map 7. *Spur lines at New Liskeard and Haileybury*

The Cobalt *Nugget* declared itself four-square behind those who wished to see their homes protected against an unsightly track.[31] And the local opposition to the spur was of course joined by the Nipissing Central Railway.

The NCR had an agreement with the town of Haileybury to pass through several of the town's streets, including the Lakeshore Road which ran north towards New Liskeard. The T&NO's proposed spur would run along the same road. If the T&NO were denied access into the town, the Nipissing Central could pass by the wharf and become the only rail access to the lake traffic. Those who were opposed to the T&NO entering the town did not have the same aversion to the Nipissing Central Railway, because the latter, powered by electricity, would be much cleaner and aesthetically more acceptable. The hearing before the Ontario Municipal and Railway Board began in Haileybury on 9 September 1909. Sixteen witnesses representing all interested parties were called to give testimony. The decision on 2 October 1909 was that the "best interests of the people are being served by the building of the spur line."[32]

The NCR could have appealed to the National Railway Board but was disinclined to do so. Given its promise of completing construction and becoming operable by November 1909, it could not afford any further delays. "We are" wrote J.W. Fitzpatrick on 7 October 1909, "at their mercy at other points—the overhead crossing and the siding at mile post 104. You will readily see that we cannot continue to conduct our irritating opposition to their project."[33] The Commission was also disinclined to continue the fight. The issue had already damaged the image of the railway: editorials in the Cobalt *Nugget* had decried the Commission's determination to run roughshod over the wishes of the people of Haileybury. Nor did the Commission see any advantage in a full-scale examination of the question of jurisdiction. In addition, there were exciting prospects of extensive mineral strikes in the Porcupine and requests for other spur lines into Elk Lake, Gowganda, and possibly even Kirkland Lake. The Haileybury spur no longer seemed so significant.

Some agreement regarding the line into the Haileybury wharf would serve both railways.

It came on 18 October 1909. The NCR agreed not to build north of Probyn Street or along Farr Avenue in the town of Haileybury without giving six month's notice. For its part, the T&NO Commission agreed that it would not build its spur into the Haileybury wharf without the same notice.[34] The path to this agreement had been eased some three weeks earlier by a memorandum of agreement regarding the Argentite location. The T&NO granted permission to the NCR to construct its desired crossing with some provisos. Most concerned the type of construction which the overhead crossing would assume, but for the chairman the most important was the premise that the T&NO agreed to this crossing "without admitting the jurisdiction of the Board of Railway Commissioners for Canada in the premises of the Commission..."[35] A statement by the Nipissing Central Railway to the president of the Haileybury Board of Trade, to the effect that the electric railway would switch freight from any industries located on its line to a point of connection with the T&NO railway between Haileybury and New Liskeard, also served to bring about an easing of tension.

The truce allowed the Nipissing Central Railway to proceed towards the completion of its projected line between Haileybury and Cobalt. It did not meet its commitment of having cars operating on the line by November 1909, but the grading and laying of track was completed by the end of that year, and the first street train ran into Haileybury from North Cobalt on 11 January 1910. The journey took six minutes.[36] That short demonstration run whetted the appetite of the Tri-town area for the electric railway. It was another three months, however, before that appetite was satisfied. Nonetheless, on 12 April 1910, the first street car to enter Haileybury passed over the Nipissing Central Line at 4:00 p.m. At 5:30 a.m., Saturday, 28 April the Nipissing Central Railway marked its official opening. On the first full day of operations the line carried some

2300 passengers. On 6 May some 3500 people travelled on the line.[37]

At that point, the subscribers of the company no doubt felt that they had invested wisely. Traffic was apparently very good, and the firm's heavy investment in lands in North Cobalt seemed likely to prove profitable as well, because the presence of the railway had already increased land values there. Furthermore, the patrons seemed to be content: according to most accounts at the time, the service was good, the fares were reasonable, and the journey on the line was quite comfortable. By the middle of March the Superintendent of the NCR, Charles Utely, declared the line's intention to expand north from Haileybury to New Liskeard, to Kerr Lake, and even to the Narrows if the mining interests in South Lorrain supported the movement.[38] It seemed that the Tri-town was being served well by two railways and that both would prosper.

The foundations of the Nipissing Central Railway were, however, weakened during 1910. Except for J.W. Fitzpatrick, who had fairly extensive land holdings in the region of New Liskeard, the company's main investors came from the town of Escanaba in northern Michigan. Both Frank Latchford (by then a federal judge) and M.J. O'Brien, a former T&NO commissioner whose many interests included a local mine, were involved in the railway; but they had been hired to lobby for the federal charter and neither held shares. Fitzpatrick quarrelled with J.B. Stack, another director, and with Utely, the superintendent of the railway. Fitzpatrick, at one point, simply took away the company's books. Stack and Utely recovered them through a court order and finally bought out Fitzpatrick's shares.[39] This discontent in management was exacerbated by the unexpected delays and expense incurred before operations had begun. By November 1910, barely six months after the trains started running, the directors of the company were actively seeking a purchaser for the enterprise.

They found one in Alex Fasken of Toronto. He had a controlling interest of the Cobalt Power Company and was probably interested in

Street view, Haileybury, showing NCR electric street car, 1917 (ONA-1991460)

Street view of NCR electric car system, New Liskeard, 1919 (ONA-1991489)

eliminating a potential competitor: the Nipissing Central Railway had the right, if not the resources, to engage in the power business. On 11 March 1911, the Fasken syndicate acquired a controlling interest in the Nipissing Central Railway for approximately $250,000. The rolling stock and line of the Nipissing Central Railway, with its land holdings in North Cobalt, were valued at approximately $500,000.[40]

One month later on 11 April 1911, the Fasken interests in the Nipissing Central Railway were purchased by the Temiskaming and Northern Ontario Railway for $250,000.[41] There has been speculation that the passage of the Nipissing Central Railway to the Commission was engineered through Fasken by the Chairman of the Commission, Jake Englehart. Englehart declared in 1909 that in his opinion the T&NO should have a monopoly of rail service in the North, and the purchase did eliminate his line's only competi-

tion.[42] The evidence would suggest, however, that no conspiracy was necessary. The town lands in North Cobalt were probably the Fasken syndicate's real objective; it was not equipped to run a railway. The NCR people, too, escaped from their growing financial and managerial difficulties. The T&NO, for its part, had acquired its first subsidiary and soon after (1912) extended its electric railway beyond Haileybury to New Liskeard. Because both railways had fallen under one management, the wharf problem was also solved. The townspeople who opposed the T&NO spur had their way. By running a spur of the NCR to the wharf, the Commission could accept freight onto the electric railway there and transship it to the T&NO spur line. For a quarter century the NCR carried freight and passengers in the Tri-town area until the depression and improved highway conditions forced its closure in 1935.

Notes

1. Latchford to Lee, 16 April 1927. ONA, B-8203. "25th Anniversary—Turning of the First Sod."
2. Browning to Latchford, 3 July 1902. *Minutes.* Pre-Commission Correspondence. ONA.
3. *Minutes,* 8 August 1902.
4. *Minutes,* 3 December 1902.
5. *AR,* 1903, p. 9.
6. *Minutes,* 3 December 1902.
7. For the T&NO, all other railways were foreign. Likewise, rolling stock or motive power from other lines were termed foreign cars or foreign engines. Of course, the T&NO was foreign to all other lines, as was its equipment.
8. *Minutes,* 3 December 1902; *AR,* 1903, p. 8.
9. *Minutes,* 9 February 1904. See also chapter 1, n. 36, p. 27 of this text.
10. *AR,* 1911, pp. 37–44.
11. *Minutes,* 20 March 1905.
12. *Minutes,* 26 January 1906, 13 February 1906.
13. *AR,* 1906, p. 6.
14. *Minutes,* 5 June 1905.
15. *Ibid.*
16. *Minutes,* 15 September 1909.
17. *Minutes,* 17 November 1909.
18. *Minutes,* 19 August 1909.
19. Act to Incorporate the Nipissing Central Railway, Chap. 112, 6–7 Edward VII.
20. Cobalt *Nugget,* 2 March 1909.
21. Cobalt *Nugget,* 5 March 1909.
22. Cobalt *Nugget,* 23 March 1909.
23. McKay to Jones, 13 March 1909. NCR File, ONA.
24. Cobalt *Nugget,* 23 March 1909.
25. *Ibid.*
26. Cobalt *Nugget,* 31 March 1909.
27. Cobalt *Nugget,* 2 April 1909.
28. Stack to Jones, 19 July 1909. NCR File, ONA.
29. E.J. Lockwood to NCR, 15 September 1909. NCR File, ONA.
30. Cobalt *Nugget,* 23 February 1909.
31. Cobalt *Nugget,* 18 August 1909.
32. Cobalt *Nugget,* 2 October 1909.
33. Fitzpatrick to Jones, 7 October 1909. NCR File, ONA.
34. Agreement of 20 November 1909 between T&NO Railway and NCR. NCR File, ONA.
35. *Ibid.*
36. Cobalt *Nugget,* 11 January 1910. North Cobalt, for a time called Port Cobalt, lies adjacent to Haileybury and about 5 miles north of Cobalt.
37. Cobalt *Nugget,* 7 May 1910.
38. Cobalt *Nugget,* 17 March 1910.
39. Writ of Summons, re Nipissing Central vs Fitzpatrick, 20 June 1910; statement of standing of stock...NCR, 7 November 1910. NCR File, ONA; Cobalt *Nugget,* 7 November 1910.
40. NCR *Minutes,* 13 June 1911. ONA.
41. *Ibid.*
42. Cobalt *Nugget,* 13 October 1909.

Chapter 5

The Porcupine Spur and the Elk Lake Branch

I N THEIR EFFORT to meet the demands of the railway and of the north, the T&NO commissioners had to manage a wide range of issues. Their meeting of 13 October 1909 was typical. The most troublesome item on the agenda was undoubtedly the appearance of local opposition to the construction of the spur line into Haileybury. As serious as that issue was becoming, it was only one of many demanding attention. The Commission also heard reports from the Chief Engineer on the surveys being made of Iroquois Falls and Win Falls as well as on his examination of the area around Coochiching Falls. The object of that examination was to estimate the amount of hydro-electric power that could be developed; the idea of electrifying the railway had not yet been abandoned, and, in any case, the Commission felt that it should keep itself abreast of all aspects of northern development. The chief engineer also reported that one of his men, Engineer True, was running final location surveys between Elk Lake and Gowganda and making a preliminary survey of possible routes between Elk Lake and the main line at Earlton. The Commission also discussed the typhoid epidemic at Cobalt, deciding that nurses should be granted free passage over the line to deal with the crisis there. There were several more routine matters to deal with—the killing of a horse by a locomotive, the need to clear brush at the Englehart yard, complaints about the delivery of telegrams, the establishment of express charges, and the authorization of a new timetable. Negotiations were still proceeding with the CPR over the union depot in North Bay. The minutes show the commissioners working systematically through this heavy agenda without delays or indecision. As they dealt with the matters at hand, they must have been aware, as was the whole North, that the region west of mileage 222 had suddenly acquired new importance. But they could not yet have known how quickly the discovery of gold in the Porcupine was about to affect them.

The first news out of the Porcupine did not cause any particular excitement. In Cobalt, the recognized centre of northern mining for about three years, the *Nugget* dutifully fulfilled its self-assumed obligation to report any finds of precious metals anywhere in the North. With the provincial mining recorder only a few miles away in Haileybury, the paper could easily keep track of new claims. Such reports, like that on 3 September

The Night Owls   These shop men termed themselves the Night Owls because they worked through the night to service the engines. Note the cowcatcher at the base of this engine. This device was designed to prevent animals from sliding under the wheels and thus prevent derailments. See photo on p. 79. (Evelyn Chivers, North Bay)

The area was already known to prospectors. The possibility of gold or other mineral deposits there had been noted in the Ontario geologist's reports from 1898 through 1902, but extensive prospecting had produced little result. Among the unsuccessful gold seekers had been Reuben Daigle, who found fame by missing fortune. Acting on a hunch, he had sunk an unproductive shaft that was later proved to have missed the great Hollinger vein by only a few feet! Northern prospectors were still inexperienced at locating or even recognizing gold-bearing ore. They knew silver, and the Cobalt strikes had made that their first objective everywhere in the northern corridor. When new discoveries of silver were made at Gowganda, most of those working in the Porcupine hills or around Night Hawk Lake moved there.

Some persevered. Among them were Tom Geddes and George Bannerman, who at last found gold in the fall of 1909. Their strike prompted the first *Nugget* stories of the Porcupine field. More discoveries followed: Harry Preston found what became the great Dome Mine; Alex Gillies and Benny Hollinger hit the vein that Daigle had so narrowly missed;[2] Bill Davidson, Clarence Dixon, Tom Middleton, Hardrock Smith, and John S. Wilson all made other important discoveries. The *Nugget* abandoned its caution, and even the very conservative Arthur Cole, mining engineer for the T&NO, wrote in his annual report for 1909 that "although hardly any development work has been done in the district, there seems to be reason to regard it as one of great promise."[3]

Before the coming of winter the Porcupine rush was on. Not everyone found gold, but an enormous number of prospectors tried; and they all needed food, shelter, clothing, and supplies. Many people entered the Porcupine intent on exploiting the potential exploiters. The result was the rapid development of towns as well as mines in

1909 of fresh prospects slightly east of Matheson (originally McDougall's Chutes), had become routine. Two weeks later, on 17 September, the *Nugget* reported that "some remarkable gold specimens" had been brought out of the area around Whitney township. A small rush began, but the paper's reports remained cautious: "...as almost everywhere in Northern Ontario the gold is in narrow veins and extremely pockety."[1]

Derailment of contractor's train caused by cows trespassing on track, near
Wawbewana, 1907 (ONA-1988096)

the Porcupine. By January 1910, three distinct settlements had taken form on the shores of Little Porcupine Lake. Within five months there were perhaps 2000 people there. The prospector Sam Wilson, whose letters to the *Nugget* are among the best first-hand accounts of the Porcupine rush, reported "500 living around the lake and three times as many in the bush."[4] There were general stores, hotels, even a bank, some under canvas. The Cobalt boom had created a new town in three years; the Porcupine was growing even faster.

It had the advantage of offering gold, a metal many times more valuable than silver. A further advantage was the publicity given by the Cobalt *Nugget*. As the special voice of northern mining, it had carried the first reports of the new rush—its editors strenuously refuted the rival claim of the Toronto *Globe*—and it made a point of publishing accounts by anyone who had visited the gold fields. The greatest advantage of the Porcupine, however, was the earlier success of Cobalt itself. That community had had to wait

for American or British investors to provide the capital necessary to exploit its mineral wealth. American capital would also enter the Porcupine as it did at the Buffalo Ankerite mine which operated between 1926 and 1956.[5] But the first development capital for the Porcupine came from within the North, from Cobalt. By 1909 silver mining there had created the first substantial supply of investment capital in Northern Ontario. Noah Timmins was one of several who had made fortunes from the Cobalt finds and were thus able to develop mines in the Porcupine. He began by financing Gillies and Hollinger in return for a share of their claim. He eventually put together the syndicate known as the Canadian Mining and Finance Company, which controlled Hollinger Gold Mines.[6] His success in the Porcupine enabled him a decade later to invest heavily in the Rouyn camp.

With rapid growth came the first government services and the need for more. Porcupine (which

IS GOING TO BOOM ALRIGHT, THE VERDICT

Sam Wilson Sizes Up the Porcupine Lake Situation to His Satisfaction
Second letter of Sam Wilson to his partner, Bub Andrews at the front.

Porcupine River

Well, she's going to boom alright, Bub, make no error about that. Why, there was twenty old time prospectors cooking a dinner on the portage below here and talking the same old way, only its not a vein eight inches wide chock full of silver, but dykes of quartz eleven feet wide and with free gold all through it.

Its good to be in the rush boy; the pitching of tents after a pull from sun up to sun down and the talk round the fire on a belly full of bacon and beans.

We'll be to Porcupine Lake tomorrow at noon and we will see what we will see. Oh, but she was a beaut of a day to paddle in was yesterday, boy. Snowing every minute of the day and blowing some, too. We put our canoe in at Wilson's Lake about half past eight with a dozen more.

Forty of us had got out at mile post 228. There's a couple of Englishmen running a little eating house near the tracks and its a saving of time when you want to pull out at first peep of day.

When you get out of Wilson Lake you strike Slim Creek. She's some slim, too, crooked as a dog's hind leg and just full of logs. Wilson and Bannerman have cut them out but you have to be some canoeman to make it out to Frederickhouse River without getting a bung up on a log, and there's seven miles of it, too.

We went about a mile south on Frederickhouse River before we camped for dinner. Its almighty muddy as all the water seems to be flat running to James Bay. Its the old time stamping ground of the right honourable gentlemen adventurers as the Hudson Bay Company still call themselves and balled after some grand duke or other when one of the royal George's was prancing around and having a good time in England. You [know] what it is to make a fire and eat in the snow, and we came away without cups, plates or sugar, like a bunch of greenhorns.

We struck Frederickhouse River when it was snowing hard and the sky like lead. As long as she did not kick up too much it didn't matter much though. There's been hundreds of dollars worth of flour and beans dumped in that lake already and a dozen or so prospectors. If you come up this way play Indian, and hug the shore. The lake gets up in a few minutes right from the bottom and runs six or seven feet high. We were lucky and were not tied up a minute.

We camped for the night in the snow about a mile south of Frederickhouse Lake on the river. Snug enough we slept, too, under three blankets.

We hadn't paddled ten minutes this morning before we met two Haileybury fellows with another wrapped up in a blanket at the bottom of the canoe. He was as white as a man can look when he is reddened up with the wind and sun. There was an other canoe behind it and a boy called to us "Nearly dead." loud enough for the sick fellow to hear. Kind of reassuring wasn't it?

We hit Night Hawk Lake early and skirted the north side into Porcupine River. She's not too bad for seven or eight miles from the mouth. Then you can hear fellars talking half an hour's paddling away its so darned crooked, and there's about four miles of it that's full of logs and the water running ten miles an hour against you.

They say all Whitney and Tisdale is staked. Bub and I guess we shall have to [go] into the reserve. Say, Bub, it looks all right to me. There's plenty of free gold all over. She's good for a boom and a few men will make fortunes and a bunch of suckers down country will get stuck. But hell, what's buying a prospect, but gambling anyway?

They are saying that Wilson is getting eighteen dogs and is going to ship out gold quartz, and Bannerman is going to get in a mill. There's sure going to be something doing and its going to be a live winter for prospectors particularly when a foot or so [of snow] gets on those big quartz veins. Watch some, they will grow then.

Well, she's getting late Bub, and the boys want to turn in.

Yours truly

Sam Wilson

Letter of prospector Sam Wilson to his partner, 3 November 1909 (Cobalt *Nugget*)

SAM WILSON RIDES OVER PORCUPINE TRAIL

Good Road Being Made by Convicts—Good Stages and Launches
—Last Part Only Bad
Second letter of Sam Wilson, Cobalt, prospector, to his partner,
Bub Andrews, at his home in Cedarville.

Shuniah Hotel, Porcupine.

Dear Bubb;—We've all heard a lot of talk about the Porcupine trail. I'll tell you what it's like. The first six miles out to Frederickhouse Lake you can ride. I used to despise the fellars going by me in rigs or stages as afoot and packing, but now we've made a nice little wad from these claims we sold last fall, why, Bubb, there's nothing to it, it gives you a contented feeling seeing the boys turning out of the road as you go by. For about half that six miles to Porcupine it's an automobile route, the rest of the way the team will have to walk. There was a Cobalter thought he could pick up a little dough running a chug car on the Kelso road but after he had been two hours under the car and one as a chauffeur he changed his mind. The lowering of the Frederickhouse Lake is no dream. You bowl along the water's edge at a spanking pace on the finest sand beach you ever saw. Every now and then the horses splash through a little trickle of water from some lake that last year was just a bay. Some day when Porcupine is the big gold camp there will be the finest race course in Northern Ontario along that beach. Up old Nighthawk, where we lay storm bound last fall for a couple of days, we chugged up in as neat a little gasoline as you will find on Lake Temiskaming. So far it had been like a picnic. From Hill's on the Porcupine River, if Hays Hammond himself took the trail he would have to walk. It's a bit sticky on the trail and until the frost binds up the roads it's not going to improve any.

But its a find broad road these fellows in the black and yellow pants have cut and dug and with a little ballast they would be as good as those in Coleman township. And that's going some. For a prospector who has been used to hiking it along the concession lines in the bush its Broadway. The city gentlemen with cosy corners in their vestibules, to women and children, to females in high heels, its a weariness of the flesh. But there's worse to follow. It isn't far but the trail be-tween Three Nations and Bobbs Lakes, where there are ferries, is as nice a bit of log balancing and mud wallowing as you'd want to find anywhere. To a man who can have his fizz every night and lots of it its worth a thousand dollars but prospectors are making it every day for less wages.

Wasn't I some pleased when my 75 pound packsack was on Mike Henessey's back in front of me instead of throwing in the mud when ever I stumbled over a root. The trail got so bad towards Bobbs Lake that I got kind of ashamed of myself. There was Mike sweating blood under the tumpline and I went up behind him all framed up to say, "Let me take it a spell, Mike?" What I did say was, "This would have been a mighty bad trail in the fly time."

I guess Mike must have been expecting me to take a spell for he dropped the sack with a sigh and "Phwat." said he. "A fine morning isn't it?" said I. "Oh h—" said Mike, and if ever I saw bloodshed it was in the Irishman's eye.

About ten minutes later I saw the gleam of water through the trees.

I yanked that packsack off Mike's shoulders like a flash. "I just got to do my stunt Mike," says I, and shouldered the pack as if I meant to hike her right into Porcupine. In a couple of minutes we hit the ferry and the lake and Mike wasn't as grateful as he might'a been.

Well Porcupine hasn't grown much. Freight at $5 and $6 a hundred weight has just arrested its development. There's a bridge over the swamp where the Porcupine river came into the lake and there's a fine new jail, though I'm told not a single prisoner has been thrown into the coop yet.

Your old pard

Sam Wilson

Letter of prospector Sam Wilson to his partner, 16 September 1910 (Cobalt *Nugget*)

"The Fighting Six" At Porcupine Lake

Among those who joined the early rush into the Porcupine Lake gold section just before the "freeze up" were six men who are well known in the north country, Shirley Craig, Bruno Boissenette, Arnold Frappier and Teddy Gledhill, and the Haileybury hockey players, Skeene Ronan and Lou Berlauquette.

The had a rough trip and not only endured hardships but passed through some really dangerous experience three of their canoes being sunk by the ice through which they were forcing their way on Frederickhouse River and two of the party narrowly escaping death by drowning.

Teddy Gledhill an old time Nome prospector has briefly touched on their experiences in these lines.

———————

TO THE FIGHTING SIX

"THE FIGHTING SIX" AT POR
CUPINE LAKE

It wasn't Services' Lone Moose Trail
　That we tramped to the Porcupine,
We weren't after the Northern Lights
　And we heard not the malamutes'
　whine

But a steady plug through muskeg
　and swamp
That started at Night Hawk Lake,
Where we left our grub and battered
　canoes
When the ice refused to break

I tell you the bunch were a happy crew
And we called them "the fighting
　six,"
'Cause there wasn't a thing they
　could not do
When they got in a devilish fix.

The trail was hard, but the harder
　it grew
The fight six just bulled it
　through
Till at last we reached the longed
　for goal
That we'd all been plugging for
And landed at noon at Wilson's trail
On the Porcupine's golden shore

We kicked it out to Wilson's find,
Gee' but 'twas good to see
A dyke risking out of the cedar swamp
And the gold' oh' hully gee'

Well we staked our claims
And they are good ones too
So the hardships count for nought
For we bulled it through when all
　looked blue
And we worked and got what we sought

And if ever again on a stampede i go
And want pals who are game to stick
You can bet your life that the ones
　I'll choose
Will be my pals the fighting six

The Fighting Six (Cobalt *Nugget* Saturday December 18, 1909)

82

Sam Wilson's letters first called Shuniah and which was also known as Pottsville) received a post office in January 1910 and a telephone line on 17 February 1910.[7] A recording office for claims was opened at Golden City.[8] The third settlement, South Porcupine or South End, although closest to the mines, was ignored. The *Nugget* duly carried a prospector's complaint at having to walk five miles (return) to collect his mail.[9] More seriously felt was the lack of a police force, especially after a prospector murdered his partner in December 1909. He went to Matheson to surrender himself to the police, relying unsuccessfully on a plea of self-defence.[10] A more common crime was theft, particularly of food. Miners were inclined to take matters into their own hands: they beat one thief badly before handing him over to the authorities.[11] Blind pigs, which do not seem to have been similarly resented, were also quick to appear. The first reported seizure of illegal liquor bound for the gold camp was made on 18 January 1910: six barrels of whisky consigned to mileage 222 and labelled "SUGAR."[12] Inspector Caldbick, whose territorial responsibility was extended into the Porcupine, made this arrest.

The region's greatest need was for transportation. Although the gold fields lay only some 30 miles west of the T&NO line as the crow flies, prospectors had to travel over 60 miles. Snow-packed roads could carry both men and machinery in the winter, but in summer the Porcupine Trail was a hard two days' journey. It led by canoe down the Frederick House River and its lake to the north end of Night Hawk Lake, then on foot to the Porcupine River and down it by canoe to Porcupine Lake. Reports that travellers had been reduced to cannibalism along the way were unfounded,[13] but the route was dangerous as well as difficult for travel and completely inadequate for freight. During the spring break-up it was simply impassable, even after one group had devised a bridge across the Frederick House River. Father Paradis, who according to Sam Wilson organized "the slickest bunch of camps on the road,"[14] made a more ambitious attempt to improve navigation by lowering the level of Frederick House Lake. Unfortunately he used too much dynamite

and turned the lake into almost a mud patch in the summer of 1910. Wilson conceded wryly that it had "the finest sand beach you ever saw,"[15] but it was harder to cross than ever. A still more inventive suggestion, to transport supplies by hot air balloons, was never acted upon. It was probably inspired by an international balloon race that passed over the Tri-town area in October 1910, during which one balloon landed by error in Ville Marie.[16] Demands for a railway or at least a road multiplied.

The road came first, and it was built by convict labour. An order-in-council on 7 June 1910 authorized a special prison camp at Matheson to which all the magistrates north of North Bay were instructed to send offenders sentenced to less than a year in jail. There were protests from labour unions, particularly in Sudbury; the *Nugget* was scornful of their argument that the camp was undignified for the prisoners.[17] Convict labour nevertheless cut the road through from Matheson to Night Hawk Lake. The result was less than satisfactory, because there was little shelter or storage at the points of transshipment from the T&NO: Matheson and Kelso (mileage 222). There were stories of travellers spending the night without shelter and of huge piles of luggage dumped into the snow beside the track.[18] When facilities were improved, they continued to be strained as traffic increased.[19] It was clear that nothing short of a rail spur would satisfy the miners.

The T&NO Commission had on 19 January 1910 directed its Chief Engineer to begin a reconnaissance of the Porcupine, but this was simply in accord with Jake Englehart's desire to be prepared and his axiom that money spent on surveys was seldom wasted.[20] In fact, he continued through most of the following summer to think that a freight road would be sufficient.[21] The Porcupine traffic would depend on general freight and passengers, not on ore shipments: it is still a truism among railwaymen that "there is no freight in gold." Besides, it was not yet clear that the mines would last long enough to justify the expense of a rail spur. Premier Whitney had similar reservation. "I suppose," he said,[22] "somebody

The Dome mine, 1911 (ONA-19911205)

will be wanting to build a railway to the moon next."

Where the T&NO hesitated to tread, others rushed in. A private syndicate led by Arthur Ferland of Haileybury offered to build an electric railway into the Porcupine from Kelso and provide hydro-electric power for the mines at the same time.[23] The provincial Cabinet, faced by a northern initiative to meet northern demands, approved the scheme on 28 July; but it set conditions. The new line was to run from Matheson, where there was better agricultural land than at Kelso; it was to be begun within 10 days and completed by 1 January 1911; it was to be under the supervision of the Ontario Railway and Municipal Board, and it was to act as a feeder to the T&NO. That last stipulation protected the T&NO from the threat of competition. Jake Englehart was concerned, not about the new line, but about the National Transcontinental Railway, which was proposing to run steamboats on the Mattagami River into the Porcupine at Timmins Landing.[24] The project of the Ferland group was ambitious and innovative, "one of the biggest jobs yet at-

tempted in the way of engineering in New Ontario," as the *Nugget* observed.[25] Its deadlines and its scheme for electrification were however not realistic.[26] In spite of being reorganized under E.A. Wallberg of Toronto, the syndicate failed to meet or even approximate its schedule. By the end of November, it had cleared less than a mile of its proposed right-of-way.

By that time the T&NO Commission was convinced that a railway should be built. The Dome mine, then operating at a depth of 50 feet, had run test drills showing that it would still be profitable at 800 feet, so its longevity was assured.[27] It planned a 40-stamp mill to be in operation by mid-1911.[28] The Hollinger mine, with comparably optimistic forecasts, proposed a 30-stamp mill for the same date. Sawmills were also being opened in the Porcupine. Satisfied that the region would continue to develop and that the private line had failed, the Commission on 30 November 1910 ordered an immediate start on the construction of its own spur into the Porcupine. It was to begin at Iroquois Falls, named to honour the 17th century victory of the local bands over the invading Iroquois war parties. Later renamed Porquis Junction, this point lies three miles north of Kelso; the surveys begun 11 months before had shown that to be the most practicable route. In the same week, the provincial cabinet cancelled the Wallberg syndicate's charter, and the T&NO bought out its interests.

The deadline for completing the new spur was set for 1 July 1911. That would meet the schedules for bringing in heavy equipment to the Dome and Hollinger mines. It would also be convenient for the Conservative government, which faced a good deal of northern dissatisfaction on the eve of a general election.[29] To meet the deadline, the Commission decided, for the first time, not to tender the construction but to build the extension using its own forces, augmented by day labour. Its Engineering Department had recently proved its ability by undertaking a major relocation and grade reduction of the main line. The end of steel was set, as it turned out temporarily, at "a point one mile west of the southerly end of the [Porcupine] lake."[30] South End (South Porcupine) was

more than compensated for its lack of a post office! Other necessary arrangements were quickly made: local contracts were let for 100,000 ties; Drs. A. Fisher and H.H. Moore were appointed to provide medical services at a rate of one dollar per man per month (double the rate set earlier for Dr. McMurtry on the main line);[31] and the provincial cabinet reserved a right-of-way through the veterans' lots that had been allocated in the region.

Construction began intensively at both ends of the line. By mid-February there were 853 men, 56 horses, and 10 cars on the job.[32] A month later 1,100 men were working on the Porcupine grade. The terrain which had been so difficult to cross on foot posed no special problems to railway construction. There were few curves and no really steep grades. The first train to serve the public over part of the line ran early in March,[33] and regular service as far as the Frederick House River began at the end of the next month. (The fare was set at 50 cents.) Steel reached South End two weeks ahead of schedule on 16 June. Just before that the Commission had agreed to extend the line for five miles west of

First train of the Porcupine branch, 9 March 1911   (Left to right) Wm. Oldham, B & B Master, and S.B. Clement, Chief Engineer, with Engine 109. (ONA-1988012)

South End to Timmins Landing (Timmins) to accommodate the Hollinger mine. The mining company in return lent the T&NO $100,000 to be repaid from the earnings of the extension.[34] To cap the success of a remarkably well-conducted operation, the Conservatives were re-elected in December, Bob Shillington of Earlton retaining his seat for Temiskaming.

A tragedy intervened. The first T&NO Commission had been concerned enough about the danger of forest fires to arrange with the Ministry of Mines and Forests for a corps of forest rangers along its line. The summer of 1911 was particularly dry and, equally dangerous, very windy. Familiarity with endemic fires in the bush led mine and railway workers to ignore the danger, even after fire destroyed the power plant at Sandy Falls and some buildings at the Dome mine. But on 11 July the winds rose to gale force, bringing uncontrolled fires to Cochrane and the Porcupine. At the Porcupine about 70 people died hideously and property damage was tremendous. Yet people for the most part buried their dead, rolled up their sleeves, cleared the rubble, and started again. The T&NO did the same. In spite of having to make three difficult rock cuttings, it opened its extended line for regular service to Timmins on 11 March 1912.

Before the first Porcupine strikes had been reported, several thousand hopeful prospectors had fanned out from Cobalt, and two promising areas had been located. One, southeast of Cobalt around the mouth of the Montreal River, was South Lorrain. Silver was found there in 1907, and several working mines quickly developed. The other area was Gowganda, 40 miles by way of Elk Lake west of the T&NO line. Discoveries there in 1908 also led to operating mines. Coming as they did on the heels of the Cobalt bonanza

Morning after the Porcupine fire, 12 July 1911 (ONA-1988227)

both developments have generally been seen as extensions of that great silver field. In fact, as mining historian Philip Smith has observed, either one of them alone would have been sufficient to create major excitement in mining circles.[35] Yet Gowganda had to wait four years before obtaining a partial railway service, and South Lorrain did not receive a branch line until 1924.

Had the Cobalt *Nugget* had its way, lines into both places would have been started early in 1909. It noted the presence in Elk Lake of two major banks, the proposed establishment of a radio service into Gowganda, the establishment of a business man's club complete with smoker at Elk Lake, and the construction by the Ontario government of a new wagon road from that lake to Gowganda.[36] A correspondent for *The Daily Mining Record* reported in September,[37] after a visit to the region, that its population had grown in a single year from fewer than 200 to almost 4000. Elk Lake in particular showed the rapid growth, the boisterous spirit, and the typical problems of a successful mining camp. A group of citizens had attempted to make it the site of a world heavyweight championship prize fight between Jack

Johnson and James Jeffries, anticipating a crowd of 20,000.[38] The fight was not held in Elk Lake, but the mayor, Jack Munro, claimed that a purse of $100,000 had been subscribed, with $20,000 more for expenses. Inspector Caldbick of the Provincial Police found his familiar target, blind pigs and brothels; in September 160 kegs of beer were dumped into the lake.[39] The *Nugget* reported on how bootleggers calculated losses from his raids as part of their overhead expenses.[40] Less enterprising in providing sanitation than entertainment, the town suffered an outbreak of typhoid fever in October.[41] And it complained, of course with the *Nugget*'s help, about inadequate transportation. Stories of how difficult it was to move freight into Elk Lake or beyond were staple items in the northern press.

The *Nugget* continually urged the extension of railways, into Gowganda and all over the north. The editors glibly suggested lines to connect the Porcupine with Sudbury and thence with Toronto.[42] In an age when steam locomotives reigned as the kings of transportation, such speculation was almost a form of public entertainment. Of course the same paper also suggested that Co-

balt might make a gift of a dreadnought to Great Britain during the naval crisis of 1909–10![43]

The T&NO commissioners could not be as fanciful. They were aware of the demands from Elk Lake and Gowganda; in addition to the *Nugget*'s urgings and those of special delegations from Elk Lake, Bob Shillington, the local member of the provincial legislature, had raised the matter with them and with the government. By March 1909 their officials had improved facilities at Englehart on the main line and on the spur from there to Charlton, from which point a wagon road ran to the silver fields. In April legislation granted the Commission authority to build as far as Gowganda if it chose to do so.[44] But in considering lines into Gowganda and South Lorrain, there was no dearth of rival projects. The Abitibi Pulp and Paper Company wanted a spur of about six miles to its new townsite at Iroquois Falls on the Abitibi River. From beyond the opposite end of the T&NO, and quite outside its original purview, came requests for a branch running south to Parry Sound.[45]

Bridge across Montreal River, Elk Lake, 1912 (ONA-19911311)

87

Hockey match at Elk Lake, 1914 (ONA-19911329)

Main Street, Elk Lake, 1914 (ONA-1911354)

Elk Lake Trail, 1913 (S.D. Lawlor, North Bay)

T&NO construction office, c. 1910   Chief Engineer Clement on extreme right. (ONA-1988076)

The Commission's unwritten rules, developed by Englehart's constant insistence, dictated that it choose projects on the basis of two tests: the ability of the proposed extension to support itself and the location of a route along which the grade and curvature would allow trains to run effectively and safely. Venture capital from the public purse had limits, and the projects undertaken must offer the best construction value available.

A line to Elk Lake and Gowganda was a different prospect from those into Kerr Lake, Charlton, Lorrain, or Kirkland Lake. Each of those had a single destination, and the choice of the best route into it was essentially a simple matter. Gowganda, however, might turn out to be a crossroad for the established mining centres of Cobalt, Sudbury, and Timmins. Like the *Nugget*, the commissioners speculated on the possibility of linking those centres and on such rather grand schemes as a line from Cobalt to Sudbury, or one from the Porcupine to Sault Ste. Marie.[46] To move beyond speculation required a knowledge, which they did not yet have, of the long-term development of Gowganda. The situation was further complicated by the prospect of competition from other railways. Both the CPR from Sudbury and the Canadian Northern from Sellwood via Shining Tree had seen wagon roads pushed into Gowganda to rival that from Charlton to Elk Lake.[47] Moreover, the T&NO could reach Gowganda from three points on its existing system: Charlton, Earlton, or South Porcupine. Determined to make the right choice, the Commission delayed. Meanwhile its engineers conducted the several requisite surveys, and the operating department maintained a close watch of traffic and mining development in order to predict the commercial viability of a branch line.

There was after all a limit to what the Commission's regular work force could handle. The engineering department was stretched to the utmost with surveys and with its continuing betterment programme. The operating department had to handle passenger and freight traffic that had exceeded all expectations, and there were almost constant demands for improved service and facilities. The *Nugget* carried many stories about overloaded passenger cars, especially during holiday periods, and complained bitterly about the inadequacy of the station at Cobalt. When a new station was built, an incident brought home forcibly the need of better security for railway property. On the night of 31 January 1910 someone attempted to blow up the station and its attached outhouse.[48] The line had to increase its security services and personnel.

A decision came in 1912. By then surveys had shown the route between the Porcupine and Gowganda to be harsh and its geological formations unpromising.[49] It was therefore eliminated, and the possibility of a link to Sault Ste. Marie along with it. Terrain also dictated that Charlton, although the closest point on the T&NO line to Elk Lake, was not the proper railhead. The grades on the line to it from Englehart were as great as 2.67%, tolerable for the traffic in forest products and limited passenger service for which it had been designed, but considered unsafe for heavy freight. A route from Earlton, 10 miles south of Englehart, proved more favourable. Although 11 miles longer, it allowed much gentler grades and curves; its operation and maintenance would be easier, and the construction cost would actually be the same.[50] The Commission called for tenders on 24 February 1912.

It had to complete the line itself, including a major span over the Montreal River. The contractor, handicapped by the exceptionally wet summer of 1912, could not meet the November deadline required. Having had the same experience in the Porcupine the year before, the engineering department was able to have the line ready for service over the 28.5 miles to Elk Lake on 5 February 1913.[51]

There it stopped short of the Gowganda fields. Further surveys were necessary, and it was still felt that Gowganda's development had "not yet been sufficient to warrant the construction of this extension."[52] Then the beginning of the First World War put a stop to all projects, including the possibility of a line to Lorrain. That spur had to wait for a decade.[53] The line was never extended beyond Elk Lake. That branch did not live up to

Commissioners and officials inspecting bridge, Montreal River, Elk Lake branch, 1912
(ONA-19911226)

Junction at Iroquois Falls on main line, 1912   The name was changed to Porquis Junction
when the town of Iroquois Falls was established on the Abitibi River. (ONA-19911281)

its initial promise, and regrets were often expressed that it had been built.

The Commission responded to one other northern request before the war. When the Abitibi Pulp and Paper Company decided to establish a mill at Iroquois Falls on the Abitibi River, it sought a branch line. The result was a unique arrangement: the company cleared the right-of-way under contract to the railway, a private contractor graded the line, and the T&NO itself did the tracklaying and ballasting.[54] A private spur, operated and maintained by the company, was added to reach the Abitibi mill. It soon became apparent that it could be confusing to have a settlement called Iroquois Falls at the mill end of the line and one called Iroquois Falls Junction at the other. Because the junction sent spurs to both the Porcupine and Iroquois Falls, the two names were combined into Porquis Junction.

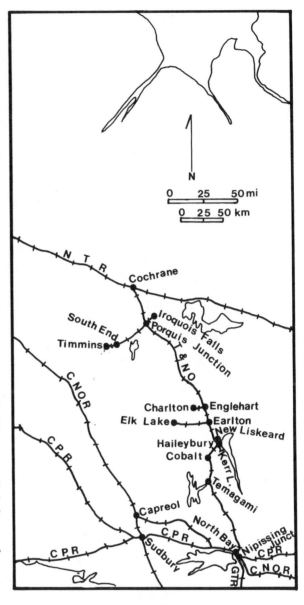

Map 8. *T&NO evolution, 1914*

Notes

1. Cobalt *Nugget*, 17 September 1909.
2. *The Book of Timmins and the Porcupine: Official Republication of the Celebration of Timmins Silver Jubilee and Porcupine Home Week*. Timmins: The Lions Club, 1937, pp. 26–32; Cobalt *Nugget*, 23 October 1909.
3. *AR*, 1909, p. 134.
4. Cobalt *Nugget*, 29 March 1910.
5. L. Carson Brown, *The Golden Porcupine*. Toronto: Ministry of Natural Resources, 4th ed., 1972, p. 12. Reprinted from *Canadian Geographical Journal*, January 1967.
6. *The Book of Timmins*, pp. 31–32.
7. Cobalt *Nugget*, 27 January 1909, 20 January 1910, 17 February 1910.
8. Cobalt *Nugget*, 19, 20 January 1910.
9. Cobalt *Nugget*, 19 February 1910.
10. Cobalt *Nugget*, 11 December 1909.
11. Cobalt *Nugget*, 1 February 1910.
12. Cobalt *Nugget*, 18 January 1910.
13. Cobalt *Nugget*, 17 February 1910.
14. Cobalt *Nugget*, 29 March 1910.
15. Cobalt *Nugget*, 16 September 1910.
16. Cobalt *Nugget*, 21, 22, 24, 26, 27 October 1910.
17. Cobalt *Nugget*, 30 August 1910.
18. Cobalt *Nugget*, 13 January 1910.
19. Cobalt *Nugget*, 6 October 1910.
20. See p. 101 of this text.
21. Cobalt *Nugget*, 28 June 1910.
22. Cobalt *Nugget*, 30 November 1910.
23. Cobalt *Nugget*, 28, 29 July and 30 August 1910.
24. Cobalt *Nugget*, 22 January and 23 August 1910.
25. Cobalt *Nugget*, 29 July 1910.
26. Cobalt *Nugget*, 4 August 1910.
27. Cobalt *Nugget*, 28, 29 September 1910.
28. Cobalt *Nugget*, 16 September 1910.
29. Cobalt *Nugget*, 3 December 1910.
30. Cobalt *Nugget*, 20 January 1910.
31. *AR*, 1902, p. 12.
32. Cobalt *Nugget*, 21 March 1910.
33. Cobalt *Nugget*, 22 January and 23 August 1910.
34. *Minutes*, 13 June 1911.

35. Smith, *Harvest from the Rock*, p. 159.
36. Cobalt *Nugget*, 13 April 1909, 28 December 1909, 5 November 1909.
37. Cobalt *Nugget*, 16 September 1909.
38. Cobalt *Nugget*, 1, 9 September 1909.
39. Cobalt *Nugget*, 11 September 1909.
40. Cobalt *Nugget*, 18 September 1909.
41. Cobalt *Nugget*, 6 October 1909.
42. Cobalt *Nugget*, 26 January 1909.
43. Cobalt *Nugget*, 12 March 1909.
44. Cobalt *Nugget*, 10 February 1909, 2 March 1909, 10, 25 April 1909, 11 September 1909.
45. Cobalt *Nugget*, 28 January 1910.
46. *AR*, 1911, pp. 10, 125–50. Cobalt *Nugget*, 26 January 1909.
47. Cobalt *Nugget*, 23 March 1909, 1 April 1909, 26 January 1910.
48. Cobalt *Nugget*, 1 February 1910.
49. *AR*, 1911, pp. 125–51.
50. *Ibid.*
51. *Minutes*, 20 February 1913; *AR*, 1913, pp. 7, 21.
52. *AR*, 1913, p. 21.
53. *AR*, 1914.
54. *AR*, 1914, p. 23.

Part Two

Into Quebec and on to the Bay

View of Mount Cheminis from the T&NO's entry point into Quebec
(ONA-1988202 Stephenson/Foerter)

Chapter 6

Kirkland Lake Gold and the First World War

PROSPECTORS FOLLOWED THE railway as it made its way north. In 1906, when steel reached Boston Creek and Dane, claims were staked at Kirkland Lake and Larder Lake. The Larder Lake discoveries were promising enough to have the T&NO Commission assign its engineering department the task of cutting bush roads into the camp from Dane. The best finds, however, were closer to the line. The brothers Bill and Jim Dusty found gold-bearing quartz at Otto Lake, just north of the new station at Dane, and in 1908 formed the Swastika Mining Company. Shortly afterward George Hurd and his son Walter began the Lucky Cross mine, just across the track. Both mines ceased operation in 1913, although they were later revived. They kept alive the hopes of a major discovery in the region, in spite of the fact that Larder Lake and Kirkland Lake had so far failed to produce anything significant. Prospectors therefore continued to search the area east of the Swastika station on the T&NO.

Among them was an Englishman, Bill Wright, and his brother-in-law, Ed Hargreaves. In July 1911 they made a discovery which led to the first significant gold producer in the Kirkland Lake region, the Wright-Hargreaves mine. Others also staked productive claims that year: Stephen Orr, George Minnacker, John Reimsbottom, C.A. McKane, Melville McDougall, Dave Elliott, "Swifty" Burnside, George and Tommy Tough, and Harry Oakes. From these and a few others staked in 1912 there developed seven major mining companies, forming what came to be known as the Main Break of the Kirkland Lake camp.

Centred for the time being around the new community of Swastika (population 450), the new camp at once demanded transportation facilities. Everyone's first choice, as always, was a railway. The T&NO Commission, already overburdened with current and projected construction, made a prompt but lukewarm response. Chief Engineer Clement reported that a spur would be possible, but the grades and curvature would be heavy, and it would cost $125,000 to build. There was already a small freight company in Kirkland Lake, run by Walter Little. Hauling freight from mine to mine, its wagons had laid out the wandering path still to be seen in the main street of Kirkland Lake. A wagon

First house built, new gold fields, Larder Lake, 1906 (ONA-1991141)

road from Swastika, which would cost only $15,000, would be enough to serve the camp; besides, it could be built by the provincial government without burdening the T&NO. "There is," Clement advised the Commission, "at present no necessity or demand for a branch line."[1] Englehart was relieved, agreed that a wagon road would suffice, and concluded that "we have done our duty."[2]

It has been observed that the "Kirkland Lake camp came into being quietly," perhaps because "it did not seem possible that there could be another Porcupine."[3] It was soon clear that the Kirkland Lake deposits were as rich as those of the Porcupine, yet the camp's growth remained slow. The explanation for that lies beyond New Ontario, in the outbreak of the First World War.

The war increased the demand for precious metals, especially gold. Most of the world's currencies were based on a gold standard, and they were now under pressure to raise capital for war production. The gold and silver mines of the northeastern corridor were an important resource

for the war effort. Many of those in the Porcupine and at Cobalt relied on cyanide in the process of ore extraction. Most of the world's supply of cyanide came from Germany, and there was concern that a shortage of it might develop. Happily, as Arthur Cole reported in 1914, all but two of the mines in New Ontario used cyanide from a Scottish firm, Cassell Cyanide Company of Glasgow. It sent representatives to Northern Ontario to ensure a steady supply, and gold production was maintained.

Paradoxically, the immediate demand for gold delayed rather than helped the development of Kirkland Lake. Only one property there —the Tough-Oakes mine—was actually in production when the war began. The others still required time and capital investment before they could bring out ore in commercial quantities. For the Canadian and Ontario governments, and therefore for the T&NO Commission, the prime goal in the years 1914–18 was that of winning the war. It had to give priority to moving the output of established mines. There were neither capital nor human resources for new construction. The new mines of Kirkland Lake would have to wait for a rail link to the main T&NO line just as they had to wait for investment capital.

The railway had to contend with a decline in civilian passenger traffic during the war, as well as in way freight and general freight. There were some bright spots. To George Lee's delight, the agriculture of the Clay Belt had a bumper crop in 1916, a year in which spring rains and summer drought ruined crops in the south. "In the Temiskaming District," he wrote, "the fall wheat crop was splendid, hay was never better, grass seed never so good." The potato crop equalled that of New Brunswick in yield and was "of a superior quality to any."[4] This was a brief success, for the Clay Belt lands do not compare with those of southern and southwestern Ontario; but it brought some traffic. More came from the transshipment of western grain at Cochrane for the Ontario market. The first substantial shipments of paper from Iroquois Falls also began in 1916. There were troop movements on the line, too, including the carriage of prisoners of war to camps at Kapuskasing and elsewhere.

Such additional traffic was not enough to maintain the net operating revenues of the T&NO, especially by the end of the war. They fell from $450,609.50 in 1917 to $60,622.74 by 1919.[5] New projects were delayed, the purchase of new equipment was postponed, and the whole betterment programme went into abeyance. But shortages of manpower and inflationary prices sent expenditures upwards. Wages, particularly in the skilled non-operating trades, rose. From 1917 to 1919 operating expenditures almost trebled. The T&NO remained solvent, but for its managers the war years were a trying time.

The men who worked the line demonstrated their commitment to the war effort. About half of them—592—subscribed to $239,450 worth of war bonds.[6] That reflected the general response of people in the northeastern corridor; the Timiskaming district subscribed for a total of $4,548,000, just over twice the objective set.[7] In 1915 the T&NO Railwaymen's Patriotic Fund was established. Collecting monthly donations, it raised $95,897.03 for the Canadian Red Cross Society and the Canadian Patriotic Fund.[8]

Mail team starting for Kirkland Lake camp, 1913, from Swastika (ONA-1988913 J. Fitzmaurice)

With the Commission's encouragement, many T&NO men enlisted in the armed forces. On 15 Ocober 1915, it set a policy designed to compensate those who enlisted.

> Resolved—Employees in service of Commission six months or more, enlisting for overseas Service be allowed following consideration:—
>
> MARRIED MEN—Three months' salary. Same to be paid to wife and family in either weekly or monthly instalments.
>
> SINGLE MEN—One month's salary. Special cases, however, such as contributing to support of mother or family will be given special consideration by Commission.
>
> Further—positions to be held open for Employees enlisting for Overseas Service.

E.L. Sherman and E.C. Shepherd were noted as the first two T&NO men to enlist after the resolution had been made public. Sherman was wounded and later returned to the T&NO; Shepherd unfortunately was killed in action. Others had already gone. Many more followed. In 1917 the Commission declared proudly that over 12 per cent of its employees had joined the colours of their respective countries.[9] The honorarium set by the 1915 resolution had by then reached a total of $13,765.16 for those who had joined the Canadian Expeditionary Force (CEF). The practice was stopped after the introduction of conscription by the Military Service Act of 1917. The Commission also maintained a Roll of Honour in the board room, listing all T&NO men who served in the CEF. Two hundred and nine names, with their trades, adorn this roll; 13 did not come home to reclaim their positions.[10]

Although no nominal record preserves the memory of T&NO men who served in the armies of their homelands abroad, the company's annual reports do observe that there were many who did so. Special mention was made in 1917 of the substantial numbers who enlisted with the Russian and Italian armed forces. Given the multicultural nature of the T&NO and New Ontario's population, it is not surprising that the Central Powers also absorbed some men who had worked on the line or in Northern Ontario. Andy MacFarlane of Englehart had been on a crew stringing telegraph wires into Cochrane. After enlisting in the CEF, MacFarlane found himself, along with a few other mounted men, responsible for a group of German prisoners. One of the prisoners eased his way close to MacFarlane, who, fearing an escape attempt, kicked the man. As it turned out, the two men had worked together on the wire-stringing crew at Cochrane![11] There is no way of telling how many men from the North served in the enemy camp; nor is there really any way to determine how many served in all the Allied armies. It can only be observed that the Great War consumed man power, even in the northernmost regions of Northern Ontario.

Throughout the war years, progress in the Kirkland Lake camp was steady if unspectacular. It was carefully observed by Mining Engineer Arthur Cole from his office in Haileybury. His annual reports noted the roadblocks that the war placed in front of gold production, notably the rising wartime costs for labour and supplies. During 1916 and 1917, the Teck-Hughes mine joined the Tough-Oakes as an actual producer; the Lake Shore mine "developed an ore shoot containing some spectacular ore on the second level under Kirkland Lake";[12] 10 other properties showed considerable activity; and the Northern Ontario Light and Power Company completed running a line some 64 miles from Cobalt into the camp and had begun operating this power line in February of 1917.[13]

The mining operations had begun to show a pattern following an easterly path towards the south side of Kirkland Lake. The mine owners and managers, who had to this point been content with a tote road from Swastika, began to press harder for a rail connection. At first they tried a letter-writing campaign. A representative from the management team of each mining concern wrote a lengthy letter to the Premier declaring that his firm had made progress and had invested heavily in the region, that this would continue, that the government should match that commitment by constructing the rail spur, and that the result would prove beneficial to the railway in terms of both freight and passsenger traffic. Their arguments were valid; no one questioned that. But these arguments were not unique either to the North or to the mining industry. Manpower shortages and transportation deficiencies were common complaints throughout the province, and while the government was sympathetic and understanding, its prime concern was the prosecution of the war. If government or the T&NO were to take action in the Kirkland Lake region, something further had to be put forward. The incentive which the mining people chose to offer was a financial commitment.

The expansion of the mining areas meant that the mines themselves would have to extend the road facilities at their expense, estimated to be about $25,000.[14] Since they would have that expense if no railway were built, and since they would prefer to have the railway, the mine operators were prepared to offer that amount as a bonus to the T&NO for building a rail spur. This offer once again brought the spur into the forefront of T&NO discussions.

For their part, the T&NO managers also felt the strains of war. One of them, George Lee, who by then held the posts of Land Agent and of commissioner, declared this frustration to the chairman:[15]

> ...we are passing through the most trying conditions that ever faced any people and do not think we are called upon to build a railway to Kirkland Lake until the war is over...we should cut out, as much as possible, all unnecessary work.

Englehart, while sympathetic to Lee's frustrations, was less impatient with the idea of a Kirkland Lake branch. Arthur Cole had recently recommended a line into the area as soon as possible. Chief Engineer Clement supported this. He added that, if the current high price of coal continued, the line should be electrified, since power had been made available through the recently completed power project of the Northern Ontario Electric Light and Power Company. If a spur was not yet feasible, its future location should be set, so that the mining people could plan their townsites.[16] Positions

had thus been reversed: Lee had urged construction in 1916, when the mine owners had first proposed the $25,000 bonus, while Clement and Cole had opposed. The two engineers changed their views because of developments in the camp; for Lee, the greater question of winning the war, which had taken some bad turns for Canada and the Allies, seems to have caused him to urge waiting until the war ended.

The chairman no doubt recognized these circumstances when he wrote to Lee on 9 February 1918. Because this letter indicates Englehart's view of the Commission's role as well as a slight chastisement of his protege, it is quoted at length.[17]

> You are right, Comm'r., that we are passing thru the most trying conditions that ever faced any people, but that does not call upon us to go to sleep—to very contrary, when conditions are worst that is the time people should get up and be doing. We must encourage the building up of that Northland (that is the common word— Greater Ontario is our word) and Kirkland Lake is an important asset in its building up. We cannot ask people to go in there as they are going and spending Thousands, yes, Hundreds of Thousands, and not render unto Caesar those things which are due to Caesar. That is paraphrasing the old, but will suit for immediate present, the new. Our duty is not performed by objecting, but it is performed by endeavoring to pacify, that is the word, 'pacify', the demands which come to us as Commissioners. It is not a personal matter, it is the people's matter—we represent the people, and if we further improve conditions, enlarge the field, then, and then only, are we performing our whole duty.
>
> The re-survey is a small matter, but it is necessary. We have a petition to that effect—we have had Committee of various Mines call upon us—we have had individuals of various Mines call. It is necessary to locate so as to have a Town and I am prepared to go up on record that Kirkland Lake, with A.A. Cole's endorsation, warrants the Branch—warrants the change, and warrants the efforts to so have

the route to meet the possibilities of a Townsite.

The Chief is now investigating possibilities of electrical power—that is the power if it can be obtained, hence surveys are required—cannot be done without necessary work.

While you say that you have submitted your views to Chairman as a member of the Commission—that is your duty, and now as you have expressed views you hold, your further duty, so appeals to Chairman, is to take before the Government, if you desire—interview the Premier —take your letter along, as also Chairman's, or transmit copies if you prefer, and after you have had opportunity [to] think matter over, Chairman will be grateful, thankful to receive your further report.

Several days later, Lee responded, denying that there had been anything personal intended in his comments and adding that if the Kirkland Lake project or any other work should receive the sanction of the Commission and the government, "You will not find any person in Ontario more willing to join, and do everything possible to make the work successful in every way, than myself."[18] Three months later, the full Commission took a strong step towards providing a rail link between Swastika and the Kirkland Lake gold camp.[19]

Considered advisable by Chairman that tenders for above contemplated extension be called for about June 1st next, which will provide for bids to be received by first week in July and work concluded in October next. In meantime Chief Engineer and Mining Engineer instructed to meet the Mine Managers and other parties with endeavour to have all interests satisfied as to the proposed location of branch. Personal interviews it is expected will produce best results.

But the day for the Kirkland Lake railway had not yet come. The cost was simply too high when combined with other needs. Estimates for the spur rose to $177,921.70, triple the cost projected in 1913.[20] The T&NO had several other expansion plans at the time—Mattagami Spur,

Lorrain, Gowganda—as well as the programme of betterments that had lapsed during the war. In addition, because T&NO traffic was expected to increase dramatically, the Chief Commissioner of the Board of Railway Commissioners, Sir Harry Drayton, had recommended additions to the North Bay terminals sufficient to accommodate an extra 1000 cars.[21] This meant 10 miles of new sidings at a cost of $125,000.

Cost alone likely prompted the Commission on 19 June 1918 to postpone construction of the Kirkland Lake spur "for the immediate present." A second consideration may have been the report of Consulting Engineer J.G.G. Kerry, who was far less sanguine of Kirkland Lake's prospects than Cole and Clement. Clement's report had conceded that the cost of building and operating the new line would be greater than the traffic would initially cover, but a loss could be justified since the spur would assist the development of a vital industry. If Cole's predictions of longevity for the camp proved accurate, then even that loss would be covered over time. Kerry disputed Cole's predictions. The life of a precious metals mine, he observed, was estimated at eight to ten years. If that rule of thumb held up, then the Kirkland camp could not justify extensive expenditures on transportation. He offered an alternative: a road for motorized vehicles. This could be built for a fraction of the cost—$100,000—and could serve both teams of horses or motorized trucks. Upon receiving Kerry's report, Englehart commented, almost wearily:[22]

In passing, just to note—there are many thoughts outlined by Mr K. as to present— future of the mines in that region—Kirkland Lake—well, we are human, and the day of the Seer has not been finally settled, to say the least. There is very much in the thoughts outlined, hence there is a very great deal for thoughtful consideration— there certainly shall be no hasty action.

Following this exchange, the matter of the Kirkland spur lay dormant for several months as the Commission occupied itself with the dozens of other matters on the main line. At the same time, the Allied offensives of 1918 began to break the German resistance on the Western Front. These led quickly to a total German retreat, followed by the Armistice of 11 November 1918. With the need to adjust to peace-time conditions, the Commission found itself busier than ever, and thus the Kirkland spur continued in the background for several months after that. When it surfaced again in April 1919, the Commission found that the mood in the region regarding transportation there had changed.

This constituted something of a shock for T&NO senior officials. In March the Commission had finally advertised, as it had planned to do in the previous year, in various journals and newspapers including eight in Northern Ontario, that tenders for the construction of the Kirkland Lake branch would be received until noon of 15 April 1919. The response to this advertisement was heavy, and as late as 10 April, Jake Englehart appeared to have been confident that the project would proceed with the full support of virtually everyone in the Kirkland region. Yet, six days later in a letter to one of the bidders, he noted that "there is just a possibility of postponement."[23] Then, in a confidential letter sent the next day to Clement, T&NO Secretary-Treasurer Maund declared that the construction of the Kirkland Lake branch "has been postponed for the immediate present."[24] Clearly something had happened in the six days between 10 and 16 April.

The first sign of change had come in a meeting in Cobalt on 10 April, between Clement and Colonel H.H. Johnson, who represented certain English financial interests in Kirkland Lake and Cobalt. Clement was clearly impressed by the man.[25]

> ... He has but recently returned [from the war] and since his arrival, has succeeded in obtaining control of the Tough-Oakes, Burnside and Sylvanite properties which will be merged into one mining company, the controlling interest of which will be held by his principals in England. Mr. Cole considers that Col. Johnson's return to Canada and the merging of these three properties will prove a very important step

in the development of the Kirkland Lake gold camp...

Because of Johnson's apparent stature, Clement listened carefully when the colonel declared that a branch of the T&NO into Kirkland Lake would be less beneficial to the mining community there than would be a "strictly first class motor road." In suggesting this a year earlier, Kerry had admitted to being less than fully qualified to predict the results and effectiveness of such a service. Johnson was not so reticent. Having been connected during the war with the British Tank Corps—itself a new institution in 1917 when tanks first appeared on the Western Front—he convinced Clement that he was "thoroughly familiar with motor transport." According to Johnson, the road could be built for $70,000 (about $10,000 to $12,000 per mile), and freight hauled over it would cost less than the railway would have to charge.

The proposition was attractive. It eliminated the capital costs, interest and amortization charges, as well as the operating deficit ($18,000 annually) that Clement predicted. There were some problems, such as the absence of a passenger service (unless passenger buses were instituted), the need to plough the road in winter, and hazards that inclement weather might produce for both the roadway and the vehicles that used it. It quickly became the hottest topic of conversation in the camps.

Ten days later, the manager of the Tough-Oakes mine, Charles Richardson, wrote to Englehart. Much had happened in that time. Richardson's letter seems to have been an attempt to soothe feelings which may have been hurt by those events and by Johnson's brusque behaviour and also that of Harry Oakes, who owned the Lakeshore mine and as part owner of Tough-Oakes was Richardson's boss.[26]

> As we understood that you were about to award the contracts for the construction of the railroad the time was necessarily somewhat short in which to get a general expression of opinion from the various people interested in the matter. However, Col. Johnson sent letters to all the mine

owners and as many others interested as possible outlining the advantages and disadvantages of both propositions. This resulted in an expression of opinion which on the part of the mine owners has been so far unanimous in favor of a motor road. A public meeting was also held in Swastika, where the sentiment was strongly in favor of the motor transport, and a similar meeting held in Kirkland Lake townsite was well attended. Col. Johnson was present and outlined and covered the ground very fully on both sides of the question and there was a general discussion by many present. The result of the vote taken was in favor of the motor road, the opposition being mostly by those who were afraid that after the agitation for some time urging your consideration in connection with the building of the branch line that a change of front might interfere with getting something done this present year.

Jake Englehart was well aware of the public meetings spoken of by Richardson. They had been covered in the northern newspapers, and the 18 April issue of *The Mining Review* carried a feature item outlining the advantages and disadvantages of both a steam railway and a motor road. Furthermore, the meeting of 17 April at the schoolhouse in Kirkland Lake—the first public meeting of the new Teck Township that had been incorporated in January—produced a series of resolutions which had been immediately wired by Johnson to the chairman.[27]

Resolution passed at a special public meeting convened by the Reeve of the Township of Teck, Mr. W.J. McLeod, and held in the schoolhouse at Kirkland Lake at 7:30 P.M. on April 17th, 1919, for the purpose of considering whether the proposed railway or a good motor road would best serve the needs of the district. *First*, that this public meeting of the citizens of Kirkland Lake convened by the Reeve, Mr. W.J. McLeod, to consider the proposed railway to be built into Kirkland Lake, hereby resolves to wire to the Railway Commission and the Government, asking that railway proposal may be reconsidered and that a first class motor

road be built immediately from Swastika to Kirkland Lake, provided that the Government undertake to maintain the said road for a period of Twenty Years, at a cost not to exceed that of maintaining the proposed branch railway line. *Second*, that nothing in this resolution shall be allowed to interfere with the immediate settlement of the question and the provision of the necessary transportation facilities at once. *Third*, that the Government be asked to provide the funds for a motor truck to be operated by the Municipality of Teck.

The energetic Johnson followed up with a visit to Jake Englehart in Toronto and then an interview with Premier Hearst. Later, Englehart, who had on a previous occasion acknowledged to Hearst that Johnson represented important interests indeed, declared that "...the only real solution would be a wagon or motor road."[28] The Premier accepted his friend's advice; the road was built; and the matter of a Swastika–Kirkland Lake branch line was once again set back. One gets the feeling from reading the correspondance that Englehart was somewhat disappointed, that he would have preferred to see the railroad extended eastward into the Kirkland Lake camp. One also has the feeling that a younger Jake Englehart would have seen that it was built. But by the spring of 1919 he had begun to lose his energy and was no longer a match for the younger and aggressive Johnson and associates.

Over three years passed before the Swastika–Kirkland Lake railway emerged again as a topic of serious discussion. In that time some significant changes had taken place in terms of the principal personalities involved. On 4 November 1919 E.C. Drury, somewhat reluctantly, had accepted the reins of power at the head of the Ontario government. During the 1919 election campaign a loosely organized group of candidates sought election under the banner of the United Farmers of Ontario (UFO). They did not expect to win, but the general agrarian discontent reflected itself at the polls in Ontario when the UFO won 45 seats. It was suddenly presented with the opportunity to form the government if it would coalesce with the 11 Labour members who had also won election to the provincial legislature. Neither the 29 Liberals nor the 26 Conservatives had sufficient strength to take control. Drury had not even sought election, but he was the generally acknowledged leader of the Farmers group; after urgings from all sides and promises of support from the Labour members, he took the oath of office as Ontario's eighth premier on 14 November 1919. He subsequently won the right to sit in the legislature in a by-election held on 16 February 1920.[29]

It was at best an awkward union, for the two allies—Farmers and Labour—held contradicting views of government and the party system. For the Labour party, the party system represented a means of obtaining power and thus was something that should be taken over; for the United Farmers, the party system was corrupt and should be replaced by some method of group government. The two also disagreed on such issues as prohibition, urbanization, wages, unions, and tariffs. The possibilities for conflict were endemic. Yet Drury managed to hold the coalition together for four years.

In T&NO country the government had no representation: Nipissing had chosen Joseph Marceau, a Liberal; Temiskaming had returned Thomas Magladery, a Conservative, and Cochrane, which had been named an electoral district in 1914, re-elected Malcolm Lang, a Liberal.[30] Drury had little personal knowledge of the North or the T&NO, and he was faced immediately with the need to replace Jake Englehart, who had already sent his resignation to Premier Hearst and was too ill to withdraw it. Drury named George Lee. It was at first a temporary appointment and an acting one, partly because it had to be made so quickly, and partly because of Lee's well-known allegiance to the Conservative party. It was an appointment that made good sense, however, for Lee was already on the Commission, had served as General Agent and Land Agent, and was familiar with a wide range of the Commission's activities. Moreover, he lived in North Bay, which

would meet the complaints that northerners were insufficiently represented on the Commission. By making the appointment both temporary and acting, Drury retained a way to cancel it easily should Lee not prove satisfactory to the government. As it turned out, George Lee proved himself to be a competent manager and fully capable of serving a master of a different political persuasion.

An even more important question concerned the fate of the Commission itself and its enterprises. It was a question which undoubtedly caused some anguish for the new premier. The basic philosophy of the United Farmers party denied that government should own and operate such enterprises. Institutions like the T&NO presented obvious possibilities for political patronage, and the UFO had campaigned against this evil. It was by no means a mere speculation that the T&NO might be sold to either the CPR or the newly created CNR, despite opposition in the North.

Drury moved slowly in this, perhaps because he wanted time to consider the matter carefully, but more likely because his government faced the problems associated with adjusting the province to a peace-time situation. As it turned out, Drury had neither the experience nor the time to make the major arrangements involved in the sale of the government railway. He did take his time; but once the decision had been reached, Drury announced it emphatically. Lee would remain as chairman, the railway would be retained by the province, and it would, furthermore, be extended northward from Cochrane as far as Island Falls and ultimately to James Bay! He made no announcement regarding the branch line to Kirkland Lake from Swastika, for that matter had been settled before he assumed office.

In Kirkland Lake itself the developments were substantial but not yet dramatic. The population had doubled to 1170 by 1919, but remained small when compared to other northern centres such as North Bay (10,692), Cobalt (4449), New Liskeard (2268), Haileybury (3743), Timmins (3843), or even Cochrane

(2655).[31] In 10 years, however, it would grow to 9915. Harbingers of that expansion began to appear in 1922, but once again events conspired to retard growth. Kirkland Lake seemed to have more than its share of hard luck in its efforts to develop. The First World War, with its demands on manpower and capital, had adversely affected the Kirkland Lake camp. Then, with the war over, the area suffered a miners' strike for several months in 1919. The trouble began in May when the miners demanded recognition of their union—the Western Federation of Miners—as well as some wage demands, such as an increase of 50 cents to a daily rate of $4.50 for underground work and $4.00 for surface labour. They also insisted on an eight-hour day, a half day for Saturdays (at full day's pay), time and a half for overtime, double pay for Sundays, and a $1.00 a day rate for rooms.[32]

The mining companies might have been prepared to give ground on the matters of wages and working hours, but recognition of the Western Federation of Miners, an international union, was a point they would not concede. The Bolshevik Revolution in Russia had thrown an immense scare into all levels of management and government in North America. The passions invoked by the "Red scare" of the post-war years are difficult to imagine. But in 1919, a year that saw strikes throughout the continent—including nearby Cobalt and the general strike in Winnipeg—feelings ran very high indeed. The entire Russian empire had collapsed following the uprising led by the Petrograd Soviet in March 1917. This had led to the Bolshevik Revolution in November and the Russian withdrawal from the war in March 1918. A civil war followed which lasted until 1922. At stake was the entire structure of Russian society which would be overturned completely if the Red forces were successful. In the minds of many western leaders, if it happened in Russia, it could happen elsewhere, including Canada. Even small protests or strikes had to be stopped short.

International labour bodies were, therefore, viewed with distrust, hatred, and fear. Faced with the local demands, the mines closed down. The mine operators declared that they

might be prepared to negotiate wages, etc. with local committees from the local mines, but would not deal with an international union. Both sides remained intransigent for several months. The strike began to falter by September as miners drifted off to other locations and men returning from the war began to seek work at home. These factors turned the tide in favour of the owners. During September some mines began hiring again, and on 15 October, a union meeting at the Miners Union Hall voted to end the strike.[33] Not a single item had been gained.

At the same time the mines faced other problems. There were changes in management, such as at the Tough-Oakes company, and changes in share structures. In one case, the Wright-Hargreaves property, the entire enterprise had been held up because one of the principals, Wright, had joined the army, and in general the camp suffered because of the dislocation that came in the wake of the war. These problems gradually sorted themselves out, and a degree of stability settled on the Kirkland Lake camp. In 1922, Arthur Cole, who had been optimistic about the area since 1918, again broached the subject of a railway. Three factors at this point contributed to the idea: geological theory, proven finds, and competition.

In 1919, H.C. Cooke of the Geological Survey of Canada concluded that, in geological terms, the terrain between Swastika and the Rouyn hills formed a single formation. He therefore renamed the entire region as the Timiskaming Series.[34] In non-academic terms this meant that the precious metal deposits found around Kirkland Lake might well continue as far east as Rouyn. Another optimistic assessment came from W.H. Goodchild of London, England, whom Cole termed "a mining geologist of the highest order, and worldwide experience." Goodchild found that the ores at Kirkland Lake were of a higher grade than those of the Porcupine, and that they were richer at deeper levels than near the surface. The main field was already more than twice as long as the famous "golden mile" of Kalgoorlie in Australia. He concluded:[35]

It will be seen, therefore, that what is at the moment Canada's second largest gold producing field is no small second, but is in fact a goldfield of the first magnitude and importance, with promise of great extensions in the near future.

Chief Engineer Cole, a professional of considerable standing himself, held the same view. Finds as rich and as deep as those at Kirkland Lake's main camp might be made along a line eastward past Larder Lake and on into the province of Quebec, "giving in all, an east and west extension of 130 miles in length, and thus increasing the probable productive prospecting area four fold."[36]

Practical results soon appeared to justify these predictions. On 18 November 1922, the General Manager of the Crown Reserve Mining Company informed George Lee that his company had been developing properties in the Larder Lake region for the past year and expected other mines would be developed there. A railway from Swastika, he said, would soon be necessary.[37] Others echoed that view, including the Cobalt *Northern Miner*. On 11 November 1922, it called upon the government to wake up and develop the two gold belts of Porcupine and Kirkland Lake, which according to the government's own geologists had a known length of 70 miles and were likely longer. A week later, the paper argued that the "truest way to open the north is to fully exploit those sections that are partially developed." Speculative construction like the James Bay extension north of Cochrane had merit, but "unless there is money to spare for both prospecting and development the prospecting had better rest for a while."[38]

> We have nine producing gold mines. Accepted authorities tell us that we have a chance for 300 in the territory adjacent to the old line. And when you get down to brass tacks you are forced to the conclusion that the reason that we are not further along the way toward the 300 is that not one mile of mining trackage has been built since 1912.

That same day the journal also alluded to the current activity in Quebec in and around Rouyn Township and warned that the CPR would likely move quickly to tap that area if it proved to have wealth. And if that happened, the CPR might also divert its line to cross into Larder Lake. The spectre of the CPR had also been raised by the *Nugget* on 10 November. It called on the T&NO to develop "the longest known continuous gold ore-bearing belt in Canada."

> It is an open secret that the northerly survey for the Kipawa to Des Quinze branch of the CPR passes this big, new gold field, at its eastern end, and it is clear that if there is to be competition, the advantage will be gained by the organization to first establish itself, not across the gold belt at any one particular point, but coursing its way along the range.

None of this was news to Lee or to the T&NO. The Commission and its officials had been kept fully apprised of the activities in Quebec by both mining interests and by the Canadian Pacific Railway. For a decade the Commission had considered moving into the sister province. Since acquiring the Nipissing Central Railway (NCR), the Commission had extended it through Cobalt to Kerr Lake and past Haileybury into New Liskeard. It could be extended further from there around the head of Lake Timiskaming and across the provincial boundary and into the Des Quinze River valley to capture the traffic from the agricultural communities there. The road had the right to run such a line by the terms of its federal charter. The war and the almost general moratorium that the Drury administration had placed on railway expansion had stopped the project.

The CPR in the meantime had extended its Kipawa branch north from the foot of Lake Temiskaming and by the end of 1922 was approaching Ville Marie. John Dresser, a leading Canadian Geologist, and Sir Stopford Brunton, another mining geologist from Montreal, both spent part of 1922 examining the area east of Larder Lake in Quebec on behalf of the Pacific Railway. During a visit with Cole that summer,

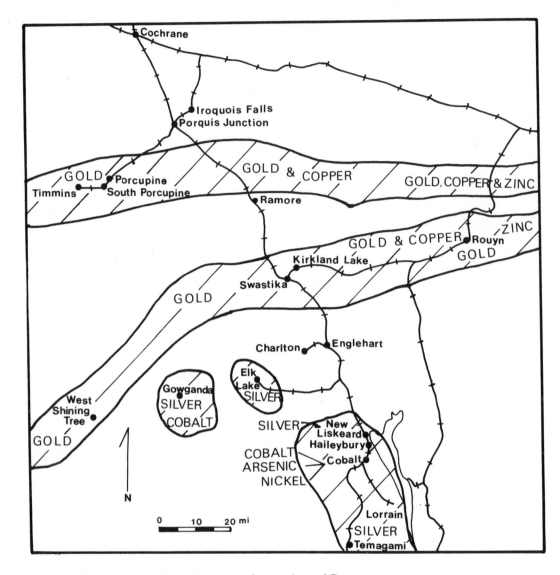

Map 9. *Mineral areas: Cobalt, Porcupine, Gowganda, and Rouyn*

Dresser declared that he intended "to report favourably on the traffic possibilities as far north as that part of the province."[39] The *Nugget* had been remarkably close to the mark.

Indeed, by the end of 1922, practical realities appeared to be bearing out the geological theory of Cooke and the mining predictions of Goodchild. Theo Denis, the Quebec Superintendent of Mines, visited the area and established a mining office at Ville Marie. He also arranged for Dr. Cooke "to spend the summer

in this area...in order to give every assistance to prospectors operating in this district." Cole, in relaying this information to Lee, observed:[40]

> Whatever the reason may have been, the mining enthusiasm which was so marked in the gold areas of Ontario, has extended over into the Province of Quebec and a great many claims have been recorded. Several of these, among them being the Thompson Chadborne, in Rouyn township, are said to have real merit.

John Ritchie, a prospector who gave his address as Box 49, Kirkland Lake, sent Lee a sketch of the claims and operating mines in the area and bluntly reminded him that miners would not wait forever on the T&NO.[41]

> We ask you and your Government urge the T&NO Ry Commissioners to construct a Branch Ry Line through the Kirkland Lake Mining Centre at the Earliest Possible Date. We have Decided to Place this Matter Before you First at the Present time trusting that it Will...have the earnest attention of yourself and of your Government at the Present time Before Seeking elsewhere for a remedy for our transportation Problems. On Behalf of the Prospectors and Property owners of the Kirkland area.

The ore-bearing ridge running from Swastika to Rouyn township was not yet a sure thing: the Kirkland Lake sector was a success, but Larder Lake was still only probable, and at Rouyn promising finds had been made but not developed. With the CPR ready at Ville Marie to strike if conditions were right, however, the T&NO Commission could not afford delay if it were to protect its hold on the northeastern corridor.

At this point the Drury government chose boldness. On 13 April 1923 Premier Drury and Chairman Lee each read a carefully prepared statement simultaneously, but 200 miles apart, the former in the Ontario Legislature and the latter at a press conference in North Bay.[42]

> It has been decided to construct a railway to Kirkland Lake, in an easterly direction from Swastika, through the Townships of Teck, Lebel, Gauthier and McVittie, to a point at or near the Crown Reserve Mine. This matter has been under con-

sideration for some time, also thorough investigation.

> The railway will be built as the NIPISSING CENTRAL RAILWAY, under a charter which we hold from the Dominion Government, to enable us to enter the Province of Quebec and proceed over to the Rouyn region, if further developments warrant it.

> The work in connection with this construction starts at once. Engineers will be in the field this coming week. Tenders will be called for and Contract let by the first of June and the work proceeded with all possible haste.

> It has been decided to investigate and lay out another Extension of the NIPISSING CENTRAL RAILWAY from New Liskeard, through the townships of Harris, Casey, Brethour, Pense, Mulligan, Skead, McFadden and McGarry—entering the Province of Quebec and joining up with the Extension from Kirkland Lake

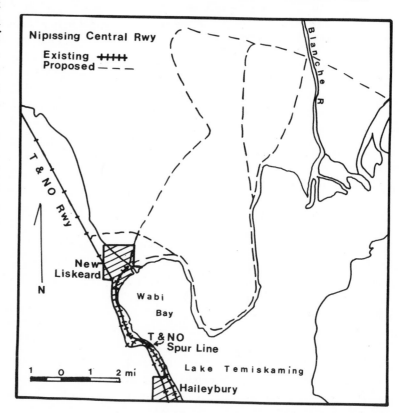

Map 10. *Proposed extension to the Nipissing Central (Radial) Railway*

Kirkland Lake, c. 1924 (ONA-1988915)

and, should investigations and developments warrant it, further recommendations will be made to the Government in due course for the construction of this railway. An alternative route will, also, be investigated by way of North Temiskaming and Nedelac Townships. The work of these investigations will, also, be undertaken at once.

Both Drury and Lee had reason to be confident about the project. It was a clearly stated declaration of government policy and in Northern Ontario at least, a very popular decision. It appeared to have been thought out very carefully and seemed to cover all possible contingencies. This time, in contrast to 1919, the mining community was solidly behind the projected railway. Furthermore, the situation in the Kirkland Lake camp had become much more settled in the intervening four years, and there were more operating mines. The chief engineer of the T&NO, S.B. Clement, now projected that the line would cover its operating costs and even recover the initial capital expenditures. It would run a distance of 25 miles to Larder Lake rather than six miles into the Kirkland Lake camp. Over that greater distance the rail-

way would be easier to construct and to maintain than a motorized road.

Indeed, the experiment with the motorized road into Kirkland had been something of a failure: the cost of freight had not been reduced as Colonel Johnson had predicted, but had remained about the same as before (i.e., approximately $3 per ton). The developments at Larder Lake (e.g., the Crown Reserve Mining Company and the Argonaut Mining Company) as well as in the 19 miles between there and Kirkland Lake provided the determining factor in the decision to build. By taking its line as far as Larder Lake the Commission would be poised, as was the Canadian Pacific Railway, only some 30 miles from the Rouyn mining district. By using the charter of the Nipissing Central Railway, the Commission had provided itself, apparently, with the option of moving into Quebec, but the option need not be exercised. The original charter had been renewed at the appropriate times since 1907, and therefore there seemed little doubt that the right to build into Quebec had been retained. There was some question, however, about the way in which this could be done. According to the

Commission's legal counsel, the Toronto firm of Tilley, Thomson and Parmenter, various railway regulations could be interpreted liberally to allow the Nipissing Central Railway to extend what was termed its main line into Quebec, but the restrictions on branch lines were more severe. Parmenter suggested, therefore, that the Commission declare the line from Swastika eastward to be the railway's main line and that operations in the Tri-town area be identified as auxiliary or branch lines of the Nipissing Central Railway.[43] The Commission followed this advice, and the unbuilt sector of the Nipissing Central Railway became its main line. This would suggest that the announced investigation of a second extension from New Liskeard into the province of Quebec was more of a smoke screen and a political gesture than a consideration with any real possibility of completion.

Tenders were called for the construction of the line from Swastika to Larder Lake. Applause for the decision came from the mining community along the proposed track, the press throughout Northern Ontario, and all community and business interests north of North Bay. In general, it can be said that this happy mood continued to prevail for the next year and a half, until the proposed extension had been completed as far as the Argonaut Mines region of Larder Lake. It was not a totally smooth ride. The construction firm to whom the contract for the line was first granted, the Sinclair brothers of Kirkland Lake, found the task too big. Largely because of undercapitilization, the Sinclair firm was forced to renege on its commitment. As a result, the contract was taken from them and granted to the construction company of Harry McLean, who had in fact been the preferred bidder, but whose bid had been higher than that of Sinclair. The McLean firm finished the line to Larder Lake in 1924.

Two minor stumbling blocks confronted the government line shortly after the joint Drury –Lee announcement. The NCR charter provided for lines to run from the towns on the west side of Lake Temiskaming southeasterly towards Lorrain, the mouth of the Montreal River, and into Quebec at the lower end of Lake Temiskaming. It was, therefore, a line designed to serve what was then the central region of the District of Nipissing. The newly proposed line, east from Swastika through Kirkland Lake

T&NO commissioners and officials, 1919   North Bay offices. (Left to right) J.L. Englehart, S.B. Clement, G.W. Lee, W.A. Griffin (Supt. of Traffic), R.F. Preston, W.H. Maund. (ONA-1988075)

and known for a time as the Windigo Lake branch, lay quite beyond the terms of the original charter. T&NO counsel, Parmenter, had warned of this and even expressed the view that the NCR had no right to build where they proposed. The Commission, however, felt that the National Board of Railway Commissioners would be flexible. They were correct. On 18 June 1923 formal approval of the Windigo branch route reached the Commission.[44] By then the second obstacle had appeared.

T&NO engineers had selected a route which included a station for the town of Kirkland Lake in Teck Township. Based on such engineering realities as drainage, curveture, and grades, they chose a station site about three quarters of a mile from the town's business centre. Many townspeople perceived the choice as being dictated by and for the mining interests, since the station, the yard, and the freight shed would all be located on the Sylvanite Gold Mines property and would be handy for the mining companies. It was less convenient for the local businesses and residents who requested a location about a half mile from the main street—Government Road.

The difference in distance was not great—a few hundred yards—but feeling ran high, and some very harsh words were spoken. The townspeople lodged a formal protest with the provincial premier and with the federal Railway Board. The strike of four years earlier had evidently not been forgotten, and there were fears that the townspeople were being manipulated. The railway became caught in the middle and the commissioners were accused of bending to the wishes of the mine owners. It was untrue. Lee declared, "Even though the Dominion Railway Commission decides to put the station some place else we would have to use that particular piece of level land for yards."[45] On 5 October 1923 the BRC approved the railway's plan and the animosity seemed to have settled since an outside body had made the decision.[46] It would, however, be only one of many headaches for Lee regarding this branch.

Notes

1. Clement to Englehart, 7 May 1913. ONA, B-93(a).
2. Englehart to Clement, 9 May 1913. ONA, B-93(a)
3. *Twenty-five years of Ontario's Mining History: A Review of Outstanding Developments in the Last Quarter of a Century,* Toronto: King's Printer, 1932, p. 13.
4. *AR,* 1916, p. 67.
5. *AR,* 1919, p. 7.
6. *AR,* 1918, p. 16.
7. *Ibid.*
8. *Ibid.*
9. *AR,* 1917, p. 16.
10. T&NO Role of Honour. ONA.
11. Interview. Bill McCallan, Englehart, 13 December 1988.
12. *AR,* 1917, p. 74.
13. Cole to Englehart, 31 March 1917. ONA, B-93(a). Rouyn Extension.
14. Mine Managers' Petition. 15 February 1917. ONA, B-93(a). Rouyn Extension.
15. Lee to Englehart, 6 February 1918. ONA, B-93(a). Rouyn Extension.
16. Report of Chief Engineer Clement. February 1918. ONA, B-93(a). Rouyn Extension.
17. Englehart to Lee, 9 February 1918. ONA, B-93(a). Rouyn Extension.
18. Lee to Englehart, 12 February 1918. ONA, B-93(a). Rouyn Extension.
19. *Minutes,* 31 May 1918.
20. Clement to Englehart, 6 May 1918. ONA, B-93(a). Rouyn Extension.
21. *Minutes,* 31 May 1918.
22. Englehart to Clement, 2 July 1918. ONA, B-93(a). Rouyn Extension.
23. Englehart to G.B. Bigy, 16 April 1919. ONA, B-93(a). Rouyn Extension.
24. Maund to Clement, 17 April 1919. ONA, B-93(a). Rouyn Extension.
25. Clement to Englehart, 11 April 1919. ONA, B-93(a). Rouyn Extension.
26. Richardson to Englehart, 20 April 1919. ONA, B-93(a). Rouyn Extension.
27. Johnson to Englehart. Telegram. 17 April 1919. ONA, B-93(a). Rouyn Extension.
28. Englehart to Ferguson, 29 April 1919. ONA, B-93(a). Rouyn Extension.
29. *Electoral History of Ontario: Candidates and Results,* pp. J5, 136.
30. *Ibid.,* pp. 268, 302, 306.
31. These population figures are all taken from the 1921 national census report.
32. Andre Wetjen and L.H.T. Irvine, *The Kirkland Lake Story: a pictorial history.* Cobalt: Highway Book Store, 1988, p. 59.
33. *Ibid.*

34. Cole to Lee, 22 April 1922. ONA, B-93(a). Rouyn Extension.
35. *Ibid.*
36. *Ibid.*
37. H.J. Stuart to Lee, 18 November 1922. ONA, B-93(a). Rouyn Extension.
38. *Northern Miner,* 18 November 1922.
39. Cole to Lee, 28 November 1922. ONA, B-93(a). Rouyn Extension.
40. *Ibid.*
41. Ritchie to Lee, 9 April 1923. ONA, B-93(a). Rouyn Extension.
42. Official Statement Handed Out by Chairman, T&NO Railway, Mr. George W. Lee, 13 April 1923. ONA, B-93(a). Rouyn Extension.
43. Parmenter to Maund, 18 April 1923. ONA, B-93(1). Main File, Volume (B) re Rouyn Extension.
44. Board of Railway Commissioners for Canada, Order No. 33791, 18 June 1923. ONA, B-93(1). Re Rouyn 1923–24.
45. Lee to G.D. O'Meara. Telegram, 21 August 1923. ONA, B-93(1). Re Rouyn 1923–24.
46. North Bay *Nugget,* 5 October 1923. The newspaper changed its location from Cobalt in 1921.

Chapter 7

Stopped at the Border

HILE HARRY MACLEAN attempted to accomplish what the Sinclair firm had been unable to do, and while the management officials of the T&NO set about the task of integrating the new branch of the Nipissing Central Railway into the general organization of the T&NO, the senior officials of the Commission maintained a careful watch on developments in the Rouyn region, where gold had been found.

The provincial geologist and others had predicted that the area of northwestern Quebec could be part of the gold-bearing range that ran eastward from Kirkland Lake, and in August of 1920 a prospector from New Liskeard, E.H. Horne, took the first step in making that prediction come true; he staked a claim on the shore of Lake Osisko in what would become the township of Rouyn. In August of 1922 Noranda Mines Limited took his claims under option and began a more careful examination of the region. In September 1922 another prospector named T.W. Powell discovered gold nearby. The Noranda Company secured an option on these claims too, and staked further claims of its own. A rush of prospectors followed, staking some 86,000 acres in the township of Rouyn and in the surrounding region by the middle of March 1923.

By the spring of 1924 two developing areas had been identified: Lake Fortune and Rouyn. In the Lake Fortune region there were four properties worthy of mention: Lake Fortune, Arndfield, Crown Reserve, and Coniagas. In Rouyn township were the Noranda Mines, which controlled both the Horne group and the Thompson Chadbourne mines, and the Powell mine. Noah Timmins, already successful in both Cobalt and Porcupine, acquired two claims south of Lake Noranda. Even more interesting for the T&NO was the news that Horne's discovery held more copper that gold. If large amounts of copper were found, the nature of the game would change greatly. It would mean that either a smelter would go up on the site or a large tonnage of ore would be shipped out to a smelter elsewhere. In either case, the freight tonnage potential for the railway would be very considerable.

There was unwelcome news as well. The CPR was reported to be considering an extension of its line from Angliers north into the Rouyn region. This startled T&NO officials until Chief Engineer Clement found that no route map had been filed with the Board of Railway Commissioners. Even so, the rumour gained enough credence to cause alarm in Northern Ontario. *The Northern Miner* of Cobalt, in an

Kirkland Lake Station with battery-operated car (ONA-1988252277)

editorial of 14 June 1924, predicted that if the CPR did extend into Rouyn, then the Montreal money people would challenge the Toronto people for supremacy in Canadian mining. The paper declared: "In Montreal the money people are an adventurous lot, enterprising and chancetaking." In comparison, said the paper, the corresponding group in Toronto lacked that adventurous spirit.

> ...the younger financial crowd of Toronto has developed into a very efficient body of bond salesmen, the best in Canada. They have forgotten how to take a chance. They know how to skim off 1 or 2 percent, but how to speculate for big money they do not know.
>
> Northern mining is going to be the big thing in Canada for a generation. The city that leads in enterprise will gather in a billion dollars in business and dividends.
>
> And the city will be Montreal unless Toronto's younger financiers learn how to speculate. The social and sentimental interests of the North, they must remember, are

just as much with Montreal as Toronto. The Toronto ties are largely legal and political.

In fact, groups in Ontario were vitally interested in the Rouyn developments. One such group was the Northern Canada Supply Company Limited, whose principal officer, D.L. Jemmett, wrote three lengthy letters to Premier Ferguson in the course of 1924 urging the Premier to investigate the Rouyn region and to authorize the construction of a railway from Larder Lake into the new gold and copper camp. Ferguson did not have to depend on information from outside persons such as Jemmett; he had access to the best possible intelligence regarding the region: the T&NO.

The principal officers of the Commission kept in very close contact with the Rouyn mining camps. Mining Engineer Cole made several trips into that region in 1924, on one occasion even flying in on the recently formed Laurentide Airways, and submitted three substantial reports to the Commission regarding developments there. Chief Engineer Clement supervised a series of expeditions into Quebec: his department, largely through the efforts of Engineer Maher, prepared a trial run into the camp, a survey of the line, and actually selected a preferred location should the line be built. At the same time George Lee saw to it that the Commission's legal counsel filed all of the appropriate applications required by the Board of Railway Commissioners in order to keep the Nipissing Central Railway's charter valid.

Carriage in and out of Rouyn was still along two competing freight roads from the Osisko Lake, one to the CPR head of steel at Angliers, and the other to the end of steel of the Nipissing Central Railway (NCR) at Larder Lake. The route to the CPR was said to be better during the summer, because it included waterways; in winter, however, the Larder Lake route was more direct and much flatter. Even so, in his report of 4 October 1924, Cole concluded that "it would be wise to postpone a decision on the possible extension of the railway until some of the extensive programmes that are now planned are more fully developed."[1]

Late in 1924 a third railway, the Canadian National expressed interest. Lee complied with their request for a copy of the T&NO blueprint of its projected line into Rouyn on 22 December 1924. Almost two weeks earlier Chief Engineer Clement had written to Lee.

> If this area develops, it is doubtful that it could be better served with railway transportation than by an extension of the NCR to Rouyn, with a connection through Cadillac to the CNR near Amos. This would place Rouyn about equal distances from Toronto and Montreal. In some respects, a connection with the CNR at Amos may not be a good thing from the standpoint of the T&NO, but it looks like the best scheme of railway development for the district, and in the long run that will probably be found to be best also from a railway standpoint.[2]

Still cautious, Lee wrote to the Premier on 8 January 1925.

> I might say to you that the CNR have approached us privately, to know if we would build into Osisko Lake and they would come that far and join us...there is no doubt that all railway eyes are on Rouyn, and particularly if it is the smelting proposition it is supposed to be.[3]

It was the smelting of copper ore that promised heavy traffic for the railway; and a smelter in the region was possible only if a railway was built. H. Chadbourne, Managing Director of Noranda Mines, met Premier Ferguson to undertake that his firm would build a smelter at Rouyn if the Ontario government would order the immediate extension of the NCR from Larder Lake to Rouyn. He confirmed the promise in a letter to Lee on 18 February 1925.[4] The initial capacity of the plant would be 500 tons of ore per day. The company would prefer to locate it on the Quebec side, but would, if a suitable one were not available there, choose a site in Ontario. It would begin construction of the plant just as soon as the railway could begin to carry material to the site. It would endeavor, furthermore, to have the smelter as soon as the railway was constructed. To assure that the Noranda group had the ability to raise the necessary $2.5 million, Chadbourne noted the names of the most heavily interested shareholders; they included significant capitalists in Montreal, Toronto, and New York, including Noah Timmins.

George Lee immediately prepared an estimate of the traffic that might result from the construction of such a smelting operation.[5] Five hundred tons of ore per day would be transported from the mines to the smelter. The railway could also expect to carry from various locations including North Bay and Haileybury some 40 tons of coke, 50 tons of limestone, 125 tons of flax, and 50 tons of blister copper. A town of about 2500 people around the smelter and a similar one in the vicinity of the mines could be expected. These towns would require general and way freight as well as construction materials and passenger services. In all the estimated total annual revenue came to $671,908. Net earnings would be approximately $134,381.80. It was a mind-boggling proposition, especially since Lee declared that his estimates in all cases were conservative.

Lee had anticipated a successful meeting between the Premier and the Noranda Mines group in February of 1925 and had, therefore, arranged concurrent discussions between the commissioners and Harry McLean, who had just finished the Swastika–Larder Lake region of the Kirkland Lake branch. This meeting had been called with considerable secrecy. In the telegram to McLean, Lee had simply asked him to consider "an interesting proposition." The proposition was this. McLean should begin immediately to bring in supplies and prepare for the construction of the line eastward from Larder Lake. No tenders would be called at this juncture; in order to take advantage of good winter conditions the Commission wanted to have everything put in place. Later, tenders might well be called for the completion of the line through to Rouyn. If McLean were successful in the bidding for that contract, he would, of course, obtain it. Otherwise, he would be paid

by the Commission for the work and effort that he had expended to that point. It was indeed a sweet deal for McLean, and, from the point of view of the Commission, it was also a sensible arrangement for McLean had proven his mettle and there was, it seems, a desire to move quietly at this point.

The Commission also had its legal counsel prepare an agreement between the Commission and Noranda Mines Limited regarding the construction of a smelter. There was a general agreement between the leading officials of both the Commission and Noranda Mines Limited except on one point. The railway wanted the smelter built in Desserat township, because it would be the most convenient for the railway's operation. Noranda, however, did not wish to be tied to a particular location; they wanted the agreement to indicate that the smelter would be built somewhere along the line of the Nipissing Central Railway. The point seemed of little consequence at the time.

Laying steel, Swastika to Larder Lake, c. 1925 (ONA-19882016 Stephenson/Foerter)

It seemed that in the Rouyn sweepstakes the Nipissing Central Railway definitely had the inside track. The principal parties in the Rouyn region were anxious to deal with the Nipissing Central Railway. Furthermore, better than 90% of all the claims staked in the Rouyn–Lake Fortune region had been made by Ontario interests.[6] In addition, the T&NO was fully prepared to begin operations: it had, as we have seen, already located a good line from Larder Lake to the Horne Mines by trial runs and surveys and even had its contractor prepared to move quickly.

The T&NO plans for the Rouyn region were soon challenged, however. There was far more at stake than the profits to be made from the carrying trade in and out of the region: there was the matter of which metropolitan centre would control the new hinterland—Toronto or Montreal and Quebec city. When the full potential of the mining region of northwestern Quebec became apparent and the carefully laid plans of the T&NO Commission regarding the development of this region also became well known, the Quebec provincial government was caught flatfooted. The Canadian National Railway was likewise ill-prepared to match the plan which Ontario and its railway had developed in conjunction with the Noranda group. The response was a rapid alliance between the Canadian National Railway and the government of Quebec. Mining Engineer Cole reported as early as 28 January 1925 that he had information that the CNR planned to build immediately into Rouyn, thus abandoning the original idea of a joint operation with the T&NO.[7] His information was that the Quebec legislature would soon initiate legislation calling for a CNR line from O'Brien to Rouyn. Then, on 19 February Chadbourne, of the Noranda group, advised Lee that he had met with Quebec government officials regarding a smelter. They, he said, would prefer that the CNR build into the region. The union between that railway and the Quebec government was apparently not yet settled, for Chadbourne understood from those same officials that they would place no obstacles in the way of a T&NO line moving into Quebec.[8]

This attitude changed sharply in the course of the next two weeks. In early March Sir Henry Thornton, President of the Canadian National Railway, announced that his company would build a railway into Rouyn by Christmas. The work would start at once by a private company. Further, he said, the government of Quebec had determined that the smelter for the Noranda Company should be built at Destor. He conveyed this information first to Murdock and Chadbourne of Noranda Mines Company. He declared to the press that a railway linking Rouyn with the Canadian National Railway was absolutely essential in order to check the drain of traffic from northwestern Quebec into Ontario. For Murdock and Chadbourne, this was shocking news. A smelter site in any of the townships of Desserat, Boischatel, or Rouyn would have suited the company, because any of those locations could be reached easily by the Nipissing Central Railway. If the smelter had to be built at Destor, considerably eastward, it would be almost impossible for an arrangement to be made with the Ontario government railway, and the Noranda group clearly wished to deal with the NCR. After a formal meeting with the officials of the Canadian National Railway, Chadbourne and Murdock sought out the Premier of Quebec, Taschereau, to see if they could secure from him a softer attitude on the part of the Quebec government. They could not.

Neither could Premier Ferguson. He wired the Quebec premier:[9]

> This Government is ready to start immediately construction of extension of Kirkland Lake Branch of Government Railway into Rouyn country and can complete line by end of present year (stop) We naturally desire to secure all possible business to take care of carrying and operating charges and have approached Noranda people with the suggestion that they erect smelter along our line in your Province where our engineers advise there are a number of suitable sites (stop) Have you any objection to smelter location above indicated (stop) Feel our line logical transportation for your mining area as business would reach Montreal and other Quebec points as quickly cheaply and fully as by proposed northern route

and would have benefit of competitive rates (stop) Want to co-operate with your government in development of your mineral field and would appreciate your favourable consideration of suggestion that will contribute to success of our Railway (stop) Please wire reply as I intend reaching conclusion and making announcement tomorrow or Monday.

Taschereau's reply of 7 February was blunt:[10]

Your telegram of 6th instant received (stop) We have completed arrangements for construction of line from Canadian National Railways to Rouyn Mining District and have received assurance that line will be completed in December next (stop) Under these circumstances we cannot favour another line.

Both premiers felt considerable pressures from interest groups, and both were anxious, political considerations aside, to tend to the best interests of their respective provinces. Since the prize at stake was located in Quebec, and since he had allied himself with a major Canadian railway system, Taschereau appeared to hold the advantage. But George Lee was convinced that the Quebec Premier was bluffing. He explained in a private memorandum to Premier Ferguson:[11]

MEMORANDUM FOR MR. FERGUSON

1. The announcement of Mr. Thornton as appears in the paper does not mean anything.
2. You will note that he says he will build from Macamick or O'Brien. This is conclusive that they have no particular line in view.
3. From any one of these points to Rouyn will be about 45 miles.
4. The Township of Privot is high land country.
5. The Lois Lake country is _____.
6. Destor Township is high land on the height of land. Railway construction from either one of these points to Rouyn through Destor would be very difficult if not impossible.
7. They have to put engineers in the field, prepare plans, file them with the Dominion Railway Commission, get their approval, and with the greatest possible haste I cannot see how this could be done before July or August. Contract could not be given or work started until this is done.
8. The most feasible and possible route, and easiest route built, would be from Amos to Rouyn, a distance of 58 miles, and this would open up a better section than either of other railways that is talked of. In any case I cannot see that there is any possible chance of them being to Rouyn before July or August 1926.
9. Regarding smelter in Destor Township, after conferring with Mr. Maher who knows the country well. This to him is the most unsuitable place that could be selected for it, and unreasonable to ask the Mining Company to build their smelter in that Township. After leaving the mine, going around the west end of Osisko Lake, there is a great elevation, probably 150 ft. The proper and reasonable thing for the Quebec Government to do would be to have the Mining Company build this smelter in the most convenient place for themselves.

The T&NO, through its subsidiary, the NCR, on the other hand, was poised to move immediately from Larder Lake, only 37 miles away. Its route and location had been chosen, its contractor was ready, its federal charter had been maintained, and it had the good will and support of the principal interests and personalities in the new camps. In light of all this and with the full support of the whole Commission, on 9 March 1925 Lee urged Ferguson to proceed with the completion of the NCR to Rouyn.

Ferguson agreed. Lee was undoubtedly pleased and excited when the following telegram reached his office in North Bay on 10 March 1925.[12]

Have just announced to Legislature that Government has instructed the T&NO Commission to resume work in extension of Larder Lake Branch and push construction with all the men and plant necessary

Cochrane, c. 1926   (Left to right) Mr. Robinson, Tom McAughey John Morris, and Mr. Burkett. John Morris was the first engineer on the James Bay Extension, 1924–26. (ONA-1988054)

to complete work at earliest possible date —Please instruct contractors at once to put on the largest possible number of men that can be economically used to insure expedition.

The response in Ontario, especially New Ontario, was highly enthusiastic. There was little reason why the new NCR extension could not be operating before the next snowfall. Such optimism underestimated the determination of the CNR, the Quebec Premier, and the Quebec government. A third winter would approach before trains would travel from Larder Lake to Rouyn.

Lee's predictions regarding the task that lay in front of the CNR were quite accurate. To comply with all of the regulations of both the Board of Railway Commissioners and the Dominion government, which now owned the CNR, would take several months. To locate a line would take several more, and to overcome the severe engineering difficulties associated with constructing through a torturous terrain would take even more. The Quebec government provided what assis-

tance it could by creating a provincial railway that would run from O'Brien—renamed Taschereau by a grateful citizenry—to Rouyn, thereby removing the jurisdiction of the Board of Railway Commissioners. The line would, when built, be handed over to the CNR. But this would not permit the CNR to get to the camp before the NCR, which had a shorter distance to run and a better route to follow. If Quebec and the CNR wished to win the race to Rouyn, they had to delay the NCR, or better yet, stop it completely. The Quebec government adopted three main tactics to delay and perhaps stop the progress of the Nipissing Central Railway: administrative, political, and legal. There began, therefore, a two and a half year process of thrust and counterthrust involving several levels and departments of government, the courts, and the two railways. These took place concurrently and began almost immediately upon it becoming clear that the NCR people meant to proceed.

Once he received Premier Ferguson's telegram of 10 March 1925, George Lee wired McLean and Clement directing them to get the line started. There followed very quickly the call for tenders and the appropriate order-in-council from the Ontario government to permit the NCR to use Crown Lands in Ontario for its right-of-way, a distance of about seven miles from Larder Lake to the provincial border. Securing the right-of-way beyond that proved much more difficult. It meant gaining permission for the use of Crown Lands and perhaps of lands which were held privately in the province of Quebec. The Quebec government offered resistance regarding both.

Two of the private owners involved were J.R. Booth's lumber company and the Riordan Pulp Corporation, both of which held timber limits which covered part of the NCR's proposed route. Both had already agreed to permit the railway to cross their limits. Under pressure from the Quebec government, both rescinded their agreement. In doing so, the Booth firm included a copy of a telegram received from G.C. Piché, the Quebec Deputy Minister of Lands and Forests.

> Please see that no felling is done in your limits in Rouyn district in connection with cutting of right-of-way and camps for railway construction until otherwise advised by us.[13]

Both companies relied on the good will of the Quebec government for timber rights and thus felt compelled to comply. Chief Forester Piché had, prior to this, issued instructions to his agent at Ville Marie to "take necessary action to prevent the T&NO Railway cutting right-of-way in the Province of Quebec to Rouyn."[14] The official hostility of the Quebec authorities was both clear and widespread.

In the meantime, Clement had filed the necessary papers and plans of the NCR's project with the Minister of Lands and Forests, Honoré Mercier. The same papers had also to be filed with the land agent at Ville Marie. Dealing with the Quebec authorities was a new experience for the Commission which was accustomed to dealing directly with the Ontario Cabinet. To assist them in approaching Quebec officials, they engaged representation in both

centres. For Ville Marie, Lee contacted J. Millard, the Mayor of Haileybury, who had a law practice in Ville Marie. In Quebec the firm of Fitzpatrick, Dupré, Gagnon and Parent, recommended by the Commission's regular counsel, agreed to act for the Commission. Parent first approached Mercier on the subject on 21 March 1925. He got a cool reception and, in reporting on that meeting, warned Lee to "get ready for a very hard fight."[15]

Parent met with Mercier and Taschereau several times, in each case presenting legal and economic arguments supplied to him by telegraph from North Bay in an attempt to wear down the Quebec objections. But he made little progress. Even the news that the NCR had a federal charter and that the Board of Railway Commissioners had approved its route map had no effect. Parent reported by telegram in 24 March 1925.[16]

> The Premier told us at the time (in the first meeting) that there was no chance of success in our project as there was already a bill passed for a railroad in that district and that there was no place for two railroads there and in allowing our demands we would be killing the CNR who had just been authorized to build a railroad through that district (stop) He said to wait for report from Hon. Mercier although he did not believe that it would change anything and that personally he was opposed to project (stop) We had other interviews with him that did not change his mind (stop) We discussed the project with him this morning, renewed all our harmonious propositions and seeing that there was no chance that way, we frankly put the question to him (stop) What are your government's conditions (stop) We are ready to meet any one (stop) The Premier answered we will not leave them go through under any consideration (stop) We replied: that you had a federal charter giving you privilege to build and that in Mr. Tilley's opinion you were covered by your charter and that it was to keep friendly understandings that you were making such step (stop) The Premier answered that he knew about your charter but that you

would have to buy the right-of-way and that the Government would not sell it and as the crown would not expropriate, you would not be able to go through (stop) That was his last word...

At the same time, in the northern Quebec woods, the NCR work crews were denied the right to cut timber in the Quebec forests even in order to build or supply their camps.

Taschereau's determination to resist the NCR stemmed from his desire to protect Quebec's interests. He had accepted the view of Sir Henry Thornton that there was not room for more than one railway into Rouyn. Thornton, of course, had his own agenda. He was concerned with protecting the interests of Montreal, and also with promoting the Canadian National Railway system. This corporation had been organized fairly recently. Between 1917 and 1922, the Canadian government had assumed ownership and control of several major and minor railway companies throughout the Dominion. Many of these, including the National Transcon-

tinental Railway (NTR), had been poorly conceived, improperly financed, and badly managed. The exigencies of the war had exacerbated these initial drawbacks and had forced the railway companies into bankruptcy, a trend that continued in the post-war years.

In an effort to salvage the sprawling railway network, the federal government had pulled the failing lines under the aegis of the government-owned Canadian National Railway system, which came to include the NTR, the Grand Trunk, the Grand Trunk Pacific, and the Canadian Northern. The new company, therefore, acquired a massive network of rail and telegraph systems. It had also acquired a massive debt. For Thornton, the Rouyn mineral resources and proposed smelter operation provided a source of freight revenue. It was, therefore, definitely in his company's interests to have freight move from Rouyn eastward to the CNR line (the former NTR) that ran to Quebec city. He had originally suggested that the NCR and CNR co-operate with both having

Swastika Junction (ONA-199121 Butler)

access. But it was soon obvious that, if such co-operation occurred and shippers had a choice of sending their goods either eastward via the CNR or westward to the T&NO, they would choose the latter. If Thornton's company was to benefit, it must be the only rail line into Rouyn. Thornton had convinced the Quebec Premier that the interests of his province and those of the CNR ran hand-in-hand.

Given these circumstances, the T&NO had to rely on its federal charter and the federal *Railway Act*. The relevant section is No. 189.

> 189.(1) No company shall take possession of, use or occupy any lands vested in the Crown, without consent of the Governor in Council. [i.e. the federal government]
>
> (2) Any railway company may, with such consent, upon such terms as the Governor in Council prescribes, take and appropriate, for the use of its railway and works, so much of the lands of the Crown lying on the route of the railway, which have not been granted or sold, as is necessary for such railway, and also so much of the public beach, or bed of any lake, river or stream, or of the land so vested covered with the waters of any such lake, river or stream as is necessary for making and completing and using its said railway and works.

On the basis of legal precedents, the T&NO counsel, R.H. Parmenter, advised that this section gave the NCR the right to acquire Crown Lands in Ontario and Quebec for the purpose of constructing its railway. Thus, after obtaining approval from the Board of Railway Commissioners for its location, profile, and plan, and after having those registered with the appropriate office at Ville Marie in Quebec, on 31 March 1925 the NCR filed a petition with the Minister of Railways and Canals for approval to use the required lands between Larder Lake and Rouyn. In essence, this meant that the NCR was requesting the federal government approval for the railway to use the lands it needed in Quebec. The assumption was that, once the Governor in Council ordered that the railway had the right to use the lands, the province of Quebec would have to make them available to the railway.

It was no secret that such an application was being made and that the province of Quebec was very much opposed to its being granted. Since the bulk of the current minority Liberal government's support came from Quebec (all 65 Quebec federal ridings had voted Liberal), the Minister of Railways and Canals, Graham Bell, was very anxious to avoid a confrontation with that province. He referred the application to the Justice Department asking if the authority of the federal government extended to Crown Lands that were vested in the province, because that authority had never before been questioned. For two months the NCR's request somehow remained submerged in the federal bureaucratic ocean. The best efforts by Parmenter, who wrote numerous times, often daily, to both the Railway and the Justice departments, could not bring it to the surface. The seriousness of the matter to the federal government was clear. On one occasion, Graham Bell declared that while he personally favoured the NCR plan, the Quebec attitude made it a delicate matter "and it would be a question of policy with the Dominion Government as to whether an Order-in-council should be pressed in the teeth of opposition of the Province of Quebec."[17] Finally, in an attempt to expedite the matter, the Ontario Premier wired directly to Prime Minister W.L.M. King, expressing his concern that no progress had been made even though the NCR had the requisite charter and Railway Board approval.[18]

> Ontario Governments view on advice of counsel is that railway is entitled *as a matter of right* to the Order applied for as refusal in the circumstances of the case would mean that your Government refuses to allow carrying out of project authorized by Parliament (stop) In this case I am unable to find any justification for refusal of your consent to a Dominion Railway entering upon Provincial Crown Lands for carrying out Dominion work (stop) Am instructed that in connection with Montreal Harbour the Dominion has successfully asserted its right to enter upon Provincial Crown Lands to enable it to carry out a Dominion undertaking (stop)...

Would be glad to be advised that Order will issue early date or have definite intimation that your Government takes the responsibility of refusal.

Ferguson's telegram, as well as a long memorandum dated 2 June 1925 regarding the NCR's case which Parmenter sent to King, Bell, and Ernest Lapointe (the Minister of Justice), certainly placed heavy pressure on the Prime Minister to take definite action. King was loath to do so, because the times were awkward. He led a minority government, it was an election year, he depended heavily on Quebec support, and he had already challenged Quebec in the Montreal Harbour affair; but he also needed support from Ontario, and he had previously confronted Ontario on the matter of hydro-electric power. Regardless of the way he leaned in the NCR case, King would offend a significant sector of the Canadian electorate, because the railway race into Rouyn had become a national issue. Newspapers in Ontario and Quebec covered the events closely. Numerous editorials, some highly partisan in nature, proclaimed the justness of one cause or the other. It was much more than a local or northern issue. The Montreal *Gazette*, *La Presse*, the Toronto *Telegram*, the *Mail and Empire*, *the Globe*, the Ottawa *Citizen*, the *Journal*, and *The Northern Miner*—as well as the small northern newspapers such as the Englehart *Times* or the North Bay *Nugget*—had all given good coverage, and most had registered opinions about the proper path that should be taken. King did not wish to be the effective arbiter. He looked for a way to pass on this responsibility to another party. His reply of 4 June to Ferguson's telegram indicated that he had found one.[19]

> Re application Nipissing Central Railway for consent of Governor in Council under Section 189 of the Railway Act to take possession of Quebec Crown Lands in connection with its proposed extension of its Larder Lake Branch into Rouyn country (stop) In view of opinion of Quebec Law Officers of the Crown on the one hand that said section refers only to Dominion Crown Lands or if not so limited is ultra vires parliament and the advice of counsel for the Ontario Government on the other hand that the Railway is entitled as a matter of right to the consent applied for, it has been decided to refer the questions involved to the Supreme Court for consideration and determination under the provisions of Section 60 of the Supreme Court Act.

Other prime ministers, including John A. Macdonald and Wilfrid Laurier, had used the courts to avoid making a decision. It is doubtful, however, that George Lee or Howard Ferguson felt any sense of appreciation for King's use of historical precedent. Parmenter might have, for it meant that he would have a chance to parade his skills in front of the Supreme Court of Canada and perhaps beyond; and he could bill the T&NO for the pleasure! He began to prepare for that event which, in spite of Quebec's efforts to delay it, took place in October 1926. The judgement came down 10 December.

The Prime Minister's actions must have been particularly disturbing to George Lee, for he had remained convinced that Premier Taschereau could be won over: and Lee certainly tried. He responded—very promptly—to any requests that the Commission's Quebec agents made, he saw to it that the Commission was represented by French-speaking counsel in Quebec, Montreal, and Ville-Marie, and he travelled with other commissioners and counsel to meet the Quebec Premier personally in his Quebec city offices on 30 March. Throughout the whole affair he exhibited an aura of calmness and confidence. When the press first began to sense a large and controversial story involving provincial and federal jurisdictions with potential racial undertones—the kind of story that will sell papers and make blood boil—reporters became more pointed, speculative, and insistent in their questions. And they sought answers from anyone connected with the affair. Lee and Ferguson consistently played the problem down and refused ever to criticize or demonstrate any harsh feelings towards Taschereau, Mercier, or Piché. On 4 April, for example, when asked by the Toronto *Star* if there was anything in the view that the NCR was

Water tower at Cheminis   It was here that the NCR remained stopped for two years.
(ONA-19882020 Stephenson/Foerter)

constitutionally barred from entering Quebec, Ferguson replied: "I don't know. We are dealing with it on the basis of the *bonne entente*. We are not fighting it on legal grounds yet." Obviously, it was desirable that others follow that lead, and on one occasion Lee admonished Commissioner Martin by telegram that "we should refrain, as far as possible, from discussing our troubles with newspapers."[20]

Somewhat surprising, given the official hostility that he and his railway encountered, is that Lee maintained the same demeanour in private. He was remarkably consistent in all correspondence with his Quebec agents, his own staff, and his own premier. In his dealing with Quebec government officials or the press, Lee consistently restricted his comments to emphasizing the correctness and fairness of the NCR position, the advantages the NCR would bring to Quebec, and the importance of co-operation, not quarrels, between the two factions. To Lee, the principal cul-

prit was not Taschereau, whom he felt was simply trying to protect his own province's vital interests. Rather, it was the President of the CNR, Sir Henry Thornton, who, in Lee's mind, had offered bad advice to the Quebec Premier about what those vital interests should be. Indeed, although he did not at any point in the correspondence say so directly, Lee appears to have felt betrayed by Thornton: Thornton had first approached the T&NO regarding a joint project and then later advised Taschereau that there was room for only one railway in the Rouyn camp and that it should be the CNR.

Lee's thoughts on the matter were outlined clearly in two memoranda to Premier Ferguson. In the first he reported on his meeting in Taschereau's office on 30 March 1925, at which the Quebec Premier made his position very clear.[21]

"Mr. Lee, I want to be very frank with you. There is not any business in there for two

126

railways, and we want the Canadian National to go in." We explained to him that on different occasions the Canadian National had asked us to go in, and had even requested it in writing. He said he did not know anything about that. He says "Charity begins at home, and we must take care of our own Province, and we have made arrangements to serve this district with a railway." He continued by saying that he wanted to be there first and for us to wait a year and then build. Three different times he asked us to wait one year...

The second, sent on 18 April 1925, was marked "Private, Confidential and Personal" and outlined both a view of the situation and suggestions about how the impasse might be broken.[22]

1. Re my letter to you this A.M. It is evidently quite apparent that the Province of Quebec is not going to allow us in, if they can stop us.

2. It is very doubtful if the Dominion Cabinet, as constituted, will go so far as to give us an Order to go through.

3. Evidently Mr. Taschereau is quite determined to block us at any cost whatsoever.

4. If the Dominion Government do give the Order, I understand that if Quebec still objects, then we have to ask the Courts to give us possession and, if the Courts do give us the possession, Quebec may still appeal to the Privy Council to have the Courts' Order set aside. From this you will see that the fight might be a long one and a very expensive one in the end.

5. Again, if we force our way in it would be one continual fight and they could, and would, embarrass us at every turn.

6. There is not the slightest doubt in my mind but that all, or at least most of the opposition has developed through Sir Henry Thornton and his Officials. I have no doubt, whatever, about this as Mr. Taschereau plainly told me Sir Henry had said "there was not room for two railways in that section".

7. A break with Quebec would be a most regrettable thing and the last thing any one of us in Ontario would want, I am sure—then, what will be the solution of our difficulties? I am sure there is some way out of it.

Let me offer this to you in STRICTEST CONFIDENCE. No person knows that I am writing this.

1. From Mattawa, on the East, on the CPR to North Bay, on the West, on the T&NO, we have two transportation systems running North—in round figures about two hundred and fifty miles—one in Quebec and one in Ontario. There is not one interprovincial connection, although we are not far apart in some places and for the general benefit of the whole country there should be and to this no person could, or should object and I think at Rouyn is the proper place to make the first one. I feel that we should put it right up to Sir Henry Thornton to carry out the spirit of the negotiations we had with his several Assistants—that both of us build to Rouyn; have a Joint terminal in Rouyn. That would let us into Rouyn and let the CNR bring Nova Scotia coal into Kirkland Lake and our Mining Districts. Insist on him recommending this to the Government of Quebec.

2. If we fail in the above and all else, my second solution would be to call a Conference with representatives of the Quebec Government, Sir Henry Thornton, yourself, Mr. Tilley and myself, and make a proposition something like this,—

A. That we go on and complete our present railway to the Quebec boundary.

B. That we go on and finish up the railway to Rouyn and sell it to the CNR Railway at cost, under an Agreement for them to take it over at cost and operate it to the Provincial line. Arrangements could be made for through passenger trains from Amos on the CNR to Swastika on the T&NO and this would not necessitate Ontario going into Quebec at all and we can hand them freight at boundary. This should overcome the objections from Quebec—if we build it for the CNR to take over.

C. Sir Henry should agree to this, as it is practically their own proposition, and

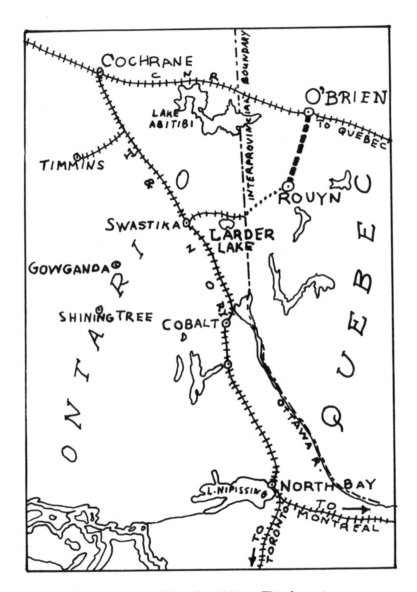

Excerpt. Ottawa Journal, 2 November 1925   This dramatic newspaper item indicates that feelings ran high and that the T&NO efforts to enter Quebec had national attention. (See also p. 129.)

TWO WAYS TO REACH ROUYN

To understand the Rouyn Mines Railway matter, as illustrated in the above cut, bear in mind the following:

1. The Ontario Government wanted, to build from Larder Lake to Rouyn, 22 miles, at its own cost.
2. The Quebec Government objected, on the ground that that would take Rouyn business into Ontario, rather than into Quebec.
3. The Dominion Government was then not called on by reason to do anything. A Rouyn railway had been offered free; if Quebec objected why not let Quebec build it?
4. Yet the King Government of the Dominion, just before a general election, passed an order-in-council authorizing an issue of five million dollars in bonds to build a Rouyn railway 45 miles long; and agreed to a contract by which the National Railways would operate it free of cost to anybody else, win or lose.
5. This order-in-council had no excuse of emergency. Sir Henry Thornton states that he wanted to pre-exempt the territory for the National Railways. But nobody could have taken it. Quebec would not let Ontario in; and the Rouyn Mines Railway Co. was a mere fiction without, capital.
6. Furthermore, the whole case was clear in March last while Parliament was sitting. The King Government could have acted then. It dared not, because discussion in Parliament of such a deal would have set Canada in a roar.
7. Two inferences are justifiable. One, that the Liberal party wanted the deal to get a slush fund; the other, that the deal was at the least a discreditable bribe to the Liberal Government of Quebec and its following.

THE WRETCHED WASTE

Bear in mind also the following facts:

1. The National Railway line from O'Brien to Quebec, the direction of which is shown in the cut, has no short cut-off to Montreal. It goes to Quebec city, not to Montreal. Any Rouyn freight or business that needs to go to Montreal must go almost clear to Quebec city before reaching a junction for Montreal. Therefore, all Rouyn business for Montreal must take a very roundabout route—nd for any places west of Montreal an utterly wasteful route freight rates.
2. On the other hand, by the Ontario Government scheme. Rouyn freight would have had a short cut into both Ontario and Quebec, via North Bay, for all points west of Montreal.

For such freight, the comparison now is as follows:

Ontario's Proposal		Thornton's Scheme	
North Bay to Swastika	165.3	North Bay to Swastika	165.2
Swastika to Rouyn	48	Swastika to Cochrane	87.8
		Cochrane to O'Brien	112.6
		O'Brien to Rouyn	48.0
Total Mileage	213.3	Total Mileage	413.7

Waste Haul—200.4 miles.

Mr. Mackenzie King's election present to Quebec means that every ton of freight from the older provinces into the new Rouyn gold camp will have to be carried almost two hundred miles farther than if it had gone in by the proposed Ontario Government road. The latter would have cost the people of Canada nothing. Mr. King's "election present" will cost the people of Canada possibly $5,000,000 in guarantee on bonds besides giving over the National Railways to the chance of losing a lot of money in operation, if Rouyn goldfield does not prove what is hoped.

Excerpt. Ottawa Journal, 2 November 1925 (continued)

surely Quebec cannot object to inter-provincial trade.

This would let Ontario people in under somewhat different conditions than if we went in, but might help solve our difficulties.

These suggestions to you for your consideration, with the sincere hope that daylight will appear in this affair.

Lee's position, then, was one of insistence upon the justness of their cause but tempered constantly by a willingness to co-operate. There was, as well, a strong desire to breach the restrictions of excessive provincial thinking. The decision to place the matter before the Courts, while it may well have had the benefit of permitting Mackenzie King to avoid making a decision, ended any possibility of *bonne entente* between Ontario and Quebec on this issue. The adversarial structure of the judicial system and the strict constitutional interpretation that the Supreme Court would have to follow meant that such factors as the nature of the population, the terrain, or the relative technological abilities of the competing railways would not enter into the final judgement. Furthermore, because King's declaration came when it did, it meant that the matter could not come before the Supreme Court until the fall session. In effect, then, the Prime Minister had made a decision: he had delayed the NCR, as Taschereau had wished. Ferguson responded angrily to King's telegram, indicating that legal precedents supported the NCR case, that to treat the NCR differently than other railways was unfair, and that to refer the affair to the Supreme Court was a waste of time and money. King refused to alter his position. Almost everyone agreed that the NCR had a winning hand in legal terms. But that was small consolation for the loss of an entire construction season. The NCR remained stopped at the border, at Cheminis, for almost two years. One wit suggested to Lee that he change the name of Cheminis to Taschereau Siding.[23]

Notes

1. Cole to Lee, 4 October 1924. ONA, B-7500(1), Main File, Vol. A. Re Investigations—Rouyn. Correspondence from October 1923 to February 1925.
2. Clement to Lee, 9 December 1924. ONA, B-7500(1), Main File, Vol. A.
3. Lee to Ferguson, 8 January 1925. ONA, B-7500(1), Main File, Vol. B. Rouyn Extension. Correspondence February 1925 to September 1925.
4. Chadbourne to Lee, 18 February 1925. ONA, B-7500(1), Main File, Vol. B.
5. Lee to Ferguson, 18 February 1925. ONA, B-7500(1), Main File, Vol. B.
6. Cole to Lee, 5 April 1924. ONA, B-7500(1), Main File, Vol. B.
7. Cole to Lee, 28 January 1925. ONA, B-7500(1), Main File, Vol. B.
8. Chadbourne to Lee Telephone conversation. 19 February 1925. ONA, B-7500(1), Main File, Vol. B.
9. Ferguson to Taschereau. Telegram. 6 February 1925. ONA, B-7500(1), Main File, Vol. B.
10. Taschereau to Ferguson. Telegram. 7 February 1925. ONA, B-75001), Main File, Vol. B.
11. Lee to Ferguson. Telegram. 7 February 1925. ONA, B-7500(1), Main File, Vol. B.
12. Ferguson to Lee. Telegram. 10 March 1925. ONA, B-7500(1), Main File, Vol. B.
13. John Black to Lee, 26 March 1925. ONA, B-7500(1), Main File, Vol. B.
14. Piché to Desjardins, 20 March 1925. ONA, B-7500(1), Main File, Vol. B.
15. Parent to Lee, 21 March 1925. ONA, B-7500(1), Main File, Vol. B.
16. Parent to Lee Telegram. 24 March 1925. ONA, B-7500(1), Main File, Vol. B.
17. Parmenter to Maund, 28 April 1925. ONA, B-7500(1), Main File, Vol. B.
18. Ferguson to King. Telegram. 30 May 1925. ONA, B-7500(1), Main File, Vol. B. (Emphasis added).
19. King to Ferguson. Telegram. 4 June 1925. ONA, B-7500(1), Main File, Vol. B. (Emphasis added).
20. Lee to Martin. Telegram. 2 April 1925. ONA, B-7500(1), Main File, Vol. B.
21. Lee to Ferguson, 30 March 1925. ONA, B-7500(1), Main File, Vol. B.
22. Lee to Ferguson, 18 April 1925. ONA, B-7500(1), Main File, Vol. B. (Emphasis in the original).
23. *Northern Miner*, 21 November 1925.

Chapter 8

From Cheminis to Rouyn

I T IS NOT surprising that King leaned towards Quebec. He was a first-time prime minister who won the Liberal leadership in 1919 following the death of Sir Wilfrid Laurier and who had won the Prime Minister's job from the Conservative Arthur Meighen in the 1921 federal election. His hold on the post was tenuous, however, for his Liberal administration, supported by 117 seats, was in a slight minority position—the first one since Confederation—facing a combined Opposition of 65 Progressives, 50 Conservatives, 2 Labour, and 1 Independent. When the Rouyn issue was dumped into his court in 1925, King faced the prospect of an election that year; the bulk of his support came from the province of Quebec where his party represented all 65 constituencies; and the provincial government of Taschereau was Liberal. King no doubt felt the need to have the full support of the Quebec Liberal machinery when the election campaign began, an event which most observers felt would begin in the late summer of that year.

Ferguson was certainly aware of King's political situation and undoubtedly understood—perhaps even sympathized with—his response to the Rouyn situation. But Ferguson also faced an election in 1925. His supporters very much favoured the NCR move into Quebec, and he could not back down in the face of federal opposition. Nor is it likely that Ferguson was inclined to do so. There is every indication that he felt that his government's railway had not only the right but also an obligation to build towards the gold and copper treasure of the Rouyn region. In declaring his position in a telegram to King, however, Ferguson walked very carefully. He eschewed any comment that could be construed as provincial chauvinism. He stressed legal precedent by observing that the federal government had already granted such a request.[1]

> Your telegram re Nipissing Central Railway received (stop) In nineteen twelve when a similar question was raised as to propriety of the Governor in Council giving consent to a Dominion Railway Company taking possession of certain lands in Toronto vested in the Crown in right of the Province of Ontario the Department of Justice advised the Dominion Government that the Section as to consent applied to Provincial as well as to Dominion lands and that the Dominion Government had no interest except as to the mere statutory condition of consent (stop) The Order in Council that was then passed recited the advice so given and granted consent expressly reserving the rights of the Crown

in right of the Province of Ontario (stop) I am advised that the Order in Council drafted in the present case contains similar terms which are entirely acceptable to the Nipissing Central Railway Company and I cannot understand why the proposal to pass it should be abandoned (stop)

He also sought to show that simple fair play supported the NCR cause.

There seems no reason for according different treatment to the Nipissing Central Railway from that given to other Dominion Railways or for throwing the matter into the Courts thereby delaying indefinitely the completion of a partly built line into Rouyn and enabling a rival Company to build first into that country though it has as yet taken no steps in that direction... I trust you will reconsider matter and not do what seems to me to be an injustice to a Dominion Railway that has shown considerable enterprise and desires to complete its line into Rouyn this year thereby opening up this portion of Canada with the least possible delay and without asking any aid from the Dominion or from the Province of Quebec.

Ferguson, although often encouraged to do so by others who declared themselves hostile to Quebec, to Taschereau, and to the federal government, refused to make pejorative comments regarding his opposition even in his correspondence with George Lee, L.F. Martin, and other persons involved. His subordinates did likewise.

In June 1925, for example, *The Northern Miner* printed a highly inflammatory article condemning the Quebec opposition to the NCR extension. According to a Toronto *Star* report,[2] the *Miner's* article declared:

Are the business men and people of Northern Ontario, in the face of Quebec's attitude, going to continue turning their millions into Montreal and the province of Quebec? Our answer, so long as Quebec maintains the narrow provincial and insular position it has laid down, is an emphatic "No"...

Not a business day passes but travellers and business emissaries from Quebec are in the north seeking our millions for the benefit of Quebec business. The time has come to decide whether these men, in the face of Quebec's attitude towards us,

New Liskeard station crossing, c. 1924 (ONA-1988627 R.J. Russell)

132

are to get our business. Shall we build up Ontario or Quebec?

When this article was shown to G.S. Henry, the acting Premier of Ontario at a time when Ferguson was out of the province, he refused to endorse the idea of a boycott of Quebec's goods and said that his "province desires to dwell in amity with her sister province." Moreover, he declared that "Quebec did not object to Ontario building the line, but only to Ontario getting in a year ahead of Quebec."[3]

Yet, while Ferguson and his associates continued to exhibit a strong loyalty to the principle of "bonne entente," they were equally steadfast in their determination to have the line built from Cheminis to Rouyn. The potential rewards for the railway and for the province appeared to be very great indeed. And since, in their view, their desire to reap those considerable rewards was totally justified, they were prepared to accept the risks and the costs of both the legal and the political contest. Consequently, the northeastern corridor became the site of a unique railway race. At stake was the railway traffic—freight and passenger—and the rewards of supplying an isolated but very wealthy segment of the country. The main action took place on three fronts: the courts, the link between Cheminis and Rouyn, and the link from O'Brien (renamed Taschereau) to Rouyn.

On 8 June 1925 the NCR directors, identical of course to the T&NO Commission, discussed developments to that point, including the exchange of telegrams between King and Ferguson. They also called the contractor, McLean, and Chief Engineer Clement into the meeting. After a three-hour discussion in what must have been a tension-charged atmosphere, the meeting agreed that the work currently in progress should be completed as quickly as possible as far as the Ontario–Quebec border. McLean would complete the task of grading to that point, but the rest of the job—track-laying and ballasting—would be done by the railway's own men, and the whole operation was to be completed by 10 September. The crews operating in Quebec were to be withdrawn, excessive

supplies disposed of to mining camps, and the tenders which had been received for construction beyond the border were to be returned unopened. Yet these men remained firm that the full line would be built, "for it was strictly understood that operations are to be continued in this matter—and that work is only suspended pending decision of the courts."[4] The NCR very quickly extended its line to the Ontario–Quebec border at Cheminis and instituted service over it to the new eastern terminus, which all expected to be temporary. The decision to establish a regular service—passenger and freight—was designed to give further credence to the Commission's firm intent to proceed further. Although stopped at the border, the NCR still provided the best rail service then available to the Rouyn camps, and the Cheminis terminus handled freight hauled to and from the Rouyn mining areas by teams of horses.

Although this method was available and certainly a better route than one by freight wagon from either the CNR railhead at O'Brien or the CPR at Angliers, it was still both awkward and costly. The Mayor of Cobalt, Dr. C.F. Armstrong, spoke for many people when he declared that "What is needed is a railway and Quebec needs it more than Ontario."[5]

> All the people on the other side of Temiskaming are strong for the Ontario railway. They want this country opened up and they have no other outlet now except across the lake. They have market gardens and farm produce, and this is their only market... The whole policy of the country must be to support the mining industry, and the mining interests have no two options about this railway line. In that respect Quebec is no different than Ontario.

To the northeast of Rouyn, the CNR gradually overcame the obstacles of the O'Brien route. The incorporation issue was handled in the 1925 session of the Quebec legislature which created the Rouyn Mines Railway. Subsequent legislation officially changed this to the "National Transcontinental Railway Branch Lines Company,"[6] but the original name was the one popularly used. Financing came through the CNR, the Quebec government, and private capital,[7] and on 3 October 1925 *The Northern Miner* reported that a contract for the construction of the Rouyn Mines Railway had been awarded jointly to the Toronto firm of Chambers, McQuigge and McCaffery and the Foley Brothers of St. Paul, Minnesota. The cost was $1,000,000. On 7 December the Toronto *Star* reported that the branch line was occupying the labours of 500–1000 men in grading and laying tracks. Problems remained, but the second runner in the railway race had begun to move.

It was a strange competition. The Rouyn Mines Railway people struggled against natural obstacles. The NCR people, well prepared with capital, completed surveys, and engineering expertise were anxious to move, confident that they could run into Rouyn in a few months. For them the problem was that of urging the matter through the courts, quickly and successfully. This task, and the fate of the entire enterprise, lay in the hands of the law firm of Tilley, Thomson and Parmenter and especially those of R.H. Parmenter, who had been handling T&NO legal work for years. It had been he who advised Lee regarding the main line requirements in 1923 and who had meticulously seen that the NCR charter had been carefully maintained and updated through the years. It was quite another matter, however, to prepare, present, and argue a case in the full judicial arena of the Supreme Court.

The issue regarding jurisdiction and the respective rights of the federal and provincial authorities was really quite simple: either the federal government had the authority to override the province regarding the use of Crown lands there, or it did not. But the implications of the decision—regardless of the winner—were potentially very far reaching in their constitutional and political consequences. Within these consequences lurked a certain irony as well, for the federal government, by its decision to use the courts to assist it over a political impasse, was actually questioning its own jurisdiction. It

Rouyn Station, c. 1927 (ONA-1988252283)

134

was Ferguson, the Ontario Premier, who insisted that the federal government had not only the right, but the obligation, to assert itself over the province in this matter. The irony runs more deeply when one notes that Ferguson stands among the provincial premiers as one who promoted provincial rights, and Mackenzie King claimed consistently that the federal government must be an instrument for promoting national unity and the national interest at the expense of the provinces if necessary.

The NCR argument can be stated easily. It was a federally chartered railway company; it had, therefore, all the rights that accrue to such a corporation; it had, furthermore, been careful to have its charter kept current by complying with all the requisite federal regulations under the federal *Railway Act*; and finally, with respect to its construction beyond Cheminis, the NCR had filed the requisite profiles and surveys with the Board of Railway Commissioners and had obtained that body's approval. The NCR asserted also that it had already incurred considerable expense in constructing 30 miles of track from Swastika to Cheminis, and that it was committed to the further expense of another 30 miles of rail from Cheminis to Rouyn. In doing so it would be serving the national interest by opening up a new and wealthy sector of the hinterland. In a similar dispute between the province of Ontario and the CPR, the Department of Justice had ruled that the federal control of Crown Lands in the province superseded provincial control. Thus, if the CPR's federal charter prevailed over the objections of the province of Ontario in 1912, then the NCR's federal charter should likewise prevail over the objections of the province of Quebec in 1925. Accordingly, the NCR had applied for a federal order-in-council that would permit the railway to use unoccupied Crown Lands in northern Quebec in order to construct its line from Cheminis to Rouyn. It was, according to the NCR argument, obligatory that the request be granted because of the precedents set in two previous judgements by the Judicial Committee of the Privy Council (*Corporation of the City of Toronto v. Bell Telephone Co.*, 1905; *Attorney General for British Columbia v. Canadian Pacific Railway, 1906*) and also by the action of the Justice department in 1912.[8]

The Attorney General for the province of Quebec had a different view. This case, prepared by G. Lanctot and Geoffrion, contended that the land in question was the public property of the province of Quebec under the *BNA Act* and as such the federal government could not extend ownership or jurisdiction over it. To support this argument, they cited several cases ranging from the famous *St. Catherine's Milling Case* of 1888 through to that of the *Attorney General for Canada v. the Attorney General of Quebec* in 1921. It was, for them, simply a matter of jurisdiction over Crown Lands, and the correctness of the NCR's behaviour was not relevant. The province of Quebec, like all the original provinces of Confederation, held ownership and jurisdiction over its Crown Lands, and, according to the Quebec lawyers, this could not be taken by the federal government.[9]

The timing of King's decision to refer the matter to the Supreme Court of Canada prevented the issue from being considered at its spring session of 1925, although the NCR people pressed for it. The case was finally heard in October and judgement given on 10 December 1925.[10] As often happens, it did not settle the matter. In handing down the judgement, the Court declared that the federal Parliament did have the right to assert its jurisdiction over provincial Crown Lands regarding railway construction. It added, however, that in the matter of the NCR's request for the use of lands in Quebec,

> ...it is not obligatory upon the Governor in Council to give his consent, and that he has, in point of law, discretion to grant or refuse such consent, as he may see fit.

This pleased no one. The Quebec group did not care for this assertion of federal jurisdiction. The NCR people did not like the discretionary aspect, because it meant that the federal government could decline to grant the required permission to use Quebec lands. King disliked

Frozen water tank at Cheminis, c. 1926   Someone forgot to turn off the pump.
(ONA-1988203 Stephenson/Foerter)

it for the same reason. Furthermore, the general political circumstances had worsened for him since June. The election of October 1925 had been disastrous for him. King and eight of his cabinet met personal defeat; the Liberal contingent dropped to 101; and the Conservatives, under Arthur Meighen, increased to 117. King was not prepared to surrender power, however, and sought to secure a seat for himself and to win the support of the 24 Progressive party members who held the balance of power in the House of Commons. It was while he was working at this task that the Supreme Court decision came down. Thus he was likely very relieved when Quebec also indicated displeasure with the Supreme Court's decision and chose to appeal to the Judicial Committee of the Privy Council in Great Britain, an option that was open to the province at that time.[11]

This appeal to the Privy Council occupied another five months, but the judgement issued on 17 May 1926 changed nothing. The Judicial Committee concurred in the judgement of the Canadian Supreme Court.[12] Since both courts had declared that the federal government possessed the right to grant the use of provincial Crown Lands to railway corporations, it could be argued that Parmenter and the NCR had won. But the courts' declaration that such action was not obligatory meant that the affair had simply been set back into the lap of Mackenzie King. His government had to decide whether or not to grant the NCR's request in the face of the full opposition of the Government of the Province of Quebec. When first faced with this question a year earlier, King had considered the circumstances of the day to be unpropitious, and he had chosen to avoid or delay making a decision. By May and June 1926, the circumstances were immeasurably worse.

King remained in power, but barely. He had secured a Commons seat for himself and had met the House on 7 January 1926. His position was precarious because the powerful Conservative opposition actually outnumbered King's Liberals by 15 seats. With support from the other groups 24 Progressives, 2 Labour, and 2 Independents —King nonetheless continued to hold office despite several efforts at motions of no-confidence. Support from the Progressives was severely threatened, however, by revelations of serious corruption and maladministration in the federal Department of Customs and Excise. A multiparty committee investigated and determined that many of these charges were valid. The minister, Jacques Bureau, resigned at King's request, but the committee recommended that several other officials be dismissed or forced to retire, and the investigations went on. In the face of these troubles, Mackenzie King was by no means anxious to be faced once again with the NCR's request for the use of Crown Lands in Quebec.

As it turned out, the NCR matter was postponed for another four months. The events of June–September 1926 in Canadian federal politics have been recounted and analysed many times and need not be narrated in detail here.[13] At the time, the principal issue before King was that of the role of the Governor General and of Canada's role in the British Empire, both prominent matters at the Imperial Conference scheduled for that fall. Indeed King and Prime Minister Hertzog of South Africa together led the movement for greater autonomy for the Dominions. The result of this conference was the famous Balfour Declaration of 1926 which appeared to satisfy the recalcitrant Dominions and which led to the Statute of Westminster five years later in 1931.

These several grand events—the customs scandal, the constitutional struggle, the summer election (won by King), the Imperial Conference—occupied the Prime Minister's time. There can be little doubt that he enjoyed strutting on the imperial stage, and it had the added advantage of permitting him to avoid unpleasant issues at home. The case of the NCR faded somewhat into the background behind the dominant national and imperial matters of the day.

But it did not go away. At the urgings of Premier Ferguson and Chairman Lee, Parmenter continued to press the federal government for a decision on the application for the use of Crown Lands in Quebec. It was clear that the federal government did not wish to make a judgement or, at least, wished to delay making one for as long a time as possible. The waiting game was not one that the NCR people enjoyed, especially since the two-year delay had given the Rouyn Mines Railway sufficient time to complete its connection between O'Brien, by then known as Taschereau, and Rouyn. Even the controlled George Lee showed his exasperation in January 1927 in a letter to the Premier.[14]

> This matter has now been dragging on for a long time, through no fault of the Government or the Commission. As the Winter is advancing something should be done, at once, to bring the matter to a head—one way or the other—as if we are not going to be allowed to proceed we should be given a chance to get whatever we have in there out before the snow goes and salvage what we can.
>
> I do not want to appear to you to be too eager in this matter but I am very anxious about it.

Over the next two months it gradually emerged that the federal government was preparing to accede to the NCR request and provide the appropriate order-in-council. Even so, Premier Ferguson feared that "we will find some conditions attached to it that will require negotiation."[15] He therefore agreed with George Lee that regardless of the terms of the order, there should be yet a further effort to placate Taschereau "because if he is still opposed to us going in there he can make it very difficult for us in the question of location, right-of-way, station grounds, operation of the railway and in many other ways."[16]

The order finally came through on 14 March 1927. The NCR moved quickly. Lee was called to Toronto to meet with Ferguson; the next day, 18 March, Ferguson wired Taschereau to arrange a meeting; that done, the T&NO's business car *Temagami* was dispatched to carry Lee and commissioner Martin to Quebec. They arrived on 20 March, and, the

Bunkhouses built in North Bay for use on the line, c. 1925 (ONA-198871 E. Everitt)

following evening, Lee prepared for Ferguson an account of that afternoon's meeting with the Quebec Premier.[17] He ended on a cautious, but somewhat hopeful note.

> He assured us the matter would be dealt with shortly and he would wire us. I do not think he will give us his consent at anytime but I also think that after the whole matter has been considered he will give us the same treatment as he would give the Canadian Pacific Railway, or any other Railway holding a Dominion Charter.
>
> It is our intention at our meeting on Thursday, at North Bay, to go on and call for tenders to be received about April 20th and feel sure that by that time we will know where we are with the Government of Quebec in the matter.

A subsequent telephone conversation revealed that both men intended that the project would proceed, but they were most anxious to do so properly and cautiously.[18]

Mr. Lee: Did you get my letter from Quebec? What did you think of it?

Mr. Ferguson: I am not surprised. Think you are quite right. Would wait a few days to see if you hear from him and if not, then advertise.

Mr. Lee: I will not do anything until I hear from you.

Mr. Ferguson: Do not make it public. I would wait a little while.

Mr. Lee: Well I intend to get authority at the meeting on Thursday to call for tenders and then I will wait until I hear from you.

Mr. Ferguson: Are you having a meeting on Thursday?

Mr. Lee: Yes.

Mr. Ferguson: Well have a Resolution put through to build the Line but say nothing about it to the Public. I will tell you when to go on with the work.

As Lee indicated they would, the commissioners—acting in their capacity as Directors of the Nipissing Central Railway—resolved on 23 March to extend the NCR some 27 miles from Cheminis to Rouyn, but the matter of calling for tenders would "be left with the President

(Lee) to deal with, when a definite decision had been reached with the Government at Toronto." Ferguson made the decision public on 1 April. In his final address to the winter session of the Ontario legislature, he announced that his government would build the T&NO into Rouyn. (In the public mind and elsewhere, no distinction was made between the T&NO and the NCR.) He added that negotiations were under way and had been for some time towards removing all obstacles.[19]

Despite Ferguson's apparent firmness and confidence, grounds for apprehension remained. Lee, so often disappointed in the past, posed three questions to the company lawyers.[20]

(a) Are there any other questions that Honourable L.A. Taschereau can raise in the event of him not arriving at an amicable agreement with us regarding right-of-way, station grounds, timber, etc., whereby he could stop us building?

(b) Can he set his own price on timber and land? If we refuse to pay it will he have to abide by the arbitration?

(c) Have we absolute right to go on and build and if the whole question was referred to arbitration is that final, or could he appeal against it in the same manner as he did about us going into Quebec?

Parmenter's conclusions, after a long and detailed analysis, probably caused Lee to have nightmares.[21] The NCR, he said, must make an offer for use of the Quebec land. Should Quebec decline the offer, the matter would "be determined by arbitration." The matter of compensation was expected, but the spectre of further legal fights must have been terrifying.

A glimmer of hope shone through on 9 April when Taschereau declared that he had no objection to a right-of-way on Crown Lands providing the matter was settled with the Minister of Crown Lands. Yet, as he made his way towards Quebec city for an arranged meeting with that minister, Honoré Mercier, George Lee must have been filled with apprehension. It was his third such trip; the others had accomplished nothing; and Mercier's background was one

of considerable Quebec chauvinism. (His father had been premier and had exhibited strong provincial rights stands.) His fears and apprehensions disappeared suddenly when he learned that Mercier—and presumably Taschereau—had decided to let the NCR move. Mercier made the Quebec position official in a letter of 19 April, declaring that Quebec would grant the requested right-of-way for a compensation of $10,000.[22]

George Lee was delighted. "For the payment of this $10,000.00," he wrote to Ferguson, "we are to receive the right-of-way through all the lands, through the province of Quebec, that are still in the Crown—for 27 miles."[23] Moreover, the NCR received "the right to cut through the timber limits of J.R. Booth and the International Paper Company and this $10,000.00 includes any dues that might be coming to the Government for any timbers or pulpwood that we cut off these limits."

I consider that this is an excellent arrangement and must say it is a better one than I anticipated when I came down. There will be no more differences between us—no arbitrations of any kind. They have agreed to meet every reasonable demand that we make and I feel sure that this settlement will be satisfactory to All Concerned.

While thrilled that the matter had been settled favourably, Lee no doubt wondered how this abrupt change came about. He did not tempt fate by speculating, however (not even in his private correspondence). Rather he simply accepted the good fortune and acted on it.

Taschereau's public explanation for the reversal was careful. The Toronto *Star* reported on 21 April that when asked about it, "Premier Taschereau...said that it did not make any difference to Quebec now as the province's own railroad to Rouyn was in operation and was two years in advance of the T&NO project." The stated reason was sufficient to permit the Premier to save face. But the abruptness and the extent of Quebec's retreat suggests that other factors pushed Taschereau into his new stance.

The dominant business interests in the Rouyn region were Ontario in their origins. This included the principal investors, such as Noah Timmins, as well as the principal suppliers. As George Lee pointed out as early as 1923, these men preferred to do business through Ontario rather than Quebec; and they had done so, even when the NCR was stalled at the border. Goods were hauled by wagon or by sleigh, depending on the season, from Cheminis into the mining regions. In the meantime, the prediction of NCR people regarding the CNR route proved accurate. The Rouyn Mines Railway progressed only slowly. Moreover, its only connection was to the main line of the old National Transcontinental Railway. Many of the suppliers were located in southern Ontario or the United States. To reach Rouyn via the CNR, goods had to be shipped first to Quebec city—180 miles east of Montreal and 500 miles from Toronto. To ship through Cheminis, even with the added costs of wagon freight from that point, might well be less expensive. To ship over a T&NO route that had

been completed through to Rouyn would be both less costly and less troublesome; this would have the effect of pleasing the consumers —i.e., the people of Rouyn—who had complained of the high costs in the region.

Concurrent with the transportation matter were two other continuing and thorny issues. One involved the final stages of the Regulation 17 imbroglio that had divided central Canada since 1912; the other was the matter of hydroelectric power in which the two provinces of Ontario and Quebec found themselves at odds with a common foe: the federal government. Taschereau was anxious to have the remnants of Regulation 17 removed because of the restrictions it placed on the French language in Ontario; Ferguson was anxious to have the railway into Rouyn; both were anxious to preserve their respective province's control over hydroelectric power at Niagara and at Beauharnois. The longstanding calmness of Lee and Ferguson and their disinclination to indulge in name calling thus paid some dividends. It made

Scene from Noranda smelter with Rouyn in the background, c. 1927 (ONA-1988252281)

140

it easier for Taschereau to accede to the request for use of Crown Lands in Quebec. Ferguson, in turn, could quietly remove Regulation 17 from Ontario's educational regulations. And thus the *bonne entente* could be, and was, re-established.

It was not completely a clear track, because the CNR had constructed its line in such a fashion that the NCR had to cross the Rouyn Mines Railway right-of-way in order to make its way into the Rouyn and Noranda bonanza region. Thornton tried to prevent them from doing so and argued that there was room for only one line. That line, he said, should be his—the CNR—"because we were the first railway there and had actually opened up the area." Such a claim must have caused Lee to grimace, having been forced to sit at the border for two years. This time, however, Thornton stood alone. He did not have the support of the Quebec Premier. Consequently, the arguments of the NCR prevailed at the Railway Board hearings. The line reached Rouyn in November 1927 and was extended to Noranda the following year.

Notes

1. Ferguson to King. Telegram. 5 June 1925. ONA, B-7500(1), Main File, Volume B. Rouyn Extension.
2. Toronto *Star*, 20 June 1925.
3. *Ibid.*
4. *Minutes*, 8 June 1925.
5. *The Canadian Mining Journal*, 1 May 1925.
6. Toronto *Telegram*, 7 December 1925.
7. Toronto *Star*, 15 September 1925.
8. Memorandum Re Nipissing Central Railway, Rouyn Branch, by Tilley, Johnston, Thomson & Parmenter. 2 June 1925. ONA, B-7500(1), Main File, Volume B. Rouyn Extension.
9. Memorandum Re taking possession of provincial lands by a federal Railway Company by Charles Lanctot, Asst. Attorney General. 12 May 1925. ONA, B-7500(1), Main Line, Volume B. Rouyn Extension.
10. *The Attorney-General of Quebec v. The Nipissing Central Railway.* Judgement of the Supreme Court of Canada. 10 December 1925. ONA, B-7500(1), Main File, Volume B. Rouyn Extension.
11. Such appeals ceased after 1949 when the Supreme Court of Canada became the final appeal court in Canadian judicial matters.
12. *The Attorney-General of Quebec v. The Nipissing Central Railway.* Judgement of the Lords of the Judicial Committee of the Privy Council, delivered 17 May 1926. ONA, B-7500(1), Main File, Volume B. Rouyn Extension.
13. A succinct and lucid account can be found in Roger Graham, ed., *The King-Byng Affair, 1926: A Question of Responsible Government.* Toronto: Copp Clark, 1967, pp. 1–3.
14. Lee to Ferguson, 6 January 1927. ONA, B-7500(1), Main File, Volume D. Rouyn Extension.
15. Ferguson to Lee, 14 March 1927. ONA, B-7500(1), Main File, Volume D. Rouyn Extension.
16. Lee to Ferguson, 11 March 1927. ONA, B-7500(1), Main File, Volume D. Rouyn Extension.
17. Lee to Ferguson, 21 March 1927. ONA, B-7500(1), Main File, Volume B. Rouyn Extension.
18. Memo of "Long Distance" Telephone Conversation with Honourable G.H. Ferguson, Tuesday, 22 March 1927. ONA, B-7500(1), Main File, Volume D. Rouyn Extension.
19. North Bay *Nugget*, 1 April 1927.
20. Lee to Tilley et al., 6 April 1927. ONA, B-7500(1), Main File, Volume D. Rouyn Extension.
21. Parmenter to Lee, 7 April 1927. ONA, B-7500(1), Main File, Volume D. Rouyn Extension.
22. Mercier to Lee, 19 April 1927. ONA, B-7500(1), Main File, Volume D. Rouyn Extension.
23. Lee to Ferguson, 21 April 1927. ONA B-7500(1) Main File, Volume D. Rouyn Extension.

Chapter 9

Towards the Abitibi Canyon

OST OF THE time the T&NO was severely practical and conservative to a fault. In 1909–10, for example, it was slow to run a branch line to Porcupine; and in 1914–18 it preferred the development of that line to the building of a new one to Kirkland Lake. In fact, the Commission took pride in its cautious, conservative approach.[1] The line had begun with very limited objectives and grew only in direct responses to clear opportunities after 1902. But in the James Bay extension, the Commission gave way to romance.

In the days of the fur trade, Hudson Bay had proved itself a better route into the interior of the continent than the St. Lawrence River. Furs, however, were not bulky in relation to their value and their carriage overland to ships in the Bay had been feasible. Wheat, on which the new trade of the West was based, was not a cargo suitable for canoes and York boats. So the route to Europe through the Bay had been neglected. New technology might change that. Perhaps railways, which had spanned the continent, pierced the barrier of the Rocky Mountains, and revolutionized the transport of bulk commodities, could run to the Bay and restore its old commercial supremacy. In the early '20s that was an article of faith in Northern Ontario, although it was possibly held with the caveat that the time was not ripe.

The Commission's early references to a James Bay line, from 1902, expressed that reservation. That reservation can only have been reinforced by the fate of a variety of utopian northern railway schemes circulating in 1900–20. The most visionary of them called for a combined rail and water route that would run from Toronto to Moose Factory, across Hudson Bay to its northwest corner, and then follow the rivers to Great Bear Lake. From there it would follow the Mackenzie River and ultimately reach the Bering Sea! Most of these plans died at the chartering stage, but a few actually began building. The Nipissing and James Bay Railway, for example, established a partial railbed just west of the town of North Bay, and the Algoma Central Railway later managed to extend from Sault Ste. Marie up the Agawa Canyon and beyond to Hearst. These were meagre results from grand designs, not likely to impress the sober judgments of the T&NO Commission, interested as it was in the principle of commercial viability. The end of the First World War, however, brought circumstances that led the Commission to overcome its reservations.

The return to a peace-time economy was complicated for Ontario by the fact that its war-

North Cobalt substation, c. 1931   This supplied the power to the NCR. John Warner at the controls.
(ONA-1988058)

time growth had confirmed it as the industrial heartland of Canada. Retooling plants and retraining employees for civilian production was a critical process. The economy's demand for natural resources, especially forest products and hydro-electric power, was expected to rise sharply; but their development required major long-term projects. Capital and labour released from military production and the armed forces were available, but the distribution system on which an industrial economy depended was in disarray.

Even before the war, Canada had greatly overextended its transcontinental railway programme. It was managed badly, and it was fraught with greed, special interests, and even some corruption. The Grand Trunk's financial problems were observed as early as 1912 or so. The Grand Trunk Railway was obliged to renege on its agreement with the T&NO regarding the Nipissing Junction spur.[2] That particular matter went into litigation and was not settled until 1922. These early warnings of impending insolvency occurred sporadically in the pre-war years but did not cause much alarm. The war made the basic

problem clear: the income of railways did not keep pace with costs. During the war, passenger travel declined because the general population was restricted in its mobility, and freight also declined because the nation's productivity was concentrated on the war effort. Moreover, the rates for both freight and passengers were controlled because of the war, yet wages and other overhead costs rose dramatically. The traditional main safety valve for leaky railway finances, government grants, became unavailable to the larger lines because of war-time commitments. They were left to meet their costs from their own resources, and this they could not do. Yet these same lines constituted a service essential to both the national economy and the nation's war effort. They could not be permitted to close down. When faced with this situation, the federal government of Robert Borden—at first a Conservative administration from 1911 to 1917, and then a Union government from 1917 to 1921—began the process of nationalizing the major lines that were failing. It took until 1922 when the new Liberal government of Mackenzie King, elected in 1921, completed the arrangements for the creation of the Canadian National Railways system. At war's end, however, the final steps had not yet been taken, and the full extent of the nationalization process had not yet been determined. The most often discussed line was the CPR. This railway had a sufficiently strong financial basis to withstand the strains of war, but there were varying opinions regarding its fate. Many people felt that it should be pulled under government control.

The T&NO was also affected. There was a body of opinion which argued that it too should be nationalized. This line had suffered from the strains of war-time demands, including fixed or declining income and rising costs, but, like the CPR, it rested on secure and stable financial bases. The T&NO did show an operating deficit by 1918, but it was small and with the coming of peace the line could expect to reverse that trend. As a government-owned provincial railway, the T&NO was in a different situation from such lines as the Grand Trunk or Canadian Northern which had private capital and private investors. Yet the idea of nationalization was in the air, and the T&NO formed an essential link between the Grand Trunk and the Canadian Northern at Nipissing Junction and the National Transcontinental at Cochrane. The case could easily be made that the national interests could best be served by integrating the T&NO into the new national railway system. The federal government did not touch this line, however, perhaps because the provincial governments of Hearst and then Drury saw it as one instrument for dealing with Ontario's post-war industrial progress.

Prior to the war, Ontario was awakening to two obvious trends: the increasing exploitation of its natural resources and the increasing urbanization of its population. The war years put the first partly on hold. The development of Kirkland Lake, for example, was forced to wait out the war, and other areas had to do likewise. Yet, concurrently, a new giant was beginning to grow in the form of Ontario Hydro. By 1917 this corporation had out distanced all privately owned hydro-electric companies and its chief

Cochrane yard   The station is flanked by the NTR (CNR) and the T&NO, whose tracks seemed poised to run north to the bay. (ONA-19911121)

architect, Sir Adam Beck, had convinced the Ontario government to authorize the giant Chippawa Project. This was to be the world's largest generating plant, designed to take advantage of the natural power of Niagra Falls.

The growth of Ontario Hydro both reflected and stimulated the general trend towards the use of electrical power by Ontario's industry. The northern region of the province, drained as it was by so many rivers, seemed a logical source. Some had already been harnessed, like the power development on the Montreal River which was currently supplying the NCR in Cobalt and the whole of the Tri-town area. More could be done. The extent to which hydro had grown in importance can be observed in the changed attitude of Jake Englehart. As chairman of the T&NO Commission, he had always been prepared to consider hydro as a source of motive power, but had invariably concluded that the T&NO could still best be run on steam power. By 1919, however, Jake had become an enthusiastic proponent of electric power, and in his last year as Chairman of the Commission urged that the railway look towards converting from steam to electricity.

The country had been somewhat dismantled by the Great War of 1914–1918. It had to be reassembled. The general name assigned to describe this enormous task was "reconstruction." In the North it was normally termed "northern development." For leadership in this massive undertaking, most Ontarians looked to the government. In 1919, the province assigned that mantle, through a general election, to the Farmer–Labour coalition of E.C. Drury. The inexperienced Premier, without a single elected member from Northern Ontario, sought assistance and guidance in the matter of northern development from the most likely source: the T&NO Commission. Rather than dismiss these political appointees, Drury chose to use them, their knowledge, and their skills. It was a move that made sense, given the government's general ignorance of the north; it was a move that was consistent with the UFO philosophy, in that it condemned patronage; it was a move that proved beneficial to Northern

Ontario, in that the North became a favourite of Drury, though it remained something of a mystery to him.

The process of reconstruction began before Drury took office. During the year that had elapsed since the Armistice of 11 November 1918, the Hearst administration had begun several projects. Among them was the decision, following the closure of the federal Prisoner of War camp at Kapuskasing, to develop a new model settlement there in order to provide farm land for returning service men. This project continued on course under the Drury government, and in time Kapuskasing emerged as a fairly large and prosperous community. The impetus that truly pushed "Kap" forward ultimately came from the timber industry, but in 1918–19 the goal was to promote agriculture, as one might expect from a Farmers' party.

Few in the North complained of the Kap experiment, but in general the energies of northerners in 1918 and 1919 were directed towards resource development, especially mining, but increasingly also forest products. Access to these resources remained a vital issue, and the best access was a railway. Thus both the government and the Commission were assaulted by demands, suggestions, and schemes all urging the benefits that would devolve from spurs, branch lines, or even major main-line expansion. The list was quite long: an extension of the Elk Lake branch to Gowganda where mining activity had been calling for rail service since 1909; a new line from Nipissing Junction to link the transcontinental lines with Parry Sound on Georgian Bay; a lengthy spur from a point near Cobalt into South Lorrain where promising silver deposits had resulted in considerable development and population growth; a branch from Swastika into Kirkland Lake and perhaps beyond to Larder Lake; an extension of the NCR eastward from New Liskeard around the head of Lake Temiskaming and into the Des Quinze River valley in the North Temiskaming region of Quebec; and a main line extension north from Cochrane to James Bay.

All of these had good arguments and good people to support them. The ultimate decision

Haileybury market, August 1918 (ONA-19911468)

rested with the government. The Hearst government had been made aware of them but had not rushed into any quick decisions. Rather, the tendency was to follow the advice of Chairman Englehart, who preached caution. Englehart himself had three projects at the top of his list: a line into Kirkland Lake, electrification of the line, and a main line extension to James Bay. The first was delayed because of the desire by the Kirkland Lake people to settle for a motor road.[3] The other two required further planning and investigation, partly to give the government some breathing space in the face of impatient demands for action. Commissioner George Lee noted the need for this in a private letter to Englehart on 19 November 1918 shortly after the armistice.[4]

> Referring to [proposed extension to James Bay] and all that has been read and said, at present time, in connection therewith, I beg to state that I feel that this is a matter that we should keep very closely in touch with the Government about, before anything is done—or given out.

It is just possible that the Government will not be in a position to contemplate extending the Railway to James Bay, at the present time. Conditions in the Country may not permit it.

I note the last paragraph of Mr. Clement's letter of the 18th inst., to you, reads as follows,—

> "It is to be hoped that during the reconstruction period, on which we are now entering, the resources of Northern Ontario will receive the attention they so well deserve."

And, in this connection would say that the resources of Northern Ontario have, in my judgement, always received every attention from the Government—and will continue to do so. I, personally, know that no person can be more interested in the development of any Country than the present Government is in connection with Northern Ontario. I think we should go hand in hand with them —no matter what the several Boards of Trade in this Country might say.

Lee was referring to a 6 November resolution of the Cochrane Board of Trade that had called for the construction of the James Bay line.[5] He also had in mind recent articles in various newspapers that had begun to call attention to the tasks that had to be taken up in the post-war years. By September of 1918 it was clear that the Central Powers were on the run and that the war would end before too long. An editorial in the Cochrane *Northland Post* on 27 September had begun to urge the James Bay extension as a top priority item for the post-war years. The paper followed this on 18 October by reproducing a letter from J.E. Woodall, the Anglican Archdeacon of Temiskaming. After concurring with the *Northland Post*'s view that such a railway would promote the exploitation of "mining possibilities, the extensive pulp limits and water power" of the region north of Cochrane, Woodall went on to advocate the region as a settlement frontier. He noted the abundance of wild berries, the presence of a "sportsman's paradise" for the "coveter of rod and gun," and the success which many had achieved in growing potatoes and other vegetables. He then quoted the remarks of his predecessor, Bishop Holmes.

Woodall! What a country! When will that line reach Moose? Toronto needs to breath sea air. Right here where we are now sitting there will be a magnificent hotel and on yonder sandy beach bathing houses and bathers galore. Coming and going from that little harbor where now there comes one ship a year there will be a daily packet steamer to and from Moose. Then think of fresh fish in Toronto and Winnipeg caught the previous day in the Bay.

Such rhetoric was not new to Lee or Englehart. Indeed both men had access to the many reports that had come back with the numerous parties of explorers, surveyors, and engineers who had traversed the northernmost reaches of the province on a fairly consistent basis for two decades. The T&NO's own reports on the region dated back to 1905 and were as current as that of Engineer Maher dated 2 November 1918.[6] Invariably, the accounts declared the potential there

to be considerable. Few people doubted this. The only real question in most minds was that of the timing of a railway to the bay.

Northerners did not stand alone in this sentiment. Several schemes had been suggested, including links from Quebec city or from points in Manitoba. The principal factor supporting the concept of an ocean-going port in the far north was that of distance. Corresponding Member of the Royal Geographical Society, Robert Bell, argued this in a paper titled "The Hudson Bay Route to Europe."[7]

The question of a feasible route to Europe, from the prairie provinces of Canada by way of Hudson Bay, is of the first importance to the Dominion, for several reasons. It is the shortest possible course from the centre of this group of provinces to Liverpool, as it follows approximately a segment of a great circle between these points. Not only is the total length the shortest, but this route affords a greater proportion of transportation by sea, with a shorter land haul than any other. More than a thousand miles of its water transportation is within the British possessions. Hudson Bay having only one opening to the ocean may be considered a mere clausum. The land portion is shorter than that by any existing line, and it passes through an even country with a very gentle slope towards the sea. The Bay and Strait are free from rocks and shoals and may be easily navigated by the largest ocean-going vessels.

Bell went on to argue, at some length, that the advent of steam and other navigational aids had swept aside the problems of the short navigation season and that the opposition to using the Bay was largely artificial or political. Most people who considered the idea felt that it was feasible and that a railhead on the Bay could not only be built but that it would be successful. Among T&NO people there was a common belief that the project, when undertaken, should run by the most direct route, from Cochrane. Chairman Englehart declared himself very impressed by Bell's article, as well as by other reports and arguments which favoured the James Bay route. In 1918 and 1919, however, his

New Liskeard Fair, September 1919   First prize to the heavy draft team of Alex Coe.
(ONA-19911484)

feeling was that other projects, such as electrification of the T&NO system, should come first. Even these would probably have to wait; the aftermath of the war was simply making so many demands that the James Bay project would have to be postponed.[8] In the meantime the T&NO should continue to explore the region, as it had been doing for 15 years, in order to prepare itself for the proper moment.

The impatience of the Cochrane group is easy to understand and appreciate. Also understandable was the general support for the idea from all the northern communities. All could hope to benefit; and, in public at least, all northerners have tended, then and since, to extend moral and verbal support for almost any northern project. The support that emerged, however, went far beyond editorial comment and the passage of resolutions. A northern delegation went to Toronto in February 1919 to assert the need of building a railway to James Bay. There were 75 delegates, variously chosen. Five went from Cobalt, for example, and included Mayor McKinnon, as well

as two men chosen by the miner's union, J. McGuire and A. McDonald, and two selected by the Board of Trade.[9] Timmins, Iroquois Falls, Matheson, Englehart, Haileybury, Elk Lake, Cobalt, North Bay, New Liskeard, and Cochrane all sent delegates.[10] The *Haileyburian* of 20 February 1919 probably exaggerated in its headline proclaiming "On-To-The-Bay Project Gathers Strength From All Parts of Ontario," but the Toronto and Hamilton boards of trade declared in favour of the project. When the delegation met with the government on 28 February (designated as "Northern Ontario Day" in the legislature), it included representatives from Brantford and Hamilton. The movement had assumed proportions that no one had expected.

It obtained no decision or promise, but it did cause the principle ministers to take notice. The Minister of Lands, Forests and Mines, Howard Ferguson, had his department join in the investigations that followed. These took the form of a special survey party led by T&NO Engineer Maher, who had already reported on the area. The survey was to include more minute reports on arable land, forest resources, and waterpower prospects, and its personnel was broadened to include men from Ferguson's department. In addition, Maher was to locate a trial line for the railway. The general sentiment regarding this project, as revealed in a flurry of correspondence among Hearst, Ferguson, Englehart, Lee, and Clement, was neatly summarized by Chief Engineer Clement.[11]

> ...there is no doubt that an extension of the T&NO Railway from Cochrane is the most practicable of the various projects for the construction of a railway to the shores of James or Hudson Bay. It involves the least capital expenditure and the construction and operation of the shortest line. It also has the advantage that it offers the most direct connection between the shores of these bays, and the industrial and commercial centres of Eastern Canada. The country, through which it would be built, offers greater possibility of an early agricultural and industrial development than that through which any of the alternative routes pass, and at Moose Factory a terminal can be built that will be entirely adequate for the shipping that may develop...

Regarding the proposed survey under Maher's direction, Clement observed that it was an intelligent plan, because the railway location that would come from it would "enable us to prepare detailed and accurate estimates of the cost of the proposed extension in time for their submission to the Government before the close of the present year." Since such surveys were required in any event, the government would be "just as far ahead as though it had made a definite decision to build the line." The plan for a survey also had the advantage of providing employment for 45–50 men for about six months, and since it was felt this kind of work would appeal to returned soldiers, the survey parties "could probably be filled exclusively by such."

At one point Lee had expressed the hope, and Englehart had agreed, that any further surveys or plans should be kept from the public so that no commitments could be inferred.[12] Such

a wish, while perhaps desirable, was hardly possible. Maher's party consisted of 45 men; efforts were made to enlist returning service men in order to assist in the integration of these men into the economy, which was a stated policy of both the government and the T&NO; and the group assembled itself in Cochrane, a town of 2500 people. The extent to which the group's presence and purpose was widely known can be surmised from the following excerpt from the Commission's minutes of 10 June 1919.

> "ON TO THE BAY" MOVEMENT, ET AL.: Mr. J. Stewart has requested permission of Supt. of Traffic to attach to the outer wall ofCochrane Station, a publicity board size 35" x 40" with glass front containing enlarged photographs of the Survey party sent out by Commission in relation to contemplated extension of road, Cochrane to James Bay.

Interest in this survey crew was clearly very high in Cochrane, and it was clearly not a secret! That interest trebled when tragedy struck the surveyors' crew on 3 June. D.W.T. Smith, a returned service man from Newmarket, drowned at the Carrying Places portage. The next day it struck again when 19-year-old Kenneth Ord of Cochrane also drowned while returning from a search for Smith's body.[13] The tragic incident shows two realities: the work and the wilderness could be dangerous, and there are few secrets in the North.

Maher's final report came to the Commission in November 1919. As might be expected, it tended to endorse the optimistic predictions of those who wanted the line built and the area developed. By then, however, the government had changed. Drury delayed making any declaration for several months. When he did, he simply extended the current policy of approving further study. He did go as far as declaring himself in favour of the project, but stopped short of commitment. His government, after all, had pledged itself to a policy of economy, even parsimony. The throne speech for 1920 included the following masterpiece of political writing.[14]

Fisherman's boat, James Bay, 1933 (ONA-1988714 E. Everitt)

The Temiskaming and Northern Ontario Railway Commission has been empowered to extend its line to James Bay, when the Lieutenant-Governor in Council shall determine that financial conditions will warrant undertaking. In adopting this measure the Legislature has declared a policy of development in the northern part of Ontario, which is designed to encourage exploration and enterprise, and eventually to bring Ontario into close touch with Hudson Bay and its commercial possibilities.

The statement left the government free to move forward or pull back on the project. It was two years before that decision was made.

During that time, Drury came to rely heavily on the opinion of the T&NO people, especially George Lee, who succeeded Englehart as chairman. Jake's health failed badly in the fall of 1919 and forced him to resign his post. This he did on 28 October, shortly after his Conservative party and his good friend Premier Hearst had lost at the polls but before the new administration took over. Hearst, reluctantly and sadly, accepted his friend's request to leave the service. Englehart then sought what physical

comfort he could in the warmer climate of Virginia, where he died the following year. Both Englehart and Hearst were likely pleased with the appointment, temporary at first and then made permanent, of Jake's protege, George Lee, to the chairmanship. Since joining the T&NO from Calabogie in 1907, Lee's commitment to the line and to the North had become very strong indeed. This can be seen in his reports regarding the land department, from his actions as a commissioner, and from his tenure as the Mayor of North Bay. Lee confirmed his northern orientation shortly after he was promoted to the joint positions of Chairman and General Manager in December 1920. At his urging, the Commission moved its Head Office from Toronto to the general office building in North Bay. Originally built in 1908, it received an addition in 1923 to accommodate some 23 office and management personnel, including Secretary-Treasurer Maund, who made the move north in 1921.

In the meantime, the pressure to build in the North continued. The T&NO and the government remained cautious. Engineer Maher had led his survey crew into the region beyond Cochrane in 1919. Engineer Clement took his crews eastward from Swastika and Kirkland Lake. Others conducted trial runs or surveys in Gowganda, North Temiskaming, Parry Sound, and Timmins. The special interest groups of each area could see that something was being done. The surveys had to be made in any event, so the government, by restricting itself to them, was not really holding up either construction or development. At the same time, it did not commit itself to action of any kind. Thus critics of any scheme could be answered as easily as proponents.

When Drury finally came down on the side of the James Bay extension, he was following the advice of the T&NO Commission and officials. Their correspondence makes it clear that they thought the time was at last ripe for the James Bay project. The portrait painted by the engineers, especially Arthur Cole, was invariably bright, suggesting that the resources were plentiful and the access relatively easy.[15] (See excerpt, p. 159 of this text.) There was also present a strong romantic thread. The emphasis lay on beauty, on the excitement surrounding an ocean port in the far north, and on the attraction of mysterious finds that would take place. It was the kind of prediction that was found commonly on the editorial pages of the various northern newspapers. But it was a stark contrast to other reports written by this same man about other areas of the North. Cole's comments regarding the line into Kirkland Lake or the Porcupine were complete with hard data regarding actual "wealth in place" and the potential for freight traffic. But Cole, like others of the T&NO such as Lee, Clement, and even Englehart, for some reason used a different yardstick to gauge the potential of the region north from Cochrane.

Outside opinions concurred in this general sentiment. Archbishop Rennison described bountiful wildlife and the presence of pulpwood resources.[16] But like Cole, he based his main argument on the belief that this vast region contained many unexplored riches. These should be found and exploited; and the best way to do

this would be to build a railway into the region in order to promote both discovery and exploitation. W. Tees Curran of the Royal Colonial Institute wrote in equally glowing terms and along the same lines.[17] He even predicted that it would be necessary to double track the section from Cochrane to James Bay! Once again his evidence tended to be circumstantial and based more on optimism than on reality. The belief seemed to be universal that this new hinterland contained rich minerals, good agricultural land, and endless forests ripe for harvesting. One particular outside commentator deserves mention, largely because his rationale was quite unique. This was W.D Cunneyworth of Ottawa, who was evidently much distressed by the recent public debates in the press and elsewhere regarding the possibility of dividing Ontario and creating a second province—or perhaps two more—in the North. Cunneyworth wrote a long, exhaustive report of his views regarding the north country.[18] These, for the most part, coincided with the views and appraisals of Cole, Clement, and Rennison et al. Beyond these, however, Cunneyworth suggested that a plot to divide the province loomed as a very real possibility, but the government could foil it by proceeding with the railway extension. This, he said, would bind "Old and New Ontario together so fast and tight" that the forces of division would dissolve. The extension of the T&NO "would set up such a volume of trade...one with the other that business and fraternal intercourse would become so solidified that...dissolution would never be undertaken."

Others, without Cunneyworth's belief in conspiracies, certainly thought of integrating the two sectors of the province more closely; and there were those who felt that southern prosperity depended heavily on the North. Prominent among them was Jake Englehart, who in August of 1920 felt well enough to offer advice to the new government.[19] No mining rights should be granted without royalties to the government, and settlers should be required to perform "the settler's duty" before receiving title. Oil was more than a possibility—bold words, considering they came from the founder of Imperial Oil. The James Bay fisheries were "alive." Water power included "Several Hundred Thousand (h.p.) between Cochrane and James Bay." The iron ore of the Belcher Islands, he wrote, promised

> A future that words will not convey—equal, if not superior to the Iron Ranges in Minnesota, and with a Railway from Cochrane to James Bay, it will not be long, a Smelter that will furnish the wherewith.

Englehart felt that his railway, the north country, and the province were intimately linked; and his salutation to Drury suggested that the North could indeed be the saviour of the province.

> That Great Railway, Temiskaming & Northern Ontario, and That Great North Country, which Possesses within its Zone Assets that will more, much more, than Retire the Entire Principal [debt] of our good, Dear Province, Ontario.

Despite all this encouragement, the government would not commit itself to immediate action. Drury introduced legislation to authorize the Commission to extend its line from Cochrane to the mouth of the Moose River, but this step was taken tentatively. The Toronto *Mail and Empire* reported the details on 5 May 1920:

> The Prime Minister explained the reasons actuating the Government in proposing the legislation at the present time in advance of any intention to proceed with early construction.
>
> "The T&NO," he said, "depends for its existence upon the Transcontinental, for which it is only a connecting link. We either have to make it self-supporting or sell it to the Dominion Government—and the latter course I do not agree with. This line, to my mind, serves an exceedingly important purpose, and so it is for us to develop it to make it a paying proposition. In extending the railway to James Bay, we will open up a country with enormous mineral resources and great areas of pulpwood. I am absolutely certain that by the opening of that country we will build up several very important paper industries

and provide traffic which will make the railway which we already have a gaining instead of a losing proposition. The mineral possibilities of that country are unknown, but they are suspected to be exceedingly rich."

> "At the present time, however," added Mr. Drury, "there is no intention of committing the Government or the Province to immediate construction. The time is inopportune for great capital development. The scarcity of money, the high price of labor and materials renders it impossible to build such an extension at the present time without saddling it with a burden it could not carry."
>
> The provision for construction when the time was opportune would, however, stimulate prospecting and exploration and supply an assurance to those who were going into that area that it was the intention of the government to give them a railway...

The Ontario legislature, in Committee of the Whole, underlined the Premier's caution by amending the James Bay Railway Bill to emphasize that the Commission could move on the matter only with the approval of the Lieutenant-Governor in Council (i.e., the government). Furthermore, the line might be constructed in sections rather than as a single large project.[20] It was, therefore, approval only for the principle of expansion. The United Farmers declined to commit themselves further than that. As winter approached, however, and as the unemployment figures rose, the government declared itself in favour of clearing a right-of-way for a distance of some 25 miles north of Cochrane.[21] This make-work project was subsequently expanded to include actually laying track for that distance.

At this point, northern public opinion began to fragment. Thus far, it had almost unanimously favoured the Cochrane to James Bay line. On 23 December 1920, *The Northern Miner* shattered that unanimity by observing that the proposed 25-mile extension north from Cochrane would do little to assist the mining industry and that it was an "affront and challenge to those endeavouring to develop the mining resources of the country."

A 25 mile line north from Cochrane presents nothing of interest to the miner. Geologists have examined the country very thoroughly, as late as last year, and have been unable to locate any formations of economical formation. The only mineral occurrence possessing possible value in the Mattagami and Abitibi country through which the James Bay Railway would extend is an iron ore deposit over 150 miles north of Cochrane...

Therefore, the mining industry of Northern Ontario believes that if the government has the money to spare for railway extensions it should put that money into lines where there is a sure traffic and a big income waiting.

Nothing that the T&NO Railway has done for the mining development of the north has proven unprofitable. The Porcupine line is the best paying section of the road on the T&NO. There is every reason to believe, and reasons to disbelieve, that this success would be duplicated if a line were run into Gowganda, Kirkland Lake, or Shining Tree...

Within three weeks, *The Northern Miner*, on 15 January 1921, announced that "all the north, with the mining communities leading" had swung into opposition against the proposed railway north of Cochrane. The one holdout "which won't play with the rest" was Cochrane. That same day the *Northern Miner* also reported that other schemes to reach the Bay were being considered. One was a road "running from the Canadian National, starting a couple of hundred miles west of Cochrane possibly from Hearst, where the Algoma Central comes in..."

The mining industry, however, did not reign totally in the North. Other primary industries also excited the imagination, and none more than the closely integrated activities of lumbering, pulp and paper, and hydro-electric power. Perhaps the most prominent of the firms that worked to exploit the North's resources in these areas was the Abitibi Power & Paper Company. It was not the first power company to enter this portion of New Ontario. Previously, however, the firms had responded to a demand for power from the new mining centres. This had been the impetus behind the Cobalt Light and Power Company and also behind the Wallberg operations along the Montreal River.

The Abitibi Canyon, recognized by all as a potential hydro source of consequence (ONA-1988208 Stephenson/Foerter)

Since the war, however, power companies became promoters and developers rather than followers. The new industrial base of the province demanded new and greater energy sources, and this industrial demand was matched by increasing domestic or household usage. In southern Ontario, this issue of hydro electric power had produced the new burgeoning publicly owned giant of Ontario Hydro. Smaller power companies lost their independence. The North, still beyond Ontario Hydro's reach, nonetheless demonstrated a similar appetite for such power. The demands from the established consumers—the mines and towns—increased sharply. The post-war development of the Porcupine region, for example, after an initial pause, made great strides, and by 1921 the mining interests there were issuing enormous demands for power. The Hollinger interests required it so badly that this firm sought to enter the hydro development field itself. New users, notably the pulp and paper companies, augmented the demand even further.

The minister of Lands, Forests and Mines in the Hearst Administration, Howard Ferguson, had adopted an aggressive approach to the development of the Ontario pulp and paper industry. His much quoted statement, "My ambition has been to see the largest paper industry in the world established in the Province," indicated the extent of this goal.[22] Ferguson had granted 1568 square miles of timber rights between 1917 and 1919. He promised two further large grants totalling 7000 square miles to the Spanish River Pulp and Paper Company and to the Abitibi Pulp and Paper Company (AP&P). These promised grants, made to assist the two firms to secure financing from their Chicago bankers, had not been advertised nor offered for tender.[23] The government changed before either the Spanish River or Abitibi deals had been finalized. A royal commission condemned the actions in 1922, and in 1923 Drury declared that the grants would not be made.[24] Even so, the two companies required power for their paper plants; and, with their financing secured, they sought to develop it. The Abitibi firm, with plants at Iroquois Falls,

Smooth Rock Falls, and Kapuskasing, made plans to develop a power station at Island Falls on the Abitibi River. AP&P also sought the hydro rights at other sites on the Abitibi River north of Cochrane. For these plans, a rail extension north of Cochrane was necessary.

Concurrently, the T&NO Commission had concluded that the railway should, for reasons of economy and reliability as well as cleanliness, convert its motive power from steam to electricity. Steam locomotion required coal, and coal had to be imported. This meant that money passed from Canada to the U.S. It also meant that Canadian railways were dependent upon their U.S. coal supplies. The T&NO statistician declared dramatically in 1919 that such dependence was unhealthy.[25] The war had demonstrated, he said, that coal could be used as a weapon as Germany had done against the small, neutral nations, and that in peace it could also be used as an economic lever.

> An ample surplus during the period of reconstruction will be an invaluable bargaining asset. The nation with coal to spare for the next two years, will have an advantage greater than could be contained in a favored-nation commercial treaty. If the United States is wise, she will use coal as the basis upon which to rear a whole new world-wide trade relation. She has the coal and with a rapidly increasing merchant marine, will be in a position to market it anywhere in the commercial world.
>
> Realizing the enormous value of coal, England is launching a vast scheme of power production. The country is being charted into regions, and each region will have a central power plant. The electric power developed will be available to every man and every industry. It is estimated that more than *50 million tons of coal* will be saved annually, of which, ninety percent will be due to the adoption of hydro-electrics.

England had recognized the dangers of dependence; Canada should also.

Hydro-electric power, in contrast, could be secured locally. There were reports, moreover, that the technology could "no longer be considered experimental."[26] Tests in both the United

Kingdom and the United States had seen electric locomotives perform well in direct competition with the steam engine. In one highly publicized toe-to-toe confrontation, witnessed by "more than 175 of the foremost electrical and steam engineers and executives of North American and European countries," an electric engine won a tug of war against two steam engines. The Erie *Despatch* of 8 November 1919, whose report included the name of "S.B. Clement, Chief Engineer, Temiscaming [sic] and Northern Ontario Railway," described the event in dramatic terms.[27]

> Truly it was a battle of giants. And the electric giant was victor. Time and time again the engineers in the steam locomotives threw open wide their throttles. Plainly they were making every effort to move forward. But without noise or apparent effort of any kind, the electric engine not only held its own, but forced the monsters backward. Those who witnessed the struggle, and they were the foremost men of their profession in the country, hailed the results of the novel and spectacular tug-of-war, a distinct victory for electricity over steam.

Six months before witnessing this spectacle in Erie Pennsylvania, Clement had summarized the operating advantages of an electrically operated engine to Jake Englehart.[28]

1. Increased tractive effort and weight of locomotive without increasing axle load and consequent stresses in track structure
2. Uniform propulsive effort and graduated tractive effort with lower maintenance cost of trailing equipment.
3. ...avoiding turning of locomotives at terminals.
4. Increased mileage of locomotive between inspections and stoppings.
5. Increased speed of freight trains on maximum grades.
6. Greater reliability in service, saving in detention.
7. Elimination of cinders, dust and ashes.
8. Elimination of danger to forests through fire from steam locomotives.

The biggest single factor was cost. According to Clement's estimation, the cost of conversion would run to $7,200,000. Although an enormous sum for the age, it would be offset by a $64,000 annual reduction in operating costs and by the reductions that would accompany an expanding traffic which the T&NO was anticipating. With these factors in mind, Clement then offered the following conclusions.

1. The electrification of the main line, North Bay to Cochrane, and the Porcupine and Iroquois Falls Branches is practicable and desirable from both an operating and financial standpoint.
2. Electrification involves the substitution of water power for imported coal fuel, and is, therefore, a proper step in the direction of the conservation of national wealth and resources.
3. The greatest reduction in operating expense, through electrification, is due to the elimination of coal fuel, and the great decrease in the cost of repairing the electric locomotives and handling them at terminals. The general tendency will be for the cost of fuel and shop labor to increase, which will be relatively more favorable to electric operation, which eliminates fuel and conserves labor.
4. Electric operation will be more attractive to passenger traffic, on account of the elimination of noise, smoke and cinders.

The adoption of electric power never took place, but in the years 1919–25 it was considered inevitable in the minds of everyone associated with the T&NO. The commission therefore expected to become a major consumer of hydroelectric power. It must, therefore, have a secure, plentiful, and dependable source of power. This sentiment was stated forcefully in the Commission's *Minutes* of 11 October 1921.

> The question of electrifying the Main Line and Branches of the Railway was discussed ... It was decided that Commission should intimate, through correspondence, that this

Railway was in a position to and should control their own power developments...

The commissioners, in adopting this resolution, may indeed have had more in mind than the control over their own power source. It is quite likely they were thinking of managing hydro-electric power in the North. The idea was not far-fetched. For 20 years the T&NO had been the principal government agency in its sector of New Ontario, and it served the North in such diverse—but necessary—fields as communications, land management, urban planning, and resource development. It may well have appeared logical, even natural, that the Commission, having abbreviated its activities by disbanding its Land branch in 1920, should expand them again by adding hydro to its responsibilities. *The Mining Review* had proffered this suggestion a year earlie, on 1 October 1920.

> And singularly enough, the Temiskaming and Northern Ontario Railway Commission is pointed to as the logical body to launch the project and to place Northern Ontario hydro development under the management of a thoroughly competent expert.
>
> Mention of the T&NO Rly in this connection is based upon two reasons, one of which is the fact that the electrification of the 300 miles or so of this Government owned railway is considered reasonably certain within the next few years, and the other is the desirability of valuable co-operation between the railway which serves the district and the organization which will direct the hydro-electric developments.

Neither the Commission itself, nor the government, ever adopted any formal policy in this connection. There was, however, an apparent unwritten assumption that the T&NO would be involved in some fashion. Its officials were highly prominent in the North and were likewise accustomed to a healthy influence at Queen's Park. T&NO engineers had, since 1905, maintained a corporate memory of reports and surveys in the area north of Cochrane, and it was in that area that most eyes were focused regarding hydro-electric power. Certainly the Blanche,

Amable du Fond, and Montreal rivers had potential, but it was to the northward flowing rivers that most people looked for the new power source: the Frederick House, the Mattagami, the Moose, and especially the Abitibi. Thus, throughout 1920 and 1921, the two issues of the James Bay extension and the development of hydro-electric power ran parallel paths and then coalesced in the Drury government's decision to approve the James Bay extension as far as the Abitibi River crossing.

Although it is difficult to say with certainty, the Commission's correspondence does suggest that its principal officers, like Clement, saw the move north from Cochrane as a way to secure access to potential power projects. *The Northern Miner*, on 15 October 1921, actually reported that the T&NO had won out over the AP&P Company and Hollinger Mines for rights to the water power at Big Bend on the Abitibi River, and that the Commission had plans that would permit it to develop and sell this power. If the Commission had indeed secured this right, said the *Northern Miner*, it should act on it at once, because power was urgently needed in the Porcupine. The story was inaccurate, and the division of water rights took quite a different turn. Neither mining journal, however, showed any surprise—or alarm—that the railway might be entering this new field.

The United Farmer party had rather a different agenda. For them the approval to proceed 70 miles north from Cochrane to the area of the Abitibi Canyon was designed to promote settlement and other activities in the forested region north of the CNR.[29] Drury's people were not prepared to extend the line into the Hudson Bay lowlands. But the government did want to take some action in the North to promote its popularity there and perhaps to derail the movement for separation. Perhaps also Drury agreed with George Lee that someone was going to build to James Bay, and that the government railway should do it first. Years later, Drury recalled his government's intentions.[30]

> Strangely, the one project which might properly have been opposed had escaped

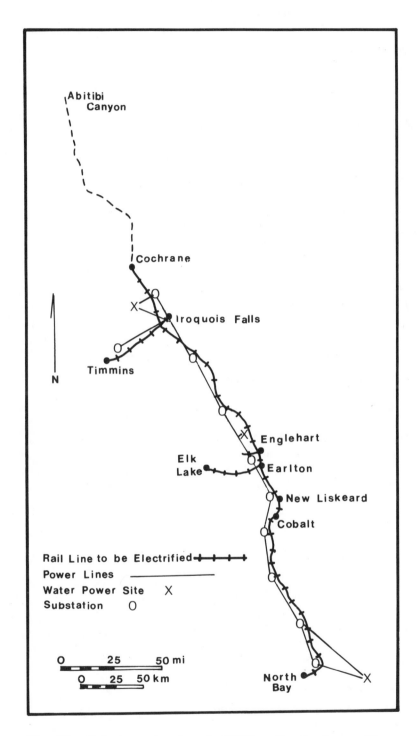

Map 11. *Hydro power sites along the T&NO* By using these and by exploiting those north of Cochrane, the Commission hoped it could electrify its railway.

The decision to extend the T.&N.O. Railway North to Moose Factory, or some other port on James Bay, opens up a vast field for conjecture as to the natural resources that now lie in the territories adjoining James and Hudson Bays. Timber, the pulp and paper industry, the fisheries, and the general tourist trade will all be important factors in building up the business of the railway, but the mining industry is likely to prove, as heretofore, by far the largest revenue producer...

With the railway completed to a point on tidewater, such as Moose Factory, it is reasonable to suppose that small steamers will be placed on these inland seas to look after the summer traffic. About the beginning of June the Spring breakup takes place in the rivers, and navigation on the bays can be resumed a few days later. This navigation can be continued with reasonable safety, for five months, or to the end of October and often into the middle of November. Navigation in the Bays is not dependant on the condition of ice in Hudson Strait. Here only three months of clear navigation can be counted on, viz, August, September and October.

The expenses of prospecting in this vast territory have hitherto been almost prohibitive. Apart from this also, the time consumed in going to and from the point where exploration was to be made, was in itself so serious an obstacle that only a few Government Exploration Parties have penetrated the interior. The result was that, even with the Government Parties, where the necessary funds were assured, the only rational method of extending the length of the exploration season, in order to make the return at all commensurate with the expenditure, was to winter in the North so as to be able to take up the work without delay as soon as the Spring breakup took place.

With the completion of the railway to a point on James Bay, and with small steamers making regular trips on the Bays, a party could outfit at tidewater and be at almost any coast point desired by the middle of June. The party would then have a clear four months for exploration before it would be necessary to make the return trip. The cost should not be excessive, considering the facilities provided. It will require only one good discovery to start the flow of fortune seekers into this great Northland and the area to be covered is so immense that many years must necessarily elapse before the mineral possibilities can be made know, even in the barest outline.

The exploration of this almost limitless Northland will be undertaken by a very different band of prospectors from those that flocked into Cobalt in the early days. The experience gained in the Cobalt, Porcupine, and Kirkland Lake Camps will be invaluable when pushing farther North. The Ontario Department of Mines has done excellent work in keeping well abreast of exploratory work with accurate geological reports and maps. The result is that today the average prospector has a good working knowledge of the geology of the above mentioned districts and is keenly alive to the value of acquiring all geological information available on the district he intends to investigate. This will make exploration much more effective, as time will not be wasted in unproductive areas, and work can be concentrated where geological conditions appear favorable. The old haphazard prospector will be superseded by a trained field man, familiar with the geological formations that are likely to be most productive. The element of chance cannot of course be eliminated but it can thus be greatly reduced.

Excerpt from letter of A.A. Cole to Chairman Lee (see n. 15)

serious criticism. On October 28, 1921, I turned the first sod on the extension of the T&NO Railway from Cochrane to Moosonee. Our information was that the new line would tap a deposit of lignite, another of glass sand, and another of china clay. We expected too that it would provide a means by which the narrow belts of excellent timber that grew along the banks of the rivers that funnelled into James Bay north of the transcontinental railway could be harvested. The timber, we thought, could be floated down the rivers to the bay and towed in rafts across its shallow waters to Moosonee and there manufactured. None of these expectations have been realized. I can see now, with the wisdom of hindsight, that the project was a mistake or at least premature.

Tenders for the actual construction were not called until December and not awarded until late January 1922. Work began about a month later. This delay of several months—the appropriate order-in-council had been issued on 18 October 1921[31]—would appear to have been occasioned by some internal disagreement regarding the rail-

way's precise route to the New Post, its proposed destination, and also by conflicts of interest among three northern giants: the T&NO, AP&P, and Hollinger Mines. At stake was control over the power development projects on the Abitibi River. These would continue to complicate the progress of the northern extension.

Notes

1. Englehart, Lee, Cole, and Clement all claimed this cautious approach as a trait of T&NO management style. See ONA, B-2557. James Bay Extension, Main File.
2. See pp. 64–67 of this text.
3. See pp. 102–104 of this text.
4. Lee to Englehart, 19 November 1918. ONA, B-2557(29-A).
5. Resolution of the Cochrane Board of Trade. 6 November 1918. AO. RG3. Ferguson Papers, Box 128.
6. Maher to Englehart, 2 November 1918. ONA, B-2557(29-A).
7. Robert Bell, "The Hudson Bay Route to Europe." Copy on file in ONA, B-2557(29-A).
8. Englehart to Gordon, 17 February 1919. ONA, B-2557(32-A).
9. *Haileyburian*, 20 February 1919.
10. *Minutes*, 12 March 1919.
11. Clement to Englehart, 12 February 1919. ONA, B-2557(32-A).
12. Lee to Englehart, 27 December 1918. ONA, B-2557(32-A).
13. *Minutes*, 10 June 1919.
14. AO. *Ontario Gazette*, 1920.
15. "Resume of James Bay Investigations & Extensions", pp. 4–5. ONA, B-2557(43) Lee's Personal File.
16. *Ibid.*, pp. 5–6.
17. *Ibid.*, pp. 7–9.
18. Cunneyworth to Drury, 15 April 1920. AO. RG3. Drury Papers, Box 45.
19. Englehart to Drury, 12 August 1920. AO. RG3. Ferguson Papers, Box 128
20. "Amendment to Bill #178—Extension T&NO Railway to James Bay." ONA, B-2557(29)a.
21. The Toronto *World*, 28 December 1920.
22. V. Nelles, *The Politics of Development*. Toronto: Find. 1974, p. 388.
23. *Ibid.*
24. Toronto *Telegram*, 23 February 1923.
25. Report of Pratt, T&NO Statistician, in Englehart to Lee et al., 4 February 1919. ONA, B-192.
26. Clement to Englehart, 7 June 1919. ONA, B-192.
27. Erie *Despatch*, 8 November 1919.
28. Clement to Englehart, 7 June 1919. ONA, B-192.
29. Lee to Drury. Private. 22 April 1920. ONA, B-2557.
30. E.C. Drury, *Farmer Premier: Memoirs of the Honourable E.C. Drury*. Toronto: M&S, 1966, p. 151.
31. Drury to Lee, 18 October 1921. ONA, B-2557(1).

Chapter 10

Salt Water at Last

EVERAL FAC-
TORS FIRST
became evident
when the Com-
mission came to
decide on the
best route to
the North. Three
possibilities pre-
sented them-
selves.

The first followed a line that ran directly north from Cochrane to Lillabelle Lake and then veered in a northwesterly direction for a time and then ran almost northerly to Oil Can Portage.

The second also ran directly north from Cochrane to Lillabelle Lake, but then veered to the northeast and crossed the Abitibi River at the Long Sault Rapids and took a north and northwesterly swing to cross the Abitibi River again at Carrying Places. At this point it met the first option and followed a northerly path to Oil Can Portage. Of these two, the easterly route was some five miles longer. Because of the double crossing of the Abitibi River and a crossing at Jawbone Creek, it would cost, according to Clement's estimates, about $500,000 more.[1] Also, the evidence of the day suggested that the easterly route ran through an area that was comprised largely of muskeg or burned-over areas; the westerly route passed through an area that contained more complete forests which the

AP&P could harvest. These factors would seem to dictate that the railway take the westerly path.

Chief Engineer Clement, however, offered a third option. Instead of beginning the extension at Cochrane, the Commission could select a point on the CNR (the old NTR) line about 25 miles west of Cochrane and build almost due north. Such a plan "would avoid the necessity of crossing any large creeks or rivers and would very materially reduce the mileage of railway to be constructed." "By utilizing the Transcontinental" in this way "the construction costs can be greatly reduced."[2]

The third alternative was clearly not to Lee's liking at all. He wired Commissioner L.T. Martin on 5 October 1921, "Privately, if Chief Engineer, while in Ottawa today, suggests to you running on Transcontinental Railway for thirty miles, then building north, do not say or do anything to encourage it."[3] The idea of depending upon the CNR for access to the North or permitting federal jurisdiction to encroach on the T&NO was anathema to Lee, regardless of the savings which might result. Martin agreed that "if such a thing were done we would, I think, lose our identity with the T&NO project North," but he wavered somewhat when he realized that a savings of $1,150,000 might result.[4] If proper running rights could be obtained, he wrote, it would be hard to justify the extra cost. Indeed, "if it is necessary for us

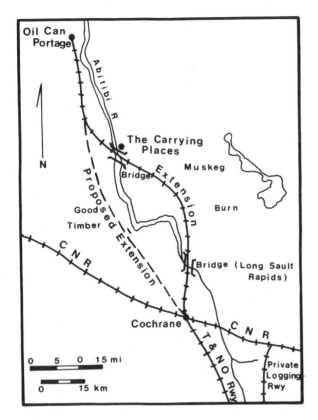

Map 12. *Routes of proposed extension from Cochrane, 1921*   The eastern route provided better access to potential hydro sites.

to reach the Long Sault Rapids we could easily build a branch line in there from Cochrane for less than half the amount saved."

Lee remained firm, however, and held the Commission and the government in line. For him, it would seem, the goal was as much the hydro sites at the Long Sault as it was the progress north towards the Bay. His enthusiasm for the eastern route which included these sites was evident in a telephone conversation with the Minister of Lands, Forests and Mines on 26 October, two days before the formal sod turning. Also evident is the strength of Lee's personality and his recently acquired status of Chairman and General Manager of the T&NO.[5]

> Mr. Lee: I got your letter; what we are doing is just exactly what he wants. Tell him that you saw me and that the finest

engineers in the world say there is more power on the Long Sault than at Iroquois Falls. 35,000 horse power can be developed on the Long Sault.

Hon. Mr. Bowman: Is that something new?

Mr. Lee: Yes—35,000 H.P.—continuous power—on the Long Sault.

If the Commission decide to electrify the railway they will use all that power, over and above what the Abitibi get.

Hon. Mr. Bowman: Does that mean that Kettle Falls will be drowned out.

Mr. Lee: Yes, the big development would drown out Kettle Falls.

As soon as the plans are ready will send them to you. Expect to call for tenders about first of December.

Hon. Mr. Drury wants the Commission to meet the Cabinet to discuss the whole thing before letting contract.

Hon. Mr. Bowman: The contract will only be for the clearing of the right-of-way.

Mr. Lee: No, for clearing of right-of-way and laying of steel.

Two days later, the Commission passed the following resolution despite the arguments in favour of the western route.[6]

> JAMES BAY EXTENSION: The easterly location was finally decided upon as the most desirable route and as the Government are agreeable to suspend present negotiations with the AP&P Co. Ltd., with regard to water powers, limits, et al until such time as Commission should be in position to definitely state their requirements in this regard, it was decided that the extension should be actively undertaken at once and arrangements perfected whereby tenders for the required construction can be called for without delay.

The great northern adventure had begun. Very quickly, however, the dream began to take on nightmarish traits. It would take 10 years to finish the job. In the case of Rouyn, there had been delays, but those had been largely man-made through administrative and litigious obstructions. In the James Bay extension, much of the delay and obstruction was the result of divine intervention. The terrain proved to be far more hostile and the climate more intimidating than the contractors had foreseen.

Not all of the obstacles facing the project emerged from natural forces, however. The twin goals of electrification and "on to the Bay" drive had coalesced to push the T&NO and the Ontario government towards this northern project. Both objectives had competitors. Rival firms, like AP&P, had ambitions in the hydro field; rival goals, such as the branch line to Larder Lake and Rouyn or an extension from Elk Lake to Gowganda, competed for the capital funds and the attention of the provincial government; and vested interests like the engine manufacturers or the coal interests sought to retard or halt any move towards electrification. Competition came also from other sectors of the province which sought development of their regions and from special-interest groups which attempted to direct government attention towards such matters as roads, prohibition, or the problems of increased urbanization.

None of these matters clouded the horizon in January of 1922 when the Commission—with the approval of the full United Farmer Cabinet —awarded the contract for constructing 70 miles of track from Cochrane to New Post to the firms of Grant Smith and Company and McDonnell Limited of Vancouver. Although such a combined bid was unusual, after an investigation by Chief Engineer Clement,[7] it was adjudged to be both bona fide and practical. The contract called for the completion of the line to the Abitibi River crossing (Mileage 44.4) by the end of 1922 and to New Post by 31 October 1923. It seemed simple enough; unlike some of the earlier construction, the potential problems seemed small. Private interests had not established themselves to any extent north of Cochrane, so the right-of-way issue was minimal. There was no need to satisfy a rival provincial government, as would be the case three years later on the Rouyn line. Nor was the terrain expected to present problems, because the full 70 miles would run through the Clay Belt to the beginnings of the James Bay lowlands. Clearing, brushing, and grubbing would be required, but the elevation changes were gradual, and there were no rock barriers to cut through. Two major water crossings of the Abitibi River had to be

Lift gang, at dinner, James Bay Extension, c. 1923 (ONA-198825134)

negotiated, but these could be accomplished by proper engineering techniques and principles. To prepare for these, the Commission contracted with the Dominion Bridge Company of Hamilton to construct the appropriate spans.[8] At the time, there appeared to be little reason why the first 70 miles could not be built on schedule.

Nor was it improper, if this were done, to think that the project would continue beyond New Post. Most people felt that the railway would soon run all the way to the Bay. In fact, by the early months of 1923, it seemed a virtual certainty that Drury's government would grant approval to embark on that road. The Grant Smith and McDonnell firms were simply the instrument by which the first leg would be completed. Much depended on the smooth completion of this first leg; that was why the contract called for completion of this segment to be ready for the Commission's control by 31 October 1923. This would accomplish two ends: it would extend the T&NO more than one third of the way towards its northern goal, and it would bring its operations into direct contact with the potential power developments at Long Sault Rapids and at Carrying Places.

The performance of Grant Smith, therefore, was a matter of considerable consequence; and the Commission watched over it anxiously. As early as March 1922, for example, the Commission noted and approved the action of the chief engineer in pressing the contractors "for expeditious performance of their contract in getting their supplies in before the winter breakup."[9] Experienced northerners would require no such urgings, nor would they need to be told that they would have to make their own arrangements regarding cutting timber. The Commission did, however, attempt to be fair to Grant Smith. On 1 May 1922 it agreed to advance $47,079.90 to cover the cost of material, on the understanding that "it was customary to consider materials delivered for use in the work as equivalent to the partial performance of the work,"[10] and a week later the Commission also agreed, after a meeting with Grant Smith, to as-

sist the contracting firm in tie and rail delivery and the construction of a yard spur.[11]

Relations between the contracting firm and the Commission nonetheless began to sour. Notice regarding construction delays was first made in June 1922, and in July the commissioners formally recorded their "dissatisfaction with the progress made by the Contractors, and instructed Mr. Clement that the contract must be carried out without any equivocation, and that he was to take the necessary steps to see that the Contractors energetically prosecuted their work."[12] The disappointment of the commissioners increased two weeks later, when they personally inspected the work on Thursday, 3 August 1922 and learned that inadequately prepared piers for the bridge at the Long Sault crossing would cause further delay. Even at this point it seemed that the Commission was prepared to be understanding, because it made extra arrangements regarding the crossing with R.H. Palmer, the Chief Engineer of the Hamilton Bridge Works firm, to facilitate the completion of this portion of the project. Moreover, Chairman Lee, while expressing the Commission's general disappointment, mitigated his remarks by congratulating the contractors' men there—J.A. Campbell, R.H. Campbell, and Alex Sunstrom—on "the effort made during the last ten days."[13]

In light of subsequent remarks, however, one suspects that Lee was reluctantly restrained during that meeting on the business car *Temagami* in Cochrane. Shortly afterwards, he wrote to the Premier on the matter.[14]

We are disappointed in this contract to some extent, because instead of having about 12 miles of track laid by this time, we should have about 18 miles. The Commission are keeping in very close touch with the matter and you will be advised from time to time, as to how it is coming on. The present Contractors did not seem to understand what they were going into when they took this contract. I doubt—by the way they are going at it—if they ever had any experience in the matter. However, they claim that they will finish in the specified time and there is not very much action we can take.

To Chief Engineer Clement, Lee was more blunt, remarking that the project had been a disaster from the beginning.[15]

Clement himself declared in mid-October that the contractors were unlikely to meet their schedule. To do so, he said, it would be necessary that track be laid and surfaced to the second crossing of the Abitibi River (Mileage 44.4) before the year's end, and that appeared improbable. He did concede that "utmost effort" might still salvage the situation, but that would require laying track and ballasting at the same time.[16] The contractors did not have a work force large enough to do that. Some 850 men were almost always on the project during 1922, but about 120 more were required. The T&NO people urged the need for more men. The contractors agreed, but said that the required men were not available. Not enough effort was being made to get them, said the T&NO people. Whichever side was correct, relations between the two grew very strained.

Even so, during the winter of 1922–23, hope of pushing the line on to the Bay remained high. In August 1922 George Lee had declared to the Minister of Lands and Forests, B. Bowman, regarding opening land for settlement parallel to the T&NO extension.[17]

We are very anxious that this matter should receive attention and the Townships in question opened up for settlement. It is the finest agricultural land in Northern Ontario and it is essential that it be opened up to the Settlers along the new Extension of the railway.

Other T&NO people shared this ambition and opinion. Arthur Cole, for example, delivered an extensive address on the subject to the Toronto Empire Club early in 1923 and sent a copy to Premier Drury.[18] W.H. Maund, the Secretary-Treasurer, dispatched a Commission resolution of 18 June 1922 to Bowman regarding the matter.

As it is understood that the Department of Lands and Forests is surveying out addi-tional Townships North from Cochrane, along the route of the Extension of the T&NO, and as the land through which the T&NO Extension, now under construction, is located from the North boundary of the Township of Blount, is clay, and well adopted for settlement, it is considered, in the interests of the Commission, that the Townships adjacent to the Extension should be opened for settlement as soon as possible, in order to furnish traffic for the Railway.

Therefore, resolved, that recommendations should be forwarded to the Department for the opening of the Townships, as surveyed, for settlement. Also, consideration given to the opening up of an additional Township immediately North of Blount, with a view to furnishing all possible traffic to the Railway.

It is likely that Lee and colleagues were prompted, to some extent at least, by the proposal to connect the CNR lines to the west by means of a line between Nakina and Longlac. This connection, which was indeed built shortly afterwards, would permit traffic from the west to divert through Sudbury to Toronto and thus reduce the trade along the T&NO. Increased activity north of Cochrane would compensate for this loss of revenue.

The full Commission continued to press this idea and in February 1923 applied to the provincial government for an order-in-council authorizing the further extension of the railway to a point near Moose Factory.[19] At the same time, it suggested to the Premier that the matter of a terminal on James Bay and the possibility of a federal subsidy should be taken up with the federal government.

The timing apparently was propitious. Premier Drury had had other parties approach him regarding development in that northern region, including a syndicate owning clay properties there, and the idea of increasing traffic appealed to him.[20] Moreover, it was an election year, and the issue of further northern development was one that Drury felt comfortable to take into a campaign. In addition, the confusion of the post-war years had subsided, and the

Abitibi River bridge, mileage 44.4, James Bay extension, 1923 (ONA-198825146)

economy had begun to prosper somewhat; hence, the idea of committing capital funds to railway construction was much more appealing. The Kirkland Lake–Larder Lake region had begun to fulfill some of its promises, and the possibility of extending into the new fields of Rouyn had also begun to receive attention. The government, therefore, provided the required orders-in-council on 27 March.[21] On 13 April 1923 Premier Drury and Chairman Lee made their joint announcement calling for railway construction from Swastika to Larder Lake and from New Post to James Bay.[22] It is safe to assume, however, that Lee and the Commission knew as early as February that such approval would be forthcoming.

With that knowledge, their irritation with the slow progress of Grant Smith and McDonnell grew sharper. The second lap could not begin, obviously, until the leg from Cochrane to New Post had been completed, at least sufficiently to carry supplies, men, and equipment. The sharpened irritation was evident in Lee's letter to Clement on 7 February. Clement, who had been assigned almost exclusively to super-

vising the northern construction, had reported the previous day as follows:[23]

When Commissioners McLaren and Martin were in my office on the 2nd. inst. I explained that the completion of the Grant Smith & Co. & McDonnell Ltd. contract before Oct. 31st, 1923 depended almost entirely upon the progress that is made on the bridge at the second crossing of the Abitibi River, Mile 44.4 and on the ballasting and train filling. The general contractors have failed to have track at the Abitibi River in time to permit the completion of the bridge before Spring. As the erection of the truss span requires false work in the river, it must now be deferred until after the Spring high water. The contractors have been instructed to have the masonry foundations of the bridge completed before June 1st, 1923, in order that the Hamilton Bridge Works Company Ltd. can then proceed with the erection of the steel work. The steel work is all fabricated and as the foundations are the critical factor, I am at present concentrating attention on them in order that they may

166

be available by the time the condition of the river permits the erection of the false work.

I may say that in repeated conversation both with Mr. J.A. and R.H. Campbell, they have assured me that they will be able to complete the work before October 31st, 1923, although in a conversation on Dec. 2nd, 1922, the latter admitted that there was a possibility that the ballasting and train filling would not be fully completed by that date, which would be due, he claimed, to the exceptionally long haul necessitated by the fact that we have been unable to locate suitable ballast pits along the route of the extension.

Lee's reply showed his frustration.[24]

The proper way is to go after those fellows rough shod. If they cannot complete the contract let them say so and get off the Line. No excuses will be taken in connection with this matter. The last paragraph of your letter is just how I thought it would end—by finding some excuse against the Commission for the delay.

Further contracts on the James Bay Extension will depend on this contract—this year. We want to take it over this Fall and we are going to take it over on the Thirty-First day of October 1923. I hope there will be no misunderstanding about this.

The contractors responded by complaints about a lack of co-operation and understanding from the Commission and its engineers. The Commission called in an outside observer, J.G. Sullivan, a Consulting Engineer from Winnipeg. He declared in favour of the Commission, stating that from "the information furnished me and from my observations on the ground, I fail to find any reason why the Contractors should complain about the treatment they are receiving at the hand of your Engineers."[25]

By then, however, it was clear that Grant Smith and McDonnell would be unable to fulfill its contract. The Commission had begun to make plans to assume control of the work, but it was still inclined to compromise. About 45 miles had been completed to operational standards, enough to reach a small settlement that was growing at Mile-

age 20 and a large power development at Island Falls (Mileage 44) begun by the Hollinger Corporation. Those would require service and the Commission wished to provide it. It therefore agreed to extend the completion date for 70 miles for a year if it could take control of the first 44.5 miles on 31 October.[26]

This agreement never took effect. On the same date that he met with the Commission on this matter, McDonnell learned of the death of his partner Ross Grant and left immediately for the funeral in Vancouver. Upon his return, he declared his desire to give up the job. Perhaps the death of his friend had shaken him too much; perhaps he realized the job had been a bad decision; perhaps, as he said, he wished to direct his attention to his affairs in Egypt. In any case, the two parties agreed to a settlement which by T&NO reckoning resulted in a loss of $81,843 to the Vancouver firms. "There is no doubt whatever," Lee wrote to Premier Ferguson, "but that the Contractors did not understand what they were going into when they signed up."[27]

Just 16 days after the abortive agreement with McDonnell, the Commission's engineering department took control of the line. The next day, 1 November 1923, the first train—officially—ran from Cochrane's Union Station north to Island Falls Junction. In this fashion, the names of Larocque, Gonier, Clute, Beaunt, Gardiner, Sucker Creek, Workman, Wiertels, Wards, Maher, Trappersville, McGuiness, and Island Falls, all originally merely flag stops an average of four miles apart, worked their way onto the T&NO timetable. Lee himself attended this first official run, but did not ride the train, driven by Engineer Hermiston and operated by Conductor E. Robinson, Fireman J. Lebarron, and Brakemen H. Smith and J. Valliere. Chief Engineer Clement and Assistant Superintendent Stewart Ryan, however, were among the 90 or so passengers aboard this first mixed train to travel a scheduled trip north of Cochrane. Some were simply along for the ride, but most were destined for the Hollinger power plant at Island Falls.

Most northern newspapers covered the event and noted that it would run thrice weekly, leaving Cochrane at 9:00 a.m., arriving at Island Falls at 11:50 a.m. as train 101, and then leaving Island Falls as Train 192 at 1:30 p.m., arriving in Cochrane at 4:20 p.m. All reporters were eager to observe that on leaving Island Falls the first southward run of Train 192 carried an Indian family from the Lake Abitibi region who were enjoying their first train ride which they experienced "with the stoicism of their race."[28] The Cochrane *Northland Post* was, as might be expected, the most effusive in its coverage. It declared, in part:[29]

> In putting in the new train, the T&NO is holding to their good record in furnishing for this local service a nice looking train which will attract undoubtedly quite a lot of traffic from those who are anxious to see the country beyond which is rich in lakes and promising scenery. On the first trip over 30 tickets were sold. The train is a mixed one and will be a great convenience to the contractors working on the Hollinger power plant at Island Falls and therefore is likely to prove a financial success besides being of great convenience.
>
> For the first 18 miles it serves a fairly settled country which will rapidly develop in fine farm lands and by the time the present work on the power plant is finished, the local traffic should have taken on such proportions as to continue to make this portion anything but a burden to the T&NO.
>
> The present inauguration of the new service north of Cochrane marks another milestone in the development here and already rumors are in the air of further power development north with a new pulp mill, which will insure the continued success of the undertaking, and will draw the attention of Southern Ontario to the importance of the good old T&NO as the best investment which the province has.

The last remark was directed at both Premier Ferguson and other northern newspapers. Ferguson and his Conservative party had managed to secure a majority in the Ontario legislature on the election of 25 June 1923. One month before the first train ran north from Cochrane, Ferguson himself had made a northern trip, and had intimated at Cochrane that the government's railway programme, in the North would be limited.[30] He agreed that the commitment made by the Drury administration to build north as far as Oil Can Portage should be honoured by his government, but for the moment, at least, he was disinclined to authorize any construction beyond that point. The first 70 miles of the northern extension would service the region known as the Clay Belt. The need for a railway beyond that distance was speculative at best, he said, while other areas of both the north and the southern regions of the province had a clearly demonstrated need for such service. The people of Canada, said Ferguson, were already labouring under a very heavy railway debt, much of which had been caused by ill-advised railway construction. The grand designs of the National Transcontinental Railway and the Canadian Northern Railway were clearly a mistake, and caution must be exercised in order to prevent a similar mistake being made in the far northern regions of northeastern Ontario.

Newspapers in the North had generally responded favourably to Ferguson's reasoning. Each of these, no doubt, had in mind particular projects such as the extension into Lorrain, or one into Gowganda, or, most certainly, the already approved route eastward from Swastika towards Kirkland Lake and Larder Lake. Only the *Northland Post* objected to this plan and termed its rivals as being "self serving" and narrow-minded in their approach.[31]

Railway construction in northeastern Ontario, at that time, was to be limited to the completion of the line north of Cochrane as far as mileage-post 70 and to the construction of the line eastward from Swastika. For the first time, the T&NO Commission had been unable to get government approval for its plans. Ferguson may not even have consulted with the Commission. George Lee and his fellow commissioners were probably disappointed with this turn of events, but they did not say so either in public or in their correspondence. Rather, they directed their efforts toward

"Young track" on the James Bay extension
(ONA-19882017 Stephenson/Foerter)

be no construction north of Mileage 70, and even the 30 miles between Island Falls and Oil Can Portage were in doubt. According to the *Ottawa Journal* of 11 March 1924, the Premier declared that "the completion of the other thirty would depend on the action of the Spruce Falls Pulp and Paper Company. If the Company decides to go ahead with its plant at Smokey Falls then the thirty miles will be completed. It is already graded. In any event the road would be kept from deteriorating".

The Spruce Falls Pulp and Paper Company did decide to build its operation at Smokey Falls, and the government did indeed agree to complete the first 70 miles of construction. The Commission entered into a contract with the firm of C.D. French & Company to take over the unfinished part of the contract of Grant Smith and Company. This contract was arranged without tender. At its meeting of 10 December 1924, the Commission agreed that this work had been completed satisfactorily.

The matter of construction north of Cochrane, at that point, took something of a different turn. Still disinclined to continue the line directly north along the Moose River to James Bay, the Ferguson government was prepared to consider the possibility of a branch line from the Abitibi River crossing westward to Smokey Falls, to take advantage of traffic from the operations of the Spruce Falls Pulp and Paper Company there. Chief Engineer Clement was directed by the Commission to see that surveys were made in order to lay out the location line from the end of steel (Mileage 68) to Smokey Falls.[32] As it turned out, the pulp and paper company decided to build its own railway from Kapuskasing to service its plant at Smokey Falls. Consequently, the T&NO Commission abandoned its plans westward and returned its attention to the further extension of its line northward.

the building of the line eastward from Swastika into Kirkland Lake, and towards the completion of the first 70 miles.

On the James Bay extension, the Commission's engineering department continued to operate with the remnants of the contractor's crews and some subcontractors. This work did not proceed satisfactorily, however, and consequently was suspended during the winter months of February and March 1924. During that time the Ferguson government considered making it a permanent stoppage. On 11 March 1924 Ferguson declared again that there would

By early 1927 the government had become more inclined to consider expansion. In the election of 1 December 1926 it had retained its majority in the Ontario legislature. The government's interest in the region was piqued also by reports of gypsum deposits on the Moose River and of china clay deposits at the foot of Long Rapids. In any event, following a discussion between Chairman Lee and Premier Ferguson in Toronto on 11 April 1927, the Premier agreed that the Commission should advertise for tenders to construct the main line northward to mileage 100.[33]

When the Commission considered the tenders at its 3 May 1927 meeting, it found that a firm known as Construction and Engineering Limited had submitted the lowest bid—$675,866. "In view of the verbal and written criticisms made by Chief Engineer Clement covering some of the unit prices quoted by the lowest tenderer," the commissioners "unanimously resolved that judging from past experience and the necessity for the completion of the work this year, as well as the proper performance of the contract, that the tender submitted by H.F. McLean Limited be accepted." The McLean bid was for $710,566. That firm, however, had already demonstrated its competence by taking over the Sinclair contract on the Kirkland Lake–Larder Lake section of the Nipissing Central Railway.

Even so, in June of that year the Commission actually went over the ground and inspected the right-of-way as far as possible for the northern extension. While there, the commissioners determined with representatives of the McLean firm the various classifications of materials and costs. Here too, it was clear that they had learned from their experience with the Grant Smith firm, because the matter of classification had been a bone of contention throughout the period of that contract. The performance of McLean on this portion

At the foot of the rapids, Abitibi Canyon, 17 August 1927 (Left to right) Messrs Maher, Clement, Kerry, Terrien, Armstrong, Durrell, and Mrs. Durrell (ONA-1988252115)

of the railway was not in fact without incident: there was a slight cost overrun, and it was completed at a slightly later date than called for by the contract. Still, the Commission was reasonably pleased with the performance, and on 18 October 1928 it considered that the contract had been completed satisfactorily.[34]

The completion of the line as far as Coral Rapids was undoubtedly pleasing to Lee and his colleagues, but they still had a strong desire to continue as far as salt water. The Commission invited its three principal engineers—Chief Engineer Clement, Mining Engineer Cole, and Consulting Engineer Kerry—as well as Superintendent of Train Service W.A. Griffin to its meeting of 17 April 1929. The chairman of the Commission explained that the Commission desired a report on the proposed extension of the present railway through to James Bay. This report was to include all developments and natural resources as well as reasons for and against the proposed extension. The report was also to include final recommendations. These men were also to give consideration to the possible extension of the T&NO line westward through the Patricia District towards the watershed north of Lake Superior.

The extensive report which these men tabled with the Commission in May of 1929 contained very little that was new.[35] It spoke of the vastness of the region and of the existence of enormous natural resources in the form of fur, game, fisheries, minerals, water power, and agriculture. The report declared that Moose Harbour was strategically located to handle traffic from the bays—that is, James Bay and Hudson Bay—at an expenditure of approximately $500,000. It declared that the two bays were navigable five months of the year and that the climate was such that living conditions, particularly in the vicinity of James Bay, are fair though somewhat severe in winter. The engineers were in favour of such an extension, which would run about 91 miles in length and could be constructed at an estimated cost of $5,537,000. They estimated further that the annual operating expense would run in the neighbourhood of $302,700 and predicted that

within a period of five years the estimated annual revenue might well run to $512,000. Subsequent to this, Chief Engineer Clement supervised the task of surveying the line and establishing a trial run north of Coral Rapids. In his report to the Commission on 28 November 1929, he declared that a location had been completed as far as Black Smith Falls and that the task would continue as far as the crossing of the Moose River. He observed that recent mineral discoveries, especially the lignite coal field, were among the most important events in the mining history of the province, and he declared further that the Commission would be justified in taking every precaution to conserve the resulting traffic to the T&NO.[36] This report was sent to the Premier.

At the 3 January 1930 meeting of the Commission, the chief engineer submitted a route map, profile, and estimates of costs of construction for the extension of the railway from Coral Rapids to Black Smith Rapids on the Abitibi River and hence to the Moose River, a total of 43.5 miles. The chairman was authorized to address the Premier directly, enclosing the planned profile and estimates of costs, and to recommend that the extension be proceeded with as soon as government deemed it possible to do so. On 28 January 1930 Chairman Lee reported that Premier Ferguson had agreed to the extension as far as the Moose River crossing and had authorized the calling of tenders. Tenders were called for at 12 noon on Tuesday, 18 February 1930.[37] Of the three bids submitted, the Commission unanimously contracted to the lowest bidder: H.F. McLean.

By the time McLean actually began the work on this project, it had become abundantly clear that the collapse of the Canadian economy, like the collapse of the world economy, was going to be both severe and lengthy. The Depression had not, by any means, reached its deepest point by the late spring of 1930, but there was considerable unemployment throughout the province. The Commission persuaded itself that depression was as good a reason as prosperity had been to press on with the James Bay extension. It could be seen

Charles Lindberg's plane taking off from Moose Factory   The famous flyer visited in the same year that he flew solo across the Atlantic, 1927. (ONA-1988715 E. Everitt)

as providing jobs in the North, and the Commission discussed the possibility on 3 July 1930 of extending the work beyond the Moose River crossing right through to tidewater at James Bay Harbour. The McLean firm would be offered this work on basically the same terms as its present contract. Towards the end of the month, George Lee secured Premier Ferguson's agreement.

Consequently, in August the Commission extended the McLean firm's contract;[38] it would complete the construction of the James Bay extension as far as the harbour on the Moose River. There seemed to be good reasons for extending the contract without calling for further tenders. The McLean Company had served the T&NO well along the Kirkland Lake–Larder Lake section of the line, it had constructed the middle portion of the James Bay extension, and it had successfully outbid its competitors for the first 45 miles of the final run into Moosonee. There was every reason for the Commission to assume that the McLean firm would continue to produce effectively for them, and it was also likely that under the circumstances it would

have again been the lowest bidder. As it turned out, the decision was a mistake. It would cost George Lee severely. But those unhappy times lay four years in the future. For the moment, the work continued.

The work crews of the McLean Company made steady progress towards and then past Coral Rapids on the shores of the Moose River. It seemed that little could stop them. The terrain, while possessing a severely harsh climate, especially in winter, did not provide insurmountable barriers. The nature of the vegetation meant that brushing, clearing, and grubbing could be done fairly quickly, and the gentle slope of the James Bay lowlands provided the work crews with a relatively easy task in preparing the road bed and in laying steel. Ballasting the track was the major problem for the contractor; good gravel was scarce in the region and had to be transported some distance.

The most serious obstacle to this final length of the James Bay extension came at the crossing of the Moose River. Here the river was divided by Murray Island into two wide and shallow channels

Moose River crossing   This photo indicates the plan to fill the right channel of the Moose River at this point and span the left channel. This task required both special engineering skills and a unique railway bridge.

Trestle at Murray Island, Moose River, being filled in, 1932 (ONA-198875 E. Everitt)

of water. To facilitate the crossing, workers closed the right-hand channel with earth fill which was drawn to the point by cars travelling over a temporary trestle that extended partway into the river. Other work crews concurrently worked to span the left channel. Begun in September 1930, this work had to be completed during the fall and winter of 1930–31; when the spring drain-offs began, the river would become torrential, strong enough to destroy the earth fill and the temporary trestle unless the blockage had been fully secured by concrete and steel pilings. During the eight months that this project required, the co-operation between the contractor and the Commission was close. The T&NO actually supplied the huge steam-powered derrick and the man to run it, Homer Blain of North Bay.[39] Equally significant was the co-operation between the Commission

173

Moose River crossing—setting the fourth span

and the Dominion Bridge Company. The Moose River crossing bridge was the third major span that the Hamilton company had provided for the Commission on the James Bay extension. With this co-operative spirit and no labour problems, this portion of the project was completed on schedule.

From that point on the route was literally downhill right to James Bay. In the summer of 1931, the Commission could take considerable solace in the fact that their line was proceeding quickly and on schedule towards the projected end of steel in the vicinity of Moose Factory. The site actually chosen for the end of steel lay several miles upstream from the mouth of the Moose River at Revillon's Post.[40] Here the river turned in such a way that it was expected its current would keep the harbour clear of ice and silt and the Smile Islands which lay off-shore would provide some protection to the settlement there. At the time, no settlement existed at that point, but one could be expected to develop there because of the activities which would be required at the end of steel. This new community would need a name, and it was towards that

end that Chairman Lee instigated research to find one. Upon learning that the Cree word "Moosoneek" translated as "at the Moose," Lee concluded that a suitable name would be "Moosonee," the final "k" being dropped to obtain a softer sound. He sent this recommendation on to the new Premier, George S. Henry, who had succeeded Ferguson in 1930. Henry concurred in the choice, and thus the name Moosonee was chosen for the community that would mark the completion of this 30-year-old dream.[41]

At this point, George Lee, as Chairman of the Commission and as a strong promoter of this particular extension for over a decade, must have been very pleased indeed. It is true that all of his ambitions with respect to the railway had not been fulfilled. Premier Ferguson had, as we have seen very early in his tenure as premier, put a halt to the northern extension of the line from Cochrane. His rationale, of course, had been that capital funds were limited and should be directed towards projects that would bring more certain and more rapid traffic to the railway. In this Ferguson was probably correct. In

174

Car 832, first school at Moosonee, 1933
(ONA-1988713 E. Everitt)

Boardwalk from station to Moose River, c. 1933
(ONA-1988725 E. Everitt)

Revillion Brothers' wharf, Moose River, 1911   Future site of Moosonee. (ONA-19911193)

addition, however, Ferguson's attitude toward the development of hydro-electric power in the province also worked to frustrate the T&NO ambitions. While his government was committed to providing power for the industrial demands of southern Ontario, even to the point of purchasing it from the sister province of Quebec where necessary, Ferguson hesitated to commit the provincial government with the responsibility of providing all such power everywhere. On the one hand, such a commitment could prove to be a political disaster should the supply of power ever fail. Few things would irritate an electorate that had grown dependent upon power as much as having that power taken from them. At the same time, in Northern Ontario, the principal consumers of hydro-electric power were the major mining companies or pulp and paper companies who, in Ferguson's mind, were quite well-equipped to provide that power for themselves. He did not feel that the Government of Ontario should subsidize those operations by providing the capital expenditure necessary to produce the requisite hydro-electric power.

The Premier and his government accordingly withdrew the government-owned railway from any activity in the hydro-electric field. Rather, the development of hydro in northeastern Ontario fell to such large northern enterprises as the Hollinger Mines, which was granted a lease to develop the power on the upper Abitibi River at the Carrying Place, and to the Abitibi Pulp and Paper Company, which had through a subsidiary begun work on the construction of a dam at the Abitibi Canyon. This project, projected to cost some 17 million dollars, had required the influence of the Premier to set it in motion. While the benefits of this project would undoubtedly accrue to the Abitibi company, it could also be noted that the capital funding came from the corporation rather than from the government and people of the province.

This development also affected another project of the T&NO, the electrification of the railway. With others in control of hydro development, it became more difficult for the T&NO to be assured of a proper supply of power for the operation of its line. In addition, during the

1920s the price of coal declined somewhat, reducing the benefits of electrification. Finally, it should be observed that the companies which manufactured steam-powered engines, when faced with the very real threat of electrification of railways, developed new technology. The result was the Mikado engine, which was much more efficient than its predecessors. These factors, then, contributed to the demise of certain T&NO ambitions. Lee, Martin, and, in particular, Clement may have regretted this development, but it was one over which they had no control.

Notes

1. Clement to Lee, 10 October 1921. ONA, B-2557(1).
2. *Ibid.*
3. Lee to Martin. Telegram. 5 October 1921. ONA, B-2557(1).
4. Martin to Lee, 5 October 1921. ONA, B-2557(1).
5. Memorandum. Long Distance Conversation, 26 October 1921. ONA, B-2557(1).
6. *Minutes*, 28 October 1921.
7. Clement to Lee, 16 January 1922. ONA, B-2557.
8. *Minutes*, 7 April 1922.
9. *Minutes*, 8 March 1922.
10. *Minutes*, 1 May 1922.
11. *Minutes*, 8 May 1922.
12. *Minutes*, 18 July 1922.
13. *Minutes*, 2–4 August 1922.
14. Lee to Drury, 22 August 1922. AO. RG3, Drury Papers, Box 128.
15. Lee to Clement, September 1922. ONA, B-2557.
16. Clement to Lee, 23 October 1922. ONA, B-2557.
17. Lee to Bowman, 26 July 1923. AO. RG3, Drury Papers, Box 128.
18. Cole to Drury, 12 February 1923. ONA, B-2557.
19. *Minutes*, 2 February 1923.
20. *Minutes*, 15 January 1923.
21. Copy of the order-in-council of 27 March 1923. ONA, B-2557(1).
22. Official Statement Handed out by Chairman, T&NO Railway, Mr. George W. Lee, April 13, 1923. ONA, B-93(a). Rouyn Extension. See p. 109 of this text.
23. Clement to Lee, 6 February 1923. ONA, B-2557. James Bay Extension, Main File.
24. Lee to Clement, 7 February 1923. ONA, B-2557. James Bay Extension, Main File.
25. *Minutes*, 7 September 1923.
26. *Minutes*, 7 September and 3 October 1923.
27. Lee to Ferguson, 17 November 1923. AO. RG3, Ferguson Papers, Box 47.
28. Toronto *Globe*, 2 November 1923.
29. *Northland Post*, 2 November 1923.
30. *Haileyburian*, 4 October 1923.
31. *Northland Post*, 2 October 1923.
32. *Minutes*, 3 February 1926.
33. *Minutes*, 13 April 1927.
34. *Minutes*, 18 October 1928.
35. "Report of the Hudson Bay Region Relative to Proposed Extension of the Temiskaming and Northern Ontario Railway from Coral Rapids to Moose Harbour" by S.B. Clement, J.G.G. King and Arthur Cole. May 1929. ONA. Engineers Reports re James Bay Extension.
36. Clement to Lee, 28 November 1929. ONA. Engineers Reports re James Bay Extension.
37. *Minutes*, 28 January 1930.
38. *Minutes*, 19 August 1930.
39. Tucker, *Steam into Wilderness*, p. 99.
40. *Minutes*, 19 August 1930.
41. Lee to Henry, 18 November 1931; Henry to Lee, 23 November 1931, AO. RG3, Henry Papers, volume 147.

Part Three

Operating the System

Telecommunications office over Noranda Station, c. 1947
On left is Madeleine Quirt (ONA. ON Communications)

Chapter 11

The Lee Years

I N THE OPEN-ING hours of 1926, Mining Engineer Arthur Cole wrote expansively to the chairman regarding the plans which the T&NO leaders held for their railway's future. (See p. 182.) The tone and tenor of this New Year's greeting indicated that great prosperity was actually expected. Cole was far too sanguine, yet the spirit contained in the message pervaded T&NO thinking at the time. The future looked good, prosperous and secure. This same sentiment was present in a letter which Lee received a year later from Harry Preston of Elk Lake, who signed himself as "Discoverer of the 1st Real Gold Mine, Resident of Northern Ontario 23 years less 12 days south of North Bay." He wrote to inform the chairman that it was a significant year.

> Don't you know that 1927 is the 25th or $^1/_4$ Century Birthday of the T&NO Ry. Was it not started in 1902. If so our great Millionaire Maker the T&NO Ry is 25 years. Therefore don't you think the City of North Bay especially should hold a big celebration and the T&NO run excursion trains. A lot of us old timers who rode on the work trains of A.R. McDonnell 25

years ago will not be here at the end of the next 25 years but there will be greater mines than now and the T&NO will look like a spider web of branch lines like southern Ontario is today. Don't you think a celebration should be held at North Bay, the starting point of the T&NO Ry. $^1/_4$ century ago.[1]

Lee, who would have known of Preston's role in finding and staking the first Dome Mine claims, responded politely that "the question you write about is now under consideration." Lee had actually been thinking of such a celebration since the previous October and arranged for it to take place on 12 September 1927.

The day itself was apparently quite a success.[2] It followed the pattern of civic celebrations of the time: it kept a rather clear distinction between the official participants and the public, and the genders were restricted to assigned roles. Premier Ferguson, accompanied by the commissioners and senior officials, toured the T&NO shops, roundhouse, and other facilities in North Bay in the morning. At noon the Premier addressed a Rotary Club luncheon to which commissioners Lee, Martin, and McLaren and Secretary-Treasurer Maund were invited. Mrs. Ferguson meanwhile addressed a special ladies luncheon at which she was the guest of honour at the Anglican Church. Naturally, Mrs. Lee, Mrs. Martin, Mrs. McLaren, and Mrs. Maund also attended. That evening

COBALT, Ontario,
Jan. 2, 1926.

Personal

George W. Lee, Esq.,
Chairman,
T.&N.O. Railway Commission,
North Bay, Ontario.

Dear Mr. Lee,

I would like to use my first letter of the New Year to express to you the hope that it may be a Happy & Prosperous one for you.

May the day not be far distant when you will be Chairman of a T.&N.O. Railway that will extend from Georgian Bay to James Bay; when passenger ships will ply regularly between Moose Factory and points on James & Hudson Bays during the summer months; when fish trains will be a frequent occurence from Moose Factory for the south; when special provision will have to be made for the tourist trade during the summer and the hunters in the autumn; when the line from Cochrane to Moose Factory will pass several large and flourishing paper and rayon mills, as well as an up-to-date government experimental farm; when Moose Factory itself will be a thriving town with fish canning factories and general outfitting headquarters for mining and prospecting parties working from the 2000 miles of coast line around James & Hudson Bays; also an airplane service station.

May this plan begin to unfold itself in 1926 and may your health be good to see its eventual consummation.

With best wishes to you and yours, I am,

(SGD) ARTHUR A COLE,

MINING ENGINEER.

COPY
PT.

Cole to Lee, New Year's greeting (ONA, B-93(a))

these same ladies acted as patronesses at a special dance, by invitation only, held in the Blue Room of the Queen's Hotel. The Cangiano Orchestra provided the music. The evening began with the "Grand March" and included special entertainment in the form of solo dances by three young local women; Margaret Angus, Edith Winters, and Loretta Swan.

Before the dance began, Premier Ferguson addressed a special dinner held also at the Anglican Church hall. Among the guests there was J.J. Scully from Montreal, General Manager of the CPR, to whom Lee had sent an invitation by telegram which ended with "... I would appreciate, very highly, knowing if you could be there that day at a banquet at six o'clock in the evening, and make a very short address." In accepting, Scully had stated that he would "not comply with the last six words of your message!"

For the general public, the T&NO sponsored a day at the movies, still something of a novelty, at both the Royal and the Crystal theatres. Free to the public, the programme included current feature pictures as well as recent documentary shorts: "Northern Ontario," "The Hollinger Gold Mines," "Gold Productions," and "The Prince of Wales in Canada." The general public was also invited to an afternoon ceremony at Memorial Park (at Ferguson Street and First Avenue, beside the North Bay Normal School). There, the Premier, on behalf of the T&NO, presented to the city of North Bay a 30-acre plot of land from the railway's holdings in the east end of the city. The intent was that it be used for park and recreation purposes. The city, in time, would name it "Lee Park."

For T&NO workers, the best news of the day came at 9:30 in the morning, when Chairman Lee sent out the following telegram to all department heads along the entire line.

> On account of the 25th Anniversary of the T&NO Railway, we will give everybody a half day holiday this afternoon. Hope everybody enjoys themselves. We will be glad to see every person at the Memorial Park—Normal School at 4 o'clock.

One suspects that the chairman wished to ensure that there would be an audience when the Premier made his gift to the city. It is perhaps worth noting that invitations to all functions were sent to Justice Latchford, who pilotted the enabling legislation for the T&NO through the provincial legislature, but he did not attend. Nor is there any record indicating that Harry Preston made it down from Elk Lake. One hopes that he did.

These years were happy ones for the T&NO and indeed for all of northeastern Ontario. The area had experienced remarkable growth since the end of the war. With money and men again available for the work in the North, many of the mines which had languished during that conflict could move to full production. This was especially true in the Kirkland Lake region, but increased mining activity throughout the North was common in the 1920s. The decade also saw a rapid growth in the demand for forest products, especially timber and pulp and paper. One of the greatest sources of demand was the enormous growth of newspapers, especially in the United States. The demand for newsprint from the northern mills grew tremendously as did the demand for building materials. Increased activity in the northern forest industries meant, in turn, heavier traffic on the T&NO.

A frosty morning at the Englehart roundhouse (ONA-19911337)

With the war's end, thousands of young men returned home to take up their lives. The resulting rise in the birth rate and the re-opening of immigration led quickly to a rising population, which led to an increasing demand for land. Ferguson, no doubt urged on by his chief northern adviser, George Lee, had considerable faith in the Clay Belt farming region and saw it as a natural place to direct the growing population of Ontario. Once again the T&NO benefited. Finally, the increase in urban population brought new demands for electric power. Consequently, the hydro developments in the North, notably at the Abitibi Canyon, expanded. Here again one of the beneficiaries of the increased activity was the T&NO. Virtually everything, then, seemed to indicate a bright, prosperous, and expanding period for the railway. One can understand, therefore, the expansive greetings of Arthur Cole to George Lee in January of 1926 and also the pride exhibited at the 25th

George W. Lee, Chairman, 1920–34
(ONA photo collection)

anniversary celebrations in North Bay. Tickets to the several functions all proudly displayed the phrase "mighty oaks from little acorns grow." As George Lee listened to the Premier make his formal donation of railway land to the city, he may well have reflected that, even as Ferguson was speaking, there were men busily working on the line north from Cochrane, and others who were, after a two-year delay, driving the rails eastward from Cheminis towards Rouyn.

The T&NO was a truly dominant institution in the northeastern corridor. It controlled, directly or indirectly, by design or by influence, virtually every feature of life there. It is difficult over six decades later to understand how all pervasive the presence of the railway really was. Every item of clothing in Sam Buckavetsky's stores, every bolt, tool, or household gadget in Cochrane's or Taylor's hardware stores, every piece of fruit or item of canned good in the Wooling's grocery store, and every street sign, block of cement, bicycle, or even automobile had reached its destination by railway. With 2100 employees, the T&NO payroll was likely as large as any in the North. Everyone who did not make a living from the T&NO was either related to or knew someone else who did. Everyone who travelled into the North, out of the North, or within the North, did so by rail. Simply by offering the normal services of a railway—passengers, freight, express, mail, telegraph, and telephone—the T&NO sustained and ordered life in the northeastern corridor.

It did more. In times of hardship or danger, people looked naturally to the railway for assistance and guidance. This was made very clear during the three tragic fires of 1911, 1916, and 1922. The only means of escape from the ravages of those fires had been the T&NO line; and the only means by which relief could be provided to those who had suffered was the railway. Any emergency was apt to involve the T&NO. In virtually all northern communities, the mining companies provided many services, ranging from first aid to recreation facilities. But the only institution which covered every community in the northeastern corridor, had facilities in all of them, and linked them was the T&NO. Train schedules, therefore, were more than memorized. They became part of one's manner of thinking. Public and private events were planned around those schedules, as were business meetings and operations.

Beyond these considerations the T&NO exercised even greater prominence because of the several tasks assigned to it, either by government direction or because its very presence called for it to take control. The Land Department, for example, had a decisive influence on the manner in which lands were distributed in the first two decades of the northeastern corridor's development. The fact that the railway had obtained mining rights to portions of its right-of-way and other areas in the North had dictated the need for its own mining engineer. Arthur Cole held that post until his retirement in 1934. During that time the mining division maintained a close connection with the mining industry, including the young Haileybury School of Mines that grew out of special classes offered by the first claims recorder, G.T. Smith. In the field of communication, the railway figured largely. Its telegraph service, although intended in the first instance for internal use, formed the only such link in the North, and its telephone facilities also served as the single means for long distance calls to move beyond the local telephone companies. It was, for example, a T&NO telephone operator who sent the tragic news south in 1922 regarding the terrible fire that swept the Timiskaming district. Through its various departments, therefore, the T&NO provided an intelligence system that covered every feature of northern life. It followed that the railway's officials had more ready access to more complete information about the North than anyone else.

It was hardly surprising that government representatives in Toronto looked naturally to the T&NO for data and advice on the region, whether for purposes of government service or for those of partisan politics. It was equally natural that political partisanship should become a common feature in the structure of the T&NO and its related services. From the earliest days, the connection between the government and the T&NO was conducted at the highest levels, with the top railway personnel communicating directly with the Premier or with members of the Cabinet. The trend, which began during the Liberal regime of Premier Ross, was more firmly and solidly entrenched during the long tenure of the Conservatives. The lines between policy and politics became somewhat blurred, and, as a result, when government members or civil servants sought advice and information from the North, it was not always possible to separate the operation of the line from the operations of the party in power. It was, in many minds, an unhealthy circumstance, but it developed in the North and in the T&NO just as it did elsewhere. Elections and their results, therefore, were events of considerable consequence; and, as shall be seen, few were as significant as that in 1934.

Even in those halcyon days of the 1920s, when the steam railway's dominant position prevailed everywhere, some rival systems operated. One was the concept of radial railways or, as they were commonly called, trolley or street car lines. They were also called "light railways" for the obvious reason that their engines and rolling stock, operating on a narrower gauge and powered by electricity, weighed far less than that of the traditional railway. They were, therefore, far easier and much less costly to stop, start, and maintain. They could not carry the heavy freight, but they were ideal for light freight, most express, and especially passenger traffic. They offered a potential solution to the transportation problems in growing urban areas. The original Nipissing Central Railway had been an attempt to apply these advantages in the North.

Having acquired this light railway in 1911, the T&NO Commission, acting as the NCR's board of directors, extended its lines southward through Cobalt to Kerr Lake and northwards past Haileybury's lakeshore to New Liskeard. It provided the main link among those communities and was the principal reason why Cobalt, Haileybury, and New Liskeard came to be viewed collectively as the Tri-town. Cobalt had emerged as the miners' heartland. It became

FIRE IN THE BUSH

Fire constituted the most terrifying prospect for northerners. In the settled communities where residents depended upon fire for heat, light, and cooking, the potential for accidents was both profuse and constant. A defective coal oil lamp, an errant cigar butt, a dropped lantern, an unwatched hearth, or dozens of other possible mishaps connected to regular routines could easily result in a significant blaze. Since the towns had been thrown up very quickly, largely with flammable building materials, and with buildings usually in close proximity to each other, such a blaze could, with frightening speed, destroy a house, a block of houses, or even an entire community. While frightening, such tragedies could be kept somewhat under control through the proper handling of lamps, stoves, lanterns, and matches, through caution and vigilance, and through rapid response in times of crisis.

But the fear of house fires paled into insignificance when compared to the terror of a full forest fire. Even constant care and vigilance could not prevent these, for most forest fires come from nature through lightning or spontaneous combustion. Nature would also extinguish them, by rain or from a natural firebreak like a body of water or a previously burned-over area, but that could take some time. To be caught in the unpredictable path of such a blaze while it raged, was a northerner's greatest dread, especially if the flames reached the tops of the trees. A crown fire could spread at 50 miles an hour. It was impossible to outrun such a terror. One could only hope for a shift in the wind or some other miracle, and in the meantime take what precautions were available. Everyone had a personal contingency plan: an escape by rail, or by boat, or actions to protect one's family and possessions as well as one could. An early resident of North Cobalt, Clara Seguin, recalled that fires were common and broke out every summer.

> It was a way of life... Once my father came down from the mines and said he had been told to evacuate... And we each took a pillow case of whatever clothes we could put in and wore three layers of clothing and got ready to take the streetcar down to the train and...away from the fire. And just before we were ready to go, the wind changed and the danger was over.[3]

On other occasions when fire seemed to be threatening, the Seguin family would, if time allowed, move their furniture to a nearby culvert of the NCR in hopes that the fire might jump over that sector. "We did that twice that year (c. 1911)."

Fortunately the fires started out small and a threatened community, with warning and grand effort, often could beat them back, usually by cutting

Hailebury fire   Mrs. Olive E. Russell and Marjorie Russell, ruins of home, 1922.
(ONA-198861, R.J. Russell)

Matheson Fire, 1916   Soldier on right bearing casket for shipment to southern Ontario.
(ONA-198891, J. Fitzmaurice)

firebreaks. Kathleen (Farmer) Houghton remembered an event from her youth near mileage 104.

🔊 Well the fires burned pretty well all September... And they used to take lunches out to the men. The mills closed everything and put the men out to fight fires... When it was my mother's turn she made great gobs of lunches and as kids we took them out so far and a man would take them and send us home because they didn't want us under foot. Fighting the fire out there, they'd have to eat out there. Twenty-four hours a day this went on, ...and they'd nothing to fight with!...they didn't have planes and water like they do now. They just kept digging ditches, and they were all smoke and their eyes were red and it was awful...[4] 🔊

This fire, however, was not controlled. It ran amuck, destroying much of Haileybury and Cobalt, killing 43 people, and leaving some 6,000 homeless. It is known as the Haileybury (or Temiskaming) fire of 1922. Six years earlier, 223 had died in devastating fires in the Matheson region. These horrible events, combined with the blazes that destroyed South Porcupine and Cochrane in 1911, are known collectively as the great fires of the northeast.[5] Following the 1916 Matheson disaster, the provincial government, despite the wartime situation, dispatched troops to the North to assist the survivors. It also es-

tablished the Northern Ontario Relief Committee to supervise and manage the assistance that poured in from the more southern regions. This committee was re-activated in 1922 when the Haileybury tragedy took place. In the various rescue and relief operations the T&NO naturally assumed a prominent role. Individual T&NO people also performed steadfastly and often courageously during these crises. Among them was engineman Jim McKerrow who stopped his train to collect refugees near Thornloe during the 1922 fire. As the people boarded his train, McKerrow noticed a woman in front of a nearby sod shack which displayed a red flag, a sign of typhoid which is highly contagious.

🔊 Big Jim runs across over there and says, "What's the matter?" She says, "My 12-year-old daughter's in there. She's got typhoid. I can't leave her. I won't leave her. What are we going to do?" Jim just rushed in, grabbed the kid up in his arms with a blanket around her..., got on the locomotive, and they went on down the track... And he never got typhoid or anything like it.[6] 🔊

The Haileybury fire was the last major forest fire catastrophe, but until more efficient methods of fire ranging developed to detect potential dangers and more effective methods of fighting fires were developed, the great dread of northerners remained.

also the commercial focus for the region along the western shores of Lake Timiskaming, for the NCR's line had the effect of turning the full shoreline and the New Liskeard farming lands into a single market area. Likewise, the easy access which the trolley cars afforded the Cobalt mines from North Cobalt and from Haileybury permitted those towns to serve as a residential centre for those who worked the mines and who wished to remove themselves and their families from the raucous environs of the mining camp. The three towns—sometimes as rivals and sometimes as co-operative partners—interacted socially and commercially. There are other instances where three or more small centres developed within a 12-mile span along the T&NO line, but in no other instance in the years before the automobile did this sort of interaction occur. The catalyst was the NCR.

Possibly because of the Tri-towns' success, a project for an extensive system of light railways in the northeastern corridor appeared in 1920–21. The *Nugget* devoted several stories to the idea—which it naturally supported—and even produced a map on its front pages to show how it could be done.[7] In all this it seems that the Commission played no role other than to observe. If anything, the commissioners likely viewed the prospects with approval. The conditions in the North had changed since Englehart had frowned on the original NCR as a potential rival. The proposed lines of 1920 would enhance the T&NO traffic, because all traffic would feed into it and they would reduce its responsibility by eliminating at least some of the pressing demands for new construction.

As events unfolded, however, the light railways of the North remained forever on the drawing board. The Ontario government, which was being urged to build such lines there and throughout the province, was also under pressure to build a network of provincial highways. It was not feasible to attempt both. After assessing the relative merits of each as links for the province's rural and urban centres, the Drury government declared for the highways. Henceforth, the light railways would meet acceptance only in the larger urban centres like Toronto, Hamilton, Ottawa, and the Lakehead, where street cars would be the mainstay of intracity travel for some 40 years. Beyond the city streets, the government concentrated on road

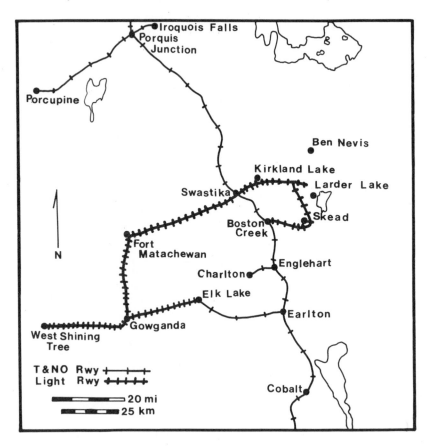

Map 13. *Proposed light railways, 1920*

Construction of James Bay Inn, Moosonee, 1931–32 (ONA-1988195 J. Hammar)

development. While the government gave most of its attention to the southern parts of the province, it was not too long before Yonge Street road, already into Muskoka, was extended to North Bay. Beyond there the progress was slow. In 1923, for example, only five miles from each end—Cochrane and North Bay—was undertaken. Yet by the end of the decade the trunk road had been pushed north as far as Cochrane. Its first official use was not propitious. A special cavalcade journeyed from Toronto to publicize the completion of the new road, which had been named the Ferguson Highway. Just beyond North Bay it suffered considerable embarrassment when one of the cars actually sank in a hole in the road and disappeared completely into the muskeg! The incident caused amusement at the time. Few viewed the new road or the cars that might run over it with anything beyond curiosity, and even fewer considered them to be a threat to the railway.

Three major developments would have to take place before the highway and the automobile would pose a serious competitive factor in T&NO thinking: a much improved internal combustion engine, an effective system of highways, and a widespread demand for cars from the general public. These would occur, but before they did two major worldwide events slowed their progress for almost 20 years: the stark economic depression of the '30s and the Second World War of the 1940s.

These two worldwide events also had drastic effects on the railway. It was some time before the full extent of the Depression and its attendant hardships came to be either recognized or admitted. Everywhere leading government officials and businessmen attempted to play down its extent and sought, desperately, to find cause for optimism. In the North, George Lee described the first year of the Depression euphemistically as one of "restricted opportunity," and the T&NO's annual report for 1930 declared that "Canada is growing even in this period of depression, and it is necessary for the improvement of business in every regard, that the operations that are contemplated for betterment and extension of railway service be maintained."[8]

The following year the Toronto *Globe* reported Lee as saying that "so far as the North is concerned, the Depression is over." That same report also reported him as saying that the T&NO "was the only railway in North America which had a profit this year."[9] Because this phrase has been much cited ever since, it is worth noting that on 18 November Lee wrote to Premier Henry: "No such words were ever used by me nor did I mention finances, in connection with the railway, while in Brantford. This statement may have been made by Judge Jones, who introduced me."[10] That same year the annual report noted that Canada had come to occupy second place in the world gold production, "having exceeded the United States in 1930," and then declared boldly that "the northern part of Ontario holds enormous possibilities of advancement and enrichment in the near future..."[11] Part of this optimism may have been inspired by the completion of the line to tidewater in James Bay by the end of 1931 and the branch's formal opening the following year.

The completion of the railway through to James Bay can be considered the T&NO's crowning achievement to date and of Lee's tenure as chairman. Once converted to the project, he pursued it tenaciously. Both Lee and the other commissioners, as well as senior railway officials, seemed to find something heroic in the idea of a salt water port for Ontario in the distant north. As the work progressed northward, with the dream overcoming one obstacle after another, it may have become almost a missionary enterprise in the minds of those who pursued it. The harsh northern climate, the miles of muskeg, the mounting costs, and the Depression's onslaught were all ignored. And as the task drew closer to completion, the commissioners grew increasingly anxious that the line be completed. They became considerably more generous in approving costs than they had been for other portions of the line. At the meeting of 11 March 1931 they agreed to an expenditure of $12,000–$15,000 to build a wooden trestle across the Moose River to assist in bridging the river. It was an unexpected cost, "but in view of the time saved and the extra convenience in going about the work, it was decided to grant the necessary authority for the building of the trestle." At that same meeting it was reported that requests had already "been received for the privilege of being present" at the official opening. The commissioners were not the only anxious observers. It was an encouraging sign.

Over the course of 1931, the progress of the James Bay extension was the single encouraging feature of the T&NO operations. The Depression had truly taken hold and had caused disruptions and anguish everywhere. Yet north from Cochrane the work continued, and so did the hope that

Last-spike ceremony, Moosonee, 1932   George W. Lee in photo, centre, just to right of microphone. (ONA-19881911 J. Hammar)

190

this division might prove successful, as other branches had done, and help restore the sense of excitement that had prevailed for the previous decade. Hope remained fairly high, for example, that the Onakawana lignite deposits would prove to be extensive and profitable. On 14 June 1932 Lee reported that "results of the tests of the lignite, which had been carried on in Germany, etc. had been received by the Department of Mines and were very interesting."[12] It was hardly the stuff upon which to build a dream, but the Commission had little else to cling to. It decided it should try to meet with the minister regarding that report "with view to affording traffic for the railway." Other factors enticed the commissioners into an optimistic frame of mind. The Hudson's Bay Company indicated it might "enter into the tourist business in earnest" by providing "boating facilities to take tourists out around the Bay" and by arranging "sleeping and eating accommodation at Factory Island";[13] the *Nugget* planned a Special Souvenir Supplement; the Ville Marie Navigation Company offered to place a boat in service in the Bay;[14] the Premier visited the line and the proposed terminus;[15] Chief Engineer Clement found it necessary to advise the contractor "not to handle any building supplies or other materials for Moose Harbour without first obtaining permission";[16] the United Church Young People's Tour Committee inquired regarding a tour of the north country as far as Moose Factory.[17]

Even combined, these items hardly provided grounds for much optimism, but the commissioners may have been buoyed up by them. In any case, they developed some elaborate plans for the new end of steel. Through the appropriate order-in-council the Commission obtained ownership of the townsite. It then prepared plans for the new town, which would be called Moosonee, and arranged for a special train to travel from Cochrane for a public auction of lots there on 10 June 1932. At the same time, a celebration was planned for the official opening on 15 July 1932. In the meantime, on 8 January 1932 the Commission determined

that the new townsite should have appropriate accommodation for the traveller. It proposed a hotel with 15–20 guest rooms, five of them with connecting baths, and for 10 bungalows with two bedrooms and a bathroom each. "It should not be fancy, but along rustic lines, and substantial." While the plans changed somewhat under the management of James Kingston, with a staff of seven, the hotel began receiving guests later that year.[18] It marked the first elaborate foray of the T&NO into the hotel and tourist industry.

The auction of 10 June proved to be a disappointing affair. Auctioneer Long could not sell a single lot. This naturally led to a considerable reduction in the upset prices and the charges to special groups such as churches. They were to receive a discount of 80% except for the Anglican Church which had been there so long that it received permission simply to occupy its land at the pleasure of the Commission.[19] Even the disappointing auction, however, could not dampen enthusiasm for the official opening.

It was a happy event, at a time when happy events were few. Moreover, a dream had been accomplished. George Lee wrote boldly in the 1931 annual report.[20]

> To the sub-Arctic Circle, Ontario's Northern frontier has been pushed back one hundred and eighty-five miles (185) by this year's completion of main line extension north of Cochrane to Moosonee at James Bay.
>
> Another Chapter written in the well-filled history of the railway's progress and achievement.

The Commission was proud of its accomplishment. To show it off, invitations were sent to the presidents of 24 different Ontario boards of trade and to the full boards of trade along the T&NO line. Also invited were various political figures, including Quebec's Premier Taschereau and Dr. Robert Manion, the federal Minister of Railways, as well as press representatives, some of the contractors, and several railway people, including Sir Henry Thornton. It was also arranged to have the event broadcast

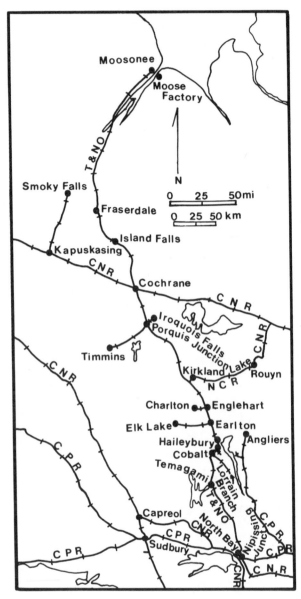

Map 14. *T&NO evolution, 1932*

over radio. Some 125 people accepted the invitations and travelled from North Bay on a special train, handsomely equipped with sleepers and diners, several of which had to be borrowed or leased from other railways.[21] The highlight came in the afternoon of 15 July, when not one but three "last spikes" were "fair and truly driven home";[22] Frank Latchford,

who had turned the first sod for the T&NO in 1902, came to hammer in the first; E.C. Drury, the UFO premier whose government had authorized the first phase of the construction, pounded in the second; and Premier G.S. Henry drove home the third.

The Moosonee party, however joyous, could divert attention only briefly from harsh reality. T&NO passenger traffic had declined 50% between 1929 and 1933, and freight had collapsed from 1,376,581 tons to 823,946 tons in that same period.[23] Nor could it be hidden that the exigencies of the Depression had forced the railway to adopt such cost-cutting measures as the lay-offs of personnel and a reduction in the hours of work afforded many of those who remained on the job. In addition, in line with the other railways of Canada, the organized labour force had been required to accept first a 10% reduction in wage rates and then a second reduction of 5% in 1933. Clearly, the expansion dreams of Arthur Cole only seven years earlier belonged to a different era.

Moreover, when economic conditions finally improved, they did so only partly as a result of the gradual turn of the business cycle. The truly big impetus came in September 1939 when Canada followed the lead of England in declaring war on Germany. Once again Canada committed its resources, almost without reservation, to the prosecution of the war. This meant a tremendous drain on both capital and manpower, just as it had done a generation earlier. The effect on the T&NO was that of restricting growth, even of restricting maintenance. Once again T&NO men who entered the military could count on their jobs when they returned, and once again the Commission urged the purchase of war bonds. This time the roll of honour was maintained at civic buildings throughout the North. In North Bay, T&NO Engineering Clerk Russell Huntington had the task of inscribing each local lad's name on a scroll maintained at city hall. He also had the sad chore of indicating those who fell. Among those who did was a Latchford man, Aubrey Cosens, whose courage was recognized when he was posthumously awarded the Victoria Cross. It was to acknowledge this further that the Commission named its first vessel on Lake Temagami in his honour. Many others also went, and most fortunately came home. Some met when they were overseas. Glenn Ruttan, in 1986, recalled an incident in Italy in 1944.[24]

> &. I was in this old bombed out building in Italy and a guy comes rappin' at the door. I opened it. He said, "Have you got any empty bottles?" He wanted to get some wine to take back [to his group]. I said, "Sure." Then I looked again. "Say, didn't I work with you for Tony Protomani?" Sure enough, it was Clayt Johnson!... I also met Eric Rutherford—from Kirkland Lake—he was a captain—I met him in Italy. &?

The Depression and the war have generally been viewed as providing almost two decades of hardship for the T&NO. Yet another view is plausible. The years of depression and war can be seen as providing the railway with an additional 20 years of prominence that might well have otherwise been denied. These years had an equally devastating effect on the railway's two major enemies: the automobile and the highway. Both also suffered retarded growth because of the Depression and the shortage of capital and manpower brought on by the war. Indeed, for them the hardship was even greater, because the railway was in place and already had a history of public acceptance.

Even so, even during the dark days of the Depression, motor vehicles and several roads in the North began to indicate the ways in which incursions could be made into the various activities of the T&NO and its attendant services by rival forms of transportation and communication. The street car portion of the Nipissing Central Railway, for example, fell on particularly difficult days in the early 1930s. Certainly a portion of the explanation for its declining ridership could be found in the reduced incomes of the persons who normally used that railway. Another explanation, however, could be found in the increased number of local roads and local motor vehicles in the Tri-town region. Like-

wise, in the early 1930s the T&NO Commission began investigating the possibility of introducing bus and truck service within its sphere of influence, partly because these might prove to be more efficient for the railway, and partly because other firms had begun to introduce these same services. In addition, in the early part of this decade the Northern Telephone Company and the T&NO conflicted. For the moment these particular inroads remained small. They can be seen, however, as harbingers of much more serious challenges that would come in the future. More immediate changes came as a result of a sharp turn in Ontario politics.

The election on 19 June 1934 was devastating for Henry's government. Redistribution had reduced the number of seats in the legislature from 112 to 90 for the only time in the history of the province. The Liberals, recently revived under the flamboyant leadership of Mitchell Stewart Hepburn, carried 65 seats, and four others were taken by candidates running under the label "Liberal-Progressives." The newly created Co-operative Commonwealth Federation (CCF), the Labour party, the United Farmers of Ontario, and an Independent took one seat each. The Conservatives retained only 17 seats, and their rejection in the North was complete: the 12 ridings from Muskoka northwards returned 11 Liberals and a Liberal-Progressive. In the northeastern corridor, all four Conservative incumbents—in Nipissing, Timiskaming, Cochrane South, and Cochrane North—were defeated by Liberals.

The campaign had been as bitter as it was decisive. The Liberals found in the government's use of patronage an issue ideally suited to Hepburn's abrasive style; they found also in the hydro and timber contracts of former premier Howard Ferguson evidence to suggest mismanagement and malfeasance. As soon as the new government took office, it launched a series of inquiries into the conduct of its predecessors. One led to the dismissal of George Drew (a future premier) as Ontario Securities Commissioner. Another declared that the former Minister of Mines, Charles McCrea, had been involved in a liquor board scandal. Still another condemned the Niagara Parks Commission. The most publicized, the Smith-Latchford Commission on the affairs of Ontario Hydro, charged both provincial and federal Conservative former ministers, George Henry and Arthur Meighen, with improper financial conduct.

It was not, however, until six weeks after the election that the T&NO became a target for Liberal scandal-hunters. Hepburn had been advised, while campaigning for Joseph Legault in Nipissing, that attacks on the railway might do him more harm than good. There was no doubt that the T&NO Commission had regularly given preference to the loyal Conservatives in awarding contracts and in making appointments and promotions. Accusations to that effect soon poured into the new premier's office from northern Liberals who felt that their time had come. The charges are borne out by the correspondence of Englehart, Lee, and other commissioners. But the new government did not really wish to change the familiar practice, it simply wished to control it; and bringing the T&NO under control would be most clearly justified if there was some evidence of mismanagement or some breach of the Commission's rules.

Such evidence appeared. Among the first to offer it was W.B. Russell, the railway's first chief engineer, who remembered his own dismissal when the government had changed from Liberal to Conservative in 1905. "Mr. Whitney's first act upon assuming office," Russell wrote to the Premier's friend, Senator W.H. McGuire, "was to wipe out the Commission & appoint another & they in turn froze out the Chief Engineer, your humble servant, along with others of my staff of Engineers." He named a specific case, the award of a contract for a bridge at the Abitibi Canyon to Dominion Construction Ltd.: "I sat in on these tenders with another firm & was of the opinion there was favoritism."[25]

Thus encouraged, Premier Hepburn on 8 August 1934 appointed a one-man commission to investigate the T&NO. Armand Racine, a Windsor lawyer who had already reported on the Niagara Parks Commission, spent a month collecting evidence. He held hearings at North Bay, questioned the T&NO commissioners and officials, and travelled the line to interview people throughout the northeastern corridor. It was soon clear that his mission was to build a case against George Lee, a case that rested heavily on errors, improprieties, and expenses in the planning and construction of the James Bay extension. On 30 August, five weeks before the report was submitted, Hepburn had already told the Toronto *Telegram* that "Mr. Lee has to go," and that the new hotel at Moosonee might as well be given "back to the Indians."

Lee was vulnerable. He had been an active Conservative, appointed to the T&NO Commission after a term as its land agent, with no formal claim to expertise as a railwayman. Named as Chairman of the Commission by E.C. Drury's UFO government, he had been confirmed when the Conservatives returned to office, and he had continued the intensely close relationship with the Premier inaugurated by Jake Englehart. Moreover, he was also General Manager in charge of the actual operation and construction of the railway and of all its other activities. In the whole system, therefore, there was no error for which he could escape responsibility. In its determination to push the railway north of the Abitibi Canyon, the Commission had ignored its own rules: it had let two contracts totalling $4,246,281 to H.F. McLean and Co. without tenders and had awarded that firm another contract on which it had not been the lowest bidder.[26]

Even Racine was unable to find corruption in these transactions, but he did denounce them as improprieties, made worse by the bad judgment of undertaking the unprofitable line to Moosonee at all. He found the whole Commission "lax and negligent," particularly in its financial management; the apparent surplus of $18,023.03 for 1933 should, if the T&NO had been paying a proper interest on funds received from the government, have been a deficit of 1,176,340.43.[27] He recommended an immediate audit, an independent survey to reorganize "every department of the railway" and another to curtail services on unprofitable branch lines.

He recommended economy measures ranging from the closing of the Moosonee Inn and the sale of the private car *Whitney* to abolishing the commissioners' stipends and restricting free passes. He wanted eight senior officials dismissed at once and named eleven others, including Mining Engineer A.A. Cole and three janitors, to be pensioned off. Above all, he recommended that George Lee be retired on pension and that the new general manager, "a practical railroad executive," should not be a member of the Commission.[28]

Lee, as he himself realized,[29] had to go. There was only one other casualty on the T&NO staff, the manager of the Moosonee Inn, who was told frankly that his political affiliation was the reason. One of Hepburn's most zealous supporters in North Bay, who told several employees that they were "gone," was merely exceeding his authority. Racine tried, unsuccessfully at the first meeting of the new Liberal Commission, to dismiss Maund, Clement, Freeman, Alford, and Hamilton (respectively the Secretary-Treasurer, Chief Engineer, Employment Agent, Purchasing Agent, and Auditor); nobody seconded his motion.[30]

While a good many of Racine's strictures hit their mark, he made no allowance for the fact that the T&NO was quite as much a public utility for the development of the North as it was a railway. Provincial advances to the Commission were not simply loans to a private company. The original hope that the railway could be sustained by land grants along its route had been confounded by the absence of suitable public land; when grants in the district of Algoma were suggested instead, they were not productive enough to pay for the construction programme that northern communities and the provincial Cabinet wanted. As a result, the railway's capital costs had been underwritten by the government. Inefficiencies and overstaffing, which were easy to condemn as

political patronage, had nonetheless maintained employment in the northeastern corridor during the Depression when no other agency was doing anything effective about it. Furthermore, Chief Engineer Clement was able to claim that the line's operating ratio—the percentage of its operating revenues spent on operating expenses—was 78.2 in 1933, better than the Canadian average of 86.2.[31]

Small wonder then that Racine's inquiry was soon regarded in the North as a partisan attack on the T&NO, and even on the North in general. The formality and publicity of his hearings in North Bay were enough to cause tension. His attempt to find scandal in the destruction of some old records looked like witch-hunting.[32] E. Lynden Longmore, a metallurgist for the Hollinger Mines, gave Racine a catalogue of the mining wealth which the T&NO had made possible.[33] Another engineer, and a Liberal besides, A.D. Campbell, reminded southerners that the railway had "served well the largest companies of the north and equally well the humblest settler."[34] Lee's position may have become politically untenable, but he had no lack of admirers in the North. Racine himself advised that Lee should be kept on as the head of a new freight solicitation department. (It is an indication of how high partisan feeling ran that this, the eighteenth of his recommendations, came to be remembered as a proposal to put Lee to work in a freight shed!) While he insisted that Lee was not well qualified to run a railway, Racine did not withhold a tribute: "Possessing an unfailing enthusiasm in the development of the vast mineral and timber resources of the north, and the development of that district generally, his work in this respect is worthy of commendation."[35] In the northeastern corridor and perhaps in the mind of George Lee, no other respect mattered much.

Notes

1. Preston to Lee, 6 January 1927, ONA, B-8203. "25th Anniversary."
2. A good sense of the proceedings and activities as well as the surrounding correspondence can be obtained from ONA, B-8203, "25th Anniversary."
3. Clara Seguin. Interview. 16 December 1987. North Bay.

4. Kathleen Houghton. Interview. 9 February 1989. North Bay.
5. For an extended account of these see Michael Barnes, *Killer in the Bush*, Toronto: Boston Mills Press, 1987.
6. Bill Ross. Interview on file at ONA. Also cited in Tucker, *Steam into Wilderness*, p. 79.
7. Cobalt *Nugget*, 12 June 1920.
8. *AR*, 1930, p. 6.
9. Toronto *Globe*, 17 November 1931.
10. Lee to Henry, 18 November 1931. AO, RG3, Henry papers, Vol. 147.
11. *AR*, 1931, pp. 5–6.
12. *Minutes*, 14 June 1932.
13. *Minutes*, 17 August 1931.
14. *Minutes*, 10 March 1931.
15. *Minutes*, 2 November 1931.
16. *Minutes*, 27 August 1931.
17. *Minutes*, 21 April 1931.
18. *Minutes*, 12 August 1932.
19. *Minutes*, 14 June 1932.
20. *AR*, 1931, p. 6.
21. *Minutes*, 26 May 1932.
22. North Bay *Nugget*, 15 July 1932.
23. *AR*, 1933, p. 16.
24. Glenn Ruttan. Interview. 10 December 1986, King Kirkland.
25. Russell to McGuire, Private. 16 July 1934. AO, RG3, Hepburn Papers, Vol. 231.
26. *Temiskaming and Northern Ontario Railway Inquiry: Report of Armand Racine*. Toronto: King's Printer, 1935 (Racine Report), pp. 10–12; See also pp. 171–172.
27. *Ibid.*, p. 16.
28. *Ibid.*, recommendations 2 and 3.
29. Lee actually confided this to his successor, A.H. Cavanagh. Bob Lee. Interview. 17 July 1991. North Bay.
30. *Minutes*, 1934.
31. Clement to Racine, 19 September 1934. ONA. Volume of statements, etc. re Racine Enquiry, Aug. 14–Sept. 13, 1934.
32. Ralph Brill. Interview. North Bay, 20 June 1991.
33. North Bay *Nugget*, 5 September 1934.
34. Porcupine *Advance*, 23 September 1934.
35. Racine Report, p. 14. 25 July 1991.

Chapter 12

Changes, Consolidation, and Expansion

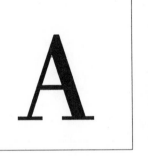

LTHOUGH POLITICALLY MOTIVATED in its creation, methods, and recommendations, the Racine Commission revealed two significant features of the T&NO Commission and its operations. The first was that it had been remarkably clean. Corruption could not be found. At most, a few of the senior personnel had on occasion received a gift of a turkey or some other small token. According to George Lee's son, the opportunities for various bribes, kickbacks, and other pay-offs had been present. He recalled his father showing him such opportunities and stressing that it would be improper to accept them, and he never did.[1] He also recalled that his father consistently emphasized that his appointment as General Manager and as Chairman had come from the Farmers' party administration. Indeed, from that point on Lee, who had been considered in 1909 as among the most active Conservatives in North Bay,[2] had largely eschewed formal political connections. He actually advised his six children against close involvement with any party.[3]

Second, the overall conduct of the railway, it seems, had been quite efficient. No one denied that the line beyond Fraserdale had been an error, and even the run into Elk Lake was considered by most T&NO officials to have been a financial miscalculation. The rest of the operations, however, were deemed to be efficient and effectively operated.

Yet it was also clear that considerable power had been vested in a single individual, regardless of the discretion with which that person exercised it. Premier Hepburn's decision to separate the two posts of chairman and general manager was logical, even if his treatment of Lee himself was unduly harsh. The Premier's immediate appointment of new commissioners could easily be defended, even commended, on the grounds of administrative responsibility and control. His appointment of himself as the new chairman was a temporary measure and received no real criticism. Nor did his appointment of Arthur Slaght, a Toronto lawyer and for a time the counsel for the Commission, and Racine, receive any criticism because it was expected that Liberals would move into those positions. The selections of C.V. Gallagher, a longstanding resident of South Porcupine and formerly the reeve of Tisdale Township, and Malcolm "Mac" Lang, formerly MLA and then MP for Temiskaming, were actually applauded in the North; both were north-erners with strong connections there, and few objected to their Liberal associations.

Hepburn's selection for the general manager's post also met general approval. There was considerable lobbying for that job on behalf of several men who were clearly competent as well as unmistakeably Liberal: M.S. Campbell, a labour conciliation lawyer from Ottawa; Latham Burns, a professional engineer from Toronto; Earl Hutchison, who could expect some reward for surrendering his Kenora seat to permit the election of Peter Heenan, whom Hepburn wanted in his cabinet; and W.G. Bullbrook, the mayor of North Bay.[4] Hepburn chose none of them but turned instead to A.H. Cavanagh, a rising star in the CNR's administrative ranks. At age 18 he had started on the T&NO in 1905, later moved to the Canadian Northern Railway, and to the CNR when that organization absorbed the Canadian Northern. He had held several posts, including his current appointment as Superintendent at Allandale, and at age 47 was due for appointment to the post of General Superintendent of North Bay.[5] Hepburn personally contacted the President of CNR, S.J. Hungerford, who agreed to grant Cavanagh a four-year leave of absence. Cavanagh then accepted Hepburn's offer.

Before doing so, however, he had apparently tested the opinion of his predecessor. Railway circles are tight and so are social connections in a small town. George Lee, according to his son, advised Cavanagh that there was no possibility of him retaining his post, and that if Cavanagh did not accept it, someone else definitely would.[6] With this assurance, Cavanagh felt comfortable in replacing George Lee. According to an interview that he gave some 40 years later, he insisted that no one else be removed.

> I told Mr. Hepburn that if...these men [Maund, Freeman, Clement et al.] were to be dismissed and replaced by men without experience or qualifications for railway work, then I wasn't prepared to take his job. He had the wrong man. But if he wanted it run strictly as a railroad, by railwaymen, I would take the position. But there would be nobody dismissed because of his political views... He took my advice and kept me on and there was nobody dismissed...[7]

This may have been the reason why Racine could not find a seconder for his motion of 10 December.

There followed the expected resignation of Hepburn as chairman, in favour of Malcolm "Mac" Lang, with Gallagher as vice-chairman. This surprised no one, but Hepburn's next move probably did. Early in 1935 he tendered his own resignation from the Commission, forced those of Slaght, Racine, and Gallagher, and through an order-in-council altered the original T&NO legislation to permit the Commission to consist of one or more persons rather than three to five. With that done, Lang became a one-man Commission, assisted by the general manager. He possessed, arguably, even more unchecked authority than Hepburn had condemned when it had been held by George Lee. Two other commissioners had served with Lee; Lang sat alone. An even further concentration of power was to come five years later.

Lang and Cavanagh found they could not work together, although they certainly tried. They were in agreement, for example, regarding the company pension plan. It began in 1922 with a $5000 contribution from the railway, and each year after that the company made a further donation of $1000. The fund, therefore, had not grown very much, and the pensions derived from it were consequently very small. Although the initiative came from the general manager, both Lang and Cavanagh agreed that an updating of the system, to include employee contributions, was in order. In 1938 they made the first move in that direction by recommending a contributory plan to the Premier, and a revised plan went into effect on 1 May 1939. It would remain a point of controversy for 20 years, as the railway and the various unions attempted to find a plan that would provide for present and future employees and at the same time include a catch-up provision for those who entered the plan rather late in their T&NO careers.[8]

Float for parade at Swastika   The sign reads "The home of the first baby born north of Cobalt, the Gateway to the Great Northern Gold Belt." When the T&NO renamed that station "Winston" during WWII, townspeople resisted the change, for their town pre-dated Hitler. (ONA-1988916 J. Fitzmaurice)

In general, Cavanagh concentrated his considerable talent and energy on operating the railway services. It was not an easy time to manage a line profitably, because the Depression would continue, with some minor periods of partial recovery, until the Second World War forced the Canadian governments into a spending spree. Yet the new general manager received solid grades from most observers, then and since, although he too had his critics. One was W.H. Price, the Conservative MLA for Toronto-Parkdale, who charged him with trying to close the Rouyn station and turn over the business to the CNR.[9] Cavanagh responded by observing that he had done no such thing and that the CNR had simply improved its service there and was thus reaping some benefits. The city of North Bay also protested against the decision to move some 15 jobs, including that of Superintendent, to Englehart.[10] Cavanagh responded to this by explaining that "with practically the entire operating and management staff located at North Bay, it resulted in a top heavy organization at one extreme end of the line." The decision to move the Superintendent's Of-

fice to Englehart, he said, was taken "to provide for a better distribution of supervision."[11]

One person who applauded the railway in general was the commanding officer of the prisoner of war camp that was established at Montieth during the Second World War. Prisoners would arrive in small groups, usually on a Sunday when traffic was light, and of course they had to be fed. One woman who had that task observed that they were normal-looking fellows, and added with a smile that she and the other women who fed them would laugh at their inclination to stand on tip toes to look over the counters at the women's legs.[12] The commanding officer was more interested in knowing in advance of the arrival of POWs, but this information was not always sent. In April 1942, for example, he observed that the T&NO would supply information to the camps about incoming POWs, information which the military had not yet supplied. He resented this, but on 16 April 1942, wrote in the camp diary words that would have made Cavanagh proud:

We are now advised by the T&NO again— good old T&NO! If it weren't for them we wouldn't know much about our prisoners' movements!—that the number will be 68 and that they will be two days or more later than the 18th. Camp leaders have been instructed to prepare for 68 or more —much to their consternation.[13]

Rail services was the natural venue for Cavanagh. His entire career had been spent in railway work and railway management, and he clearly took pride in doing it well. There was good reason for many retired T&NO men to pay him the ultimate compliment: "He was a railroader!"[14]

Lang, for his part, looked beyond the railway and as chairman sought to enhance the T&NO presence in the North. In this he was adhering to the unwritten but often expressed view that the Commission should promote development in the North and generally pursue goals and activities that would benefit the region. It actually could have been a good arrangement, but the two men neglected to cordon off the limits to their respec-

tive spheres of influence. When the two fields of responsibility met, Lang and Cavanagh could easily clash, because their ideas and their methods did not mesh. Two instances will illustrate: the role of buses and discipline.

In 1935 the T&NO changed its main-line passenger scheduling and directed its through-line traffic from Cochrane to Timmins. It was a logical move, because the two towns had travelled in opposite directions in recent years. The decline in the timber industry had reduced the status of Cochrane, while Timmins had continued to develop and grow because the gold market remained strong even during the Depression. Henceforth, then, passenger trains travelled directly from North Bay to Timmins, switching off the main line at Porquis Junction. In reporting this to the Premier, Lang noted that the change served the larger population of Timmins "with the main line train." Through arrangements with the CNR, he declared proudly, the over-night train would leave Toronto later than before (11:00 instead of 9:30 p.m.) thereby giving northerners the "advantage of [a] full evening in Toronto to attend theatres, hockey games, etc."[15] Local service continued to Cochrane and thence to Moosonee, but the new schedule turned Timmins into the principal northern terminus.

Two years later, following protests from Cochrane calling for a re-instatement of the former train schedule, connections between Porquis and Cochrane were supplemented by a bus schedule. In this the chairman concurred with the general manager, because it made sense both socially and commercially. Such a bus service became possible in 1937–38. In response to requests from miners in the Porcupine and Larder Lake areas for better local train scheduling which would permit them to get to and from work more easily, the T&NO chose to use buses rather than alter the train schedule. The provincial government supported this and much more by passing the necessary amendments to the railway's legislation, permitting it to acquire and operate not only buses but also coaches, trucks, and airplanes throughout the province.[16]

A.H. Cavanagh   "He was a railroader."

Lang and Cavanagh held varying views regarding these extensive new mandates. For the general manager, the bus line should be used merely to supplement the railway in such runs as the commuter service for miners (e.g., between Timmins and Pamour) or the connecting link for train passengers between Porquis and Cochrane. The Chairman viewed the extended authorities as completely new endeavours. The matter reached conflict proportions when Lang determined to extend the T&NO service beyond its short runs to the east of Kirkland Lake (e.g., between Larder Lake and the nearby mines) and add a special run between Swastika and Kirkland Lake, where the local McLellan Bus Line had been operating since 1923. This was a significant step beyond the ancillary role that Cavanagh saw for the bus service, and he opposed it. The McLellan firm also protested, through legal counsel, to the Premier. They argued that they had worked hard to build up their business, that there was insufficient business for two bus lines, and that it was unfair for a government body to compete in this fashion.[17] McLellan's position received support from people and businesses in the town. This reached sufficient proportion for a concerned Liberal party member, upon visiting a friend in Kirkland Lake, to warn the Premier of the situation.

> ...well informed people here tell me that there is a great deal of indignation and that a number of merchants and mine operators are cancelling their freight, and trucking their supplies into Kirkland Lake and Swastika in an attempt to boycott the T.&N.O. Naturally I realize that in the long run they will come back to the railway, but what worries me is that it is not the T.&N.O. or Mac Lang but the Government who are blamed by everybody. For this reason I felt that I should bring the matter to your attention. It could be very easily straightened out without cold bloodedly putting the McLellan Company out of business.[18]

But Lang persevered. T&NO bus service began in 1938. It was less than a success and closed in 1940 after Lang left office. The concept and the authority of the 1937–38 legisla-

tion and order-in-council remained in place regarding the additional means of transport, however, and would be picked up later.

The issue which brought things to a head, however, came in 1939. Over Cavanagh's protests, Lang chose to re-hire a brakeman who had been dismissed for violation of Rule G, which concerned the use of liquor. By doing so, Lang made a serious challenge to the General Manager's authority, because a violation of the non-drinking regulation was extremely serious. Even so, it was something Cavanagh could accept since the individual had been out of the service for eight months and had re-entered as a new employee. Then the brakeman involved attempted to have his full seniority re-instated as well. It became a special cause for Charles Beattie of the Canadian Association of Railway Employees, who wanted to establish his organization in the T&NO. The other unions did not support him, but they did use the issue to seek some reduction of Cavanagh's authority. Cavanagh's stance in the liquor case was unassailable, but between the two men, there was a general preference for Lang who was more flexible. Union spokesmen, therefore, wrote to Hepburn in favour of the chairman; so did the three northern members of the provincial legislature, who indicated to Hepburn their belief that the General Manager was "inclined to be arbitrary."[19] Cavanagh felt his position untenable. In March 1940 Hepburn had to make a choice between the two men. He decided to retain the services of the experienced railway administrator and dispense with those of the chairman. Lang's resignation was requested and received, though with considerable bitterness.

It may well have been, as Albert Tucker suggests in *Steam into Wilderness*,[20] that Hepburn's choice resulted from internal divisions in the Liberal party caused by his quarrel with Prime Minister Mackenzie King. Lang was perceived as belonging to the King wing of the party, as were the sitting Liberals in the North, and this may have caused Hepburn to turn on Lang. Or the cause may have been more personal. Hepburn's health by this time had depreciated greatly, and he may simply have grown weary of northern

201

An early T&NO bus, at Pamour, 1938 (ONA-5135312)

affairs. This has been a common malady among southern politicians. Even so, it is difficult to explain his next action, although it was certainly dramatic. Having forced out Lang, Hepburn replaced him with Cavanagh! Thus, Cavanagh became both General Manager and the Commission, with no potential opposition or check to his decisions. Theoretically, he even had to negotiate with himself regarding his salary, his duties, and his expenses! This situation continued until 1944.

In the meantime, Hepburn suddenly resigned as Premier in 1942 and was replaced by Gordon Conant, who was replaced the following year at a convention which chose Harry Nixon. The badly divided Liberal party finished a distant third with 15 seats in the 1943 provincial election behind George Drew's Conservatives (38 seats) and the Co-operative Commonwealth Federation (CCF), which took 34 seats. After a year of assessing conditions throughout the province, Drew chose to re-establish the T&NO Commission.

Ironically, with the change of government, Cavanagh, concerned about his position, sought

the advice and assistance of George Lee.[21] So did Premier Drew, but for a different purpose: he wished to have Lee's opinions with respect to reorganizing the Commission. Finally, in 1944 he announced the new arrangement without consulting his commission/general manager. Indeed, Cavanagh actually learned of the news on the radio. His own position as general manager was confirmed by letter a few days later, but he no longer sat on the Commission. Rather, two northerners—Robert Potter of Matheson and Reginald Aubert of Englehart—would be led by a new Chairman, Colonel C.E. Reynolds.[22] Reynolds came originally from Sault Ste. Marie. He had engaged in various business operations with moderate success. He was active, however, in the Canadian Corps Association where he had met George Drew and it was this connection that pulled him into the T&NO.

Drew had good cause for making the change. The extensive concentration of authority in one man was sufficient by itself. As Drew pointed out in a letter to Cavanagh on 21 August 1944, the original legislation had provided for a "commission distinct from management."[23] There were other reasons as well. Complaints from the unions regarding the general manager's attitude had continued. A petition of 4 October 1943, from Gowganda Lodge No. 815 of the Brotherhood of Railroad Trainmen urged that the new premier "at his earliest possible convenience discontinue this Totalitarian form of Administration now in effect on the T&NO Ry and establish a form of Administration more in keeping with our Democratic way of life."[24] This declaration was something of an overstatement and was actually designed, as were other petitions at the same time, to make the case for including union representation on the Commission; yet it was also a further indication of hostility between the general manager and labour. Whether or not Cavanagh had been heavy-handed in his treatment of employees, such complaints from an area of the country that had voted solidly for the CCF Party probably had an effect on the new premier. Drew had fences to mend with organized labour. There was an administrative reason also. The effect of placing Cavanagh alone at the top of the T&NO was proving to be that the Premier's Office was the only channel for opposition or even discussion regarding his actions. This had become apparent over the previous two years.

In 1942, Cavanagh had indicated his intention of closing the Elk Lake branch of the railway and had further proposed cutting the service on the Moosonee branch from Moose River Crossing to Moosonee, a stretch of 44.3 miles.[25] Premier Hepburn agreed to the Elk Lake closure,[26] but public protest and disapproving press coverage had delayed it. Similar protest arose regarding the Moosonee branch. There, it was supported by a letter from the Minister of National Defence who urged that wartime exigencies called for keeping the line open,[27] and another from the manager of the James Bay District of the Hudson's Bay Company, who explained that such closure would seriously affect his company.[28] That line also stayed open. The closures would have made economic sense, because both sectors were los-

ing money, and Cavanagh had a mandate to run an effective and efficient operation. He sought to do so, but in this he completely misunderstood the position of the T&NO in the North. One could not tamper with it too much. Cavanagh was indeed a railroader, but the T&NO had to be more. It always had been.

In announcing the restoration of the Commission and Cavanagh's exclusion from it, the Premier acknowledged the longstanding view of the Commission by northerners.

> The Temiskaming and Northern Ontario Railway is much more than a successful railway. It is intended as a basis of development in the north. The powers of the commission are very wide and it is the hope of the government that the commission will make recommendations for the opening of new territory and the extension of operations of the railway which will produce greatly increased opportunities for new population throughout the whole of the area with which it is connected.[29]

It is also likely that Drew saw the T&NO as a means to promote, through patronage at least, the Conservative party in the North where he had, as yet, no sitting members. Certainly the selection of the new chairman resulted from patronage and friendship, although the Premier insisted that the new full-time chairman had "wide experience in Northern Ontario."[30] The new chairman took Drew's words very much to heart. His enthusiasm for new projects and related enterprises was prodigious. He was bound to conflict with the strong-minded and dedicated railroader, A.H. Cavanagh. It came less than 18 months later. Before that happened, however, the two men managed to collaborate on three issues of significance: the Onakawana lignite dream, the conversion of motive power to diesel, and a change in the corporate name.

The lignite deposits at Onakawana had been a topic of speculation and hope since they were first reported early in the century. If some way were found to harness this fuel resource, it would provide a justification for the Moosonee extension, it would bring prosperity to Cochrane, it would save the T&NO much money in fuel costs, it would reduce the dependency of all northern railroads on foreign coal, and it would bring much applause to the government that found the solution. The Hepburn administration sought to exploit the deposits but was disappointed when a 1933 report outlined the problems. It would be necessary to process the lignite to remove its excessive moisture and to customize the boilers and fuel boxes of the steam engines in order to burn it. Another report in 1938 was more optimistic and suggested that within five years a million tons of coal could be available from Onakawana.[31] With the coming of the war, interest increased and the Hepburn government conducted further tests, including a trial run with a modified engine and a specially treated portion of lignite. Hepburn himself visited the Onakawana fields and announced a further quarter-million-dollar programme to extract the coal. Despite the expenditures, which continued for a time after the change of government, and despite the hopes of virtually everyone involved, in 1946 the new Minister of Lands and Forests, Leslie Frost, announced that the development of the lignite deposit at Onakawana was economically unsound. Even if the process of reclamation were successful, the price of the fuel would be about $24–$28 a ton, at a time when imported coal cost $8.[32] The time had not yet come for Onakawana.

Neither Reynolds nor Cavanagh complained of Frost's decision. Both of them, however, were aware that the railway faced severe new challenges as it entered the post-war era. For 15 years the Depression and the Second World War had retarded the progress of highway development. The former had been a period when capital funding simply was not available; then the war had directed capital into armaments and concurrently, through rationing of gasoline, had greatly restricted highway travel. That ended in 1945. To meet the challenges from the new mediums, the T&NO had to find ways to increase its business and to reduce costs.

A solution to the latter appeared in the form of the diesel engine. The advantages of the new technology—the first major innovation, along with automatic block signals, since the Mikado engine,[33]—appeared prodigious to railway managers. The new engines were cleaner, used cheaper fuel, needed less maintenance,

Map 15. *T&NO stations, 1944*   A crowded line!

204

The last steam run, 24, 25 June 1957   At South Porcupine (ONA-19882615)

Crew for the last run on steam
(Left to right) Conductor Charles Spence,
Fireman Cliff Shubert, Engineer Tom
Muldoon, Trainmen Ed Kenny and
Horace Aubry. (ONA-1988266)

and required less manpower. Conversion to diesel motive power would require expenditures for new engines, for track alterations such as longer sidings, and for new repair shops, but the financial benefits would greatly outweigh these. The men who worked the line, who feared the supersession of old skills and the loss of jobs, were less enthusiastic;[34] the issue led to a national rail strike in 1951. Yet the change came, and the T&NO had completely dieselized within a decade, among the first railways in the country to do so. Engineman Tom Muldoon, who had joined the T&NO in 1911 and had been the first to drive Engine No. 701, took that same engine on the last steam run on 24, 25 June 1957.

By then, however, it was called Ontario Northland. Cavanagh had sought a name change since 1942, when he wrote to Premier Conant to advise him of the difficulties which the T&NO was experiencing with another line with the same initials: the Texas and New Orleans Railway.[35] This observation normally causes a smile on the face of the listener, but the matter was not one to laugh at. The cost of car hire in that period was very small.[36] Thus, it was to a line's advantage to retain and use another's rolling stock. According to Evelyn Chivers, a former office worker who recalled the controversy, it was a matter of some consequence.

> ♄ They'd [the Texas line] confiscate all the boxcars...they kept every boxcar that went into the states... In those four years [1942–1946] they [T&NO] tried to get their boxcars back, but they weren't being successful. [The initials were the same] but the name "Temiskaming" was on the boxcar, and yet Texas would take it...[37] ♞

Several years passed without action, although it continued to be a priority for the general manager. He experienced some opposition from Colonel G.G. Blackstock, Deputy to the Premier, who expressed the view that such a change would irritate those who had grown fond of the old name and confuse other lines who would not relate to

the new one. It would also cause some awkwardness regarding the use of old stationary, the painting of the new name on rolling stock, and the need for legislation.[38] One gets the impression that Blackstock simply did not want to be bothered. Cavanagh persisted, however, and added that a new name would describe more accurately the Commission's range of activities. This apparently won him the requisite support, including that of the chairman. The Drew government passed the appropriate legislation and the new name became effective on 9 April 1946. The change by and large was received either with approval or with some nostalgic regrets, but the general consensus was that the new name better reflected the nature of the enterprise and furthermore that the confusion with the American line had made it necessary in any event.[39]

Alterations in the corporate structure and in the nature of the public persona of the government enterprise followed the change of name. They were preceded by the departure of Cavanagh. In many ways this was inevitable. His position was similar to that of George Lee in 1934. He had been selected by the previous government whose premier had wielded harsh personal attacks on the new premier, he had acquired enormous power, and, although he had eschewed political involvement, he was still identified with the old order. He also quarrelled with Reynolds, who had the ear of the Premier. Like Lee, he would have to go, although Drew did not shout it to the press. Rather, after a private meeting with the Provincial Secretary, Roland Michener (later, Canada's Governor-General) and the Minister of Tourism, G.A. Welsh, Cavanagh tendered his resignation.[40] He did not go willingly, but he went. He was replaced by Archie Freeman, who had narrowly escaped dismissal in 1934, who had served as Cavanagh's assistant since 1944, and who was described as being a "supporter of this government."[41] It was also remarked that the appointment of Freeman, who had started in the days of Jake Englehart as a clerk and rose to the company's top post, had "made quite an impression" on the railway's staff. "With diligence and industry"[42] any one of them could also rise to the top. In fact, Lee had already done so, and subsequently appointments to the general manager's post have all been made from within the company: Alvin Jardine, E.A. Frith, R.O. (Bob) Beattie, F.S. (Stu) Clifford, Peter Dyment.

Other organizational changes followed. Perhaps the most significant concerned the role of Colonel Reynolds, who had, since becoming Chairman of the Commission, reported directly to the Premier. Drew altered that, first by interposing the Provincial Secretary as the conduit which would relay Reynold's reports to the Cabinet and then by adding a cabinet minister, G.A. Welsh, to the Commission as Vice-Chairman. Over time and with the retirement of Reynolds in 1962, the connection between the Commission and the government of the day evolved to its present form. The Commission reports through its chairman to the Minister of Northern Affairs. The management group, headed by the president and CEO (the title was changed from general manager in 1990), reports to the chairman and the Commission. Partisan politics has likewise declined since the peak reached in 1934. The Peterson government, admittedly, replaced the existing Commission when it secured office, but only when those sitting had completed their terms. Indeed the Chairman, J.W. Spooner from Timmins, a former Conservative cabinet minister, was offered, and accepted, an extension of his term at that post. The Rae government, which displaced that of David Peterson in 1990, has continued this trend. As terms expired, three sitting members have been replaced on the current Commission. It has also become firmly established, 90 years after the first Commission met in Toronto, that all commissioners shall represent the North.

Concurrent with these management alterations were changes in Ontario Northland's public persona. The name change was the most obvious. It had been observed that the new name would reflect more accurately the corporation's actual activities which had grown and changed. Certainly the term "Temiskaming" in the name had been anachronistic ever since the line had extended far beyond its original goal of reaching out

to the two small Lake Timiskaming hamlets of New Liskeard and Haileybury. Yet the new name really reflected not simply what the company was doing but also what its new chairman intended that it would do. He set forth these intentions in a long memorandum to his friend, Premier Drew, on 18 August 1945.[43]

The war in the Pacific had ended only a week earlier, but many had already begun to think in terms of adjusting the country to peacetime conditions. Colonel Reynolds certainly felt that Northern Ontario and its government railway could and should figure largely in the creation of the new order. The richness of the region, which Reynolds had discovered in the year since his appointment, in mineral, forest and hydro wealth as well as its agricultural potential, made it a major player in any government post-war plans. It also possessed, he noted, a railway, a system of highways, and strategically located settlements. Only an "influx of settlers was needed to assure their permanency." He added a further dimension by observing that the recreational aspects of life in the North should be exploited. "To put it crudely," he wrote, "the chance to barter good air and sunshine for American dollars...is given to us and should not be missed."

In addressing his thoughts to the Premier, Reynolds claimed to be suggesting short-term projects to provide early returns in the form of employment, and long-term undertakings to assist the present population, expand it, and lay the groundwork of prosperity for the future. His suggestions included recommendations regarding highways, agriculture, forestry, hunting, fisheries, and tourism. In doing so, he touched on features that crossed several government departments, but being "one on the ground and directly responsible to yourself," he felt a right, even an obligation, to do so; the responsibilities of the several departments were "so intimately connected with questions which fall within my special province..." This long dispatch setting forth the enthusiasms of C.E. Reynolds may well have been the impetus that pushed Drew into distancing himself from the Chairman by

Cartoon   From 1946 to 1966 Ontario Northland had an internal publication, *The Quarterly*. This cartoon, submitted by Russ Huntington, was rejected as "too suggestive." Currently the *Chevron* also appears quarterly. (Jack Huntington, North Bay)

Ontario Northland boat lines, Temagami, 1953 (ONA-51B)

the insertion of the Provincial Secretary and, later, a cabinet minister.

For the railway itself, Reynolds suggested several projects. One was track relocation and improvement for the first 32 miles out of North Bay and some smaller sections as well, which would reduce wear on track, engines, and rolling stock and concurrently provide immediate employment opportunities during the post-war transition. Improved passenger service was also a priority, since such travel, he felt, could be expected to grow with the wartime restrictions removed. Also needed was new rolling stock, none having been acquired since the war began. He did not mention it, but some heavy maintenance of way work was also needed. The war years, with the reduced manpower available, had seen this task kept to a minimum, especially on the Moosonee subdivision. He also called for the addition of a sanitary department and a first aid officer.

His memorandum proposed extended highway services, including the acquisition of a bus run between Cochrane and Hearst, where the CNR had permitted its rail passenger service to lag badly, as well as another run between North Bay and Ottawa, currently owned but not operated by Colonial Coach lines. As roads were upgraded or built in the North, such as the proposed highway from Timmins to Sudbury, the bus service on them should be reserved to the Commission.

The Commission had acted wisely, he felt, when it had in 1944 secured the assets of the Temagami Navigation Company, which had evidently been unable to serve "the rapidly developing tourist business at Temagami." In taking this first step into marine services, the Commission clearly intended to "barter good air and sunshine for American dollars" and tourist spending in general. At the time of writing, Reynolds observed, the docks in Temagami had been rebuilt completely and new buildings were close to completion. These included a general office building with a restaurant and observation gallery on the second floor, as well as warehouses, an icehouse, and a motor repair shop.

The Commission had already purchased four passenger motor boats and a light landing craft, but more service items would be required, because there was a "crying need...for additional hotel and cabin accommodation on the lake." Likewise, after also acquiring the assets of the Nipissing Navigation Company, the Commission had ordered a 100-foot, steel-hulled, diesel-powered craft for service on Lake Nipissing "with a view to developing the magnificent tourist country at the headwaters of the French River." This was the *Chief Commanda*. Jack Huntington, whose father, Russell Huntington, was an engineering draftsman with the T&NO, related how it was named.

> When they were going to buy the original *Chief Commanda*, apparently they sent up the engineering plans of the boat, and from those...my father was asked to make a painting of an actual boat, to see what it would actually look like, because the plans did not give any idea... So he did... I remember the picture very clearly...he painted it travelling through the water on Lake Nipissing from those engineering plans... When he got it finished, he said, "It looks too bare. We should have a name on it"...and he put on the name *Chief Commanda*... When he brought the painting back down and [Cavanagh and Reynolds] saw it, they were so taken with the name...that my father in essence indirectly named the boat... I can remember him saying...that he liked the name Commanda, which is a township just out here between Sturgeon Falls and North Bay.[44]

In naming its new passenger vessel on Lake Temagami, the Commission was more systematic. It was called the *Aubrey Cosens* to commemorate a former T&NO employee whose bravery during the war had been recognized by the awarding of a Victoria Cross, the highest military honour in the British Empire. Regrettably, the award had to be made posthumously.

Launch of the first Chief Commanda of Callander, 20 August 1946 (ONA-1988072)

On both of these two great lakes the Commission led the way in promoting both tourism and summer cottaging and camping, because their vessels provided access to the more remote sections. On Lake Temagami, fairly deep and narrow and heavily spotted with islands, people found that they could obtain their own access using small boats and even canoes, and, in time, Ontario Northland, having "jump-started" the region's summer economy, backed out of marine service there. Lake Nipissing, a rather shallow lake with a broad expanse of open water, remained too treacherous for the transport of extensive supplies by small craft for a longer period. In the '40s and '50s, therefore, the *Chief* provided the basic means by which the cottage and resort sector of the French River was opened up and developed, as its parent, the T&NO, had done on a grander scale for the North in general. Even the advent of greater numbers of larger, privately owned boats did not supplant it. In 1975 the Commission launched a much improved and more stable craft, the *Chief Commanda II*, for the Lake Nipissing marine service.

In seeking to "barter good air and sunshine for American dollars," Reynolds planned to pull tourists well into the North.

> As tourists are attracted to Moosonee where accommodation next season will be ready for them, motor boats will be acquired. These will be of two types—those suitable for the estuary to the mouth of the Moose River and a more stable type for the navigation of James Bay. The sea trout and blue geese, as well as the historic and scenic coast of the area are bound to have strong tourist attraction.[45]

It is likely that the colonel regretted the decision of the Hepburn government 10 years earlier to sell the James Bay Inn which the Commission had built at considerable cost.

Notes

1. Bob Lee, Interview. 17 July 1991. North Bay.
2. Anson Garde, *Gateway to Silverland*. Toronto: Emerson Press, 1909, p. 11.
3. Bob Lee, Interview. 17 July 1991. North Bay.
4. Tucker, *Steam into Wilderness*, pp. 119–20.
5. *Ibid.*, p. 120.

6. Bob Lee, Interview. 17 July 1991. North Bay.

7. A.H. Cavanagh, Interview. May 1974. North Bay. Quoted in Tucker, *Steam into Wilderness*, p. 124.

8. *Ibid.*, pp. 169–75.

9. Comments of W.H. Price, Ottawa *Journal.* 5 April 1935.

10. H.C. Pilkey, City Clerk, to Hepburn. Telegram. 2 October 1935. AO, RG3, Hepburn Papers, Box 193.

11. Cavanagh to Pilley, 3 October 1935. AO, RG3, Hepburn Papers, Box 193.

12. Mrs. Laila Nicholson, Interview. 8 December 1986. Timmins.

13. Secret War Diary of Canadian Provost Corps, (CA) A., Headquarters Staff, Internment Camp "Q" (No. 23) M.D.2 Monteith, Ontario, NAC, RG24, C17, Vols. 15, 329, Folder 1.

14. C.L. Bailey, Interview. 30 September 1988. North Bay.

15. Lang to Hepburn, 19 February 1935. AO, RG3, Hepburn Papers, Box 250.

16. Application for Incorporation...Northern Canada Transportation. 18 May 1937. AO, RG4, series 4-02 File 12, Box 12. 1938; Conant to Magone, 10 February 1938. AO, RG4, Series 4-02. File 12, Box 12. 1938. See also Memorandum to Hepburn by J.P. Bickell, 30 March 1936. AO, RG3, Hepburn Papers, Box 263.

17. M.G. Hunt to Hepburn, 12 October 1938. AO, RG3, Hepburn Papers, Box 295.

18. Bethune Smith to Hepburn. Private. 1 August 1938. AO, RG3, Hepburn Papers. Box 285.

19. Tucker, *Steam into Wilderness*, p. 146.

20. *Ibid.*, p. 141.

21. Bob Lee, Interview. 17 July 1991. North Bay.

22. North Bay *Nugget*, 16 August 1944.

23. Drew to Cavanagh, 21 August 1944. AO, RG3, Drew Papers, Box 451.

24. Petition of the Brotherhood of Railway Trainmen No. 815, 4 October 1943. AO, RG3, Drew Papers, Box 451.

25. A.A. Casselman and E. McLaren to Drew, 8 October 1943. AO, RG3, Drew Papers, Box 451.

26. Memorandum, Reynolds to Drew, 2 February 1948. AO, RG3, Drew Papers, Box 451. This long memo (14 pages) summarizes the correspondence regarding the intended closure of the two sections of the railway.

27. *Ibid.*

28. *Ibid.*

29. North Bay *Nugget*, 16 August 1944.

30. *Ibid.*

31. Tucker, *Steam into Wilderness*, p. 138.

32. Frost to Harold Wills, 31 May 1946. AO, RG3, Drew Papers, Box 450.

33. The T&NO purchased several Mikado engines in the 1920s. See Frank N. Vollhardt, *The Locomotives of the Ontario Northland Railway.* Calgary: The Calgary Group of British Railway Modelers of North America, 1985, pp. 6–9.

34. See pp. 307–309 of this text.

35. Cavanagh to Conant, 2 February 1943, AO, RG3, Drew Papers, Box 451.

36. See p. 254 of this text.

37. Evelyn Chivers, Interview. 15 June 1991. North Bay.

38. Blackstock to Reynolds, 23 July 1945. AO, RG3, Drew Papers, Box 451.

39. North Bay *Nugget*, 26, 27 March 1946.

40. Tucker, *Steam into Wilderness*, pp. 165–66.

41. Young to Drew, 28 March 1947. AO, RG3, Drew Papers, Box 451.

42. *Ibid.*

43. Reynolds to Drew, 18 August 1945. AO, RG3, Drew Papers, Box 451.

44. Jack Huntington, Interview. 17 May 1986. North Bay.

45. Reynolds to Drew, 18 August 1945. AO, RG3, Drew Papers, Box 451.

Chapter 13

Old Trends and New Directions

HE VARIETY OF the Chairman's ambitions recalled the T&NO's past. Ancillary and auxiliary tasks, great and small, had formed part of the Commission's duties almost from the beginning. Several have been noted already. There were others. Mining Engineer Cole, for example, supervised a mineral testing laboratory in Haileybury, George Lee for years promoted northern agriculture, the Commission had built the road into Larder Lake from Dane in 1906, and that same year the Commission determined to add lunch-counter facilities to the Temagami station as an assistance to tourists. In fact, the decision to include Lake Temagami on the original line had been made with tourism in mind. The Commission had a representative on the Northern Ontario Relief Committee that had been created to deal with the tragedies resulting from the horrible fires that swept through Matheson in 1916 and through the Haileybury area in 1922. Such activities had fallen by default to the T&NO. No other significant enterprise had existed to take them on.

A different tone, however, characterized the post-war years. Rather, Reynolds and the Commission, as Lang had done a decade before in a limited way, actually sought out opportunities and on occasion had to challenge for that right in the face of contending rivals. When the Commission obtained the right to acquire trucks, buses, boats, and airplanes, it was by no means the only participant in any of those commercial activities. In 1945, upon learning that Austin Airways of Nicholson, Ontario, had applied for a license to operate in Northern Ontario, including Moosonee, Reynolds wrote to the federal Air Transport Board to object to that license being exclusive.[1] The T&NO's plans for the North, he said, included air service, and he urged that Austin not obtain a monopoly in the field. As it turned out, Austin received a license but not a monopoly, but the Commission stayed out of the field for a quarter century. That the intent was present in 1945, however, is clear from a special memorandum published in pamphlet form by the Commission and titled *Airport Planning and Development*. It was intended to provide a basis for discussion of airport plans by "progressive communities who foresee the need of planning NOW for local air centres."[2]

The project did not proceed very far. Air travel will not develop much on its own. There must be concurrent ground links to the airports. In 1945 only the rail links of the T&NO connected the North. In an editorial titled "The Air Age Means Very Little to Us," the Timmins *Press* of 23 January 1946 observed that

Polar Bear Express at Moosonee Station, c. 1980 (ONA-SIPB)

the Polar Bear Express. At first the term was a pejorative one for the regular run along the Moosonee subdivision, one of the least desirable on the line. Yet there was always a romantic element to the run that carried one to the end of steel and close to the James Bay frontier. In creating a special excursion train to Moosonee during the summer months and calling it the Polar Bear Express, the Commission turned a liability into an asset and created one of the most frequently travelled tourist activities in the North.[3] The regular service, which runs only thrice weekly, came to be called the Little Bear. The Santa Claus Express of more recent years runs in the weeks just before Christmas and takes youngsters from several northern locations for a short ride of some 20 miles up the track to the "North Pole."

highway connections were scanty and that the trains were "notoriously unpunctual." Until such time as ground and air schedules could be co-ordinated, air travel would be of little value, socially or commercially. For Ontario Northland that time came in 1971 when norOntair became the air wing of the Commission. The plans for air travel did not develop in 1944–45, but the Commission had tested the waters and made its presence known in this field and in others. This condition has prevailed for almost half a century. Ontario Northland has continued to expand its range of activities, sometimes in the face of opposition, and occasionally because it continues to be a natural, if temporary, repository for the particular responsibility.

The Commission was able, for example, to enter the tourist and travel agency business in ways that others could not. Perhaps the most notable instance of this has been the marketing of

At the same time, the original enterprise, the railway itself, continued to function. Until the mid-1960s the Commission was reasonably successful in retaining its passenger traffic. After that, highway traffic tended to dominate. The line tried several counter-measures, but with limited success. One involved a separation of passenger and express traffic, both of which were under attack from highway competition.

ᘛ We took all the express off the passenger trains, because we wanted to speed up the passenger trains. Old 46 and 47, the old day train: it was handling two or three cars of express,...a couple of carloads of mail [and passengers], and it was stopping at New Liskeard, Uno Park, Thornloe, and Earlton to pick cans of milk to take into Korman's Dairy and items like that.[4] ᘚ

214

The express freight really slowed down the passenger service.

   ❧ That old train would come into Porquis...[with] two or three express cars, a mail car, and we'd have to transship it all. We'd take one mail car and put it on the little local to come to Cochrane—the [main] train went to Timmins. Then there's...you know those old wagons with the big wheels...they'd be *loaded* down with express. At Christmas it was nothing to be two to three hours at Porquis Junction transferring express from one train to the other.

   ... So [to speed up service] we started running in a short train, an *express* train, with just express. It was a *beautiful* damn train. It would leave Toronto—priority—only four to five cars—and be in Timmins the next morning... We put in a terminal manager at North Bay, New Liskeard, Timmins, and Cochrane just to look after all this freight. The concept was great!... But we found out it cost us more to run the train than the revenues we were getting for it.

   What we had in effect tried to do was take all the revenue from a passenger train and split that revenue. Half of the revenue was supposed to support another train and the revenue left behind was supposed to support the passenger train, and it didn't work. It did not work... The express train disappeared altogether. ❧

Since the express traffic ended up travelling by road, the ONR picked up some of it through its subsidiary truck lines—at the time, Star Transfer—and some of the passenger traffic no doubt also fell to the bus lines, but the consequences for the trains were serious. Highway 11, the old Ferguson Highway, had been considerably improved in the '50s. Not only was it paved throughout its length for the first time, it

was also straightened, and the steeper grades were reduced. By 1963 it also by-passed the communities—notably the Tri-towns—which had caused delays for automobile traffic. As northerners acquired more and more cars, they took to the highways increasingly. The railways suffered accordingly.

Fortune smiled on the ONR, temporarily at least, when substantial new mineral finds opened up three new and lucrative mines: Sherman (1955), Adams (1963), and Kidd Creek (1967). That the traffic from them could best be served by rail was good news for the ONR, especially since much of it travelled in efficient and profitable unit trains. The railway experienced, therefore, a minor building boom as branches went into those three locations. Yet the province's northern road building programme continued to deliver severe body blows to the railway. Stations closed, passenger runs ceased in some cases, as on the Elk Lake and Rouyn branches, and some complete branches closed totally: Charlton, Lorrain, Iroquois Falls, and Elk Lake. Most recently, the Timmins branch ceased carrying trains beyond Halnor. Then in 1990 the railway absorbed yet another heavy punch when the Adams and Sherman mines both announced imminent closure. The rail services staff, which had at one time numbered close to 2000, fell to 500 people.

One sector of the Commission's activities emerged in a somewhat spectacular fashion in the post-war world: Ontario Northland Telecommunications. Known officially as Ontario Northland Communications after the corporate name change in 1946, and later as Telecommunications, it continued, during the 1950s, to be called T&T, as it had been since the annual report carried its first account of Telegraph and Telephone activities for the year 1906. The T&NO enabling legislation of 1902 had included the authority to establish "electric telegraph and telephone lines through and along the whole line of the...railway and such branches and works as may be necessary for the efficient and convenient operation of the railway..." This provision recognized that the telegraph and the telephone had become necessary

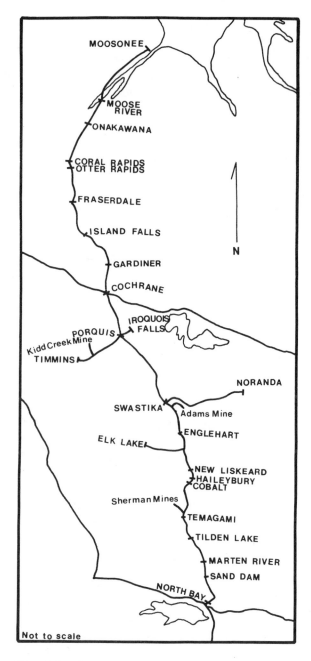

MOOSONEE

MOOSE
RIVER

ONAKAWANA

CORAL RAPIDS
OTTER RAPIDS

FRASERDALE

ISLAND FALLS

GARDINER

N

COCHRANE

IROQUOIS
FALLS

PORQUIS
Kidd Creek Mine
TIMMINS

NORANDA

SWASTIKA
Adams Mine

ENGLEHART

ELK LAKE

NEW LISKEARD
HAILEYBURY
COBALT

Sherman Mines

TEMAGAMI

TILDEN LAKE

MARTEN RIVER
SAND DAM

NORTH BAY

Not to scale

Map 16. *ONR stations, 1971* Highway competition had taken its toll.

to the operation of a railway. It did not confer a monopoly of either on the T&NO.

Telegraph technology developed independently of railways, although its first practical application in North America took place in 1844

on the Baltimore and Ohio Railway when Samuel B. Morse tested his new equipment. It was first used for train dispatching on 22 September 1851.[5] By the time the T&NO began, telephone technology was in place and had been since the creation of the Bell Telephone Company in 1877, a year after Alexander G. Bell made his famous first call to his assistant, Thomas A. Watson.[6] Railways had adopted the new technology, especially the telegraph, because it constituted a marvellous advance in the field of railway signals. The expression often heard among railway men that "it's better than smoke signals" is intended to be humorously euphemistic, but, in fact, before the telegraph, signal systems for train movement were indeed limited to the field of vision of the crews, dispatchers, and agents. It had quickly become a necessary feature, and the T&NO legislation recognized that. The first commissioners also knew that the telegraph had a commercial value, and made the necessary arrangements to link their lines with other telegraph companies.

The telephone sector of the T&NO, like the telegraph, was also set in place originally for internal use. In this the telegraph was dominant for seven decades, although decreasingly so after the Second World War. A principal consideration was cost. The telegraph required the installation of a single copper wire. The telephone required two such wires, and that provided only a single circuit. It was more intricate and much more expensive to set in place, to maintain, and to operate. The telegraph was also just as fast as the telephone for railway purposes. Most items coming over the wire had to be written down. This certainly applied to train orders which were the single most important form of message.[7] It would take the receiving operator the same length of time to write out the message whether it came by telegraph or telephone. In addition, until the late 1960s when dial telephones and direct distance dialing (DDD) became common, a call would require the intervention of a telephone operator, and even then, in an age of less sophisticated circuits and numerous party lines, there might not be an open line. It was simply too uncertain to

Earlton Station, Eddie Audet (ONA-1988276 Audet)

rely on telephones. The single disadvantage of the telegraph was the need for both sender and receiver to be skilled at using Morse code. The first line to be established, therefore, was the telegraph. These were often established in a rather primitive fashion, since speed was essential and the line might, at first, be strung from trees or be inadequately spaced. In time, however, the proper poles and careful placement were completed. With the required poles already in place the extra line for telephone service could easily be added.

In 1905, with trains just beginning to move and the telephone still incidental to their operation, there were signs of its future importance. These took two forms: the presence of local telephone firms in towns along the right-of-way, and the interest shown by the still very young but already quite large Bell Telephone Company. Bell inquired regarding the possibility of its using the T&NO pole lines to construct its system into northeastern Ontario. In response, the Commission on 12 April 1905 made three vital and far-reaching decisions. First, it determined to "take the necessary steps to inaugurate a telephone system in connection with the line between North

Bay and New Liskeard." Second, the chairman "was authorized to write the Bell Telephone in reply to a communication received from them stating that the Commissioners propose having its own office in North Bay, and asking price for making connection." Third, the chairman was further "authorized to communicate with the independent companies along the same lines..." The Commission thus staked its claim to the commercial telephone business. That business at this stage was and would for many years remain relatively small—even trivial—if compared to the railway industry. It would have been easier for the Commission simply to have made carrier arrangements with both the Bell company and the local firms for the use of its pole lines. Since that group of commissioners had been in place for less than a month after assuming control from the previous Commission, and since they sat as a part-time body, such a move would have been understandable.

Instead, dealings with Bell Telephone proceeded quickly, and by the end of the year the T&NO had achieved, in principle, its first long-distance interchange agreement a year before its telephone line had actually been strung. Two

Order of Railroad Telegraphers banquet (ONA-1988211 Duke)

factors seem to have inspired this vital decision. One was likely the lucrative nature of the business. Companies that confined their commercial activities to either telegraph or telephone were profitable, and, compared to many areas, the field was not labour intensive. For a railway that already had set the poles and the lines in place, the endeavour could be even more profitable. The other was certainly the desire to retain and protect the T&NO's sphere of operations. Here, as in so many features, Chairman Englehart set the tone. He would later demand the T&NO's prerogative with respect to rail traffic when dealing with the NCR and the line into the Porcupine; he and his colleagues also accepted responsibility regarding townsites, land management, and mining policy. It was quite in character, therefore, that they would choose an active rather than a passive role in the telephone field. Over the decades, three factors marked the evolution of the T&T department: the desire to "defend its turf," improved technology, and consumer demand. Occasionally these would interact; at other times a single factor would dominate; throughout, the dominant

theme was that of the T&NO retaining, as much as possible, control of its own activities.

Another early arrangement demonstrated that the Commission intended to protect its turf. The Gillies Brothers lumber company wished to run a telephone line for the use of its fire rangers along the T&NO telephone poles. Gillies had to agree not to extend its line to any other party and to not connect its lines with any system "except the Commission's telephone system when completed."[8] Future agreements with mining companies or brokerage firms and other businesses who sought connections with outside locations like head offices or stock exchanges followed this principle. The next year, contractual arrangements were made with two druggists, L.A. Wismer in New Liskeard and Budd and Ramshaw in Haileybury, "to take care of the commercial telegraph and telephone business of the Commission."[9] They were seen as agents for the T&NO; they did not own the local telephone business. This marked the T&NO's first entry into the local telephone field.

Independent telephone companies had nevertheless emerged in the North with rather remarkable speed. These firms provided a central switchboard, controlled by an operator, for a specific local area. The Rural Telephone Company, for example, served a limited number of subscribers around Heaslip.[10] Most were content with this, but others had greater ambitions. Among those whose plans could conflict with the T&NO were the Haileybury & Cobalt Telephone Company and the New Liskeard-based Temiskaming Telephone Company. Here too the Commission consistently asserted its status. Both companies, for example, strung wires which crossed those of the Commission. These conformed to the law regarding specifications and were considered safe, but the Commission felt compelled to notify the two firms "that they have no right to so string wires across the Commission's track without permission and that they will be held responsible for any damages which may arise on account of the wires being so placed."[11] Likewise, a temporary agreement with the Temiskaming Company gave that firm the "privilege of putting in telephones at stations between New Liskeard and Cobalt" but "as soon as the Commission's trunk line is completed all trunk line business must be done through our [T&NO] offices."[12]

As the various northern communities grew and the demand for telephone service grew with them, the T&NO played a double role. It operated the long distance trunk line that connected the North's telephones with the rest of the world, and it also operated local switchboards in several places such as South Porcupine and Kirkland Lake. Northerners viewed it as a viable alternative to other local firms. In 1929, for example, Matheson's town council invited the T&NO to bid for the local telephone service there.[13] By that time its principal competitor was Northern Telephone (NT), a company that ran several local operations and wished to connect these and indeed the whole north by leasing the T&NO lines. In response the Commission considered buying its rival,[14] but settled for a firm refusal to lease its lines while agreeing to provide NT with circuits to handle local business.[15] Northern Telephone mounted

a more serious challenge to the T&NO telephone territory in 1935 when it applied for federal permission to enter the long distance telephone business directly. Indeed, on 6 June 1935 the bill to incorporate the Northern Telephone Company with powers to operate "anywhere in the Dominion of Canada" received first reading in the Senate.[16]

The Commission feared that such a charter would be "highly detrimental" to its long distance operations and approved expenditures to assist "every possible effort" in preventing it from being granted.[17] In this case, Northern Telephone withdrew its application shortly afterwards, following an understanding arranged by Chairman Lang, which would increase its percentage on the long distance business that originated from its subscribers.[18] Matters rested there for over 10 years.

The end of the war brought a crisis in this field. The post-war demand for telephone service was expected to be great. The T&T department, organized as Ontario Northland Communications (Ontario Northland Telecommunications–ONT) under E.A. Frith, was inadequate for the task. So was NT, Frith told the Commission's meeting of 25 June 1946, for its equipment was also largely obsolete in the emerging technology. Only if one organization had full control and was prepared to make a heavy capital investment could modernization be accomplished. In Frith's opinion, only Ontario Northland or Bell Telephone could handle it. If Ontario Northland chose to proceed, he said, it would need at least new switchboards at Timmins and Noranda—at $200,000 each—for toll service, and Northern Telephone would need similar improvements for the local service. At this point the Commission had to make a clear choice. It could abandon the commercial side of the telephone operation and concentrate on the rail operations, which at that point were experiencing something of a renaissance, or it could view the new demands and challenges as an opportunity.

The Commission's Minutes do not record emotions, but one has the feeling that the magnitude of the task intimidated them. They did agree, however, that they should not proceed

Opening ceremonies for the new telecommunications office at Noranda, 1950
(Left to right standing) Mary Rayworth, Chief Operator, Margaret Hollee, Supervisor.
(ONA-ON Telecommunications)

without an "organization of considerable magnitude" to handle it. They also agreed that Commissioner Potter should explore the possibility, once again, of buying Northern Telephone. One also has the feeling that had Englehart been present, the response would have been much firmer and much more assertive. It was an outsider appointed to the Commission as a representative from the Cabinet, Roland Michener, who gave pause by indicating that such a heavy expenditure was a "matter of policy." He was inclined to seek either approval or guidance from the provincial government. In the end, the Englehart approach prevailed, but it took more time. Northern Telephone refused to sell, but Frith secured agreement to build the new switchboards, first at Noranda, and then Timmins. In addition, his department was charged with connecting Cochrane and Hearst with long distance cables. The CNR had chosen, at least in that area, to decline the telephone business.

It was a busy time for the Communications division—and it was exciting, as an era of expansion usually is. With resources inferior to those of its larger colleague, Bell Telephone, the communications groundsmen, linemen, cable splicers, and office people not only linked the North with new equipment but also sought to prevent "an isolation." This meant simply a break-down of the long distance equipment which would leave a community without an outside link. They also had a bit of luck, inspired by world events. In particular, the Russian acquisition of the atomic bomb and then the hydrogen bomb inspired the American government to establish two defence systems. One was the Strategic Air Command and the other was the placement in the Canadian north and far north of radar installations to provide warnings of a possible Russian air attack from that quarter. Three early warning lines evolved: the Pine Tree Line, which included Ramore; the Mid-

Canada Line, which ran through Moosonee; and the Distant Early Warning Line (DEW), which tracked across the Canadian Arctic. All branches of Ontario Northland benefited from the heavy defence contracts, both U.S.A. and Canadian, that grew from these grand projects. One might almost say that those contracts did for telecommunications what the Cobalt silver strike had done for the rail line.

Yet, in the telecommunications field technological growth remained in advance of Ontario Northland's work. In the early 1950s the Commission's forces modernized the facilities, updating the lines through the vacuum tube technology which permitted the use of up to 17 voice circuits on a pair of copper wires. This was a significant step forward, but even as they were set up, they were a technological generation behind, for the industry's leading edge had begun to move away from the copper wires towards a non-physical conductor: microwave. Denied the resources to engage immediately in this new field, Ontario Northland sought to defend its territory. Bell Telephone had moved fully to the microwave system, because it had a far greater capacity than the copper wires. Bell constructed a series of microwave towers throughout the northeastern corridor, but, by contractual agreements with Ontario Northland, the larger firm confined its use of these to its trans-Canada traffic. Bell refrained from using its superior equipment to pick up traffic from what ONT considered as its territory. But such agreements are finite. Ontario Northland had to upgrade again if it wished to stay in the telecommunications business, especially after CN-CP Telecommunications was formed in 1960.

A *modus vivendi* had developed whereby the major players in the communications business in the North—ONT, Northern Telephone, and Bell Telephone—refrained from intruding in the others' spheres. In 1947 Ontario Northland had agreed to refrain from competing for local telephone business, and Northern Telephone declared it would leave long distance business to the Commission.[19] This agreement was a natural step beyond the deal which Lang had made with NT a decade earlier, when that firm agreed to withdraw its application for a long distance charter. And in 1961 Bell representatives, whose firm controlled operations in northwestern Ontario, declared that "any change in the status quo would be only by mutual consent of the three interested parties"—the Commission, the Bell Company, and Northern Telephone.[20] Those arrangements were soon threatened by the new microwave technology.

Once again the Commission needed a heavy expenditure in time, manpower, and money to gird itself for the task of upgrading its system to meet the steadily increasing demands of northerners for better telephone service. Those costs could have been avoided by accepting Bell's offer to lease to the Commission a radio channel "between North Bay and Cochrane over the microwave system which they now operate in ONR territory."[21] Once again, in the T&NO tradition, Frith declared against the offer and in favour of ONT building its own microwave system. This time, having secured the province's support, the Commission did not waver.

> This matter given very thorough consideration and in view of the very great potential benefit that could accrue to the Commission through owning its own communications system, particularly in respect to expansion and growth, it was approved that offer of Bell Telephone Company to lease a channel between North Bay and Cochrane to ONR Communications, be declined and that the Commission proceed to provide their own facilities.

There followed yet another period of expansion which witnessed the Commission reassert its claim through the highly exciting and highly profitable new technology. The pattern of thrust and counter-thrust has continued for 30 years. The Commission continued to assert its right to engage in the telecommunications industry, to its territorial prerogatives in the northeastern corridor, and to its control of long distance business there. But the turf battles became more frequent and involved competitors, technology, and demand.

An early hi-rail car on its own turntable, 1927 (ONA-1988252104)

Roadmaster Art Houghton with hi-rail car during microwave construction, Mileage 32, Moosonee branch, c. 1963 (ONA-SITEL)

One took the form of resistance to a "friendly take-over" by Bell in 1979–80;[22] another was the need to upgrade once again by adopting digital technology and direct distance dialing (DDD). There have been as well fairly regular negotiations regarding the division of revenues, especially with Northern Telephone, the traditional rival and since 1966 a subsidiary of Bell. In the early days of this competition, there was little differential between long distance and local business in terms of potential profits. This feature likely was the reason why NT agreed to the arrangements of 1935 and 1947 which limited it to local service while the Commission retained the long distance field. This applied, it is noted, only within what might be termed the core area of the northeast. On the periphery, Ontario Northland continued, and still continues, to provide some local telephone service, as at Marten River, Bear Island, Moose Factory, and Moosonee. In the present commercial state of communications, however, the long distance element is far more lucrative, and many firms argue that local phone service must be subsidised from the revenues of the long distance operations. Where the same firm controls both, this can be arranged fairly easily. In the core area of ONT, NT argues for a greater share of the long distance revenue.

The most recent challenge is a combination of demand and technology. To accommodate itself to the increasing hunger of both society and business for better and faster communications, the industry has introduced another major technological change: fibre optics. This involves the use of multiple glass prisms to carry the signal. It means a change back to a physical conductor, but it is one that is equipped to carry a much larger quotient of messages. Also, because the fibre optics line is buried in the ground, the new system eliminates the disturbances that can foul the atmosphere. It is therefore much more dependable. It is also far more expensive and requires a heavy capital outlay. Thus far ONT has, once again, chosen to meet this challenge and to remain in the game.

The current situation of Ontario Northland Telecommunications is somewhat anomalous. It has been, in recent years, the darling of the Commission in that it is a true profit maker, it helps to subsidize other operations, it keeps business and money in the North, and it is an up-to-date, state-of-the-art operation. As such it is a major player in the North and in the industry. Yet it can also been seen as remarkably vulnerable. There have been offers to buy it from both Bell and its subsidiary, NT. It is also surrounded and even infiltrated: to the south, the west, and the northwest it is flanked by Bell Telephone; to the east ranges Northern Quebec Telephone, a Bell subsidiary; in the centre, CN-CP Telecommunications is present, through agreement with ONT; and, also in the centre, its traditional rival, NT, operates extensively in the local telephone field. In this fashion it stands as something of an island, but it continues to protect its territory.

That territory has actually expanded. The microwave technology resulted in two significant developments. One was the inclusion of television signals. Television pre-dated the microwave, of course, but early northern stations could service only their immediate areas. Within the corridor, stations like CKGN in North Bay had a limited range, and the homes in that range were likewise limited to that single station. Northerners, throughout the '50s and '60s, when they visited Toronto or other southern centres, were regularly somewhat awed by the range of home TV entertainment enjoyed by people there. The microwave technology that entered the North with vigour in the '70s changed that by providing enlarged viewing options. The other development was the geographical expansion of ONT into areas outside the corridor: beyond Moosonee to Fort Albany, Kashechewan, Attawapiskat, and Winisk on the west coast of James Bay, and west from Cochrane, beyond Kapuskasing and Hearst to Flynn Lake.

This territorial expansion has also applied to other Commission activities, through several agreements concluded in recent years. The rail services, despite the absorption of several severe

Snow plow stuck at Kenabeek, 1927 (ONA-19881812 D. Ruttan)

Hannah Bay Goose Camp   This tourist facility continues to "barter fresh air for American dollars." (ONA-1988224 A.E. Simms)

blows, will expand. Specifically, the ONR will assume 145 miles of the old National Transcontinental Railway (currently the CNR) between Cochrane and Calstock, some 15 miles beyond Hearst. Ontario Northland will also extend its influence into the southern parts of the province through its recent acquisition of some scheduled routes of Gray Coach Bus Lines. Similarly, through its agreements with Star Transfer, Ontario Northland already sends equipment and vehicles well beyond the northeastern corridor. In 1974, after acquiring the Owen Sound Navigation Company at the behest of the provincial government, the Commission placed the *Chi-Cheemaun* in service. This vessel permitted the Commission to perform its assigned task of providing ferry service on Georgian Bay between Tobermory and South Baymouth on Manitoulin Island. In 1989 the *Nindawayma* was added to this service. It joined the *Chief Commanda II* on Lake Nipissing and the *Manitou* which carries

passengers and freight between Moosonee and Moose Factory. In 1985 Ontario Northland, through norOntair, became the first airline anywhere to introduce the Dash-8 aircraft into commercial air service. Here too the Commission has extended its activity beyond its traditional territory. Described by an internal report in 1962 as ancillary services, the several transportation and communications functions of Ontario Northland have evolved into significant ventures. Each has its own venue, its own departmental structure, its own mission, and each has a remarkable degree of autonomy. Each purports, within the confines of its particular industry, to enhance its own service and viability. Combined, they form Ontario Northland which seeks, as did the T&NO, to provide links within the North and between the North and the rest of the world. It has been applauded; it has been criticized. Yet it remains as it began: the northern connection.

Notes

1. Reynolds to the Secretary, Air Transport Board, 27 November 1945. AO, RG3, Drew Papers, Box 451.
2. *Airport Planning and Development*, T&NO pamphlet. November 1944. ONA.
3. The excursions began running twice a week in 1968.
4. Bob Moore. Interview. 17–18 October 1988. On line to Moosonee.
5. Robert G. Burnet, "The Railway Telegraph and Telephone" in *Canadian Rail*, #425, Nov.–Dec. 1991, pp. 183–84.
6. Van Waterford, *All About Telephones*. 2nd ed. Blue Ridge Summit, Pa: Tab Books, n.d., pp. 3–4.
7. See pp. 225–256 of this text.
8. *AR*, 1905; p. 91.
9. *Minutes*, 15 May 1906.
10. *Minutes*, 16 July 1910.
11. *Minutes*, 3 August 1906.
12. *Minutes*, 28 September 1905.
13. *Minutes*, 18 November 1929.
14. *Minutes*, 28 January 1930.
15. *Minutes*, 16 August 1932.
16. *Bill N2. An Act to incorporate Northern Telephone Company*. Read a first time, Thursday, 6th June, 1935. Ottawa: King's Printer, 1935. AO, RG3, Hepburn Papers, Box 250.
17. *Minutes*, 10 June 1935.
18. *Minutes*, 22 June 1935.
19. *Minutes* 15 March 1947.
20. *Minutes*, 14 June 1961.
21. *Minutes*, 6 November 1961.
22. P.A. Dyment. Interview. 27 December 1991.

Part Four

Working on the Railway

Engineman G.E. Belanger,
1919 (ONA-19881419)

Chapter 14

A Prominent Presence

FOR OVER A century in Canada and for about half that in the northern corridor, railways and railway technology dominated the transportation fields. To a significant extent Ontario Northland continues to hold that status north of Cochrane. It has been made clear that the T&NO/ONR has always been more than a railway, but it is equally clear that, during its first 50 years, the public perception of the organization was that of a railway. For that time the term ancillary services applied to such activities as the telegraph, the land department, and the mining division. At present the term is anachronistic, because the past three decades have seen such additions as the marine, trucking, busing, airline, and telecommunications divisions emerge and grow. Concurrently, the rail division has declined in terms of its personnel, its traffic, and its revenues. There are today many people in the North who have seldom or indeed never travelled by train, and in many respects the future of this medium of transportation is uncertain. Yet, for much of this century and especially in the days of steam locomotion, the railway dominated business, travel, and even conversation.

• • •

Perhaps it is best to begin by stating the obvious. Operating a railway involves moving very heavy and very expensive equipment over a track which is also very heavy and very costly. It is potentially very dangerous. To cope with these four factors—weight, movement, cost, and danger—train operations involved two vital and constant trends: consistent effort to maintain the way (i.e., the road bed and the track) and a strict disciplinary approach to operating rules.

First, however, the line had to be built. It began with the task of selecting a route and creating the road bed. The route should be the most direct one possible, and yet one that avoided excessive grades and curves. Because of cost, tunnels and rock cuts should be kept to a minimum. The T&NO avoided tunnels completely. Likewise, water crossings should be avoided if possible for large railway bridges are costly, difficult to build, and awkward to set in place.

The T&NO's first Chief Engineer, W.B. Russell, supervised, apparently with considerable skill, the requisite exploration survey and then the establishment of a profile and a trial run for that railway. Such preparatory work is absolutely essential. A surveyor charged with the task of locating a railway right-of-way must work under two sets of restrictions. The first stems from the technology. That is, he must find a route which permits the construction of a line that has, if possible, no more than one per cent grade and a ten-degree curvature. Specifications greater than

Surveyors Peter Maher, Bert Price, and Ab O'Donnell near the Abitibi Canyon, c. 1914
(S.D. Lawlor, North Bay)

Engineer Maher and his crew, c. 1914 (S.D. Lawlor, North Bay)

230

those render the operation of the railway either awkward or dangerous. The second concerns the terrain. In locating the right-of-way, the engineer must somehow avoid extreme changes in altitude, excessive length, and excessive water crossings. At the same time, he must attempt to run the right-of-way over ground which is as solid as possible, avoiding swamps and potential sinkholes. It can be done, but in the diverse and rugged terrain of the Shield, which embodies forests, muskeg, swamps, and either harsh or rolling hills, the chore is difficult. The need to keep the right-of-way as straight and as short as possible becomes clear when one considers the process which was involved in constructing the railway itself.

The first step involved clearing, close cutting, and grubbing. That is, a crew had to clear the brush to a width of 99 feet (1.5 chains), cut it close to the ground, and pull the stumps, the latter requiring either special stump-pulling devices or the use of horses. From there the process followed an established procedure: (1) grading, (2) laying the ties, (3) laying the rails, (4) butting the rails together, (5) spiking the rails, (6) setting the gauge, (7) rough lining, (8) dumping the ballast, (9) fine lining, and (10) trimming. It seems simple enough, but each step required precision, extensive manpower, and often some special equipment. The gauge (i.e., the distance between the rails) was firmly set in the 1830s at 4 feet 8.5 inches; the grade had to be level; and the ties were set with 24-inch centres (which explains why it is so difficult to walk the track).

A vital feature of the process was ballasting. One engineer explained it.[1]

> ஃ You dump the ballast on top [i.e., after the track had been set in place], and bury the track; and then you jack the track up through the ballast, and then tamp it under the ties.
>
> [The ballast does not go down first] because you can't get it level...you'd get lumps in it.
>
> You do not grade first. Normally we have about a foot or six inches of ballast on a subgrade. It depends on

Grading at 65th mile   Red pine forest, Temagami Forest Reserve (ONA-199114)

231

what we have to work with. If it's the
main line, and we have deep ballast,
we'll sometimes put out about six
inches of ballast and spread that.

But back in the old days, they
wouldn't use ballast for a subgrade.
[At that time] they would put the ties
down—and the rail on it. Then they
came on with a railway car—and bear in
mind, this ballast comes from a special
pit and the easiest way to get it there
[i.e., to the construction site] is by rail
car. In those days, they would have
used what we call a Hart car. We now
use a hopper. A hopper has doors that
open on the bottom of the car and the
ballast simply falls out onto the track. A
Hart car operated differently. The doors
released at the side and the ballast—in
those days it was gravel—would pile
up on the side of the track, and this
would then have to be shovelled into the
centre.

Much of the T&NO was built by contractors,
but the T&NO people had to know how to do the
job. There were repairs that had to be made at
times, and from its earliest days the T&NO Commission adopted a policy that extra sidings or
small spurs for particular mines or other businesses like pulp operations were to be done by
the company's own forces. In some special instances, such as the Porcupine branch, the T&NO
undertook to do a major job as well. Thus the
company had its own skilled and knowledgeable
personnel, as well as the requisite machinery,
equipment, and tools. Likewise, the railway maintained its own ballast or gravel pits at points along
the line. Throughout the era of construction, the
T&NO also reserved timber rights in some spots
in order to ensure a supply of ties.

Because construction costs were so high, and
because the distances between destinations were
so great—at least at first—it was illogical to build
two sets of rails, side by side. It made more sense
to use the same set of rails to carry traffic in both
directions. To permit trains travelling in opposite
directions on the same track, it was necessary to

construct short sections of track, connected to the
main line at both ends but lying beside it, where
one of the trains could wait while the other
passed. The use of such sidings had the obvious
advantage of reducing construction and maintenance costs.[2] But it also increased the danger.
Once again, the operation of the line required
care and caution. The sidings had to be used
properly in order that "the meet" be done safely.

One final consideration requires comment.
Because rolling stock is so heavy, it is difficult to
stop, and, although brakes are installed on all engines and used frequently, it is impossible to stop
a train quickly. A full train travelling at track
speed would in most cases take better than a mile
to stop. Trains travelling under control would
need less.[3] When it was necessary to stop a train
on the main line, the flags (or flares) which would
call for the engineman to do so would be placed at
least a mile up the track from the point where the
stop must be complete. Any T&NO man would
know that 169 telegraph pole lengths constituted
a mile. Engines and rolling stock also must be
moved from track to track in the yard or onto the
sidings on the main line. Stopping and starting a
locomotive, on the line or in the yard, especially
one that has a heavy load, is costly, time consuming, awkward, and hard on the engine.[4] Thus it
makes sense to minimize the number of times this
must be done. To provide for these considerations, there developed a system of signals to assist
the men who operated the line. Arm signals
would normally suffice in daylight; at night the
signals were made using lanterns. There too the
operation had to be precise, clear, and strictly
controlled. Combined, these considerations meant
that an idea or concept that was eminently simple,
namely, the movement of goods and people over
two steel rails, became extremely complicated in
its operation.

The railway was also very labour intensive.
Each aspect of its movement and maintenance
had to be done manually, and every labourer,
tradesman, craftsman, clerk, or manager had to
follow set procedures. Yet the railway experienced its golden age at a time when the general
population was not highly literate. It would be

Steam shovel loading ballast train, c. 1903 (ONA-199117)

Track laying, Elk Lake branch, 1912 (ONA-19911246)

inaccurate to say that in 1900 or so illiteracy ran rampant, but the literacy rate was much lower than today. Most youngsters left school before completing eighth grade, for example, and only a minority pursued formal schooling beyond age 16. The organizers of a railway, therefore, had to take this complex and potentially dangerous organism and reduce its operations to a series of separate, yet related steps. The resulting system had four integral characteristics.

1. A clear division of responsibilities,
2. A set of very clear, and very firm rules,
3. An extensive and precise hierarchy, and
4. A system of rigid discipline.

By the time that the T&NO Railway came onto the scene, the systems had been worked out and the Commission simply adopted the operating rules which then predominated.

Among the developments which had evolved over the years was that of a clear division of responsibility. Thus, when the contracts for construction were first let for the T&NO and when the Macdonell firm began its construction in 1902, the Commission itself actually had no control over what went on even along its own right-of-way. During construction the contractor was in control. Of course, the contracting firm did work in a close relationship with the Commission's principal engineer, but Russell's primary task was to ensure that the railway was being constructed in accordance with specifications and to iron out any difficulties which might arise regarding the interpretation of the terms of the contract. At this juncture, the only department of the T&NO which actually functioned was the Engineering Department, which had the double task of (1) supervising the construction and (2) conducting the requisite surveys into areas beyond the range of the first contract. This situation pertained until 16 January 1905 when the Commission assumed control over the line as it then stood between North Bay and New Liskeard. For the first several months, the Engineering Department performed the task of running the trains, but as soon as the necessary arrangements could be made, the task was turned over to a newly created Operating Department. By this time, of course, the construction boom had begun in earnest. For the next three decades the Engineering Department would have some kind of construction job constantly before it. The Engineering Department also attended to the building of stations, sheds, shelters, section houses, or water towers. In many instances the Commission contracted for these facilities, but the Engineering Department still had the task of supervision.

This basic division continued for many years. Indeed, in some ways it is still in place, although the names and various structures within the Ontario Northland organization have changed considerably. That is, one department was charged with responsibility for seeing to the construction of new lines or branch lines; this was the Engineering Department. The other, had responsibility for operating those sections of the railway which had been completed. The two were quite independent of each other. Indeed, each was actually quite jealous of its own area. As a result, there was a degree of competition between the two internal departments. Such a division, however, was absolutely essential. There could be no doubt whatever regarding the ultimate responsibility and authority. To have any doubt or any room for interpretation would be too dangerous. Orders to move equipment could come from only one source.

Although there could be no overlapping of responsibilities, there was, by the very nature of the organization, a strong overlapping of information and knowledge, both mechanical and social. In this way, then, personnel within the Engineering and Operating departments might well be interchanged. The distinctions in the respective roles of the two departments, however, could never be permitted to blur.

The actual task of getting the track down and secured, and then allowing the trains to operate over them, while vitally significant, marked only a single stage. Other tasks immediately presented themselves. The commissioners had been far-sighted enough to ensure that, once the operations began, there would be sufficient motive

Culverts   Proper drainage is essential along any length of track, for excessive moisture can cause serious problems. If it freezes and thus causes expansion, it will disrupt the roadbed, the ties, and the track. If it results in a run-off, it can wash away the ballast, and this also disrupts the roadbed. Proper culverts provided one means of controlling drainage in a terrain that included extensive waterways, muskeg, marshland, and swamp. Over 2000 culverts of varying size can be found along the T&NO/ONR line. (ONA-1991150)

power as well as rolling stock for the initial operations. Both motive power and rolling stock, however, required heavy maintenance. Likewise, these had to be augmented and altered as the needs of the railway grew and as the demands of the consumer changed. The railway's capital construction also required considerable maintenance: i.e., the track, the railbed, and the right-of-way. All of this required a heavy capital investment and it all had to be maintained, as did the stations, warehouses, and repair shops. In addition, the railway had a commercial side.

The best known, though by no means the most profitable, sector of the commercial side of the railway was passenger services. In its simplest form, this meant that the T&NO had to acquire proper passenger coaches, build suitable passenger facilities at the various stations, prepare a sensible tariff to cover the appropriate cost of rail passage, acquire and train the requisite staff, and then set about the business of carrying passengers

along the entire length of the line. That people in the North would take advantage of the passenger service was never in doubt. Even before the T&NO began operating its own trains in January 1905, many people travelled when they could on terms arranged between themselves and the contractor. Prospectors in particular were inclined to take the work trains as far north as they could. Others from the towns of Haileybury and New Liskeard also used the work trains when they could, to travel to and from North Bay. The first service provided by the T&NO itself was that of a mixed train, thrice weekly, carrying both passengers and freight between North Bay and New Liskeard. When it became apparent that the early silver strikes in Cobalt would indeed turn into a new bonanza, it required no real planning on the part of the T&NO officials to provide for passenger service to that region. Clearly the market was there. At other points along the way, it was not so obvious.

It is likely impossible to exaggerate the full significance of the railway to such a virgin territory. The terrain through which the T&NO passed was particularly rough and wild. To travel through it on foot was a task that most people simply avoided. Had the railway not made its way through this region, it is likely that persons would have continued to avoid it. However, the railway having become a reality, people did enter the region, and having done so wished to have as much benefit from the railway as possible. To travel on foot, even over established footpaths, would take 25 to 30 minutes per mile. The two early towns of Haileybury and New Liskeard, therefore, were actually more than three hours apart. Roads were scarce, difficult to maintain, and often impassable with any type of freight load. No one wanted to walk, or drive a team of horses to carry freight, if they could use the railway. Consequently, there was a strong desire to have trains stop as close as possible to one's home or place of business, but not everyone could be accommodated.

The T&NO tried to satisfy as many demands as possible, at the same time paying due regard to common sense, the commercial return, and railway technology. Regarding the last, for example, steam engines required water and fuel at set distances, which varied according to engine class, tonnage, grades, and rail conditions. It was not uncommon for people to collect themselves in proximity to these fueling points. A community could naturally be expected to grow around a divisional point. Once the line reached Cochrane in 1908, it stretched some 240 miles from the southern terminus in North Bay. The decision to place the divisional point of the line at a halfway location guaranteed that a community would grow at White River Crossing on the Blanche River. Subsequently, White River Crossing was renamed Englehart. Other considerations figured in the selection of particular stopping points. The first stop on the way north, for example, lay very close to the town limits of North Bay. This was North Bay Junction, the point at which the T&NO met the CPR. For a brief period a station was maintained at this point to serve the east end of the town. The next stop at Trout Mills, on Trout Lake, existed to serve the tiny community which had been begun to develop around the mill of the Milne Lumber Company. At the close of 1932, when the T&NO could boast of operating some 670 miles of track, there was a total of 133 individual stops along the way. Each of these had its own genesis.

For passenger purposes, as many as 50% were merely flag stops. Based on the schedule put into effect on 13 May 1934,[5] for example, the passenger train would stop at the 13 points between North Bay and Temagami only if passengers on the train were ticketed to one of them, such as Mulock or Tomiko, or if the station exhibited the proper flag indicating that there were passengers waiting at one of those places. Likewise, between Porquis Junction and Timmins, eight of the eleven scheduled stops were actually merely flag stops.

An even greater proportion of the T&NO activities concerned the carriage of freight. Indeed, in terms of income, the freight sector has always been the more profitable. The annual report for 1905 includes the following passage.[6]

> Until the commencement of tourist traffic very little business offered except the outward movement of timber, but during the latter half of the year the outward movement of pulpwood and ore and the inward movement of tourists for Temagami and passenger traffic and general merchandise for the Cobalt mining district has been considerable as also general business for the rapidly growing farming district around and north of New Liskeard.

Tourist and passenger traffic, pulpwood and general merchandise shipments grew greatly after 1905. The Commission responded to this challenge rather well in its response to demands for additional railway construction. Concurrently, as demand grew, the passenger sector also expanded to include dining, sleeping, and news services. Similar expansion came in the railway's internal organization.

Gradually the T&NO added the full range of railway services including express, telegraph, and telephone. The T&NO, in addition, established both a land department and a mining division. All of these required either expansion or the establishment, or both, of particular physical structures. The nature and location of these, once again, related directly to the four factors of weight, movement, danger, and cost. The physical presence of the railway was ponderous. It also tended to be permanent, or certainly longstanding. The actual rail line, because of its sheer weight as well as because of the time, effort, and cost associated with it, has a sense of permanence about it. In the same fashion, other physical structures, designed and built to supplement the line, tended to throw off a similar sense of permanence and stability. In the course of the first decade and a half after the railway's inception, the T&NO's physical presence steadily evolved.

Each major decision carried in its wake widespread commercial and social consequences. In 1904, for example, when the commissioners determined that the southern terminus of the railway would indeed be North Bay rather than Nipissing Junction, the town council of North Bay undoubtedly breathed a collective sigh of relief, for that decision meant that North Bay would receive the benefits of being the transshipment point between the T&NO and all foreign railways. Also, by declaring North Bay to be its southern terminal point, the Commission had automatically decreed that North Bay would have a railway yard. There followed an equally significant event: the decision to locate its main repair and service operations there. This meant that the T&NO would construct and operate a major service centre including repair shops, a wheelhouse, and a roundhouse. Over time, as the railway continued to expand its operations, these T&NO landmarks in North Bay alone came to employ some 300 people by 1930. A few years later, in 1908, another landmark appeared in North Bay with the decision to build a

T&NO general office building, North Bay, 1908   When construction of the T&NO began, North Bay had a population of 4000, by far the largest community in northeastern Ontario. In 1911 this had grown to 8000. Much of this growth can be attributed to the T&NO and the town's "Gateway to the North" location. At the time of its construction, the T&NO office building was arguably the most imposing structure in the town. The office, the yard, the stores building, the machine shop, and the roundhouse—not shown here—all combine as testimony of the T&NO as the largest employer in North Bay. (ONA-1991164)

general office building in that town. Twelve years later this building replaced the Toronto offices as the principal headquarters for the entire Commission. And in 1923, that same building was expanded by 40% to accommodate the head office staff.

These marked a firm and concrete indication that the railway was committed to the North. It might be argued that mining companies made similar commitments when they built their mines and sunk their shafts, but mining companies would maintain their capital investment only as long as the ore produced a profit. Since the average lifespan of a mine was considered to be about 10 years, the extent of the mining companies' commitment was limited, both in fiscal investment and in the minds of the people who congregated around it. Some mines, such as the Dome and the Hollinger, went on much longer than 10 years, but their initial construction and the enthusiasm surrounding it was none the less tempered by the possibility that the veins would run out and the mines would close. With the railway, the thinking was quite different.

No other community profited to the extent that North Bay did, but there were other centres where the T&NO railway established a prominent presence. Railway yards and roundhouses graced other terminal points, including Timmins, Cochrane, and Noranda. Englehart, as the railway's main divisional point, likewise enjoyed both a rail yard and a roundhouse. While the principal repair centre remained at North Bay, significant subsidiary depots were formed at Cochrane, Rouyn, and Englehart.

Few people in the northern towns would likely have understood the full significance of these structures, in terms of either their financial benefit or the role which those buildings played in the operation of the railway. Such would not be the case with another prominent fixture along the railway: the stations. Since the T&NO at one time or another operated more than 135 such stations, and since the Commission had very early on established a policy of having work done locally if possible, the construction of these stations provided a considerable boon to the local economy of the northeast. The stations also, in the first several

Englehart roundhouse and turntable, 1908 (ONA-1991178)

Temagami Station and grounds, 1912   This station, nicely flowered, replaced the structures which burned in 1909. (ONA-1991283)

decades of the railway's existence, served as something of a social centre. People commonly met trains to greet friends or business associates who were travelling by train, but beyond that it was by no means infrequent that persons would simply gather at the station to meet incoming trains simply to see who else was there and for the social pleasure involved. "Meet me at the station" was a term that prevailed in the towns of the North as elsewhere during the railway's golden age.

Every station, it seems, was unique in some fashion. The Englehart station, for example, for more than 25 years had the distinction of possessing special greenhouses which not only promoted the beauty of that particular station, but which also provided for experimental farming in northeastern Ontario. Even after the greenhouse feature of Englehart was cancelled following the Racine investigation in 1934, a series of station agents there continued—and still continue—to take special interest in its beautification.

The heavy expense and effort connected with railway construction and the care of rolling stock and motive power was matched by the need to maintain the track, the roadbed, and the right-of-way itself. Indeed, an entire department known as Maintenance of Way held this responsibility. Over the years this department has been slotted into several different administrative areas, but its task has always been the same: to keep the right-of-way safe and efficient. The sheer weight of the locomotives and rolling stock subjected the track, the ties, and the railbed to constant abuse. The way was also exposed to natural hazards. Steel rails naturally contract in cold weather and expand in hot weather. This will not normally cause a problem if the rails are properly spaced when first spiked down. But ties can move if exposed to extreme pressure, and if the ties move, the rail moves also. Northeastern Ontario possesses a climate of extremes in terms of heat, cold, snow, and rain. A loose spike, or a slightly off-centred rail, could result in a derailment. A washout along the track in the spring runoff could easily result in a far more serious accident. The maintenance of way gangs were to prevent this. Accordingly, the T&NO, like all railways, divided its line into sections. These extended in the early days only about three or four miles. Each section became the

Section houses and agent's house, Matheson (ONA-198873 E. Everitt)

Krugerdorf, c. 1956   Section house (right), loading pulpwood with team of horses (centre), Section Gang bunkhouse (above centre). Bracket on top of poles is for 550-V powerline, installed in 1950, for power before hydro supplied it for block signals. (ONA-199124 Butler)

responsibility of a group of men, under the direction of a foreman, known as a Section Gang. Most sections, as can be imagined, were located at some distance from the small communities that existed along the way. Consequently, the men who formed the section gangs often lived at some distance from their own homes, which required that accommodations be provided for them. These took the form of bunkhouses for the men and a special house for the section foreman. These too formed a portion of the railway's physical presence wherever its tracks ran.

Some tasks necessary for the proper maintenance of the way could be accomplished only in good weather. This would include the laying of new rail or the replacement of worn ties. It would also include the replacement of ballast where it was necessary. This work was done between May and November by groups of men known as Extra Gangs. Like the section men, the extra gangs lived along the line near the spots where they were working. They too had to be provided with accommodation, but in their case it normally took the form of special residential cars designed to accommodate a group of perhaps 30 men working on each gang. These extra gangs were also used, again on a seasonal basis, to work on what were known as betterments. It should not be suggested that the original construction of any part of the

T&NO was inferior. Indeed, the work was, in the end at least, invariably very good. Yet as the line assumed greater proportions and as the traffic over it grew more and more extensive, it became clear that certain portions of it were sometimes inadequate for the task expected. One early example was that of the Widdifield Diversion. This was in fact a major project, but it was undertaken simply because the original line had been expected to carry much less freight than that which very quickly developed, largely because of the Cobalt bonanza. Consequently, the T&NO Engineering Department undertook the task of diverting the original rail line slightly to the east in order to provide a better grade. Also, it was desirable, as the technology of railways gradually developed, to incorporate improvements into the T&NO. This might take such forms as a sturdier or longer rail, the insertion of more durable culverts, or the erection of a new bridge. The T&NO, like all railways, required constant construction, reconstruction, and improvements. Throughout the first 40 years or so, this work required large numbers of men, because the jobs were extremely labour intensive.

The railway's prominent presence in the North gave it certain societal responsibilities. This factor had a double role. The first is somewhat ephemeral. It tended to engender among

T&NO Float   When the city of North Bay celebrated its Old Home Week in 1925, the T&NO presence, already strong in the town, was also prominent in the parade. (Evelyn Chivers, North Bay)

senior officials and wage-roll employees alike a sense of duty which bordered on a proprietary and collective interest in the North. Thus, while the commercial benefits of the railway were certainly present, as was the railway's developmental or colonization role, there existed also a sense of mission which went beyond these. T&NO officialdom was very sensitive to the North, to its needs, and to its people. Consequently, the T&NO provided the best source of intelligence or information regarding the North to those who were unfamiliar with it. Therefore, railway officials were in constant contact with government and entrepreneurs in such activities as mining, lumbering, tourism, settlement, and hydro. This link with outside government and entrepreneurs was certainly important, for it was through them that the railway could promote not only its own activities but also activities throughout the northeast. Railway people, however, also recognized—as did almost everyone who paid any interest to the North—that the railway's most vital feature was its presence as a lifeline for the people who lived there.

On a day-to-day basis, northerners depended to an amazing degree on the facilities of the T&NO. It was the railway that carried them into the North in the first place; it was the railway that carried them out should they wish to visit friends or to leave. All manufactured goods, ranging from dishes for the kitchen table to clothing, and any mechanical device, such as wagons or, later on, automobiles, came in by rail. Mail, food, clothing, prescription drugs, confectionaries, newspapers, indeed every item which one used on a daily or regular basis, entered the North on the T&NO. The same general atmosphere pertained regarding the business and industrial sector of the North. All machinery, all supplies, all medicines, all building supplies, all business mail, indeed all items which business and commerce used on a daily or regular basis arrived at their destination by way of the T&NO. Conversely, all of the products of the mines or the forests exited the North to their market by way of the T&NO. The safety, the security, the general well-being of northerners and northern communities rested directly on the two steel tracks which connected northern points with the rest of Ontario's society.

Widdifield Station, tram from McCordick Camp, Mileage 16.5, c. 1905 (ONA-19882212 A.E. Simms)

242

Cochrane coalchute, 1910 (ONA, *AR* 1910, #149, 19911149)

It is unlikely that the 10-year-old who gazed longingly at a bicycle in Marshall Ecclestone Hardware, or the young boy who checked the mailbox every day for his hockey photos from the Quaker Oats Company, or the young mother who bought baby supplies at Leggett's Drugstore, or the teenagers who purchased the appropriate clothing from Buckavetsky's Store, or any of the thousands of persons who made purchases or sales on a daily basis, thought in terms of the way in which those goods and services had reached them. Yet in a very real way, the railway formed a vital part of every person's life.

While the railway likely had only a subconscious presence in the minds of northerners on a daily basis, its significance came into sharper focus during times of personal crisis. Almost every railroader, for example, has a story to tell about close calls with expectant mothers. Virtually all of these stories, happily, ended with a pleasing result. Happy results often attended other critical situations as well, as, for example, when someone was injured and had to be rushed for care either by handcar or by train to the closest hospital facility. In times of general crisis, the railway's presence became even more prominent, perhaps even dominant. At such times, there was a natural tendency to look for leadership and assistance from the railway and railway personnel.

Among the upper echelons of the T&NO hierarchy, this sense of responsibility was not only accepted, it was embraced. In the annual reports, the chairman and the department heads emphasized this aspect of the railway's role in the North. The records of the Commission contain many such indications of this strong sense of duty and responsibility. What these records do not show, however, is the extent to which that same sense of duty penetrated throughout the full organization. Extensive interviews with past, and longstanding, employees of the T&NO reveal three principal characteristics. One is that virtually all former employees possessed a sense of pride in the work they had done on the railway. The second is that those same persons were then, and remain, quite prepared to indicate any displeasures that they felt regarding their employer, as well as a

The 1103   This engine, with 4-8-4 running gear, was partly designed by the T&NO. The last steam engine to be purchased, it arrived in 1937 and was scrapped in 1957. (S.D. Lawlor, North Bay)

willingness to indicate instances of events or actions which they perceived to have resulted in either unfair treatment or improper action. There was, for example, a general recognition of the skill and admiration for Chairman George Lee. Yet there was also a certain resentment towards both Lee and other leading officials regarding the bonuses which the Commission had granted themselves in the early years of the Depression. T&NO men, therefore, do not look back on their days with the line only in happy and nostalgic ways. They can be very critical and sometimes quite resentful in their criticism. Yet, among them all, there was a desire to be perceived as having done the job correctly, as well as a feeling that the work they were doing was important. And regardless of the particular role that they played, there was pride in having accomplished a portion of the task which kept the track clear, the trains running, and the North free from isolation.

Notes

1. George Payne. Interview. 15 August 1990. North Bay.
2. Spurs differ from sidings in that only one end is connected to the main track. The join is controlled by a set of switches which dictate whether an approaching train will remain on the main line or be diverted onto the spur or siding. The task of "switching" was assigned to the brakemen (trainmen).
3. Track speed varied according to conditions. Under control means that the engineman must be able to stop his train within the range of his vision.
4. The engines and rolling stock were equipped with devices which "coupled" each car to the next, the full line of cars constituting a train. To break the connection, the trainman would "pull the pin" that held the two cars together, or insert it to complete a connection. To make up a train, the yard crews had to link the cars required for a particular unit, a task that meant collecting cars from different spots in the rail yard. This process required considerable switching and coupling (or uncoupling). It also meant moving the engine and the cars that were connected to it to different spots. This practice was known as "shunting." "To pull the pin," because it meant severing a connection, came also to mean to retire from the service.
5. ONA. Train Schedules. A.E. Simms Collection.
6. *AR*, 1905, pp. 13–14.

Chapter 15

Preparing to Roll

HE MOST VIS-
IBLE sector of
the T&NO work-
place were the
train trades. In
the days of
steam, each crew
consisted of five
men: an engine-
man, a fireman,
a conductor, and
two trainmen, commonly known as brakemen.
The engineman, often called simply the engineer,
had the task of driving or operating the engine, as
well as the responsibility for insuring that the
"switching" was done for that end of the train.
With him rode the fireman, whose task was that
of keeping the "steam up" on the train, by keeping the fires hot. On freight trains one of the
brakemen also rode the front-end. The conductor
was responsible for the train: everything behind
the engine. He assured that the freight cars were
handled properly, and, on passenger or mixed
trains, he had the responsibility of ticket control
and treatment of passengers. There was considerable paper work involved, because the conductor had the job of managing the freight, and the
way bills had to be organized and filed as the
train moved along the line. The van at the end of
the train served as his office. The brakemen provided the essential link, through a set of signals,
between the front-end and the van, commonly
called the caboose. Their duties also included the

switching at sidings along the way, at junction
points, or in the yards of the several stations. On
passenger trains, both brakemen rode in the
back of the train, in the van.

Although there was a certain degree of mix-
ing among crews, most crews tended to operate as
a unit, and consequently there developed a sub-
stantive degree of comradeship and teamwork
among them. Crews would take two or three turns
each week over their particular run—between
North Bay and Englehart or between Englehart
and Cochrane, for example, or over one of the
branch lines—to a maximum mileage of between
3800 and 4200 miles per month. Each man on
the crew would very quickly become intimately familiar with that sector of the line and with all of its
idiosyncrasies and characteristics. Furthermore,
those men would also become very well known to
the persons who lived along the line or worked at
the various railway establishments in their sector.

All T&NO employees were subject to the
seniority and "bumping" system common to
all railways. Jobs belonged to the person who
had both the qualifications and the greater seniority. Beginning trainmen or other running
crew positions could expect to be "bumped"
about the line for a few years, and because
they would have to go wherever the job was
located—usually to relieve staff because of illness or vacation—the running crews in general
became very familiar with every part of the
T&NO railway system. It sometimes had an

awkward effect on the family of the man who would "deadhead" to the open job. Quite frequently a fireman would have a home in North Bay but work out of Cochrane, while the man he bumped in Cochrane would have his home there but would be taking runs out of Timmins. It was a situation which most regretted, but all accepted as part of the job. The bumping system applied to all railway positions and had the effect of establishing personal links across the entire system among the men and women whose livelihoods depended on the railway. It also had the incidental effect of increasing a sense of general comradeship among them.

In the public mind, the running crew tended to personify the railway, because it was they who were most visible to outsiders. Indeed, the position which was identified in the public mind most closely with the railways was that of the engineman, or engineer, and the symbol for any railway, the cap worn by the men in the front-end. It was an image which most of the men tended to enjoy, and some cultivated. Bob Moore, who finished his career as a company director, began as a fireman and then an engineer. In his days of running the engine, he would, when passing his family's house near Island Falls, give an extra toot on the whistle to his mother who would come to the door and wave as his train rode by. He also remarked, somewhat nostalgically, that when bringing his train either into Moosonee or into Cochrane on the northern run, he would give an extra blast on the whistle "just to let everybody know that Bob Moore was in town." Cultivated or not, the engineers and running crews, in general, presented this palladin image. Yet it was an image which did not go unchallenged, or unqualified, by other people on the railway itself.

Indeed each of the major divisions—Transportation, Engineering, and Mechanical—contended that its particular role was the most vital. All three were vital for none could function without the other two. Intellectually, every member of every division would agree with that, but emotionally there was a strong attachment to one's own area, and rivalries developed. If

that rivalry served to sharpen a particular division's desire to do the job well, it was very healthy: if it led to sluggishness or resentment, it was deleterious to the system. Fortunately, the former tended to prevail. In any event, the running crews were regularly reminded that they might toot their whistles all they chose, but they could run nowhere without a properly maintained track and properly cared for engines and rolling stock. There were, of course, other functionaries on the railway whose assistance was absolutely essential. Indeed, it could be argued that no link in the chain of railway command or duty could be eliminated.

Because the whole process of a railway's operation is so closely integrated, it is difficult—no, impossible—to designate a definite starting point. Yet, perhaps it began with the call-boys,

Engineman R.L. (Bob) Moore, 1953
(ONA-19881461 Hermeston)

A typical van (Kelly Morgan, North Bay)

who had the task of advising each member of the running crew two hours in advance of the starting time of his run. If the member of the crew to be called had a telephone, this posed little problem. In the days of steam, however, and especially in the '20s when many people did not have telephones and in the '30s when many people could not afford them, the call-boy would go directly to the person's home. He was required, however, only to visit those homes within one and a half miles of the rail yard. Those who lived beyond that limit and did not have a telephone had to make arrangements for some way to receive the call. This normally meant enlisting the assistance of someone who lived within the one-and-a-half-mile radius. It was vital (and remains so) that all telephone lines into the homes of running crews be kept open during the two hour or so period before scheduled trains, no doubt to the chagrin of many resident teenagers. Also, for obvious reasons, the term call-boy was discontinued rather

than extended when it became normal for women office workers to make the calls to the running crews.

When they arrived at the yard, always at least 30 minutes before the scheduled departure, the train crew had to inspect its train. The brakemen would arrange to have their van attached at the end. For many years each crew had its own particular van, where they would keep their own belongings. The engineer would ensure that his engine was in order, and the conductor would deal with the paperwork required for the train.

It should be noted that the train had already been assembled and the necessary train orders had been cut by the time the running crew arrived. Also, the yard office had prepared the way bills and indicated what had to be carried. Clearly several vital decisions and a considerable amount of work had been done before the crew arrived. The most significant decisions actually were made at the chief dispatcher's office in Englehart, where decisions were made regarding the trains, scheduled and extra, that would operate each day. The train schedules were issued in the name of the commission, but actually were established by senior rail officials. The most prominent of these was the superintendent of rail transportation. He had full authority over all rail services with the T&NO. The schedule, when it was compiled, would be based on the demand for freight and passengers. As demand changed, the schedules would be altered and reissued from time to time as the T&NO attempted to adjust to supply and demand from the public. Extra trains were dispatched according to particular requirements, such as the need to send empty cars to points where they were needed.

Even with scheduled trains, there were day-to-day and seasonal variations which affected the railway's operations. Among them were the characteristics of a particular crew. Ed Simms served as Operator, Dispatcher, and Chief Dispatcher. He observed that the person making up the traffic pattern must take several factors into account.[1]

> No, you can't see them [the trains] but the operators are your eyes and ears and they have to report when a train goes by...
>
> And you get to know [as operator or dispatcher] how long it takes a train to go from one point to another... If he's [the engineman] got a tonnage train [i.e., fully loaded] it'll take him so long to go that [distance], and if he's only got a few cars on, well he can do it pretty quick...
>
> And you get to know...different engineers. One engineer will go from North Bay to Tomiko, for example, in an hour and two minutes; some other engineer, you know it's going to take him an hour and ten minutes; he just won't do it any faster. So you look and see who the engineer is, and how many cars he's got on, and what tonnage it is, and how many units [or what kind of engine] and say, "Well,

he'll be at Temagami at 10:10." Another train [from the north] you'll look and say, "Oh, he should be at Temagami at 10:10 too." So that's where the meet's going to be.

Occasionally, a unique circumstance would affect the day's train movement. Simms encountered one while serving in North Bay.[2]

> There was one day I was working, and they had a bunch of skiers on the train. They were going out to Widdifield. They were going to ski back...take all their equipment, go out to Widdifield and ski back... They left North Bay... I calculated the length of time they would lose, unloading all those skiers and getting started again on the hill[3] with that heavy train, that they'd lose an hour and a half.
>
> So I put out a train order at Temagami for them to run an hour and a half late from Temagami on, even though they'd left North Bay on time... By the time he got to Temagami he was more than that. So I guessed right that time.

In addition to the scheduled trains, from time to time it would be necessary to run extra freight trains, simply because the various items of rolling stock might have to be moved to different locations on the line, or perhaps excessively heavy traffic would leave the various yards with some cars of freight that could not be absorbed by the motive power of the regularly scheduled trains. These would be moved as conditions permitted and as motive power was available.

> They used to save up the empty cars going to Kapuskasing for paper... They'd save them up in North Bay and run one train of empties from North Bay right through to Cochrane. Well, we'd take them to Cochrane and CN would handle them as they felt like it... They used to take

Yard Office staff, c. 1928 (Evelyn Chivers, North Bay)

maybe 100 cars with one steam engine...but they were empties.

... When we bought those four 1100s,[4] they were basically for passengers—but some of those passenger trains did not operate on the week-ends—so they'd take one of those units, those steam engines, and send a big train up to Cochrane with it, and it would be back in time to handle a passenger train on Monday morning.[5] ❧

Similar provisions would have to be made whenever the various yards seemed to be getting cluttered. These decisions involved the trainmaster, the yardmaster, and the chief dispatcher. A certain amount of give and take was required.

❧ ...the yardmaster at North Bay, for example, would tell the chief dispatcher, "I have 150 cars here in the yard for the North." Then it was up to the chief dispatcher to move them. But the trainmaster had a certain authority too... If the yardmaster complained to him that "My yard is getting full and the chief dispatcher won't run a train," you'd be hearing from him pretty soon, saying, "Why are you not running a train to get rid of that stuff; they can't move their own cars!" But you had equal authority [i.e., the chief dispatcher and trainmaster] so you had to give and take.[6] ❧

The chief dispatcher could also expect to receive instructions from time to time to fit in a variety of other special train services for specific

Head Office staff, c. 1928 (Evelyn Chivers, North Bay)

events or occasions. During both world wars, for example, the T&NO carried special troop trains, as did all the lines of Canada. Prisoners of war also moved over the T&NO to Kapuskasing during the First World War and to Monteith during the Second World War. Except for the large contingents that were moved for repatriation at war's end, the prisoners tended to come into the North only in small numbers; thus special trains were not involved. Of course, everyone on the line knew when POWs were on a particular train, because the names of all the stations had to be hidden while the train was there to prevent the prisoners from learning where they were. Other special trains included special excursions by politicians or journalists or for sporting and social events such as the T&NO picnics. The most elaborate was the special train that carried the large party of visitors

and officials north to Moosonee in 1932 to drive home the last spikes.

This task of moving the various trains—scheduled and extra—over the entire line rested with the chief dispatcher. Clearly the most obvious problem facing him was that of ensuring that the trains, running in both directions, would not collide. This meant that he had to gauge the relative speed of each, take into account the class of each train, and ensure that the proper train would take the siding when trains moving in opposite directions would meet. The *Uniform Code of Operating Rules* dictated that certain classes of trains were superior to others.[7] Passenger trains, for example, were superior to freight trains. Also, one direction was superior to the other. On the T&NO, north was inferior to south on the main line, while west was superior to east on the Kirkland Lake branch, and east was superior to west on the branch into the Porcupine. This caused some confusion, because it meant that east was a superior direction on one branch line and inferior on the other. Ultimately, to erase this confusion, it was determined that trains moving towards North Bay from any point were to be considered as southbound trains, while those moving away from North Bay were to be considered as northbound trains. Thus, a train moving from Timmins to Porquis Junction, although moving eastward, was considered to be a southbound train, which on the T&NO was the superior direction.

In selecting the location for the various meets, the chief dispatcher had to take into account all of these considerations, and at the same time try to maintain the published schedule. Having several trains scheduled for any particular day, the chief dispatcher would then cut train orders for each particular train.[8] These were then translated onto the running sheet, a large board located in the chief dispatcher's office in Englehart. It had (and has, for it has not changed since the line was first constructed) two parts: one showing southbound trains and the other showing the northbound trains with their respective times of departure and arrival at the several stations along the line.

If all went well, and if the chief dispatcher had estimated correctly, all trains would run on schedule. But any one of a number of regular or unexpected circumstances could throw that schedule into disarray. It might be an event like the skiers on their way to Widdifield, or it might be the result of a greasy track, or of a train being sent out with insufficient power or some other unforeseen event. When that occurred, the paramount rule was that of safety. It was far preferable to have a train—any train—sit idly but safely on a siding than to have a collision or a derailment. This might indeed cause some wits to suggest that

Repair shop personnel Clearly many had a hand in preparing an engine for the line and maintaining it. (Evelyn Chivers, North Bay)

251

North Bay shop men, c. 1918 (ONA-51 Pers.)

T&NO actually meant "time no object" but delays were preferable to accidents.

Once the chief dispatcher had determined the train orders, several other events were set automatically in motion: e.g., who would go out, what work would be done in the shops, and what work would be done in the yards. Running crews operated out of any location from which a train originated: North Bay, Englehart, Timmins, Cochrane, and Rouyn. Their shifts were determined by the regular board, which was simply a list of the men on the various crews who would rotate in order for the various runs. Should any of them be ill or absent for any reason, their place would be assumed by someone taken from the spare board. Based on this rotation, the call-boys would notify the men of their starting time. In the shops, the workforce would be assigned tasks directed towards ensuring that engines were available for the

trains required for these runs. Likewise, the Car Department would have the job of ensuring that the proper rolling stock was available for the freight which had to be carried along the line. Every rail yard would receive orders directing that the several scheduled or extra trains would collect the cars that had been delivered to that particular yard. The yard crews, therefore, under the direction of the yard master, who operated out of the yard office, would have the task of "spotting" cars or lining up a series of cars, which could be attached to a train coming from a foreign railway; or they would have the task of making up the train if it originated from that particular yard. In yards along the way, as for example at Englehart, cars would have to be spotted for inclusion on a train travelling in either direction.

An examination of timetable number 62, which became effective on 1 May 1927, illustrates the task which faced the chief dispatcher.[9] It shows, for example, that in the North Bay subdivision, seven trains of various class, ran north between North Bay and Englehart, while another six travelled south. Eight travelled north from Englehart to Cochrane, and a further eight travelled south between Cochrane and Englehart on the Englehart subdivision. In addition to this main line traffic, trains from six subdivisions had to be integrated into the flow of traffic. Furthermore, a total of four trains—two eastbound and two westbound—on the Nipissing Central railway joined the T&NO at Swastika. At 12:01 a.m. on Sunday, 19 February 1928 these runs were extended to include runs from Rouyn. Worthy of note are the special instructions on these schedules. For example, the rule that southbound freight trains between Tomiko and Trout Mills must not follow any train until 20 minutes had elapsed was clearly a safety feature set in place to emphasize the need for caution on the relatively steep grade at the south end of the main line between Tomiko and Trout Mills. The task of organizing all of these trains appears ominous. Ed Simms, who served as Chief Dispatcher from 1969 until his retirement 10 years later, and whose father held that position previously, commented on the pressure of this task.[10]

≈ Oh there's tremendous pressure on a person. There's no doubt about that. I mean, you're responsible for thousands of tons. For example, you're putting out train orders and...a train order might take...five minutes to issue to everybody, and sometimes it's put out to three, four, or five different offices and each one has to repeat that —and as they repeat it you check that they are repeating it correctly. You'd have a real lousy day when you'd put out maybe 125 orders in a eight-hour shift. You were busy, no doubt about it. And there were a lot of days, day after day after day, that you'd do that, because the traffic was such at that particular time.

That was stressful. When you'd go home—if you were working 4 to 12...there was no sense in you going to bed as soon as you got home, because you probably wouldn't sleep. You're keyed up...the adrenalin is still flowing then. What I used to do was go home and read the newspaper...for an hour and then go to sleep with no problem at all.

But a lot of fellows—like my Dad —it was very hard on him and he ended up having high blood pressure and he didn't last hardly any time. At one time, you know, there...were no retired chief dispatchers at all. They died very shortly after. Either died on the job or shortly after. ≈

None of the train orders could have any effect, however, unless the engines and the rolling stock were fit to travel. This responsibility rested with the larger Mechanical Department. Its task was quite simple: to maintain the equipment and to repair it when broken. The performance of this task was, however, anything but simple. The physical structures included the repair shops, the round house, and attendant offices, and the workforce was very large. Steam engines and rolling stock were not only heavy, but required regular maintenance of a specialized nature. Every task was essential: the ash pit man who cleaned the fires and got the engines ready; the trimmer who filled the oil cans, made sure the lanterns had oil in them and ensured that the lubricators were ready; the greaser who made sure the sand domes were full; the hostler who moved the engines in and out of the shops. Some two dozen specialized crafts and trades, ranging from the boilermaker through the machinists and smiths (i.e., blacksmith, tinsmith, etc.) were quartered, in shifts, in the shops. None of the rolling stock (i.e., freight, box, flat, passenger, sleeping, or dining cars) could move onto the line unless cleared by the Car Department. Likewise, the engineer also had to have clearance.

Before the train crew arrived for its run, therefore, a great deal of preparatory work had been done. More would take place before they left.

    Then when you back down the yard [with the engine] to pick up your train, there's another group of people [that] comes into play—the yard office... There were the car checkers who had to go out and check all the cars, and car clerks who looked after the car numbers, way bill clerks who looked after the way bills—i.e., where these cars were going and where they came from and how long they were on our line...[11]

The last brings attention to yet another specialized group, the Car Hire Department. All rolling stock and motive power was compatible with all railways. This had tremendous advantages, because it avoided much costly transshipping of goods between lines. Boxcars did not have to be unloaded, for example, for it was a simple matter to cut off a car and direct it onto another—or foreign—railway. It meant, however, that the T&NO would lose the use and the control of that car while it remained on the foreign line. Likewise, the T&NO could use foreign cars which made their way onto its track.

Railways had to pay a small fee for the time that they kept a foreign car: "It wasn't very much—$2 a day or something like that. It was [there] only to keep someone from using a car for a summer cottage or something like that."[12] Actually, it could lead to abuses like that complained of by Cavanagh and others regarding the Texas and New Orleans Railway, but until the arrival of computers it was not really possible to alter the system. It had to depend largely on good will. Then in the 1970s the system, through computerization, changed to charging a car hire rate that was truly significant, based on mileage and an hourly rate.[13] It made for better equipment use.

Conductor Orville Nicholls described his view of the train originating procedure. One is struck by its complexity.[14]

    We got called. They gave you a two-hour call, and you were on duty 15 minutes before the time you were called for. So, if you were called for 10 o'clock in the morning, you'd be on duty at 9:45. We usually got down...10–15 minutes ahead of that time.

Then they would tell you what train you were on... Even if you were on a regular train you got called...that was the call-boy's job. The yardmaster would notify him that he wanted a crew and...give him a list of the crew that was to go to work, both the front-end and the tail-end...

He [the yardmaster] would also notify the billing clerk, because he would have to arrange all the bills for the train that was going out—and they would send a checker down. He would check the cars and bring up the list of all the cars on the train. They would sort the bills out in order...and then when you got down—as I say you were on duty 15 minutes [ahead]—you would have to get your orders, check your orders, get the bills—as a conductor you'd have to get the bills for the train.

The tail-end brakeman would walk the train and make sure there was nothing wrong...release any hand brakes that he would find on the train and make sure everything was ready. When he got to the tail-end—before they had electric lights—he would put the oil markers on the tail-end of the van. If it was cold weather, he'd get a fire going in the van, get it warmed up.

The conductor then would get his orders and he would take one set down to the engineman, read the orders with the engineman, make sure

Sample train order, 30 July 1953
Sent to all trains, this order warned of activity on the track so that enginemen could be under control as they approached Mileage 104. Note that trains from Timmins are termed "southbound" even though they would be moving east. Note also that numbers are written in both figures and words. Clarity was essential. (ONA)

Sample train order, 30 June 1948
This is also a general warning. The siding at Bushnell is partially occupied. Trains taking to that siding for a meet would have to allow for that. (ONA)

Sample train order, 7 January 1952
This calls for a "meet." Since both trains are of the same class, No. 414 (which received this order and is travelling south) had superiority over 411, which is travelling north. 411 will take the siding at Tomiko. 414, however, must be under control as it approaches the meet. (ONA)

Sample train order, 7 January 1952
No. 414 has received new orders—wired to Temagami—since leaving Englehart. Such changes were common and were based on information received during the day at the Dispatching Office. All changed conditions had to be reported so that the various train orders could be adjusted. (ONA)

that he understood them, and they would talk over anything—like if there was a regular train on the road and they had no meet on him—the dispatcher might say, "This train is on time, make your own meet." He would do that often on purpose, because you might be delayed getting out of the yard, and he didn't want to hold the regular train up, so you would have to go on your own.

After that was all set—the car checkers, of course, would give a brake test from the tail-end... Before radio, he would wave his arm back and forth and the engineman would be looking back and he would set the brake up... There'd be lanterns at night. After the brake was on, he would give him a signal to release the brake and he would make sure that the brakes released.

... And then if it was time to go, you would pull out. They'd pull out slowly so the conductor could get on the tail-end... 🏵

Bill Ross's remarks concerning this same operation bear noting, because they indicate a few points regarding the early days on the TNO.[15]

🏵 Whenever you were leaving a terminal, you got what we used to call the "flimsies." That's what they called your train orders. You see, they were made on a very, very light paper... Well then, much as I hate to say this, although its true in many, many cases, a lot of the men weren't too well educated in the first place. In the second place, they weren't too well versed in what was needed of them, so the engineers and the conductor would read the orders, one to the other, which you were required to do by the rules. 🏵

It is likely impossible to exaggerate the importance of the train orders,[16] for the safety of the train—its crew, its cargo, and its passengers—depended upon their accuracy, especially re-

garding the meets. Occasionally, the enginemen were left to arrange their own meets, which they would do based on the train orders, their knowledge of the line, and the schedule of oncoming trains. This would occur only on slow-traffic days, and never when it involved a meet by two passenger trains. During the construction period on the Moosonee line, trains would sometimes make "smoke meets." The two enginemen watched for the approaching smoke and the one moving in the inferior direction would take to a siding at the appropriate point. Such meets would be possible, of course, only on clear days! The need for absolute adherence to train orders and to the uniform code of operating rules formed part of the mentality of all running crews. To ignore them meant risking one's safety and indeed the lives of others. There was considerable anxiety regarding any engineman who tended to play fast and loose with the rules and a definite inclination to report infractions.[17] While all agreed on the need for strict obedience to the rules, there were likely times when it was frustrating, for it could lead to some very long and very uncomfortable runs.[18]

In due course, the conductor would receive the requisite train orders, and the engineman would then move the train out of the yard and onto the main track. Even here, special rules applied in that all switching in the yard must be done by the yard crews. The brakemen on the running crews could certainly perform this task, but the rules forbade it. There had to be a clear—very, very clear—line of responsibility. By assigning specific tasks to specific positions, the system hoped to prevent errors; if an error occurred, the same system could determine responsibility. Indeed, this emphasis on a very precise division of responsibility can be observed throughout the railway's psyche. Like the bumping system, it was recognized as necessary, and it was strictly applied, even if at times it resulted in an awkward distribution of work. A former chief dispatcher was discussing its application to his job when he said the following, but the sentiment he expresses applied in all areas of the railway when movement of rolling stock was involved.[19]

❧ As a dispatcher, for example, if you didn't have a lot of trains running, you weren't very busy. For example, on a Sunday, or on Christmas Day,...you might not do anything for five hours at a time; but there were other days when you were really over-worked. But you couldn't give it to somebody else to do.

Like, you have a piece of railway, and there's a lot of trains operating there, so you have a lot of train orders to put out. You can't give part of it to somebody else; you just have to do it all yourself... One mind has to do it, that's all there is to it. ❧

Notes

1. A.E. Simms. Interview. 27 February 1989. North Bay. In this quotation, Ed Simms refers to "a tonnage" train. Each engine had the capacity to pull a specific weight or tonnage. It was possible for engines to pull a little more than their weight or tonnage, but in such cases the engineman might have trouble on steep grades or in slippery conditions, and this could cause delays.

    Various speed limits applied to the various parts of the line. For a period of time the T&NO imposed a general speed limit of 24 mph, but that was a temporary rule. *Track speed* depended upon the track and upon the type of train. Passenger trains, for example, had higher speed limits. For some areas and some conditions, this speed was included on the published train schedule. Needless to say, the hope was that all enginemen would have their trains under control at all times, but in railway jargon, the term *under control* had a very specific meaning, namely that the engineman must be able to stop his train within one-half the distance of his field of vision. On the road this was not always possible because of curves, etc. There the engineman was required to be under control for the expected—i.e., what was in his train orders. No one can be prepared for the unexpected.

2. *Ibid.*
3. This is a reference to the long and rather sharp grade that develops as the line moves out of North Bay. As shown on p. 261 of this text. Widdifield lies part way up.
4. The nature of the T&NO motive power and its evolution is described nicely in Frank N. Vollhardt's, *The Locomotives of the Ontario Northland Railway.* Calgary, 1985.
5. A.E. Simms. Interview. 27 February 1989. North Bay.

6. *Ibid.*
7. The *Uniform Code of Operating Rules* contained the rules for all train movements on a railway, and the same code applied throughout the country. It still does. Two methods are used to teach these rules to all who must know them: a system of classes run by Rules Instructors, and a period of actual work experience under the supervision of an experienced person. Variations from the code may occur, but only to provide for greater safety. The rule regarding flagging, for example, calls for flares (fusees) to be set a mile from the point where the train must stop. When the trains became faster and heavier after dieselization, the ONR, in the 1970s, decreed that the distance for flagging would be 3000 yds. This was allowed. A reduction would not be.
8. See pp. 255–256 of this text.
9. Train schedules. A.E. Simms Collection. ONA.
10. A.E. Simms. Interview. 27 February 1989. North Bay.
11. Bob Moore. Interview. 22 May 1987. North Bay.
12. Ken Moorehead. Interview. 12 September 1988. North Bay.
13. *Ibid.*
14. Orville Nichols. Interview. 27 February 1988.
15. Bill Ross Jr. Interview. 1974. On file at ONA.
16. Several copies of each train order were required—dispatcher, operator, conductor, engineman—so onion skin paper was used, because that made it easier to make several copies using carbon paper.
17. See pp. 281–282 of this text.
18. See pp. 285–286 of this text.
19. A.E. Simms. Interview. 27 February 1989. North Bay.

Chapter 16

On the Line

O NCE THEY WERE out of the yard and onto the main line, the running crew might well have experienced a sense of freedom and independence. On a clear day with a good engine and a fast freight and clear train orders, there was undoubtedly often a strong sense of exhilaration, especially in the front-end where everything lay open and clear before the engineer, the fireman, and the front-end brakeman. Yet the crew and the train were remarkably vulnerable. Each man knew that up the line at several places there were trains moving southward. At some point they would meet. Also they were at the mercy of the weather. Not all days were crisp and clear. Snow or rain, if heavy enough, would blind them; even a light moisture could make the tracks greasy, and a light snowfall—one that was insufficiently heavy to require a snowplow—might serve to cause snow swirls which could blind the driver or could cover the ties enough to hide defects.

Defects could occur from many different causes. Extremes of temperature, either hot or cold, resulted in either expansion or contraction of the track. Excessive rains might cause a washout. And there was, of course, a certain amount of wear and tear on the track caused by the passage of many trains, each weighing thousands of tons, on a regular basis. The problem of slippage, possibly caused by a light rain which rendered the track greasy, was particularly poignant in sectors where there were steep grades. One such sector was that known as the Summit, located just north of North Bay;[1] another substantial grade could be found in the Tri-town region;[2] the third, and generally acknowledged as the most severe, was that on the Kirland Lake branch between Cheminis and Northland Park. Caution and slow speeds were essential when trains were proceeding down these grades. The reverse was true for trains travelling in the opposite direction, for in those cases the fireman would be required to build up a truly full head of steam, and the engineer would have to use all of his driving skills if the train were to make the grade. At times they were not successful, perhaps because of bad luck, perhaps because of inexperience, perhaps because their tonnage was too great for their engine. This then required the use of a tactic known as "doubling." It was most likely to occur on the Rouyn branch, at least according to Ed Simms.[3]

When I was working on the Rouyn branch, I'd come home, and I'd get a ride on a freight train, and I'd get on the engine, so I saw what they did on the engine, remembered it. Like I remember in the 500-class units they'd be pulling more than they could really handle over some of [the] bigger hills. One of the big hills was at Northlands Park—from Larder Lake up to Northlands Park—quite a steep grade...

Well, they would run that engine until it wouldn't move another inch—it'd just chatter... Well, then they'd stop—and they'd cut off the first 10 cars..., force them over to the next siding, come back and get that [i.e., the rest of the train], take it over, couple up, and away they'd go again. 🐿

Doubling certainly occurred at the Summit but,

🐿 I think the grades on the Kirkland Lake branch are steeper...[and] they don't get a run at them, you see. This [the Summit] is a pretty steep grade; there's no doubt about that, but trains did not stall on the hill up to Tomiko the way they did in the Rouyn branch. Practically every freight train that ever came out of Rouyn for years...stalled on the hill and had to double into Northlands Park...and sometimes #47, the passenger train.

On a Sunday, they always had a lot of passenger cars on, and it was heavy pulling. If they had a lot of snow that night..., not yet enough for a snowplow but enough, that train would have to double too. He'd get part way up and he'd stall, so he'd have to cut off the first part of the train, take it up to the top of the hill, come back, get the rest. Now that's bad when a passenger train has to do this, because the minute he stalls, he's late, right off the bat, and maybe he was already an hour and a half late out of the station. 🐿

Most agree that the grades around Cheminis Mountain and Northlands Park were the most awkward for the steam engines, but

the reason for more trains stalling there than at the Summit may have been the result of greater attention being paid to the Summit problem, which was, after all, part of the main line and a much busier sector. There it was common to double the motive power out of North Bay as far as the Summit. The extra unit was called the pusher. Former conductor, C.L. Bailey, worked that task from time to time. If a particular train were especially heavy, "they'd double head the train out of here [North Bay] and...cut him off at the Summit...he'd [the pusher] come back to North Bay."[4] When coupling up the train, the crew would add the second engine.[5]

🐿 One would face north and the other [the pusher] would be facing south, both together, tender to tender... [At the Summit] you'd cut the heading engine off and run it down the track, and the other fellow [the pusher] would come, and you'd put him in the siding. 🐿

At that point, the pusher would be uncoupled from the train, pulled up the track somewhat, and when the switch to the siding was closed, the pusher (facing south) would return to North Bay yards, perhaps to assist another train. The first engine would then back down from its position on the main track into the siding (after the switch was thrown), connect onto the train, and proceed north.

Even when the pusher was used, a crew might have to double to make the Summit, perhaps even double twice and take only one third of the train to the top at a time. Conductor Bailey observed that one year—perhaps 1945 or 1946—the region was struck particularly hard by army worms. This small plague had the effect of causing the engine's wheels to slip badly and force doubling on that run.[6]

The act of doubling was not particularly difficult, but it was time consuming, and the delay would not have been figured into the crew's train orders. There was a certain pressure to avoid the tactic and also some pride in being able to do so.[7]

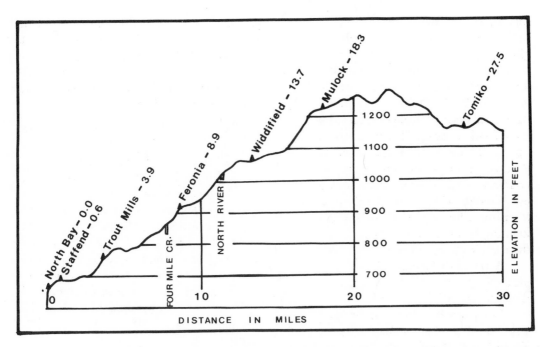

T&NO Profile, Mileage 0 (North Bay) to Mileage 27.5 (Tomiko)

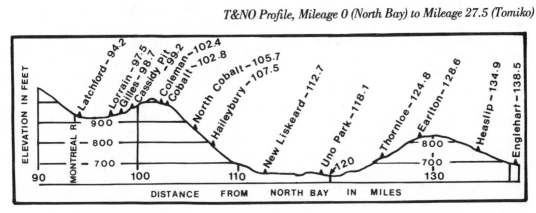

T&NO Profile, Mileage 90 to Mileage 138.5 (Englehart)

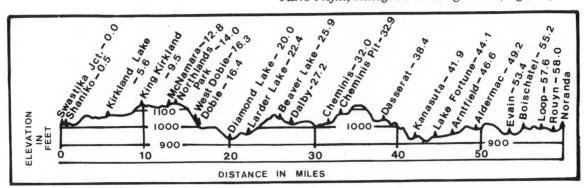

T&NO Profile, Kirkland Lake Subdivision

There were two things [necessary] to get over these hills with a single engine, providing...the tonnage wasn't over what the engine could handle. The engineer, the way he ran that engine, and also the fireman. If he didn't have a full head of steam—we called it a full *head* of steam. That means right up to...the capacity of the boiler. If you don't have enough steam, of course you lose power... So it took a combination of the two—the fireman keeping it hot and the engineman knowing how to run that thing. That's the combination you need.

A lot of the times these trains stalled on the hill because they died...for steam.

You never backed down, because you'd never get your steam up again. You'd just sit there, you'd bring your steam back up—get her hot again. Then...you'd double... And that really [could foul things up]

... Not only your own schedule, but the southbound train, or any other train—they'd be waiting for you somewhere...or there could be a passenger train—you might be trying to get to Mulock for [a meet with] a passenger train...it could lay out the passenger train. Then you could be sure you're going to hear from somebody! Somebody would be down to see you in very short order.

Beyond his train orders, the engineer had no definite knowledge of other activities on the line in either direction. Yet there were safeguards against the unforeseen. The most obvious was the general rule that if one were uncertain about proceeding, he should not. Also, speed limits were set and enforced. Another safeguard lay in the fact that the T&NO, like all railways, had to keep numerous employees located along the line itself.

Some were there for mechanical reasons. Steam engines required water and fuel. The amount of each needed varied according to the size of the engine and the tonnage of the train. To provide for these requirements, water tanks were set every 25 miles or so and coal every 70 miles. Also along the line there were the section forces, or section gangs.

... We'd leave North Bay—there was a section gang at Feronia which is Mileage 8, Widdifield, Mulock, Tomiko, Osborne, Diver, Bushnell, Redwater... All those places had section gangs of five or six men [including the foreman], which maintained the track. As you get farther north, north of Englehart, the gangs are spread out a bit more...and north of Cochrane, back in the old days of steam, each gang was responsible north of Coral [Rapids] for about 40 miles of track.[8]

The work of the section forces was acknowledged to be both difficult and lonely.

[They] made sure the track was lined. They had to change ties. All the ties were changed manually... [They would] jack the track up, make sure it was level, get everything in good shape. All summer they worked like slaves out there—through the heat, the flies, and the rain. [They'd] get everything in perfect shape.

And then, about mid-December or the 1st of January, when the frost sets in, the track starts to heave. Then they're working like slaves again... They have to start shimming the track to keep it level...

Then comes Spring—March, April, and maybe May—the frost starts going out of the roadbed and they'd have to work like slaves again, to get those shims out... It was a continuing thing, every year; fix the track up in the summer time.

And they'd change rails. They had to go out and inspect—quite often —before the train [went through] to

262

Freight shed, North Bay (ONA-198808)

make sure—to check for broken rails...[9] ❧

The maintenance-of-way section gangs provided the first line of defense for the train crews, the engines, and the rolling stock against the vagaries of the northern climate. It was they who would patrol their particular section by motorcar (and before that by hand car) and occasionally on foot. It was they who would, upon finding something untoward on the track, warn of the danger and, of course, repair it. It was an important job and one which the men took seriously; but it was also a lonely job and, apart from some of the labouring jobs in the yard or in the shops, was the lowest paid. The section foreman was provided with a small house to which he could bring his family. The five-man crew, however, lived in the section house or bunkhouse.[10] Sections located fairly close to one of the northern communities could visit those towns, but those located at a distance were required to occupy themselves during their off hours pretty much as bunkhouse men everywhere did. But men can restrict them-selves only for so long to such activities as reading, playing cards, and trading stories. An occasional visit from the crews on the way freight or other sporadic visitors were certainly welcome, and all visitors were treated pleasantly. Many of the train crews remember the section gangs as being among the most hospitable people anywhere. On occasion, men on the various sections would engage in a bit of hunting, or a bit of fishing, or perhaps some sightseeing. It was forbidden for the members of the section gang to take their motorcar beyond the limits of their own section, but this rule was sometimes, if not routinely, overlooked by the section foremen and possibly by the roadmaster. On one occasion, at least, this practice resulted in something of an awkward situation.

❧ It was overlooked as long as he didn't burn excessive gas or drink or take bad risks. At the same time, if he got caught, you had to discipline or do something with him.

Now back in 1967, in May, there was a section guy out, early, early in the morning, about 6 a.m., going down the track [on the motorcar] with the intention of shooting a moose—at mileage 162 [on the Island Falls Subdivision] He got down to Mileage 151...[there] the water had come way up on one of the tracks it was going through a culvert, but the culvert had a hole in it...the gravel [i.e., ballast] was going down the hole, the water was carrying it away and the track was hanging there! And the train was due in three hours. So he went back and reported.

Now. What do you do with the guy?... You report the discipline because you have to set an example for the rest of the motor car operators,

Herb King, B & B Foreman at Tomiko water tank, c. 1930 (ONA-19881917 J. Hammor)

that you're not supposed to have that car out after hours. Yet he probably saved a whole train and probably some lives![11]

The maintenance-of-way people could not prevent severe natural disasters such as the one discovered at mileage 151. Certainly the man who reported the washout there should be commended. It is also possible that the washout would have been discovered by section forces who might well have conducted a survey of that section before the train arrived. That is something which will never be known.

Nor could the maintenance-of-way men protect against mechanical breakdowns on the train itself.

Back in 1966... I was coming up [to Moose Factory] and we came around the curve...at Onakawana and made one helluva rough stop. I was sitting with...Fred Winter...a mountie at Moosonee. Don Dingwall was the engineer. I said "Geez, that guy's getting rougher all the time!"

Well, what had happened—we had two cars of ballast on—these old Hart cars, old ballast cars. The axle had burned off one car, and we had dragged it. Some of the ties, you can still see some of the marks on those ties—tho' most of the ties have been changed...that's where the axle broke down, and we went around the curve, and when it hit the switch, the car derailed. Luckily we were only going about 10 mph.

Q. Those ties haven't been changed since 1966?

Well the life of a tie is 25–30 years... These were not cut sufficiently, so it didn't weaken them, but a lot of them have been changed.

So we got around the curve, took a look and assessed the damage... There was no way we could move. We couldn't move the car—we couldn't lift the car,...

I sort of took charge... I came back to the train and recruited about 15 Indian boys, and...got on the phone and got the section gangs to come from behind us with all their shovels and picks they had. And we emptied that car—of the gravel then we got the jacks out. We jacked the car up, put some ties underneath it, skidded it along to a little spur, and repaired the track as well as we could and moved on to Moosonee. We lost about seven hours...

So I went back to the dining car and—Adrian Florent was the chef... And I said, "I want enough sandwiches for 20 men." "Well, I don't know if I have enough bread." "Well, dig out whatever you got, because these guys are hungry and they earned it." So he made up a good load of sandwiches and took them up. The boys all had some coffee and some sandwiches, dug back and emptied the car of gravel. I forget what time we

got to Moosonee, it was six or seven hours later than we should have been.

But we were lucky. We were very, very fortunate.

Q. Because you were going so slowly?

Well, we'd normally be going about 40 or 50 mph...but he had to slow up, because we had to stop at Onakawana. The siding is this side of where the stop was going to be—but the car jumped, it broke the air line, and the brakes went into emergency stop. Lucky... We could have dumped the whole train, coaches and all.

Q. A "Q and A" [Investigation]?

Certainly the train crew were questioned, because they're supposed to have a running inspection. But it's pretty hard, coming along in the fall with a bit of snow, on straight track you can look back all you want, and you can't tell if there's smoke or what it is... You really can't tell.

Bridge and building (B & B) crew at Kenabeck, 1927 (ONA-1988182 D. Ruttan)

Section men at Kenabeek, 1927   Dan Ruttan, Ed Ruttan, Ralph Peever. (ONA-1988181 D. Ruttan)

Sometimes...you can smell the smoke from a journal and sometimes you can't. And that time we didn't.[12] 🐦

Despite the persistent emphasis on the need to watch for irregularities along the way and the same emphasis on the need to adhere strictly to the rules, such accidents occurred. Subconsciously all T&NO people were aware of this harsh reality, and all feared the consequences of a truly serious one. Everyone's worst nightmare was a head-on collision. If it happened, the effect on the entire line was funereal. Isabelle Labreche recalled an incident from 1965. This was a head-on collision at mileage 9.3 on the Kirkland Lake subdivision (near King Kirkland), when the Work Extra Train 1516 met Extra Train 1303 East. Two men, Foreman C. Huston and Wingman A. Webster, were killed, and Engineman A. Wallace (all on the eastbound train) was badly hurt.

🐦 On the night of February 21st, there was a snow storm...and the train crews were busy in the yard trying to get the trains moving. A snowplow crew was sent out to plow the track, and I cannot recall much else happening during the day, except that later on, probably in the afternoon, word was spreading around the office in Englehart that something had gone wrong and that the dispatching office could not tell where one of the trains was. This was quite unusual as they normally knew exactly where all moving equipment was located at all times.

Since the superintendent's office staff is located [or was at that time] on the same floor as the dispatching office, there was a lot of whispering going around, and people were gathering at different desks to talk about the mysterious movements and trying to figure out what could have happened. I recall a group of us being at the roadmaster's desk and discussing all possibilities. The plow crew was made up of section crews along with a roadmaster who went along, so they

266

were quite concerned. It was sort of like being at a funeral wake where everyone just stood around and whispered. There was no work going on, people were sort of in shock, especially after word came out that there had been a head-on collision, and there were fatalities.

I was speaking with a brakeman recently who worked in the Englehart yard that day, and he said that the snow was so deep that the yard engine had to push the outgoing trains to get them started on their trip out of town.

The other frightening incident that sticks in my mind quite clearly was the time the machine was plowing snow in Englehart yard and a section man [C. Plante] was helping the machine operator by cleaning and throwing switches, and the snow was so heavy and blowing so bad that Mr. Plante somehow fell down and the machine ran over him, severing his leg. I was working in the assistant superintendent's office which was located right above the yard tracks and you could hear the screaming of this man. The office clerk [Karl Redden] ran out and applied a tourniquet and saved his life. This was a terrible experience and was on everyone's mind for some time after. Apparently, the noise of the machine and being bundled up for the cold, Mr. Plante didn't hear the machine coming close to him.[13]

The main protection for the train, as Isabelle notes in her recollection, came from the string of operators, or telegraphers, who were located at each station along the right-of-way. Their task was that of maintaining contact, via the telegraph, with the dispatchers and chief dispatcher in Englehart. It was they who kept

The sons of Charles Ruttan   It was common for children to follow the father into the T&NO. Among the more striking instances is the Ruttan family, from which eight of ten sons followed the father (Charles), at least for a time, into T&NO service. Six sons are shown here at Kenabeek in 1944. Charles, Dan, Verndon, Howard, Wesley, and Vernon. (ONA-1988814 D. Ruttan)

A meeting of telegraphers, Cobalt, c. 1930 (ONA-1988226 Sandwith)

the central dispatching office informed of the progress of trains in their sector. If one were late, or if it experienced some mechanical difficulties, or if it in any way threatened safety or scheduling, the operator would transmit this data to other dispatchers. This new information, which the dispatchers received from various points along the way, would result in the chief dispatcher, or the dispatchers, issuing new train orders from time to time. Thus a meet which had been scheduled for a siding at Latchford might be changed and occur at Cobalt instead. If an operator received new train orders for a train approaching his station, and if that station were simply a flag stop, it would be the duty of the operator to flag the train down and give its crew the new orders.

Until the introduction of the automatic block signals (ABS), the operators were indeed the only link between the running crews and the central dispatching centre or indeed anyone else on the railway, and even after ABS came into play the operators continued to provide a vital link between the trains and the operations branch. It was a job, therefore, of considerable importance, and

it was also one which required particular skill. Telephones certainly existed, even from the first days of the T&NO, but their usage was greatly restricted, partly because there were so few of them in place, and partly because their use was considerably more expensive than the telegraph. As a result, the principle means of intercompany communication was the telegraph, based on Morse code. The ability to use Morse on the telegraph was not common. It required extensive and constant practice. It also required that the person receiving the messages be able to type, at least as fast as the person who was sending. Both skills were essential for an operator. Of the two principle tasks—sending and receiving—receiving was the more difficult.

≈ It's a lot harder to receive, to understand what's coming... It doesn't take you long to get to know how to use the key and send, but its a different situation to listen to it. That's why, when you're learning this, what usually happens is you get somebody to send messages to you and you keep copying and copying day after day after day, and eventually you get better. Then you go over to the ticket office, for example, and sit there, to one side, all day long, just copying whatever is going over the line—to get practice.

And you eventually pick it up, but unless you work hard at it, you don't get really expert.

You've heard of Mel Hicks—his Dad was a tremendous operator...

Oh, there's been some wonderful operators on the road. We've had some smart alecks though...always seemed to try to overpower the junior telegrapher.

There was an old fellow—he worked at Larder Lake, Bill Denman his name was, and he had no fingers, except the thumb and little finger on his right hand—and to write he used to put an elastic around his wrist [and in-sert the pencil through it to give it some stability]...his writing wasn't too good, but you could read it.

And he used to send on the key, and it was pretty wicked sometimes to understand it.

...partway through his career he was working at Porquis, and George Arnet was also working there as a junior telegrapher...the operator in North Bay [apparently] thought, "I'll fix that fellow," [i.e., young Arnet] and he started sending as fast as he could go, and of course George couldn't keep up.

But Bill Denman happened to be in the office, and the typewriter was sitting on the safe on one side of the room and the key was over on the other side. So he [Bill] goes over and opens the key and tells him, "Faster." And goes back to the typewriter, and types away...you know,

Collision at Connaught, 23 January 1965 This was a railroader's greatest fear. Fortunately it was rare. (ONA-199224 Boston)

269

the fellow could be four sentences ahead of him on the key but Bill could still remember... And he'd go back and send "Faster, faster." And he eventually got the fellow so rattled, he didn't know what to do (laughter). But he did it on purpose you see...[14] 🐾

The operator might also serve as the station agent in the smaller stations. This was the case at places like Widdifield or Uno Park or Connaught. At the larger and more active points, like Cobalt, Porquis, or Timmins, the corps of workers was much larger and included the station agent, the express agent, and the operators, as well as a few others who handled freight or baggage. In these centres, the telegrams would go out by way of messengers. In smaller places, the operator would have to deliver them himself if he had someone—like a station agent—to tend the key.

Like the section men, the station agent's life could be lonely, but he did have greater contact with the rest of the line, and of course he normally also had his family with him. It could also, at times, be dangerous. On one occasion, the operator at Larder Lake, Tom Jonkin, was held up by robbers who made off with three bricks of gold, at $35,000 a brick.[15] Tom received considerable ribbing about the incident, because the robbers left him bound. Even so, he was far more fortunate than the night operator who was murdered at Redwater in 1909.[16] W.J. Dyston was killed in a quarrel with two young section men, named Morin (21) and Cornish (25). Conductor Nixon, whose train was at Redwater at the time, witnessed the fight, but it took place so quickly, he "was unable to intervene."

This event illustrated both the isolation of the smaller agencies as well as the vulnerability of a train and its crew. The *Nugget* reported:[17]

> The operator being dead, Nixon was unable to get running orders and had to flag his train slowly to Diver, sixteen miles away, where the news of the tragedy was wired to North Bay. The despatcher at North Bay reports incident happening at 5:33 p.m., which must have been about the time that Dyston was assaulted.
>
> A queer jumble of letters, half-formed and incoherent, came over the wire which the despatcher was unable to piece together, and found afterwards that Dyston's key at Redwater had been opened and remained open two hours after tragedy, so that the Redwater key must have been the one which attracted his attention suggesting that Dyston must have crawled to the key in an endeavor to warn his chief of his condition, but his brain failed to respond to the call and death came before he could report tragedy.

Fortunately, the tragedy of Dyston at Redwater was a rarity. Yet, after listening to Ed Simms discuss the manner in which the T&NO treated gold and silver, one wonders why there were not more robberies.

🐾 When I was working in Schumacher, the people from McIntyre mine would come down in an armoured truck, and they would unload maybe two or three safes with maybe two bricks of gold in each one, and they had the big bricks—they were $70,000 bricks—and they would unload two or three of them out on the express track, come in and have you sign the receipt for them.

Now...this was an armoured truck that came in. It had a guard there with a sawed-off shotgun and all this stuff.

You'd sign...and away they'd go.

It's sitting out there...as far as they were concerned, of course, it was now your responsibility...but there didn't seem to be any way of looking after these things.

If anyone had wanted to go and steal a brick of gold, it would have been very easy, except for the weight of them.

I suppose that's what took place at Larder Lake [i.e., with Tom Jonkin]. They [the mining staff] brought it down

At Mileage 19.25, Ramore subdivision, c. 1956   Note the wooden walkway on top of the car. (ONA-199125 Butler)

there...and he's all alone there. What can he do about it?

Precious metals were treated different [in those days]. When we lived in Widdifield, my grandmother lived in North Bay, and I would go down there on the local that would go through Widdifield about 4:30...to visit her for a while. I don't know how old I'd be—5, 6, 7. And in the baggage car at that time they'd have bricks of silver that they'd picked up at Cobalt—a pile of it...Each brick would be 1' x 6" x 6" or something like that—they'd have them crisscrossed so they wouldn't slide too much... And of course I was young enough in those days that I'd like to play with them...couldn't lift them of course...and I'd get to North Bay and my hands'd be black from the silver!

But that was a common occurrence on that train, maybe 2–3 times a week...there were no guards or anything like that.[18] ❧

Train crews began their voyages several times every day from each of the divisional and subdivisional points. As they proceeded towards their respective destinations, operators filled the wires with information, dispatchers responded with altered train orders, maintenance-of-way people operated to keep the track secure. The safe and efficient operations of these trains, however, depended also on a strict adherence to the *Uniform Code of Operating Rules* and an equally strict adherence to any refinements or any local regulations which were called for on the T&NO itself. For the most part the rules were indeed followed. And when they were not followed, the person who broke them was punished. The most severe, and swift, punishment was applied to those who broke Rule G. For obvious reasons, the use of alcohol while on duty was strictly and categorically forbidden.

271

The admonitions against drinking on the job met with general agreement among railroaders.

    ❧ You can't booze and railroad, because its your life and somebody else's. So many things can happen. Everything you do...well you can't stop a boxcar;...when you're switching and kicking boxcars, you gotta be alert. Like the old saying goes, "If you're not [alert], you're gonna get hurt."[19] ❧

Yet because of the closeness that developed among the men, there was a reticence to report the offenders. While there were, at the height of the T&NO's prominence, some 2000 employees, the men generally worked in groups, and there was an inclination to protect the group's members. It has already been noted that the train crews often came to work as a team. The same tendency applied among section men, operators, station personnel, yard men, and work crews. Thus there developed the paradoxical situation where the fracturing of Rule G was viewed with disapproval and yet

    ❧ There were a lot of fellows that violated Rule G that...got away with it...because the rest of the crew covered up for them. They were a unit, and they covered for one another come hell or high water...

    I knew of some of the fellows. I was fortunate enough that I never worked with one of the boozers. I never had to. I was never subjected to it. I knew who they were. We all knew who they were. The superintendent knew who they were... There are no secrets on the line...not one. It was just catching some of the fellows...I don't think it was a huge problem. I can remember back in 1949, 1950, I could...count the real offenders on one hand...on the whole system...[20] ❧

It should not be assumed that railroaders were abstainers, though certainly some were. Like other northerners, they would certainly

On the baggage cart (Malcolm Clark, North Bay)

take a drink, and the circumstances were often amusing. One story that circulates the line is likely apocryphal, but it bears telling for it is a typical railroader's tale. Apparently a load of whisky was stored in a freight shed at Porquis Junction during prohibition days, which would make it between 1916 and 1926. In any event, the authorities not only locked the supply at Porquis in the shed but also stationed a guard who actually sat on the barrel. The floor of a railway storage shed sits some four feet off the ground to make it level with a boxcar opening; so one enterprising chap crept under the shed, drilled a hole through the floor, and through the barrel, and thus obtained his own supply. It is likely not true, but Bill Ross recounted two tales that could be.[21] In one case in 1928 or so, a group of men from the work car known as a Ditcher "got feeling good" and stole an organ from the church at Earlton and brought it onto their boarding car. One of the men apparently got the idea that he was a musician and wanted music on the boarding car. They were not fired, but "they had the devil of a time getting it out" of the car. "In fact no one could ever figure out how they got it into the car around that narrow

opening and railing." On another occasion in
the early '40s, men in the Rouyn bunkhouse
made a powerful punch consisting of alcohol,
wine, and maraschino cherries. While they sat
around drinking, playing cards, and singing, a
Salvation Army Captain came to visit. He declined the punch, of course, but made the mistake of accepting a dish of the cherries!

Punishments for infractions of the rules
normally took the form of demerit points. These
were issued on the basis of a merit system
worked out by a man named Brown. Thus it
was common to hear someone say that they had
a certain number of "Brownie" points. Only a
few of the people involved with the movement
of trains did not receive at least some brownie
points. As one engineer remarked, "We called
them company shares. Everybody had a few
company shares at one time or another. We all
did."[22] It is characteristic of the system that the
points were applied for any rule violation
whether or not the infraction resulted in a mishap. The penalty would be as severe whether or
not something happened. The system was the
same throughout the T&NO/ONR organization
regardless of the trade: sixty demerits could result in dismissal. All aspects of the jobs were
covered. For example, missing a shift or constant tardiness could result in demerits. Of
course the rules were strictest when concerned
with the movement of trains, and thus those
people involved, such as the dispatchers and
running trades, were more likely to be disci-
plined by the Brownie system. Other forms of
discipline could be used, such as suspensions,
demotions, or transfers, but the Brownie, or demerit, system always remained in place. It was
not unforgiving; it permitted good performance
to compensate for mistakes. A complete year
without incident would wipe out 10 points.
Also, while the acquisition of 60 demerits could
indeed lead to dismissal, the ultimate penalty
was by no means automatic. Transfers to different jobs or temporary suspensions might be applied instead. Indeed, few were let go simply
through the application of the Brownie system.

A conductor patrolling his train
(Malcolm Clark, North Bay)

Stories about the system abound. Some are
really quite humourous and possibly apocryphal. At one point, for example, when
W.H. Griffin was superintendent and was observed to be limping, someone remarked that
"he must have dropped a bag of demerits on his
foot." Another story tells of the time that Buck
Newell was in to see the superintendent because he had piled up so many demerits. The
superintendent is said to have remarked, "I
don't know what we're going to do with you;
you've got 55 demerit marks!" According to
tradition, Buck simply shrugged and said,
"That's simple. Just wipe them out and we'll
start all over again!"

In some instances, the incident was as
much embarrassing as anything else.

&✥ Back in 1947 or 1948, Donald
R. Dingwall...was the engineer and
Ernie Swales...was the fireman [on a
run to Moosonee]. They stopped at
mileage 165. Jardine was the superintendent, with his private car at the
back of the train...[they] had to set a
couple of cars onto the siding. So the
brakeman made the cut.

It was dark, it was in the fall, the
train was late...and the [brakeman] said,
"O.K." to Dingwall with his lantern. He

[Dingwall] opened the throttle, closed his window, and went right to Moosonee. He left the superintendent, the coaches, and everything sitting at mileage 165! He still had about 10 cars behind him...funny he didn't notice that he was feeling light... Well, he gets to Moosonee and everybody [on the platform at the station] was pointing back and waving their arms.

He [Dingwall] kept looking back and says to Ernie Swales—the station was on his [Dingwall's] side and Dingwall was looking back for a signal for the brakeman to tell him when to stop—"I don't see any brakeman!" Ernie Swales said, "You better stop pretty soon or we'll be off the track. We're a mile by the station now!"

Then [Dingwall] twigged to what had happened...

What did he do? He put those box cars over in the yard track and went back and got the train. Well, they say that Jardine was just walking up and down...just tearing his hair out!

I came up to work there about a week or so later, and I said to Dingwall, "Did you put in for 'doubling' for that?"—doubling, you know, means that he had run up, then 20 miles back...there'd be all those extra miles [on his time sheet].

He said, "You're damn right I did. They gave me 30 demerit marks. I thought I better put something in!"

You can imagine how embarrassed he must have been...[also, it could have been tragic because] he could have dropped off the end of the track, into Butler Creek... Poor old Don, it took him a long time to live that one down.[23] ❧

A dozen years later, Moore himself narrowly escaped experiencing a similar embarrassment.

❧ About 1960, I went to Moosonee with one of our Montreal Locomotive Works engines. We used to go up Saturday and back Monday. And we had [on the fuel tanks] a floating gauge rather than a sight glass. The float gauge would sometimes stick and not give you an accurate reading. I put a bit of fuel in at Moosonee, but I thought...I had lots of fuel to get to Cochrane.

Archie Freeman [the general manager] was in the private car on the tail-end. And I was at mileage 22, going along merrily, when one cylinder stopped, another one stopped—16 cylinders ran out of gas, one at a time...and I had 21 miles to go! ❧

At that point they were coasting, close towards Gardiner where the train was supposed to stop anyway. He remembered that about a quarter mile past Gardiner there was a fuel shack on the edge of the track and a road from there into one of the lumber camps.

❧ So I said to Ernie Johnson, the brakeman, "when we stop [at Gardiner], as soon as we stop...we'll be over that little knoll...you turn the angle cocks and the hosebag, pick the pin, and we'll drift down to that little shack and...we'll break in and get a barrel of fuel oil." We stopped, and I put the engine at just the last minute so he could get the pin. He didn't get it. He couldn't pull it. The thing had stretched out.

So I said, "I'll crank it." So I took the crank to it. So I turned the starter...and there was just enough vibration that he got the pin. And the engine started to move, and it rolled down the quarter mile to this shack. We broke in, got a barrel of fuel oil...fixed her up, backed up, and away we went.

Forty minutes I lost. Got into Cochrane. I said, "I'm going to get hell for this, I know." But Mr. Freeman said to Arnold Gillespie, the conductor, "No problem. We ran out of fuel."[24] ❧

Apart from the obvious good fortune that surrounded Bob Moore at the time, the incident also showed that he, like all running crew personnel, had an intimate knowledge of the road. It was this which permitted him to improvise to obtain the required fuel and thus avoid both demerits and embarrassment with the ONR; and it was this, combined with his personal relationships on the northern run, which allowed him to replace the fuel and repair the lock on the shed and thus avoid an extensive investigation (or "Q and A"). Such a knowledge of the road, and the people along it, provided the running crew with a set of tools—a set of instincts really—to help them sense the unusual and react to it, as in the case just noted. This knowledge also assisted greatly in the general operation of trains.

> ❧ You had to know the railbed, because with the slack action of the train, you could pull that train all apart...if you didn't know the roadbed.
>
> Like going into a dip or a hollow, the engineman has to know. He ties the brake down a little bit in order to drag the train out, so it won't run in on him. The same thing applies when he starts up another grade, everything starts to pull out on him... That's the slack action. You could pull a train apart that way...if you got a lot of heavy loads on the tail-end of a train, you can rip the thing right apart.[25] ❧

By "knowing the road," the engineman could, by a judicious use of brake and throttle on knolls, hills, curves, and gulleys, keep the train strung out straight, with the couplings between the cars extended. A sudden change in movement would cause the couplings to open violently (if speeding up too fast) or to close (if there was a sharp speed reduction or a stop). This would happen often in the yards, of course, where it was a matter of routine to shunt cars to particular spots (called spotting) in order to keep the yard orderly

and organized or to line them up as part of a train. It would also happen if a train had to double on a hill, cut or collect cars at sidings, or even simply pull into a siding and stop. These actions, however, all took place at slow speeds, and they were also expected. This controlled slack action caused little damage or danger. To hear those openings close, however, as a line of perhaps 11 cars was shunted to meet another line of perhaps 15, was (and is) a somewhat awesome sound.

Should such slack action take place at higher speeds of perhaps 50 mph, it could lead to a broken coupling—or perhaps worse—and that might not only rip the train apart, as Orv Nichols said, but it could also result in separate sectors of the train running out of control. Controlling slack action was also an important feature of driving a passenger train.

The slack action could have a devastating effect on the tail-end, which might be pulling the business car. Orville Nichols remembered one such instance when he was firing for George Gubb.

> ❧ Coming south [from Englehart] you have a heavy grade from Liskeard through to Cobalt, then it eases off over to Latchford, and out of Latchford you get another hill, and it eases off from those, and you hit another out of Temagami. Then it's fairly level right from mileage 68...til you get...south of the Osborne Straight (mileage 35), then you start to climb again...up into Tomiko, then you go down a little dip, and then you climb up again south of Tomiko before you get to Mulock, you've got two little grades there. You go over one and down through a little dip and back up another one. I got a kick out of Col. Reynolds. (Chuckles) I was coming down with George Gubb one Sunday morning, and they put on the private car, with Col. Reynolds, on the tail-end. And George was a little angry because we were actually that much

Maintaining the way   Various activities.
(Malcolm Clark, North Bay)

[i.e., the weight of the private car] over tonnage for the engine we had.

It was a bad day. There'd been a bit of sprinkling rain, and the rail was slippery. We started up. (Chuckles) We got over Cobalt hill all right and started out of Latchford, and the engine started to slip—we were running out of sand. It was a steam engine, and we stalled... I said to George, "I'll go back and we'll take half of it to the hill." He said, "No. We'll slack a little bit, use a bit of sand on the rail and lift again."

We did that seven times on that hill! You can imagine the jerking and jarring that went on in that private car! (Laughter) Col. Reynolds had visitors back there with him. And this all during the night. We left Englehart at 11:30 or so. (More chuckles) This went on all night. We never got into North Bay till quarter to eight in the morning.[26]

When George Gubb put his engine away and returned to the platform, Colonel Reynolds was waiting! The outcome of that meeting is not known.

Notes

1. See p. 261 of this text.
2. *Ibid.*
3. A.E. Simms. Interview. 27 February 1989. North Bay.
4. C.L. Bailey. Interview. 30 September 1988. North Bay.
5. *Ibid.*
6. *Ibid.*
7. Bob Moore. Interview. 22 May 1987. North Bay.
8. *Ibid.*
9. Bob Moore. Interview. 9 July 1986. North Bay.
10. See pp. 53, 138, 240 of this text.
11. Bob Moore. Interview. 17 October 1988. On line to Moosonee.
12. *Ibid.*
13. Isabelle Labreche. Interview. 19 December 1991, North Bay.
14. A.E. Simms. Interview. 27 February 1989.
15. *Ibid.*
16. Cobalt *Nugget*, 22 December 1909.
17. *Ibid.*
18. A.E. Simms. Interview. 27 February 1989.
19. C.L. Bailey. Interview. 30 September 1988.
20. Bob Moore. Interview. 22 May 1987. North Bay.
21. Bill Ross Jr. Interview. 1974. On file at ONA.
22. Bob Moore. Interview. 17, 18 October 1988. On line to Moosonee.
23. *Ibid.*
24. *Ibid.*
25. Orville Nichols. Interview. 27 February 1988.
26. *Ibid.*

Chapter 17

Still on the line

OFTEN THE EN-GINEMAN and the conductor would prefer to work the freight runs rather than the passenger trains. As one said, "It was easier to talk to freight." For the engineer it also meant less need for concern regarding the ride. Bill Ross had the following experience.

    I was the spare engineer [c. 1946 or 1947], and I got 46 and 47. That was the day-passenger train out of here... I went up on it and I did pretty good... Coming back down that night we were a bit late—making up a little time—and [we] came racing into... Temagami. There was a coal chute and a water tank there...and we had a big 1100... It was the practice and the habit to fill up the coal box first and then back up for water, so I did.

    At Englehart, before I left...the conductor had come up and he said, "Now Bill...we have the chairman of the road on there in a private car..." "Oh," I said, "that's fine. I wonder where he'd like his soup spilled," which was a standard joke among railway men, young engineers in particular, when they first got their job running...on a passenger train. Where would they like to have the passengers' soup spilled in the diner. Well I don't know now, there was a conductor—and I was pretty sure of him as a friend...—and there was a brakeman standing there. Now I don't know which one took it back to the chairman.

    Anyway, we stop at Temagami on the way south. I had been hitting the high spots on the way down and—of course it wasn't 24 mph then. It was a way up higher, 55–60 on passenger... We pulled down and made a nice spot for coal, back up for water, and we're not even spotted for water, and Bang! All the air goes, and everything goes in emergency and the train stops in a heap. So I get her pumped off again, back up, take water. We get started out of there again. Of course we're late, and I make up some more time. We get into North Bay, back over to the CNR, cut the engine off, go to the shop.

    Next morning the telephone rings about 9 o'clock. "That you, Bill?" "Yeah." "You're pulled out of passenger service." "I am? Why?" "Rough handling of the passenger train." "Oh. Well, if it must be, it must be." Then I said, "Where did it happen?"

"Well," he said, "He cited one place, at Earlton."

I said "That's right. The express messenger forgot to put the milk cans off, and pulled the air on me there...and the other place would be Temagami?"

He said, "Yeah. What happened there?"

I said, "Somebody on the train pulled the emergency valve back there..." I found out later that there was a drunk back there and he pulled that little velvet cord. (Laughs) Mr. Reynolds was the chairman, and he used to call his wife "Mommy." And when the train went into emergency, the big heavy car pulled the train out with a snap, knocked an ashtray over and broke it, and scared Mommy.

So I was pulled out of passenger service. For three months. It didn't hurt me any because we didn't get that many trips on passenger. (Chuckles)[1] ❧

Both Bill Ross and his wife were of the opinion that the remark about spilling the soup had been passed on and that this—when combined with the two sudden stops—had led to the discipline. "He wasn't a railroader...so he didn't realize" that the remark regarding the soup was really quite harmless. Indeed, Reynolds was not a railway man. He owed his appointment largely to his connections with Premier George Drew. The two men had been connected through the Canadian Corps Association; they had both served in the First World War; in 1944 they both held the rank of Colonel. Reynolds was also a staunch Conservative. At the time of his appointment as Chairman of the T&NO Commission, he had, after a five-year venture into the sawmill business in British Columbia, founded a cement contracting company in Ontario but spent most of his time with the Canadian Corps Association.[2] He was not really a railroad man, and he may well indeed have misunderstood Bill Ross's innocent remark. Yet the incident was exemplary of the watchfulness that T&NO officials had over their trains.

Bill Ross's remark that Reynold's was "not a railroader" carries with it certain nuances. In this

Cochrane Station crew, 1936   (Left to right) J.E. Ballantyne, Ryder, Bill Landsdell, George Gorman, A.T. King, J.M. Nelson, B.A. Harkness. (ONA-1988249 B. Landsdell)

Fraserdale Station, c. 1931 (ONA-1988079)

instance, it was something akin to forgiveness, in that because he was not a railroader he could not be expected to understand the railroader's way of doing things. Therefore, he should not be judged too harshly. Conversely Conductor Bailey summarized A.H. Cavanaugh, the General Manager, by saying, "Well, he was a railroader." One has the feeling that Cavanaugh could never hope to receive higher praise.

The two stories indicate that there was indeed a desire to keep the runs smooth, especially on the passenger trains. The infractions noted resulted in some discomfort, not danger. Much more serious, much more frightening, were instances of carelessness, particularly carelessness on a regular basis. Because "there were no secrets on the line," everyone knew which engine men were inclined to ignore the rules or to act in an unsafe manner. Such men were feared.

  This particular engineer—I'm not going to give you his name because [of] his family—he'd just take them [the train orders] and put the orders in his pocket...he'd be leaving North Bay here on the hill. He'd set the engine—there was a big lever...that you cut off—and he set that down there, he opened up the throttle, he put his feet up...put the orders in here [gestures to a place in front of him]. And he'd lay back and lots of times he was sleeping going up there, and you were shovelling coal to beat the band... If you asked him, he'd say, "You never mind the orders, you'll be busy down in the kitchen." [i.e., firing the engine].[3]

Orville Nichols also had harsh words to say about one man whom he, and many others, considered to be reckless.

  You never knew what you were going to run into... In Temagami, we come in there one night and there was a train working on the main line... We came in, and we were running ahead of the passenger train, and he [the passenger train] would follow the passing track. We had to flag the passenger train behind us.

281

A fellow named *X* was the engineer on the passenger train—old 49—I had dropped off to go flagging just in case we did get stuck, and he ran right by me. He hit the torpedoes, he seen [sic] my fusee and just ran right by me. Bill Barnhart was the conductor on the tail-end of our train, and fortunately they had got pulled onto the siding and clear...the passenger train would have hit our van if we hadn't moved.

We turned him in several times for doing that same thing. He'd run by flag after flag like that. Its a wonder the man hadn't killed someone, or killed himself.

Q. That must have scared you.

Oh, it did. Often... Another time we had a meet at...the first siding north of Temagami, and we were running ahead of the passenger train. *X* was the engineman [of the passenger train], and we didn't see any sign of this other train [i.e., the one they were supposed to meet]. He [the other train] was to take the siding. We didn't see any sign. What we didn't know was that he only had a tiny little train on, and he was in the south end of the siding, but we couldn't see it because there's a curve on that siding. So we pulled into the siding, and I get a whistle to go flagging. It was because they [i.e., our train] couldn't get all the way in to the siding, because of this other train sitting in there.

So I grabbed the flagging kit and headed back and got back as far as the mile board, put down my torpedoes, and started to run away, and I had a fusee lit in my hand, and he [passenger train] came around the corner. And he went sailing right by me.

The other train had decided to back out far enough to let us out, realizing we would flag him [the passenger train] and hold him up. The van was just pulling in to clear and the conductor lined the switch, and he [passenger train] went by and he just about clipped the taillight off the corner of the van, that's how close it was...he was given some demerit marks for that... Yet he done that time after time. The fireman'd turn him in... He was a bad man... We were afraid of that fella every time we had a meet on him...he'd disregard flags time after time.

And you know there was no communication the way there is today. There were no radios. They did start to put phone booths up at the ends of sidings so you could call the dispatcher. But that was just certain sidings; other places you had to use that long pole and cords to try and make your contacts... We had some bad men.[4] ☙

He quickly added, however, "then you had some very good men... Most of the men...valued their own life too."

In the instance just given, an awkward situation had developed because the south bound train had pulled into the siding—its orders called for it to pass the northbound train (i.e., the inferior direction) and there was not enough room for the two trains on the siding until the former backed up a little. To correct this bad situation, the passenger train (southbound) was flagged and should have stopped. This should have been sufficient to keep the train line-up in order. Some luck—and possibly the anticipation of that particular engineman's behaviour (i.e., the one operating the passenger train)—prevented a disaster.

Such prompt action was expected on the part of the running trades. Indeed, they took pride in their ability to correct awkward situations or to accommodate to inclement weather or faulty track or some other unforeseen contingency. Perhaps the single most severe difficulty concerned communication, even among the running crew itself, in the days before radios. It sometimes meant climbing along the top of the train!

&. It used to be that all the cars had running boards along the top of them [in the middle]. And if the conductor got a little worried about something and he didn't want to pull the air, he'd come over the top of the train.

I've done it many times when we were having problems on the road...we [had to] double into Johnson —that was on the Latchford hill, south of Latchford...and [because of the time it would take for doubling] we were going to be short of time for meeting the passenger train.

I cut the train in half, and then, when I gave him [the engineman] the signal to go ahead, I climbed the car, got up on top and ran ahead up through the cars—over the top—to get to the engine to put him in the siding, and then get the flagging kit,...flag the passenger train and hold him there while we went back and got the other half of the train...it used to happen quite often.[5] ❧

Every railway man emphasizes the importance of following the rules strictly and of obeying any and all signals. Missing even one can lead to a mishap, and because the equipment is so very heavy, any mishap could be serious. Most, it seems, experienced at least one mishap which would be termed minor. On one occasion the dispatcher sent out

&. ...a second section of Train 109, which at that time was the mixed train...we were ordered as a second section...to run as a snowplow from [North Bay] to Englehart...

All you had [on this second section] was the plow, the engine, and the van... He [the mixed train] was due out at 9:30 a.m... We were ordered from 1 o'clock to run as a second section. So he was showing the green flags and the green lights, displaying signals for a second section, so other trains and the section men would be looking for us.

The reason they did that was because they had forgotten to on the line-up—just before 8:00 a.m. the dispatcher gives a line-up of all the cars on the road, and they forgot to put the plow on the line-up. So when they were getting the 109 ready...they ran him as a first section. Now, the first section shows green flags for the second section—in fact you could run four sections if you wanted, or five sections, and every one but the last one would show green flags... So they ran us as a second section of 109.

Len Monahagn was the engineer, and he'd never worked the south end [i.e., North Bay to Englehart]; he'd always worked out of Englehart... He was cautious, because he was on strange track... They had run him down from Englehart the night before. An engineman had taken sick—a south-end engineman—on the way up and...booked sick [there]. So they used Len to bring the train back [to North Bay] from Englehart. [Then] rather than pay him deadhead to go home, they put him on [to take] the plow.

We were given a meet on 418 [the paper train] at Mulock... And he told [the man on the plow, which runs directly in front of the engine],..."the yard limit board is practically at the switch at Mulock, so you make sure to give me a whistle at the mile board so I'll slow down."

[But] the man on the plow forgot to give him the whistle at the mile board and he didn't blow till he got to the yard limit board. By that time, we were going over the switch...we couldn't get in the siding. We were going up the main line! [It was quite serious because] 418 was coming down

283

Snow plow   The plow is placed in front of the engine. Thus the engineman, who has control of the engine, has greatly reduced vision. Indeed, swirling snow could eliminate vision to the point where the enginemen could see neither in front nor his mate on his right side (i.e., the fireman). He had to depend on the man in the plow for signals. The man in the plow could control only the plow's apertures by lowering or raising the blade. It could be stressful. (ONA-199126 Butler)

the main line and hadn't got down far enough to line—You see, normally, a [superior] train, if he gets there first, will line the switch for the meet...for the other train to take the siding. The timing was bad...if we had been a couple of minutes later, they would have had the switch lined for us...and everybody would have been safe.

But instead of that, [418] was just coming to a stop. The plow foreman blew the whistle for the yard limit board [which was almost on top of the switch for the siding], and then [he] realized what had happened and put the train into emergency, but it was too late and the plow ended up on top of [i.e., between] the two engines.[6]

The men on the front-ends of both trains and the man in the plow were shaken up somewhat by the head-on collision but not seriously injured, likely because the southbound train (418) had stopped and the northbound train had been thrown into emergency stop, and with a cautious engineman had probably not been travelling too fast anyway. Orville Nichols, who was in 109's van—which was actually directly behind the engine—was less fortunate.

I had just pulled up my parka hood, and thank God for that, because that's what saved my life. I had gone to the tail-end, to the van, and I heard the whistle. I thought we were at the mile board, so I got up and pulled my parka up, and we hit! I went the full length of the van and into the cupboards. If I hadn't had that parka hood up, I'd have been killed... As it was, the doctor thought I had broken my neck, because I was completely paralysed at the time... The very fact that I was standing up at the end of the van was the reason I got hurt so badly.[7] 🦤

Following the collision, 418 simply backed up a bit, and the plow fell off it clear of the passing track, so 109 also backed up and pulled onto the passing track (i.e., the siding) till the vans of the two trains were parallel. They then transferred Nichols to 418 which brought him to North Bay. It is a measure of the state of communications at the time that, since the railway people neglected to call his wife, she was not aware of the incident until two days later, when one of the nurses, Miss Foley, called to tell her about it. Of course, it was not uncommon for one of the running crews to be away from home for several days, so Mrs. Nichols would have had no reason to inquire.

Separation within families was quite common because of the nature of the work, and the people involved no doubt grew to live with it, but it could get worrisome at times of personal or family crisis. It was more severe in the earlier days before telephones became common and before the North was covered by a network of roads as well as the railway. In 1928, for example, engineer Bill Ross received word that he would be working on the Elk Lake branch.

🦤 I went to the foreman and asked him if I could be excused from going in there. We were working the spare list. He said, "No. Every time you fellows have to go away...you book sick or something." Well, I had never done that, but there were two or three other fellows that had... So he made me go in there. There was no motor road in there, and we didn't have a car anyway. And once you got in there, you laid in there over night...and here I was all the time expecting a wire from my wife or her mother or somebody

stating that my wife was in the hospital or the baby had come or something, and I'm tied up in there. Well, you know what a young fellow is like, his first born. And it was bad there for a couple of weeks. Boy, I worried and worried. And no operator, no way of getting a wire or a telephone call or anything like that. (Chuckles) The power plant had gone out in there too...but we survived it.[8] 🦤

It was a girl!

A few years earlier Bob Cameron, who worked as a section man near Matheson, experienced the unexpected while driving his motor car.

🦤 I used to go down to Loiselle's farm down here and get two quarts of milk every evening...we got a lineup on trains that would be operating that afternoon, and there was one supposed to be out of Englehart at 3:30... I was coming back home, went in and got the two quarts of milk, and had them on the windshield in the front of the motor car, and we still had plenty of time. It was only 2:30, and that train wasn't supposed to be out of Englehart until 3:30. So I got up close to the road here that comes into the railway, stopped, and I listened...and didn't hear nothin' at all; so I started up again. I didn't get very far, and here's a locomotive in front of us. Whoa boy! I said, "Jump, boys, jump!" And I stayed about 5 seconds and cut the switch on the motorcar and...I could see tools flying over the boys' heads when that locomotive smashed the car...that'd be about '44 or '45.[9] 🦤

Strict adherence to the rules was essential, but, when combined with a little bad weather, some minor equipment failure, and a touch of misfortune, the rules could lead to an excessively long and arduous run.

We left Englehart one day with one of the 1100s...a passenger engine on a train of freight. We had a meet at Uno Park, and we sat at Uno Park for 12 hours. (Chuckles)

The train broke down, and we couldn't get our phone to work. You had long poles with hooks on the end, and you put your wire on these ends and they hooked up to the line to get hold of the dispatcher. What we didn't realize [was that] there was a break in the wire on our phone cord, so we couldn't get hold of the dispatcher. We sat there all that time till a train finally came along, and he stopped to deliver orders to us because we'd run out of date—after 12 hours, if you're 12 hours late, then you're out of date.

We had been running as a regular train, but [because we were out of date] they had to run us as an extra, from there into North Bay... [And as an extra train we] became an inferior train and therefore [we] had to make way for all others, except—in this case—other extra trains [travelling north], because south was the superior direction.

We got to Liskeard, and, of course, they had a red board on there, so we stopped. Of course, we had to get water anyway. So we watered up the engine and checked the train over. We had set two cars off at Uno Park that were running hot journals. [We] got our orders...and went over to Coleman, which is part of the siding at Cobalt, [because we] had another meet there. [We] took the siding, and...were there for seven hours.

It was 17 below when we left Englehart, so you'll realize that what was happening to us was that the train sat so long at the siding that this [lubricant] in the bottom of the journal boxes would freeze up, and when you'd move,...your journal would run

hot, so you'd have a "hot box" and you'd have to set the car off.

We finally got going again. We got to Redwater and we stopped [there] for five hours. We had three meets there. We sat on the siding for those three meets. By the time we met them, we couldn't get out of there because of the passenger train [which was due by then]. We had to sit there and wait for him...

I always laughed at old Pop Garde [when] I think of that trip. When we finally did get going, we didn't have anything else to meet till we got to North Bay. We were coming down the Osborne straight and we were having a heck of a time, because every time we got a long delay, the train would freeze up, and it would take quite a while to get it warmed up.

We came around the Osborne Straight, and at the south end...is a little rock cut and quite a bad curve, for which pretty well every engineer would slow down to about 30 mph., and widen on it after he got past there, and make a run for the hill at Jocko.

The fireman went over to Bill Garde—we had that 1100—we must have been going 60 mph...he said to Bill, "When are you going to put the brake on?"

Bill walked over to his side and said, "Do you think we're going to make it?"

And he never touched the brake at all! We made it. We sure rocked a bit! I think the one side of the engine lifted right off the rails!...always enjoyed working with Pop Garde.[10]

Trips like the one described by Orv Nichols were something of a rarity, but it was not uncommon for the men who rode the trains to experience harsh or unusual conditions and circumstances. Included among the more unusual would be the experience of Malcolm

Unloading baggage, Moosonee   Note the dogs. Baggageman holding rope is Malcolm Clark Sr., c. 1950. (Malcolm Clark, North Bay)

Clarke, the baggageman on the Moosonee subdivision in 1946 or so.

   Joe Friday was an Indian lad who later worked for the ONR, but before that he was [living] on Sheep Ash River at mileage 62...he'd come down [from Moosonee] in the fall, come out at Christmas, go back in after Christmas, and stay there till spring. When breakup would start in the spring, we'd start looking [for him]—"Well, so and so [several native families like that of Joe Friday would follow the same pattern from various points along the Moosonee run] should be out pretty soon." And sure enough, they'd be out—their tents, their kids, their dogs, and their furs. [They'd] all hop on the train...the dogs would go in the baggage cars [with] their furs and tents.

[The dogs were not in cages. They were just tied in the baggage car.] They'd howl and roar and yell...they'd be O.K....just don't go too near them! The [owner] would look after them. He'd tie them up, so the baggage man wouldn't have to go near them.

One baggage man—unfortunately he's dead now—his name was Malcolm Clark, in 1946 or so, there were three or four dogs in the baggage car. They were howling, and they got on his nerves, so he took a piece of hard grease—now this hard grease, it comes in cakes and is used for journal boxes on cars. There's always a good supply of it in every baggage car. This was before we had roller bearings. Old Malcie threw a couple of chunks of hard grease at the dogs, and they fought over it. They just gulped it and swallowed it!

An hour later, he was a sorry guy. They got diarrhoea!... The smell, he couldn't even stay!... When we got to Moosonee, we got a hose in there and hot water and flushed the whole thing out.

I said, "Good for you Malcie, you won't do that again![11] 🐾

C.L. Bailey also had an unusual experience.

🐾 [One time] at New Liskeard...a car of bananas was going through New Liskeard to Kirkland Lake. So we get the bananas on the train and lo and behold, we're going up through Earlton —it's a big curve [there]—and we see [from the front-end] that the car's on fire!

Boxcar living
(Malcolm Clark, North Bay)

288

They were heated with charcoal burners. There was nothing we could do. We had nothing to fight it with.

So we go into Englehart... I'm on the head-end—I was the brakeman then. I cut the car off and went down the centre lead. Abby Simms was the chief dispatcher [stationed at Englehart]. I can remember this as if it was yesterday. They used to keep those old hoses in the station—you know, all folded up.

Abby said, "Turn the water on!"

Hah! It was a sin—full of holes. So there was that car of bananas on fire; and the insulation in the cars...was like horse hair. Burned all the car on the inside and roasted all the bananas.[12] ☙

More often than not, however, the unexpected and the harsh occurred as a result of the extremes of the northern climate. In this regard, the men of the T&NO—running crews, section men, yardmen, and all other—came to expect the unexpected. There was a limit, of course, to the ways in which they could prepare themselves, but in general the men would be as ready as possible for inclement weather or for unexpected mishaps or emergencies. Those who rode the front-end, for example, knew full well that on a blustery winter day, or in any period of snow fall, a circumstance that could emerge quite suddenly, they could expect to get wet and cold.

☙ We'd leave here in the wintertime, 35, 40 below zero with the snowplow tacked on the head-end, and you had an old canvas side curtain on the locomotives in those days—they weren't vestibule cabs. And they'd be flapping in the wind until we pulled them in and piled a little coal on them to keep the snow from coming up from underneath... By the time we'd get 35 miles on the road, the fireman would be pretty well soaked wet because you would have to get down into what we

called the kitchen, which was down where the coal box was, and put the coal on the fire to produce the steam. Well, then you come to a water tank, and if you had a good tail-end crew, they would take water for you, and you would clean your fire if it needed it, which nine times out of ten it did because it was clinkered. And then you would carry on, and the most amazing thing of the whole bunch, of the whole operation, you would be dead tired; maybe you'd be plowing all the passing tracks and spurs that you could on the way up and, you'd be tired out. You'd be 14, maybe 15, hours going up, and soaking wet, and you would have by this time cursed every operational management right from the big man right down to the guy that shovels snow on the switches, you might say, not because of any personal enmity, just because you were tired and angry.[13] ☙

☙ We went north with the snowplow one time and you couldn't see the coal on the deck at all—it was all covered with snow...when the curtain [of the cab] got froze...the snow would come in on your back...[it would melt] every time you stoked the fire... I got off at Englehart, walked over to the bunkhouse,...took my over-alls off, and they stood up on the floor![14] ☙

Indeed all front-end men would have had the experience of frozen clothing because of the alternation of heat and cold in the cab. Clearly, the men, knowing this, would be ready with proper clothing. They would usually be prepared as well with a generous supply of food. There were three reasons for this. One was the fact that even a fast run, and one that was on time, would be fairly lengthy. For example, the shortest possible outing would be one like a run from North Bay to Englehart or from Englehart to Cochrane on a passenger train. Then, upon reaching their destination, the crew would turn around almost immediately and bring another train back to their home base. It was a procedure called "doubling." Even that, however, would take a minimum of 20 hours. The second was the possibility that a run—any run—might be extended beyond its schedule because of bad weather, mechanical failure, or untoward circumstances. On a way freight it was almost certain! The third resulted from such organizational realities as the possibility of special trains—or second and third sections of regular trains—being run, and the use of the spare board to fill in for the regular board. Always a possibility, again, was the need for a man to do a second "trick" because of unexpected book-offs by the regular crew because of illness, fatigue, or personal reasons. Thus, it was fairly common to take a run which might, in the end, keep them away from home for several days. To prepare for these various contingencies, the men on the train would commonly, if not as a rule, carry some substantial supplies with them.

Some of the actions which they took in this regard showed considerable ingenuity.

Cathy McDonald in dining car of the residence cars at New Liskeard, 1933 (ONA-1988194 J. Hammer)

❧ There was never a lunch bucket in my knowledge that was made anywhere else for the running crews except in the tin shop in North Bay, in the old roundhouse. Vic Tynan was down there for many many years, Len Dawberman worked in the tin shop...all these guys would custom make the lunch buckets for the engine crews. Not too many for the tail-end—the conductors and brakemen. They had what they called a telescope. It was a thing about 24" long by 8" or 9" deep...by 14", 15" wide, and a cover that fit over it, with a strap. That's what they carried their lunches in. But the enginemen had to have this particular box made—lunch box that would fit in the seat box [on the engine]. [That] was where you sat. You opened it up and put your lunch in that.

Sometimes, you'd be...out for two or three days...leaving North Bay on

415 or 417 (at night)—you'd leave there, say, at 7 o'clock at night. If you turned right back from Englehart, you could be back at seven or eight or nine the next morning. But if you were on the old way freight, where you stopped at every little siding—the old 209 and 210 was that little train that used to run out of North Bay with a little coach behind it—then you'd be gone for two days. If you went out on a plow and spreader, you'd be gone for three or four days. So the lunch box had to be full of food.

You got a two-hour call...then you knew where you were going and when you were going to go. So you had to be pretty adept at getting this thing full of food.

Q. What kind of food would be all right for two days?

We didn't have much refrigeration in those days. In fact, we had practically none...

Number one, you'd have sandwiches to eat on the road. The runs then were between six and seven hours [i.e., between North Bay and Englehart]. With diesels today, four hours; but with steam engines you had to stop at Tomiko to take water,...at Redwater to take water,...at Temagami to take coal and water, and water at New Liskeard, so it took a lot longer with the old steam engines...

You'd get to Englehart and you were fine. You were at the terminal. So you'd be six or seven hours going north and you'd have sandwiches, a thermos of tea or—you didn't really need a thermos because—if you were stopping somewhere—we'd have a little tea pail—you'd open the fire box door and put the water in there over the hot fire—the water'd be boiling in two or three minutes. It'd make an excellent cup of tea—almost as good as over a camp fire, you know, where the ashes are falling in! (Chuckles)

So when you got to Englehart, normally you'd have potatoes in a little dish, that were cooked, so you'd fry up some potatoes, you'd have bacon and eggs, have a small steak and whatever veggies you want to put in there. And that would be your heavy meal, when you got there. Always bacon and eggs... Would cook in the bunkhouse when you got the Englehart.

Q. That's 1950 or so. What was it like earlier?

It didn't change much.

Q. They didn't have electricity earlier on.

They had stoves—coal stoves. In 1946 I worked out of Cochrane to Moosonee. We had a little bunkhouse on this side of the track... We had a great big, cast-iron, pot-bellied stove, fired by hard coal. It was the nicest warming thing you've ever seen in your life when you've been out on a cold winter's night...

We used to have these little galvanized pots...would hold about a quart, maybe a quart and a half. The night before or early in the morning before we left on a run coming to Moosonee, we'd buy some round steak or stewing beef, get some carrots, some onions, some turnips, put them all together in this pot with some salt and pepper, put them up on the engine... It was where all the valves came out...[and beside the valves] was the bare part of the boiler. You'd set this thing up there... We'd normally eat about Island Falls, which is about 2.5–3 hours out of Cochrane. But about an hour after the thing was put up there, the smell was mmmm! But we used to cook that way. We'd cook these stews, and we'd stop and have a hot stew.

On a steam locomotive you had to stop and have your lunch. So at Island Falls we'd stop and do our freighting. Then we'd pull up ahead a little bit and stop there and have our lunch— and lunch was a hot meal. We'd generally cook enough stew that we'd have it for lunch going down the next day on the way back.[15] ❧

Another engineer, C.L. Bailey, also spoke of the habit of cooking on the boiler.

❧ That's where the enginemen would put their [food]. Because it was hot up there. That's where all you gauges were in front of you. You got your stoker there, and it's hot. They'd put their stuff up there... They'd even take...oxyl and water, put it up there and have a drink of oxyl... I remember, I worked with a fella, George Drubb. He used to call it "bull-ur-ina!" "Let's have a drink of bullurina," [he'd say]. That was oxyl cubes and hot water.[16] ❧

The practice of cooking on the boiler or of stopping for a cup of tea from time to time with section men was a recognized and accepted part of the milieu of the train crew's activities, and few managers would have questioned it. It was only on the more relaxed atmosphere of the Island Falls subdivision, however, that certain other activities would have been tolerated. There the mood remains quite different—even today—than elsewhere on the line; simply, the railway remains largely the single mode of entry and exit for that area. Thus, the crews there would be more likely to stop anywhere for pas-

sengers, or mail, or supplies, or perhaps just for conversation. On occasion the crew might stop simply to do some fishing.[17] It is unlikely that the last would have received official approbation, although that it took place was almost certainly known by officialdom. As all employees—past and present—emphasize, there are no secrets on the line.

In the event of a mishap, minor or major, two groups of men would be dispatched to the scene. One would be the T&NO policemen who would have the job of ensuring that the area of the accident was secured and that any cargo, equipment, or supplies would not be stolen or pilfered. The second would be a work crew whose job was to restore the scene to order. This might be the simple task of correcting a derailment. If this were simple enough, it might require only a small crew armed with a set of levers that would be used to lift the car back up onto the track. More complicated work, from more severe accidents, would require the use of more extensive equipment and a large crew of men.

Section man and hand car　Each section had its hand car; later a motor car. (Malcolm Clark, North Bay)

❧ I remember one time, 1948 I guess it was, they piled paper train into the creek at Uno Park. And it was cold. It was almost 50 below when we left Englehart.

We got down there and...well, Mr. *Jardine himself* [the speaker's emphasis]—we had the private car on the end [of the work train]—he went out and gathered up broken debris and that from inside the box cars and piled [it] up... "Come on, Orville, [he said], let's get a fire going." In those days you used to work straight through. There was no such thing as eight hours or twelve hours, you went right through. And we worked 72 hours straight, without a break, getting the main line clear...

So he [Jardine] said, "Let's go back into Liskeard and have a rest"... so both auxiliary crews—north end and south end—we all went back into Liskeard... There was no other person on the road that'd do what he [Jardine] did that day...

He came into the van and said, "Okay fellows, the cook says he's got some food ready for you there. Oh, by the way...I left an empty whiskey bottle sitting on the table there...well you can just throw it out"... Well it was full and he had some glasses sitting there... Needless to say, it was empty when we left!

It was breaking a rule, yes, but he realized that we had been on duty for 72 hours...and we weren't going anywhere. We were going in the siding and he told us, "You're not going back out for 12 hours." There was lots of work to do yet [on that accident]. We had just cleared the main line...

That was the kind of person he was...a really fine person.[18] ❧

Every mishap had to be investigated, and this consisted of two parts. One was the on-sight inspection; the other was an official inquiry in which men connected with the incident would be questioned. Usually referred to as a "Q and A," this procedure would invariably lead to a determination of blame. Thus, in addition to the work crew and the railway police, an investigation team could be expected at every sight as well, and often this meant the presence of the superintendent, who was described as "the most powerful man, on the line, under the general manager." Based after 1935 in Englehart,

❧ He was responsible for everything that happened on that railway...your enginemen, after they got out of the roundhouse and were on the line, he [the superintendent] was responsible for [them]. All your dispatching staff, your operators, your section men, your section foremen, your section crews, your trainmen, your conductors, your enginemen, your firemen, all your B and B staff—everything—all your agents, all

Superintendent Alvin Jardine   "The fellow that we worried about was the superintendent." (ONA-516M)

your shed men—they all came under the superintendent. ❧

The importance of the superintendent could be expressed in a different way. As one former engineman put it, the chairman and the general manager may well have been important figures, but

❧ As far as we were concerned, the fellow that we worried about was the superintendent. We never worried about the general manager. I guess the superintendent worried about the general manager! That's the way we looked at it. All those years in Transportation, the superintendent was the fellow we had to look out for.[19] ❧

With that heavy responsibility went the need for the superintendent to know what had happened in the case of serious accidents. He travelled by private car with a small entourage to assist him. One man who filled, for a time, the role of private secretary to the superintendent was Ralph Brill. He concedes that it was a good job, but it did have some demanding features.

  In 1942 I went to Englehart as private secretary to the superintendent... As [such] you travelled in the private car—old 99. Mr. Jardine had just been appointed—I forget when, but he had not been on the job very long. George Sewell was secretary—he joined with me. We did have another man, a good shorthand man and a good typist. So was I. They needed that because any investigation that the superintendent did had to be taken down in shorthand, verbatim, which I did. We travelled quite a lot on the private car between points on the T&NO/ONR—wrecks particularly...

[We'd] be gone for days... I remember one wreck at Val Gagne—well, up that way... It was January 1st, in the morning—'45, '46, or '47... And we got finished that wreck, and pulled in [to Englehart] I think the next day, and the station agent came and said there had been another wreck—at Tomiko...so we...got up, got the engine crew and everything and came down to Tomiko.[20]

While accidents or break-downs could not be predicted, certain general trends could be anticipated. One of these was the need to repair cars which were left along the line because of "hot boxes." This was more prevalent in cold weather. It could reach almost epidemic proportions.

  One day we left Englehart with a train of pulpwood, and of course a train in those days was maybe 28–30 or 32 cars—loaded cars of pulpwood; that was a full tonnage train. It's all one steam engine could handle. And I've seen us arrive in North Bay, [and] we'd set off 14 of them—with hot boxes.[21]

These cars had to be repaired and put back into service as quickly as possible, for to leave them on sidings would risk late deliveries, spoilage, and pilfering. Furthermore, each car represented a substantial investment, and therefore it was good business as well as good sense to keep them in service. It was especially urgent if a "foreign" car was crippled, because every day it sat on the track increased its car-hire charges. The T&NO, therefore, maintained "travelling crews [of workmen] that did nothing but run up along the line fixing cars so they could bring them in."[22]

Two general characteristics would seem to have prevailed among all sectors of all trades and crafts on the T&NO. First, although there were periods—often extended periods—of considerable, sometimes frenzied, activity, there were also long periods of very light activity. All members of the running crews, for example, faced periods when there was little to do except sit as the train made its way along the line. The yard crews, shopmen, office staff, agents, operators, and dispatchers all experienced times on the job which were relatively quiet. The section men, extra gangs, special work crews, and troubleshooters also had periods when they may have had little to do. In those cases, even when the work was extensive, their isolated circumstances on residence work cars where there was little to do during the off hours meant even longer periods of inactivity.

The second characteristic was the tendency of all railway people to be rule oriented. It was a tendency which was encouraged by the *Uniform Code of Operating Rules* and the corresponding need of all persons to be intimately familiar with those portions of the rules that pertained to their tasks. It was vital, in an industry which was so heavy and so potentially dangerous, that every person in the complicated process of railway operation should remember to perform his particular task and to perform it both well and at the proper time in the requisite sequence. He must not be distracted. It was this which created the need for so many separate jobs. Likewise, most of

Conductor, Sam Farmer, one of a well-known T&NO/ONR family (Malcolm Clark, North Bay)

the railway trades, crafts, and roles were guided by collective agreements negotiated through union representatives. Here too there was a strong emphasis upon rules and an encouragement—this time by the union's officials—for the men to comply strictly to the terms of the agreement.

It has been observed that the men of the T&NO generally possessed a strong sense of duty to their particular jobs and a similarly strong sense of responsibility to the North in general. Those remarks stand up under scrutiny. But it can also be noted that the men also possessed a perfectly natural sense of self-interest. The self-interest tended to exhibit itself in the manner in which the T&NO men—as with railway men everywhere, one expects—followed the "rules of the game." And because of their rules' orientation and the nature (and often the location) of their jobs, they played those rules with considerable skill and imagination. It has already been observed that they knew and largely accepted the

regulations surrounding the bumping system. At the heart of that system was the seniority list for each trade and craft; and *everyone* knew his exact place on that list. Phrases like "eight hours is as good as a year" were commonly heard when men discussed their respective places on their various seniority lists. Consequently, it is hardly surprising that every one, even 50 or more years after the event, could recall the exact date of his first day on the job and usually the circumstances surrounding the manner in which he came to be hired in some detail. Bill Ross Jr., nicknamed "Pulpwood Junior" because his father had been known as "Pulpwood Ross," recalled in 1974 an event from 1924.

    I was out of a job and I had applied down here... There was no vacancy at the time for a fireman. There was a friend of ours—my family's—he was a foreman on the gang...and he says, "Oh, Bill, are you working?

295

Earlton Junction   At this point, c. 1932, the automobile did not appear as a serious threat. (ONA-19882710 Audet)

I says, "No, I'm not, Mr. Webber."

He said, "Why don't you come down and see a fellow now and then. I might have a job for you."

I said, "Do you have a job for me?"

He said, "No, I don't now. You come down and see me tomorrow, and be bloody well dressed for work, in your working clothes."

So I went there and I got the job.

...when it came time, they wanted to send me up to a place called Cassidy Pit, mileage 99, watching a shovel—that is, night work. So when Mr. Tom Ross, the master mechanic came to see me, I was over at the...old icehouse... I was working in there and he came to see me and he said, "I got a job for you. I want you to go up tonight to watch the locomotives in the shovel at Cassidy Pit.

"Well," I said, "Mr. Webber gave me a job when you didn't have one. I can't leave without seeing him." He said, "Where's Mr. Webber?" "He's

way down in the east yard." That was a mile away. I guess Tom Ross was...a fair man, but he was a crank at times.

So he said, "All right, I'll go down and see him."

So down the yard he goes, and he comes back in awhile, with Mr. Webber, and Sam [Webber] said, "You didn't have to do that, Bill. All you had to do was go. It would have been all right."

So forever after that, Mr. Ross—who is no relation—always brought that up when I was in the office. I was the only damn man that made him walk a mile to hire me![23] 🐾

A man's first day on the job was an important event. Likewise, the terms "first in, first out" and "first on, first off" had special meaning for those whose names appeared on either the regular board or the spare board. Everyone knew these terms, and indeed among the most interested were the railway wives who would, daily one expects, ask the question, "Where do you stand?" Their husbands' place on the board not only determined the family income at that point, it also served to set the wife's immediate task, for it would invariably be she who would prepare the man's food supply for his run. These women also were as conversant as any of the men with the rules that governed the workplace as well as with the means by which these rules could be manipulated by the regular crews, usually to the disadvantage of the men on the spare board.

    We had 14 through-freight crews on here at one time...and it was often you'd come in and you'd be "first out" because the other crews were out on the road...

We worked on a first in, first out... As you came in you went to the tail-end of the list, and everybody that came in behind you went in behind you. In other words, you didn't have any assigned jobs. You were on through freight, and whether there was an extra train or a regular train you still maintained your turn...

"First in" meant first in off the road... The regular board also worked on the basis of "first in, first out."

If you were on the spare board, and if there were no extra shifts, you did not work...

There was no such thing as paid vacations or paid holidays.

So the last few weeks before Christmas and New Year's, the regular crews would work everything, and the spare board would sit quiet... I've seen me sit on the spare board 16 turns out and be there for days...without moving.

Q. Did you resent that?

We did at the time because we knew what was taking place. There was no time and a half or anything for working the holidays, so the regular crews would work everything, knowing that they could then book off at Christmas and New Year's and still make their mileage.

And you would be so hungry to go to work that you would go to work...no matter what day it was—Christmas or New Year's or anything else, and the regular men knew that. They put you right on the spot. You worked [those special holidays] or else you didn't eat.[24]

Another engineer spoke of this same circumstance.

    The spare board had many names. It was called the spare list, the starvation board—and it could be a starvation board! We found working the spare board before Christmas—that was when it was a starvation board because that was when all the old regular enginemen would work steadily to make a Christmas pay...the spare board was designed to provide a spare fireman, or a spare engineer, or whatever—for the regular men when they wanted off. It could be for illness...vacation or whatever. The spare board that was maintained in North Bay was a pretty fair-sized [one] because [it] supplied all the relief requirements in Timmins, Rouyn, and Cochrane...there was a spare board in Englehart but...unless we were short in North Bay, they just supplied the men for their own requirements in Englehart.

At busy times of year—in the summertime, with vacations and the work trains being out—everybody was working. Then the spare board was extensive. There could be as many as 10–15 men on the spare board.

At Christmas time, or before Christmas—that two week period from the 1st of December—when the old firemen and hoggers were working on their Christmas pay—the spare board would be cut down to about three or four men.[25]

   When I got up in that senior position, they were starting to pay us time and a half on holidays, so a lot of the men would work those days. Sometimes they would scheme—booking rest here and there—so they knew their turn was going to be on that day.

Like I've seen men get to Englehart and there'd be a train waiting for them. Normally they'd turn right around and come back with that train. But they would go into Englehart and book eight hours rest so a couple of crews would "scoop them"... [That is,] go by them [on the board]. They'd [i.e., the other crews] come in and wouldn't book rest so they would go by them [i.e., those who did book rest] and that would maybe leave them home for Christmas...

Q. I imagine that sometimes the scheming backfired.

Oh, it often did! (Chuckles) They'd run a couple of extra trains.[26]

The manipulation involved more than just the Christmas holiday period.

   We worked by miles...we didn't work by hours. Four-thousand and two-hundred miles was a conductor's mileage, and a brakeman's was 3900. And he could make—if he was classed as a conductor and was used as a conductor —on the spare board he could go 4200 miles with no carry-over.

Carry-over? Well...you could go out [on a run] with 4199 miles [already done]...and make that trip and not have to carry the rest of that mileage [over to] the next booking period. You see, we all had different times of our mileage—different periods...we all didn't get our mileage in at [the same] time. We're all at different times. Enginemen were the same too.

You see, if you get 4200 miles, you're automatically off [till the next booking period—i.e., month]. Then a spare man goes in, and he runs the job. But some fellows would skinive around. They'd have around 4189 miles, and they'd go out [on a long run] and make that extra mileage, and they wouldn't have to put it in their book when they started again.

Q. It was a kind of overtime?

For sure, but the spare man who was next up to get the job, he wouldn't get it because that [regular] fellow had already gone out.

Q. Was there bitterness?

Well, yeah, a little bit, because some of them cheated on mileage—because that means a job for someone else. [The idea of the booking period was that] you get your mileage in, then somebody's got to replace you—so it could be a spare conductor [who would get the work]...

See, you used to keep a little book on your mileage...so if I got to 3800 or 3900 miles before my booking time, I'd have two or three days off. I'd come off and a spare man would have my job. It was creating jobs for other men. That's what the idea was.

At one time they had no mileage [limit]. You could work the clock around...It could be [dangerous] but some of the fellows—well, the money...[27]

Some attempts at manipulation involved an effort simply to avoid awkward or unfavorable conditions. Among these was the way freight. Quite simply, this meant a train that delivered and collected freight of all kinds at all points along the right-of-way. In many instances the stops involved the collection of milk tins set at the various stops by the local farmers for delivery to the closest dairy, and thus there evolved the term "milk run." It was by no means unique to the T&NO; it applied on every line in the country. It is also a term that has come to mean any journey—on any mode of

298

transport—that involves numerous stops. In the T&NO's early days, the way freight formed an important portion of the company's business, and, for the people along the way, the importance of this service cannot be exaggerated. Yet, for the men who worked the trains, the way freight run was the least desirable, because it took the longest and because of the extensive switching—at many of the stops it would be necessary to cut off, or to add, cars—it was a more arduous trip. It was for good reason that the train was termed "the Struggler," because the run from North Bay to Englehart could take 10 hours in 1912—if it ran on time! The passenger train made the same trip in less than six hours and was much more likely to be on time. There was always the temptation, then, to use whatever means were available to avoid it in favour of the faster tricks. Another circumstance that most would try to avoid was "deadheading." This meant travelling to a job on one's own time and without pay. Should a regular man be called upon to do it, he might try to book off or avoid it in some way. A spare man would be more likely to accept it willingly because he often needed the work.

Older employees would sometimes use their seniority to take on extra work.

> & Some of the older fellows with good seniority would bump to go where the money was—they would live out of bunk houses and work the high mileage jobs so that they could get their miles in by 18 days or so and have the rest of the month...north of Cochrane was a high mileage run.
>
> Bumping was just taken as part of the game. You might be upset, but you accepted it as part of the game.
>
> Between 1946 and 1951 there was a great deal of bumping, but it levelled off by 1951 as the new men who had come on in 1946 or so after the war began to settle in.[28] &

Some of the tactics regarding carry-overs, taking excessive tricks without proper rest, or the seasonal hardships for the spare board people certainly caused some resentments. But these were simply a few of the ways that T&NO people used the system to personal advantage, and the resentment came because the tactics tended to subvert the purpose for the rules being in place. And in the process, others were sometimes hurt. There was nothing subversive, however, in some of the men bidding—through the proper channels—for positions which suited their own circumstances or which served their own needs. It has been noted, for example, that in some of the stations, the operator would act also as the agent for tickets and for express. Those positions carried with them some further remuneration in the form of a percentage payment based on the express handled. One man who sought these out was E.A. Audet, who had a large family and who felt the corresponding need—or desire—to secure this extra income. As he developed in his seniority, he also secured the right to claim a wider variety of positions, of course; but quite early in his long T&NO career, he developed an inclination to bid on relieving agent's positions in the smaller or more remote areas because of the potential commissions.[29]

Bidding for more desirable circumstances was actually quite a common practice. Motives varied. Certainly income was a factor, and the men would sometimes seek out positions for that purpose. Occasionally one would "strike it rich" by accident, as was the case of the express agent who happened to be in Moosonee, not normally considered a plum job, when the federal government chose to construct the Mid-Canada line, a precursor to the Distant Early Warning (DEW) line. Tons of supplies and equipment, all sent as express, flowed through the Moosonee station, and the agent received a commission on all of it. But this was an aberration. Normally the men who sought extra income did so through bidding or through bumping. The same methods would be used to seek positions for other reasons. One was security or at least a degree of certainty. One family, for example, stayed at the Island Falls section

T&NO Car 99 (on left) and school car   The T&NO loaned its car, formerly the superintendent's business car, to provide more living space for the teacher's family. The teacher, Andy Clement, was a familiar figure on the line. (ONA Clement)

for years because the circumstances there—a school close by and steady work with little danger of being bumped—suited them. Others would establish a base, as Clem Ruttan did for a time at Mulock where he built a small house, and from there seek work on the extra gang on a seasonal basis. Arnold Sullivan, while pleased to have been born in Elk Lake, sought positions based from Englehart.

The general trend was that of taking posts in the more isolated spots or the more northern locations and then, as one's seniority grew, moving either southward or to the larger centres. This tendency towards movement, it might be noted, had the effect of making the men familiar with the people and the system everywhere along the line. This would be advantageous in that the railway

thus had people, many people, who would have first-hand experience in many sectors. It also contributed towards a sense of belonging. Such effects, however, were incidental and resulted from accident, not design. The men moved for their own reasons, not the company's. In general, they were certainly prepared to give good measure; and most, it seems, recognized their role and took a certain pride in performing it properly. But the railway was also considered as an institution that, while certainly of benefit to the North in general, could be used for one's personal advantage.

The examples, anecdotes, and stories used to illustrate the nature of the T&NO railway have been drawn largely from the steam era or from the years that surrounded the process of dieselization, which was fully completed in 1957. This results partly from a desire to include the recollections of people who have worked the line and are now living in retirement. These people, some of whom have regrettably died since offering their experiences, worked the line at a time when the conditions and technology differed quite radically from the conditions that currently pertain. They described, therefore, an era in the T&NO/ONR's past which was unique to them. The experiences of the current generation can be recorded somewhat more fully by that generation's scribe. The choice rested partly also on the reality that the musings and experiences of those years tend to be representative of and common to the whole era of the railway's first 50 or 60 years. The mechanics and technology of the line did not undergo many dramatic changes in that time.

Notes

1. Bill Ross, 1974. Interview on file at ONA.
2. Tucker, *Steam into Wilderness*, p. 153.
3. Bill Ross, 1974. Interview on file at ONA.
4. Orville Nichols. Interview. 27 February 1988. North Bay.
5. *Ibid.*
6. *Ibid.*
7. *Ibid.*
8. Bill Ross. 1974. Interview on file at ONA.
9. Bob Cameron. 1974. Interview on file at ONA.
10. Orville Nichols. Interview. 27 February 1988.
11. Bob Moore. Interview. 17–18 October 1988. On line to Moosonee.
12. C.L. Bailey. Interview. 30 September 1988. North Bay.
13. Bill Ross. 1974. Interview on file at ONA.
14. Clinton Bainbridge. 1974. Interview on file at ONA.
15. Bill Moore. Interview. 17–18 October 1988. On line to Moosonee.
16. C.L. Bailey. Interview. 30 September 1988. North Bay.
17. Bill Moore, Interview. 17–18 October 1988. On line to Moosonee.
18. Orville Nichols. Interview. 27 February 1988. North Bay.
19. Bob Moore. Interview. 17–18 October 1988. On line to Moosonee.
20. Ralph Brill. Interview. 12 June 1991. North Bay.
21. Orville Nichols. Interview. 27 February 1988. North Bay.
22. *Ibid.*
23. Bill Ross. 1974. Interview on file at ONA.
24. Orville Nichols. Interview. 27 February 1988.
25. Bob Moore. Interview. 2 August 1988. North Bay.
26. Orville Nichols. Interview. 27 February 1988.
27. C.L. Bailey. Interview. 30 September 1988. North Bay.
28. Bob Moore. Interview. 9 July 1986. North Bay.
29. E.A. Audet. Interview. 5 July 1991. North Bay.

Chapter 18

The Decade of Change

HE MECHAN-
ICS AND tech-
nology of the
line did not un-
dergo many dra-
matic changes
during its first
four decades.
Between 1945
and 1960, how-
ever, the T&NO,
like all Canadian railways, faced new challenges. Specifically, this meant facing competition from two fields of transportation which had
been in their infancy 20 years earlier: highway
travel and air travel. Their significance had become apparent, but for two decades their development had been retarded by the Depression of
the 1930s and then by the Second World War
and the post-war confusion. It is not intended
here to analyse the impact of automobiles,
trucks, buses, and airplanes on Canadian society; rather, it should be noted simply that competition from these grew immeasurably, and
their burgeoning new competition greatly affected the T&NO in two ways.

First, it certainly challenged the railway's
business, because the new competitors provided a
clear alternative where none had existed before.
Second, these newcomers forced the railways, including the T&NO, to improve their service and
efficiency. The need for greater efficiency led di-

rectly to some truly dramatic alterations in the
technology and the delivery systems of railways.
These, in turn, had some remarkable—some
would say devastating—consequences for the men
and women who looked to the T&NO for their careers and for their livelihoods. It was a nationwide
phenomenon, of course, and it manifested itself
somewhat differently on each of the nation's railways. For the T&NO, the decisive decade was the
one which followed the Commission's decision to
change its motive power from steam to diesel.

The real drama came because of the *extent*
of the changes. There had always been some
change and some improvement, because management had always hoped to increase efficiency and the men always sought to improve
their working conditions. One instance was the
Commission's inclination at various times to investigate the possibility of converting to electricity. By 1925 or so this had become something
of a red herring because the capital costs of
such a conversion were simply too staggering,
but it was nonetheless raised by Armand
Racine during his investigations of 1934. Likewise, the hopes of using the Onakawana lignite
deposits as a source of fuel had a truly long lifespan. First suggested in the years before the
James Bay extension had even been begun, this
dream was revived periodically until about
1945. After obtaining power in 1943, the Conservative government of George Drew invested

rather heavily in the project. Men who were present during this experiment smile at it:

&⁊ They spent hundreds of thousands of dollars there, because all this coal that they have at Onakawana is all under water, and its down deep. And what it actually is, you could see. You could pick up a chunk of it and you could see the bark of the trees...it hadn't been compressed long enough.

And they were going to process it, and they had steam pipes and steam coils and all this, to dry it out... They had a great big pile of it. They'd been loading it out on cars for tests...[1] ⁊

Bill Ross was up there as relieving fireman and decided to try a load of the lignite in his engine. He and the engineer, Peck Hermiston, loaded the tender as high as they could "because it was very light [coal]," and they got the steam up for the trip.

&⁊ This was at night—pitch black night... So we get the highball to go, and he opens the throttle, and there was the most magnificent display of fireworks you ever saw! The stack was completely full and all the clouds—you know the white steam that you normally see—were all sparks, all over.

And this was up in an area where the fire hazard was very very great in the summertime, and this was summertime, and I was scared skinny because I was afraid fires were going to start all over... And the heat of that stuff was terrific. The pop valves—what we call the pop valves on a steam locomotive or the release valves for excess pressure—they opened up—three of them were blown— I had the injector on—and the firebox door was wide open and sparks belching out...(Chuckles)

Eventually we got it cooled down...and went into Cochrane...the next morning the watchman came in

to call me and said, "Bill, whatever happened?"

I said, "Why?"

He said, "Never in all your life [have you] brought such a dirty fire as you did last night!...there was four inches of clinkers on it. I had to put the water to it to break it up and [clean it out]." That was my last experience with lignite coal.[2] ⁊

The provincial government and the T&NO went to considerable expense during the war years to harness this potential fuel source. The operation included a large drying plant, a big chimney stack and boilers, and the requisite appendages, including a rail spur. The railway also purchased four special steam engines—the engine on display in Lee Park in North Bay was one—to use the cured lignite along the T&NO. The process was inadequate to the task of curing the troubles like those experienced by Bill Ross, however, and the operation was shut down.[3] Lignite is a form of coal that is about 500 years premature. "By the time they get the thing [the Onakawana plant] going," said one man, "it's going to be just right. 500 years!" The project never really had any chance of success, but to condemn it outright is probably unfair because the exigencies of war call for bold measures. This one simply did not—could not—work out.

Improvements in railway technology occurred gradually during the first half of the 20th century. Hand cars, for example, were motorized, a considerable boon to the section forces and the roadmaster. Other minor refinements also took place. In the 1920s T&NO people began adapting highway vehicles for use on the railway. These hi-rail vehicles—so called because they could operate on either highways or rails—also grew more efficient and sophisticated over the years.

Engines also experienced increasing efficiency. The first four engines of the T&NO (numbered 101–105) came from the Canadian Locomotive Company in 1903, weighed 133,650 pounds, and had 56-inch driving wheels. Three years later four more engines

Ontario Northland Railway Yards showing turntable, roundhouse, and new diesel shops,
North Bay, c. 1952 (ONA-1988038)

came north. They were a touch heavier—by 350 pounds—and two of them (numbers 107 and 108) had 62-inch drivers, and thus were marginally more powerful. All of these passed out of service by 1920 and thus did not "receive improvements such as piston valves or superheaters" as did later purchases.[4] Such minor improvements took place throughout the steam era but with rare exceptions did not really affect the nature of the jobs of the front-end men except in a marginal fashion. Likewise, refinements in rolling stock such as the change from wooden to metal boxcars or improved facilities on the passenger cars had little effect. Certainly these advances increased the durability of the freight cars and contributed towards a more contented passenger clientele. For the men on the line, however, their respective roles and the manner in which they performed these roles changed very little.

Towards the end of the steam era, significant forward steps came in two areas of train movement: signals and the method of fuelling. In the former, improvement came in two forms. One was

the adoption of coloured light signals in the yards and station areas along the line. Previously, the signal posts displayed arms, using the semaphore system, to direct the crews to stop or to proceed with their trains. In their place the railways installed posts which displayed the signals for movement by using coloured lights (red, green, yellow). It had the advantage of clarity and of use in day and night. The other was the introduction of a system known as automatic block signals (ABS). The greatest fear of any railroader has always been that of collisions between different sections of rolling stock, especially two engines moving toward one another. Even on the wide open road, men working the track or operating the trains must be wary of the unexpected, and since the contact of train crews with other crews or other railroaders working the same track can be, at best, sporadic, there has been constant thought applied to reducing the instances of unexpected developments. ABS seeks to do this by dividing the track into blocks of varying lengths. An electric impulse is sent through each block. The entry of a train into the block breaks the circuit and this results in a

305

Engines 1302 and 1303 in new ONR diesel shop, c. 1953 (ONA-1988040)

Air dump cars, lengthening siding at Freeman, c. 1956 (ONA-199123 Butler)

signal at each end of the block, indicating that there is something in there. Trains approaching from either end, upon reaching the beginning of the block, are thus warned of the presence of the train there. Both of these signals improvements were installed in the early 1950s.

The other was the development, at about the same time, of the stoker furnace. For years, the fireman had to shovel the coal into the firebox by hand, using a beaver-tail lever with his foot while shovelling, to open and close the door. Since they fed the fire by hand, the men called this type of firebox a "hand bomber." It could be an arduous job. The men estimated that they would shovel 12 tons of coal a trip, one way. Thus, they applauded the introduction of the stoker engine which, to some degree, fed the coal mechanically into the firebox. The fireman still had to operate the required valves and learn some techniques, but it was a vast improvement on the hand bomber. One man remembered remarking that "This is it, we've arrived, you can't get any better than this!"

The fuel issue, however, went far beyond the hardships of the firemen. Coal had to be imported, and thus the supply was occasionally in jeopardy. The difficulties that the T&NO had experienced in obtaining supplies from the United States during the First World War had underlined this point. The problem of heavy costs and transportation emphasized this problem further. The consumption of coal, as the testimony of the firemen would attest, was prodigious, and the need to run special coal trains to the several fuel depots added to the difficulties of yardmen, operators, and dispatchers who had a schedule of operations that was already tight. Furthermore, the use of coal was dirty and awkward. These factors inclined the Commission to seek alternatives, and, in 1918–1919, Chairman Jake Englehart had been converted to the idea of electrification of the line. This consideration had been a major factor in the decision to build the line north of Cochrane in order to tap into the hydro resources of the northern rivers. The reduction of prices and the easier access of supply following the war's end in 1918 and the subsequent development of a more

fuel efficient engine—the Mikado—stayed off the enthusiasm for conversion to electricity. When similar difficulties arose some 20 years later during the Second World War, there were renewed efforts to solve them, such as the unsuccessful experiments with Onakawana lignite.

What evolved instead was the development of the diesel powered locomotive, which had the advantages—over steam powered engines—of cleanliness, reduced fuel costs, and greater power. In addition, there were reduced labour requirements because the diesel engine eliminated the fireman. Strong efforts were made to prevent this, but without success. The railroads of Canada chose to adopt the new system, a conversion process that took almost 15 years. The T&NO, by then renamed Ontario Northland, sent out its final steam run in 1957, and was among the first railways in the country to be fully dieselized. By then the full impact of the new technology had become apparent.

A few years earlier, when the first diesels began to run north, in many centres school children were taken from their classrooms on special trips to the rail yard to see the new engines. Generally, from the adult world, the new machines received high praise and were termed harbingers of the future. In most cases, however, the children were singularly unimpressed, because by then—1947—the railway had already ceased to be the prominent influence that it had once been in the daily lives of northerners. One youngster recalled the event.

    It was really no big deal. In fact, I couldn't understand what all the fuss was about. We walked over to the station. It was only a short walk—maybe three blocks—from Golden Avenue school (in South Porcupine). We saw the new engine. I remember thinking that it didn't look very much like a train—but to me it was just another piece of machinery that the grown-ups had come up with for some reason.

Mind you, I was only 9 or 10 at the time and had never been on a train up there. I think I had been on

The Northlander, 1986   Following the VIA reductions, this train provided the only remaining passenger service between Toronto and New Ontario. (R.J. Surtees, North Bay)

Noranda Yard, 1988   This once busy centre currently dispatches only one freight a day. (R.J. Surtees, North Bay)

one before we moved up north but never up there. We had a car, and the road to Timmins—both roads—where we usually went shopping, was pretty good. Even when we went south—to visit relatives—we went by car. Most of my friends were the same way.[5] 🐦

For the men on the line, however, it was indeed "a big deal."

🐦 People have said, "One thing about modernization, it never hurt railroaders."

We were the first hurt. And we were hurt the worst...where we had one steam engine hauling the train, when diesels came in they put two and three of them together—they were hauling two and three trains [i.e., the equivalent of two or three trains] at one time with one crew. So instead of three crews working, there was one... And we lost the fireman. Right now they're running trains with three men. We had five...[6] 🐦

The seniority list confirms what Nichols said. The list for 1946 shows 180 men who worked the front-end; the list for 1986 has only 51 names. It was with cause that the men felt concern. Apprehension ranged rather widely for two reasons. Some of the older men—those in their late 50's or early 60's—looked at the new engines with some fear, because it was a completely new task. Others objected to the diesels because they just did not look right, the way a train engine should look! This sentiment prevailed among much of the non-railway public as well. The greatest apprehension, however, resulted from the potential job loss. It was a nationwide concern. On the T&NO, the fears were allayed somewhat for no general lay-offs took place. For a time, some men retained their jobs as firemen, but over time the front-end workforce gradually reduced itself through natural attrition such as retirements and resignations. It did mean, though, that no new men were hired, and there were simply no opportunities for peo-

ple to move onto the front-end by way of the fireman's job as many had done in the past.

The fate of the firemen formed only one aspect of the dieselization process. Its impact was felt almost everywhere. It was clear that the need for the steam engine repair shop had passed. The boilermaker's trade—at least on the railway—had gone the way of the harnessmaker. Other trades, like the machinists, underwent dramatic changes or were eliminated completely. Those jobs had become redundant and so had the buildings where they were carried out. It was also clear that the nature and configuration of the diesel engines did not conform to the organization of the roundhouses. Thus, throughout the system, parts of the T&NO/ONR physical presence began to fall. The shops remained, but in a new form and in new buildings. The old ones were torn down, as were the roundhouses, and with them went the jobs that they housed. As Orville Nichols remarked ruefully,

🐦 The railroad saved money on labour because you reduced [the number of jobs]. Well, take even the ONR Shops down here and the old roundhouse, there were 200–300 men worked every shift down there—what do you see down there now, with diesels?[7] 🐦

With diesels, the ONR could run trains of much greater length. One man remarked that he had once taken a train of 155 cars with a diesel; this was much greater than the 38 or so that would follow a steam engine. The effect was three-fold. First, the need for fewer trains meant that fewer men were needed to operate them. Second, it meant that there were fewer meets, which had the happy effects of reducing the danger somewhat and of simultaneously reducing the stress on the dispatchers and operators, in particular, and to some extent on everyone else. Third, it meant that the sidings had to be longer, because when the meets did occur, it very likely was a longer train than before that had to take to the siding. The ONR's workforce had, for a time,

The eatery known as the Meechim, on the Little Bear, Moosonee branch, 1988   On this sector, rail services remain a lifeline. (R.J. Surtees, North Bay)

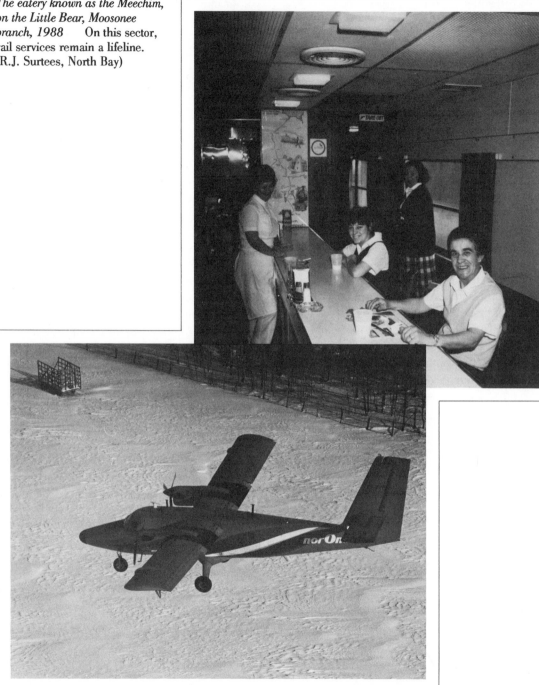

The first of norOntair's planes, the Twin Otter, landing at Earlton Airport, c. 1975   In this, the first paint scheme, the body of the plane was orange, and the loon was purple and white. The present paint scheme for all ON's fleets (trains, buses, trucks, planes) is gold, royal blue, and light blue. (ON AirServices)

an increased role in the obvious need to extend the length of many of the sidings.

With the passing of the steam age, the water towers and coal chutes along the way, as well as the large coal yards, also disappeared from the northern landscape. And with them went the jobs related to their operation and maintenance. Since coal no longer had to be moved about the line to the various coaling stations this meant as well a further decline in the total number of trains that coursed the tracks.

The maintenance-of-way men also experienced a change about the same time. The decline in the number of trains caused by the advent of the diesels likely had little effect on the section forces. The total weight of the traffic—and therefore the wear on the track—did not change much as a direct result of dieselization; indeed, it might be observed that with fewer trains to worry about, the effect for the sections would have been to improve their lot. They had to work around fewer obstacles and be wary of fewer dangers. Other factors, occurring concurrently with the process of dieselization, however, affected the role and the conditions of these men. The least significant, yet still important, of these was the decision finally to adopt the use of creosote to preserve the railway's ties. It was not a new idea and had been broached in the 1920s. Other railways had already adopted the process. The practice of coating the tie with the oily tar finish had one purpose: to extend the life of the tie and to reduce, therefore, the number that had to be replaced. The T&NO hesitated for years before adopting it. It was expensive and ties were readily available—at low cost—along the T&NO right-of-way. Indeed, the railway had its own timber stands, largely for that purpose. And in the North, where fire had ravaged so widely and so wildly on several occasions, it was considered unwise to give fire another potential fuel by creosoting the ties. Rising costs, depletion of the ready supply, and reduced fire hazards changed that thinking. By gradually setting the treated ties in place, the ONR achieved the benefits of creosoted ties and concurrently reduced the section man's workload since fewer ties had to be replaced.

More significant was the change to rock ballasting. This process began in the '50s but picked up greatly after 1962, largely through the promotional efforts of Chief Engineer George Payne. Rock ballast is somewhat heavier and more porous than the gravel it replaced. Thus there is far better drainage which means that the roadbed holds together far better. And this, in turn, means that less heaving occurs against the ties and the rails. There again, the result was a reduction in the work of the section men. An organizational change contributed to this trend as well. That is, the task of replacing ties—large numbers of ties—was transferred from the section gangs to the extra gangs and was performed on a seasonal basis. Previously the section men had often performed that job for their particular stretch of track. As a general consequence of these several factors, the railway extended the length of its sections. Where they had been seven or eight miles in length, they became 20–30 miles long, and this in turn meant that the total section forces declined from about 450 men to 120 or so.

Other considerations contributed to the drastic reduction of the railway's manpower requirements. The most prominent by far was the decline in passenger and freight traffic as a result of competition for the carrying trade from highway vehicles. In 1929 the government of Ontario proudly published a booklet titled *The Ferguson Highway. Beauty Spots and Points of Interest in Northern Ontario.* It begins:

> The Ferguson Highway, so named in honour of Premier Ferguson of Ontario, provides a splendid road for motor travel from Severn Bridge to Cochrane, the latter being five hundred miles north of Toronto...

After describing the road from Toronto to North Bay, it continues innocently.

> Proceeding a distance of five miles farther, the tourist arrives at the entrance gates to the new portion of the Highway known as Cooks Mills, Mileage 236, where the Forestry Department *registers the name and address of*

New Head Office of Ontario Northland, 1987 (ONA-2491112)

*P.A. Dyment, General Manager, and J.W. Spooner, Chairman, at the
opening of the new Head Office building in North Bay, 1987* (ON photo)

every tourist entering the territory leading to the magnificent Temagami Forest Reserve.[8]

Almost 10 years later the practice of registering travellers continued. The curious reader may well have asked why such registration took place. Had he heard the story of how one of the cars in Premier Ferguson's motorcade of three years earlier had sunk completely into the muskeg while travelling this highway, then the need for such registration would have been obvious!

At a time when the railway was at the zenith of its commercial success and at the peak of its prominence in the North, the highways of the region—and it is generous to term them highways—remained in their infancy. For the next two decades, this remained relatively unchanged. The late 1920s were a prosperous period for all of North America, and the enthusiastic authors of *The Ferguson Highway* might be excused somewhat for the deceptions which they perpetrated in that little booklet. There was indeed every indication that the good times would continue and that tourists, settlers, and entrepreneurs would make their way north, would use the Ferguson Highway, and would in this fashion promote the economic boom in New Ontario that had been in place since the turn of the century.

But the boom did not continue. In the same year that this little pamphlet appeared, there began the worst economic disaster of the modern age. It would last 10 years and hurt everyone. Among those hardest hit was the provincial government which had responsibility for the construction of roads in the province. The provincial road building programme had been financed largely through special taxes placed on gasoline used by automobiles and by fees levied for licences for those same automobiles. During the Depression the general public greatly reduced the number of automobiles which they purchased and concurrently reduced the amount of gasoline consumed. Many who owned automobiles already also declined to purchase the required licence plates each year simply because they felt they could not afford it, and most often the authorities simply ignored

this minor breach of the law. The fiscal base for the road building programme, therefore, was greatly eroded. Furthermore, the general tax base for the province also declined, and there was at the same time an increasing need for expenditures of a social nature because there were so many people unemployed. Although the social programmes of the day were minor compared to the current system, they still placed a drain on the provincial treasury. For 10 years the province lacked a capital base to use for building roads except as occasional and temporary make-work programmes. Road building languished for this period simply because the required monies were not available. Responsibility for local roads rested with the various municipalities, but these were equally short of money for that purpose.

Economic conditions improved somewhat at the end of the 1930s, largely because of the heavy government expenditures on the war effort beginning in September of 1939. As had been the case during the First World War, however, the principal preoccupation of government, indeed of everyone, was the prosecution of that war. Any capital that was available was applied to the war effort. Little was available for roads, unless those roads were directly related to the war effort. Thus the Ferguson Highway languished throughout this 15-year period. It continued to languish somewhat for a few years after the war ended as well, since it took that long for the economy to convert itself, once again, from wartime to peacetime conditions. In 1947 the roads between North Bay and Cochrane, between Timmins and Matheson, and between Swastika and Cheminis were certainly better than they had been in 1929, and some progress had been made in the vehicles that travelled over them. Nonetheless a journey over the northern highways continued to be an adventure, and for most passenger vehicles it was an arduous one. Under good conditions, an automobile trip from North Bay to Cochrane today (1992) can be accomplished with relative comfort in approximately four hours, and slightly less if the driver has a heavy foot. In

Laying continuous welded rail near Feronia, 1988 (R.J. Surtees, North Bay)

Changing ties, mileage 31, near Cheminis, 1988 (R.J. Surtees, North Bay)

1947 the same journey could not be accomplished in less than a full day, and most people would break the journey into two days. Much of the road—about two-thirds—had not been paved, and many of the hills were so steep and the curves in the road so numerous that the vehicles of the day would often break down. Standard equipment for vehicles which attempted long northern trips included water containers, because radiators overheated on a regular basis.

In the 1950s, the economic conditions reversed, and the province of Ontario embarked on a highly ambitious road building programme. Much of the work was done in southern Ontario, but the North also benefited from the new expenditure. By the end of the decade, northern roads had achieved a state approximating their present condition. Automobiles had also become more comfortable and more durable. Buses and trucks had undergone similar improvements. All three could be found in increasing numbers on northern highways. Highway transport had become a viable alternative to the Ontario Northland Railway which was no longer the only lifeline for the North. The highway challenge continued and grew and would appear to be a clear winner.

Yet the railway remains. It may be rather heavily propped up by government subsidies, but it remains. It remains because, in addition to those subsidies, there are still some tasks for which the railway would appear to be better suited than any other mode of transportation. It remains also because the railway has taken steps to make itself more efficient and cost-conscious. Some of the methods used have already been noted. One that has not and which has had an enormous effect on the workplace has been an increased dependence upon mechanization. Some of the developments have been quite ingenious. The process of laying track is an extensive one and, considering the weight and bulk of the ballast, ties, tie plates, and rails, a surprisingly delicate one. Yet in their need to fight back against the new competition, railroaders and railroad engineers have managed to mechanize much of it. There is a machine which will remove the ties, another which will insert them, and yet another which will perform the required tamping of the ballast between the ties. It would be illogical to provide each section gang with a set of these machines. They are simply too expensive. Rather this task was, for the most part, taken from the sections and assigned to special extra gangs who undertake the wholesale replacement of ties for a substantial portion of the railway when this is required. This mechanization contributed to the decision to extend the distance covered by each section crew. In addition to mechanizing much of the work related to the maintenance of way, the ONR has also sought to improve its railbed and track. Once again the motivation has been a desire to increase efficiency, reduce costs and, concurrently, improve the ride on the rails. One early improvement in this regard, as the traffic grew in the days of steam, was the move to a heavier grade of steel rails. The first tracks were 80-lb. rails, then 90 lbs., and finally 115 lbs. This heavier track costs more but has more durability and thus greater longevity. One problem that remained was the joint between the rails. Chief Engineer George Payne explained it in layman's terms.

“ As rail heats up it gets fatter,...it gets longer... That's why on each 39-foot rail, when we lay it, we leave a quarter-inch between them. Because it will expand to fill that gap. This will create a pressure and the rail might buckle. If that happens, and the train comes along, you'll have a derailment. That's why we put all the anchors [i.e., tie sections] in—we try to anchor that rail and relieve the stress on the rail and transfer the stress from the rail to the tie. The tie is buried in rock ballast and there's a nice shoulder on it that holds it from moving. So the whole track structure is anchored down by the anchors, and by the ballast to try to keep it from buckling...when it buckles it's the whole track structure that buckles. It's all tied together.[9] ❧

This structure of the track, anchors, ties, and ballast forming a unit works quite well. It must work, for railways have been effective transportation systems for almost two centuries. But even structures as heavy and secure as railbeds can weaken. Ties can have flaws or just wear out, for example, and when flaws develop they must be repaired. The section men or extra gangs which perform those repairs have certain restrictions. It has already been noted that they must clear the track in the event of traffic. In addition, their work is also restricted by the weather because of the connections among the rail, tie, and ballast.

❧ When we have a hot day with the sun out...we just tell our guys, "Don't touch the track," because if they touch some of that ballast—that ballast is just how it's holding things—if they decide to jack things up, and lift things or change ties, then they disturb that ballast, and disturb some of the forces that are holding that thing together from buckling. So we say, "Hey, don't touch it." It's too hot, too much pressure from that rail. There might be too much pressure. Every time we have a sun kink, that's where it happens, where someone has loosened some ballast.

Q. That's called a "sun kink"?

Yeah. We call them "sun kinks" or "track buckling." It's expansion that really causes it but we call them "sun kinks."

Q. Is it worse in the summer or the winter?

Oh, the summer. In the winter you get the opposite. The problem is, you see, if we could just loosen off all the joints—you must remember that rail contracts, the same as it expands. So what's happening in the wintertime is that all that rail is shrinking. Everything is held together by...there's

three bolts holding everything together at the end of each rail, and if you don't adjust your rail so there's a happy balance between expansion and contraction, you get a pull-apart. You'll shear those bolts off if you get enough pressure so those bolts'll not hold anymore and they'll shear and then the rail will come right apart at the joint.

The result is the same. You get a train on the ground.[10] ❧

The most recent innovation—though a very costly one—in railway track technology is the evolution of continuous welded rail (CWR). The intent is to eliminate the rail joints to prevent buckling and, at the same time, provide a safer and much smoother ride.

❧ ...all of those years we've put a quarter-inch gap at the end of every 39-foot rail to make up for all this expansion. Now we weld everything together in one string...we box anchor every second tie, and we transfer the stress into the tie and we hold the rail from getting longer... We don't care if it fattens...we put in these quarter-mile strings now—we've got a piece of rail that's a quarter mile long—we'll weld those together.

So there's not even a joint every quarter mile—perhaps joints at switches—but there could be 10 miles of track without a joint.[11] ❧

Another innovation has been the practice of lubricating the track. Initially the intent had been to reduce the wear on the rolling stock's wheels, but the use of lubricants on the track had an unexpected advantage.

❧ There are several ways of lubricating rail, but we do it by means of our wayside lubricators... This thing is fastened right on the rail. There's a distributer bar fastened right on the rail that squirts a little bit of oil out on the gate side only on the head of the rail just

Boston Creek, 1986 (R.J. Surtees, North Bay)

below the top, on the inside of it—puts a little squirt of grease on there, and then the wheel comes along and picks up that little piece of grease and carries it along. The tank is just to hold the grease in. That big tank there is full of grease, and there's a little pump in there that is activated—these are all mechanical greases that we've got. The pump is activated by a little treadle that the railway car's wheel hits. It hits it and pushes down and turns a little gear and pumps a little grease—and the grease just squirts out on the rail—on the edge of the rail. And the wheel picks it up and carries it on down the track. So we are, in effect, greasing the rail,...that saves wear on the rail and on the wheel.

Also we found out we're saving about 15–20% on our fuel costs just by this greasing. So we put a lot more emphasis on them since we found out. We thought we were saving the wheels and

the rail, then we found out we were saving fuel like crazy, according to those answers anyway. So we're being a little more sophisticated with our maintenance on these things. There are other ways of doing it. You can have a hi-rail car with a little...special dolly that goes along behind it and sweeps it on as it goes up the track. Or you can have on-board lubrication on a locomotive or a special lube car. We don't have those yet, but there's a lot of experimentation going on across the country on different ways of doing it.

We burn somewhere in the neighbourhood of nine million gallons of diesel fuel a year, so if you can save 10% on that, it's a lot of money.[12] 🐾

Among the roles assigned to the maintenance-of-way forces were those of lining and surfacing the track. Here too mechanization has come to the ONR.

317

❧ Its pretty self-explanatory. Surface —we make a nice flat surface and we line track to make it straight. We can do it manually, but we don't do that anymore. We use special tamping machines that come along and tamp underneath the tie—its a machine that has four big tamping feet about 4 inches wide—and hydraulicly push down and vibrate under the ties to squeeze the rock under the ties. The same unit has a jack on it that measures how high to lift and lifts up the rail a little bit and tamps at it to make a nice smooth surface.

Now surfacing and lining is something we do all the time on all track...

The single most important thing to do is lining. If you're off-line, the train action...would put you out-of-line even worse and end up with a rough ride and...make holes in the track.[13] ❧

The lining can now be done by using a machine, which permits one crew to line three or four miles in a day. When done manually, in a good day a much larger crew with much more equipment could manage about one-half mile. The effect of these various responses to the challenge of highway competition has had a truly remarkable affect on the ONR workforce, in two ways.

First, the workforce has been greatly reduced. At one point, the total T&NO workforce consisted of almost 2200 men. In 1987 it numbered less than 800. Second, the work became far less strenuous than it once was. It is commonplace for oldtimers in any craft, trade, or profession to observe that the newer circumstances of their particular job have become less demanding than they once were. Some of this attitude may result simply from a highly selective memory, but often times much of it is quite accurate. And in the case of railroading, it would seem that the current groups of running crews, section forces, dispatchers, etc. do indeed have tasks that are less demanding. But the jobs remain essentially unchanged in that

Matheson, 1986 (R.J. Surtees, North Bay)

the way must continue to be maintained, the train orders must be accurate and precise, and the trains must roll efficiently and safely. Undoubtedly, there are regrets that the traffic has thinned so much, but it is unlikely that anyone would prefer to return to the old ways and the old conditions. In the meantime, among the current crews, there are likely men like Gerald "Rule Book" Ireland who was a "real stickler" on the rules; like Johnny "Honey Bee" Anderson, whose hobby was raising bees and who once indicated a desire to cross his bees with fireflies so he could have them working day and night; like Johnny "Jump Up" Bellemew whose habit of jumping up suddenly resulted in a scar when he once shot up and hit the throttle rest; or like Orville "the Owl" Buffet, so called because of his heavy and bushy eye brows. One difference, however, if the trend at the Matheson station and elsewhere continues, may be that some of the nicknames will belong to women.

Notes

1. Bill Ross. 1974. Interview on file at ONA.
2. *Ibid.*
3. See p. 204 of this text.
4. Vollhardt, *Locomotives of the Ontario Northland Railway*, p. 2.
5. Author's recollection.
6. Orville Nichols. Interview. 27 February 1988. North Bay.
7. *Ibid.*
8. Ontario, *The Ferguson Highway*. Department of Northern Development, Toronto, 1929. p. 6. Emphasis added.
9. George Payne with Ken Moorehead. Interview. 12 September 1988. On the line, near Feronia.
10. *Ibid.*
11. *Ibid.*
12. George Payne. Interview. 12 September 1988. North Bay.
13. *Ibid.*

Afterword

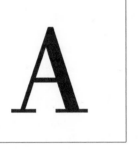A S ONTARIO NORTHLAND begins its tenth decade, the metamorphosis continues. Trains still roll, of course, for there remain certain sectors within the northeastern corridor's economy which either choose or require this mode of conveyance. The unit trains from Noranda and from Kidd Creek are two examples; and north from Cochrane the railway's regular mixed trains still form that region's principal lifeline. Consequently, the passenger runs, although severely limited, will continue on the main line. Indeed, the Ontario Northland run between Toronto and Cochrane, and thence to Hearst, constitutes the only rail passenger service through that elongated area. Freights also cover that sector on an as needed basis. The mixed train between Moosonee and Cochrane will continue, five days a week, and the special excursion train, the Polar Bear Express, will also run in 1992. Thus, while longstanding stations such as those at Timmins, Cobalt, and Haileybury have closed, new structures have appeared at Englehart and North Bay. The latter location, opened in 1990 and called simply *The Station*, is the first such facility which the T&NO/ONR has actually operated at its southern terminus. Hitherto, apart from briefly main-

taining a small station at North Bay Junction (where the T&NO met the CPR), the Commission relied throughout its past on first the CPR and then the CNR for its station facilities in North Bay.

Rail service, however, has clearly dwindled in relative importance. The reverse is the case with the Commission's highway enterprises. Indeed, the new stations have been designed to accommodate both rail and bus traffic, and the latter is clearly in the ascendancy. Begun in 1938, this branch sputtered badly at first, and until the end of the Second World War, consisted basically of a commuter service designed to augment the railway's passenger schedules. Progress in highway construction and vehicles permitted this service to expand, however, and it gradually grew from its commuter beginnings to develop regular runs of some distance. These at first were also tied to the railway's needs in that they tended to fit into or supplement the railway's scheduled trains; in time, however, the buses moved beyond that to their own commercial ends, a development which placed them in direct competition with the Commission's own trains. Ontario Northland Bus Lines expanded beyond the northeastern corridor and pushed its scheduled runs to Sudbury, Sault Ste. Marie, and Hearst. Recently this division extended the presence of the company's chevron, its symbol since 1974, southward as well through the acquisition in 1991 of certain scheduled runs and equipment from the Gray

321

Coach Bus Lines. This firm had expressed a desire to restructure itself in a fashion that would have been deleterious to some northern communities. Ontario Northland's longstanding commitment to service the North naturally inclined it to step into this partial vacuum. As a result, the bus lines department obtained 30 buses, a terminal in Barrie, and the former Gray Coach routes to Toronto from both North Bay and Sudbury.

Concurrent with the emergence of the bus lines, a trucking division also emerged at Ontario Northland. Road transport of various kinds has always had a role in the North. Here too, at first, it was connected directly to the railway and consisted of moving goods and passengers from the railhead to an inland location. The development of roads and the emergence of motorized vehicles increasingly infringed on the carriage of what had been exclusively railway commodities: way freight and express. Trucking firms ate into the railway's traffic, and the railway itself felt compelled to enter this field. Ultimately the trend to "put it on rubber" resulted in a trucking division within the Commission's activities. Currently known as Star Transfer, this Ontario Northland subsidiary operates throughout the northeastern corridor and beyond through interlocking agreements with other carriers.

The development of highway transportation had a further effect on the North and on Ontario Northland. By the 1960s the difficulties regarding air travel which the Timmins *Press* had complained of in 1946 no longer pertained.[1] Ground transport via train, bus, and private automobile had developed sufficiently in the North so that landing strips ceased to be isolated. Regular flights could be scheduled because passengers, no longer totally dependent upon unpredictable train schedules, could make their way to airports with a high degree of certainty. This progress in highway travel may have hurt the viability of rail passenger services, but it concurrently created an environment favourable for commercial air travel. Accordingly, the demand for speed in the transportation of passengers and light freight grew among northerners just as it did elsewhere.

In 1968 the Ontario government responded to this demand with its "Highways in the Skies" program which saw nine new air strips developed in Northern Ontario. Three years later a further response was the invitation to properly licensed airline companies for proposals to provide air service in the North. In a manner reminiscent of George Lee's use of the NCR charter, Ontario Northland officials dusted off its airline licence, obtained in 1938,[2] and submitted the successful bid. The new air travel department, named norOntair, sent out its preinaugural flight on 14 October 1971, beginning in Sudbury and setting down in Earlton, Timmins, and Sault Ste. Marie. Using first some temporary equipment and then Twin Otters, the new firm grew steadily, if somewhat haltingly, for over a decade. Here too the Commission could soon claim a degree of initiative and innovation as improving technology permitted the jet engine to enter the field of the smaller commercial aircraft. The annual report for 1985 declared proudly:

> When norOntair introduced the Dash-8 aircraft of de Haviland of Canada, it was the first airline to do so. The performance of this aircraft during 1985, its first full year of service, reinforces the correctness of the Commission in making this decision. It has proven to be extremely popular among passengers and very effective. In a single day its route includes Sault Ste. Marie, Sudbury, Timmins, Kapuskasing, Timmins, Kapuskasing, Timmins, Sudbury, Sault Ste. Marie, Thunder Bay and Sault Ste. Marie. So reliable is this airplane that it is considered likely that its workload can be expanded beyond even this impressive schedule.[3]

In 1992, the 91st year of the Commission's life, this Ontario Northland subsidiary will continue the traditional task of connecting the North, both within and without.

As these words are written, the Commission's Marine Services division remains largely inactive. With the advent of spring, however, the various vessels will receive the requisite attention to permit them to perform their limited but worthy roles on three northern waterways: the Moose River (the *Manitou*), Lake Nipissing (the *Chief Commanda II*) and Georgian Bay (the *Chi-Cheemaun* and the *Nindawayma*). The least prominent, physically, of the Commission's enterprises, Ontario Northland Telecommunications, will continue to exert the most pervading influence through its telephone and television technology. Already very good, these are likely to improve further through the continued transfer from microwave to fibre optics technology.

Throughout its past Ontario Northland has accepted a special, almost proprietary, sense of responsibility towards the North and concurrently has inspired a sense of pride in having met that responsibility. In this regard, perhaps the last word should go to the current president, Peter Dyment, who reviewed the several enterprises and then added:

> ❧ I think that tells you something about Ontario Northland. That we could in Ontario Northland recognize that we were the communicating link among the communities of the North, and between the North and the world, and use those different mediums as our methods of communicating... ranging from trains, with their very

slow advance in technology, to telecommunications which has probably the most frequent technological change of any medium. Ontario Northland was able to embrace both [rates of change] and do well at them; to hire people from the North to work with both those technologies.

We have a telecommunications system as contemporary as any in North America—it always has been—and better than many. Our railway has kept pace technologically with other railways. We were one of the first to be dieselized. We have a thoroughly modern shop. We've kept pace there. We had the first Dash-8 to fly anywhere commercially in the world. In terms of being contemporary and technologically capable, a group of northerners have said, "We can do it. And not just in one field. Not just in mining or harvesting forest products. We're pretty good in the transportation business."[4] ❧

One gets the feeling that Jake Englehart would approve.

Notes

1. See p. 214 of this text.
2. See p. 200 of this text.
3. *AR*, 1985, p. 16.

4. P.A. Dyment. Interview. 27 December 1991. North Bay.

Index